INSIGHT GUIDES

GReaT RIVeR
CRUISeS Europe
& The Nile

APA PUBLICATIONS
Part of the Langenscheidt Publishing Group

INSIGHT GUIDE
GReaT RIVeR CRUISeS EUROPE & THE NILE

Editorial
Managing Editor
Tom Le Bas
Consultant Editors
Douglas Ward
Sue Bryant
Editorial Director
Brian Bell

Distribution

UK & Ireland
GeoCenter International Ltd
The Viables Centre, Harrow Way
Basingstoke, Hants RG22 4BJ
Fax: (44) 1256 817988

United States
Langenscheidt Publishers, Inc.
36–36 33rd Street, 4th Floor
Long Island City, New York 11106
Fax: 1 (718) 784 0640

Australia
Universal Publications
1 Waterloo Road
Macquarie Park, NSW 2113
Fax: (61) 2 9888 9074

New Zealand
Hema Maps New Zealand Ltd (HNZ)
Unit D, 24 Ra ORA Drive
East Tamaki, Auckland
Fax: (64) 9 273 6479

Worldwide
Apa Publications GmbH & Co.
Verlag KG (Singapore branch)
38 Joo Koon Road, Singapore 628990
Tel: (65) 6865 1600. Fax: (65) 6861 6438

Printing

Insight Print Services (Pte) Ltd
38 Joo Koon Road, Singapore 628990
Tel: (65) 6865 1600. Fax: (65) 6861 6438

ABOUT THIS BOOK

The first Insight Guide pioneered the use of creative full-colour photography in guidebooks in 1970. Since then, we have expanded our range to cater for our readers' need not only for reliable information about their chosen destination but also for a real understanding of that destination. Now, when the internet can supply inexhaustible (but not always reliable) facts, our books marry text and pictures to provide that much more elusive quality: knowledge. To achieve this, they rely heavily on the authority of locally based writers and photographers.

Insight Guide: Great River Cruises, a companion to Insight's ocean cruising guides to the Mediterranean, the Caribbean, and North America and Alaska, is structured to help people get the most from their cruise:

◆ The **Features** section, indicated by a yellow bar at the top of each page, covers the background to the river cruise industry, with descriptive accounts of how to choose a cruise, and what to expect once you are on board.

◆ The main **Places** section, indicated by a blue bar, is a complete guide to the rivers and the ports of call along them. Major ports of call and their sights are detailed in two- or four-page photographic essays.

◆ The **Travel Tips** listings section, with an orange bar, provides full information on booking your trip, facilities on board, full country-by-country practical information, and an invaluable list of river cruise vessels. An easy-to-find contents list for Travel Tips is printed on the back flap, which also serves as a bookmark.

ABOVE: taking it easy on deck.

The contributors

This Insight Guide, a first in its field, was put together by **Tom Le Bas**, an editor at Insight Guides' London office. He also wrote sections of the Danube and Russia chapters and contributed several photographs.

The book was originally conceived by **Douglas Ward**, President of the Maritime Evaluations Group, author of the Berlitz *Complete Guide to Cruising and Cruise Ships* (now in its 21st year), and a highly respected authority on all aspects of ocean and river cruising. He has been the subject of three television documentaries and has appeared as an international cruise industry expert on CNN, *Good Morning America*, and on TV shows in numerous other countries. Ward wrote the Introduction, and provided the text on much of the Danube, Rhine and Elbe rivers, as well as smaller sections on other waterways. He also compiled the list of river cruise vessels, with ratings, at the back of the book, and provided more than 20 photographs.

Sue Bryant, a London-based specialist cruise writer, wrote the History and Features chapters, the chapters on France, French Barge Cruises, Scotland and Ireland, Italy, Portugal, Russia and the Nile, as well as parts of the Danube, Rhine and Elbe, and also helped with editing the text on other chapters. She also compiled the first three sections of Travel Tips. Bryant has edited *Cruise Traveller* magazine since its launch in 2001 and has contributed to a total of 18 guidebooks, including two on ocean cruising for Insight Guides. She writes regularly about cruising for numerous magazines and newspapers, including the *Daily Express*, *Cruise Passenger, Deckchair* and *Food & Travel*, and appears on various BBC news programmes as a commentator on the industry.

Anthony Lambert, a London-based travel writer, helped with editing and research of the Places section. The 14 Ports of Call summaries were compiled by **Paula Soper**, and designed by **Alan Gooch** and **Corrie Wingate**. Overall design was by **Klaus Geisler**. The extensive picture research was managed by **Hilary Genin**; the images which bring the text to life were sourced from a wide range of photographers and photo libraries.

Neil Titman proofread the text, and **Helen Peters** compiled the index.

The main places of interest in the Places section are coordinated by number with a full-colour map (e.g. ❶), and a symbol at the top of every right-hand page tells you where to find the map.

INSIGHT GUIDE
GReat RIVER CRUISES EUROPE & The Nile

CONTENTS

Travel Tips

Ports of Call Highlights

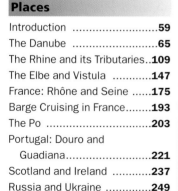

Places

THE BEST OF RIVER CRUISING

From major cities to remote villages, from Scotland to the Nile and Portugal to Russia, a run-down of some river cruise highlights

MAJOR PORTS OF CALL

- **Vienna (Danube)** The Austrian capital exudes centuries of culture and refinement. *See pages 82–5*
- **Bratislava (Danube)** Explore the handsome old town and its castle. *See pages 88–9*
- **Budapest (Danube)** With its magnificent setting right on the river, Budapest is a highlight of any middle Danube cruise. *See pages 92–5*
- **Cologne (Rhine)** Germany's fourth-largest city has a vast cathedral and excellent museums. *See pages 128–9*
- **Prague (Elbe)** One of Europe's most attractive cities, Prague marks the start or finish of most Elbe cruises *See pages 152–5*
- **Amsterdam (Rhine cruises)** Unique, picturesque, bursting with life, Amsterdam is a perennial favourite *See pages 132–3*
- **Paris (Seine)** The endlessly fascinating City of Light is the embarkation point for cruises down the Seine. *See pages 182–5*
- **Venice (Po)** Like no other city on earth. *See pages 208–11*
- **Porto (Douro)** A beautiful city at the end of a beautiful river. *See pages 224–5*
- **Moscow** Edgy, exciting, memorable and full of interest, Moscow is a vivid introduction to Russia. *See pages 260–3*
- **St Petersburg** Beguiles with its harmonious architecture and northern light. *See pages 270–3*
- **Cairo** Full of fascinating sights, colour and atmosphere. *See pages 300–1*
- **Luxor** Gateway to the awe-inspiring sights of Upper Egypt. *See pages 310–3*

OTHER PORTS OF INTEREST

- **Nuremberg, Germany (Danube)** Gorgeous medieval centre, close to stunning river scenery. *See pages 71–2*
- **Dürnstein, Austria (Danube)** Beautiful, historic small town, with Melk Abbey nearby. *See pages 78–9, 77*
- **Heidelberg, Germany (Neckar)** One of Germany's top sights, Heidelberg is, unusually, both picturesque and lively. *See pages 138–40*
- **Dresden, Germany (Elbe)** The opening of the new cathedral symbolises the rebirth of this handsome city. *See pages 158–9*
- **Toruń, Poland (Vistula)** Could have been lifted from a film set, with Gothic squares, medieval houses and churches *See pages 169–70*
- **Avignon, France (Rhône)** Encircled by medieval walls, sunny Avignon is one of the most pleasant of all French cities *See page 180*
- **Verona, Italy (Po)** The fabulous Arena is just one highlight of this Italian beauty. *See pages 213–4*
- **Kostroma, Russia (Volga)** An attractive city with a spellbinding monastery. *See page 259*
- **Kiev, Ukraine (Dnieper)** Much to spur interest at the start of a Dnieper cruise. *See pages 280–2*

THE BEST RIVER SCENERY

●**The Wachau Valley** One of the most appealing stretches on the Danube. *See pages 78–9*

●**The Danube Bend** The mighty Danube loops through enchanting scenery as it encounters the impenetrable block of the Börzsöny and Cserhát Hills to the north of Budapest. *See page 87*

●**The Iron Gates** Another Danubian highlight, a dramatic gorge on the Serbian/ Romanian border. *See pages 99–100*

●**The Rhine between Mainz and Koblenz** This famous stretch is the Rhine at its most romantic – with brooding castles, picturesque towns and vineyards. *See pages 118–125*

●**The Elbe south of Dresden** The Elbe carves its way through the "Little Switzerland" of limestone hills around Bad Schandau. *See pages 156–7*

●**The Rhône from Vienne to Tournon** A rugged stretch of southern France. *See pages 179–80*

●**The Douro from Peso da Regua to Pinhão** Terraced hillsides covered in vines, and tranquil small towns in north Portugal's backwaters. *See pages 226–8*

●**The Caledonian Canal and Loch Ness** Part of the Great Glen bisecting Scotland, in the midst of fabulous Highland scenery. *See pages 241–2*

●**Lake Onega and Kizhi Island** A sparsely populated, very beautiful region of dark forests and remote villages. Kizhi Island is a UNESCO World Heritage Site. *See pages 265–7*

●**The Nile between Aswan and Luxor** This attractive stretch of Upper Egypt includes the fabulous ancient site of Kom Ombo. *See pages 307–9*

LEFT: the Rhine flows through the heart of Cologne. **BELOW LEFT:** Prague's astronomical clock.
BELOW: glorious scenery on the middle Rhine. **BELOW RIGHT:** relaxing on deck on a Nile cruise.

PRACTICAL TIPS

Research which cruise suits you best. There are degrees of luxury and style on board river cruisers, so think about whether you want a formal or informal atmosphere, lavish or more modest dining and, probably most important, whether you want an only English-speaking cruise or whether you prefer to travel with other nationalities.

Be culturally aware. A degree of tolerance is required on a multi-national river cruise. People of other nationalities may smoke more than you are used to, or make more noise, or have a different attitude to queuing!

Book excursions ahead. Many operators include excursions as part of the package, but for those who don't, it's worth signing up for anything you are interested in as soon as possible. Assuming you are reasonably mobile, try to arrange both coach tours and walking excursions. Many cruise vessels offer evening excursions to concerts and recitals, too.

Things you might need. Binoculars; spare camera film (particularly in Egypt and Russia, where quality cannot be guaranteed); a hat that won't blow off in the breeze; good walking shoes. It is also a good idea to bring a supply of euros and a few US dollars.

WHY TAKE A RIVER CRUISE?

Douglas Ward, the world's foremost authority on cruising,

outlines the appeal of a European river cruise

A river cruise represents life in the slow lane, sailing along at a gentle pace, soaking up the scenery, with plentiful opportunities to explore riverside towns and cities en route. It is a supremely calming experience, an antidote to the pressures of life in a fast-paced world, in surroundings that are comfortable without being fussy or pretentious, with good food and enjoyable company. A cruise provides luxurious and convenient access to destinations that is hard to match on other means of transport: Whether you want to explore the stately Volga, the magnificent Rhine or the "blue" Danube, to say nothing of the vast Dnepr, the Elbe, the Rhône, the Po, the Douro or the incomparable River Nile – there's an amazing array of itineraries, destinations, river cruise vessels and operators from which to choose.

Well over 1 million people take a river cruise somewhere in the world each year, with Europe and the Nile the most popular destinations. The itineraries on offer are always full of interest, taking in some of Europe's most fascinating towns and cities.

A river cruise is very different from an ocean cruise. For a start, you are in almost constant sight of land, and stops are far more frequent than they are at sea. The vessels are like small, friendly, floating inns, whereas ocean-going ships tend to be bigger, flashier, busier and livelier, the crew practised in the art of moving up to 4,000 people from one port to another and getting them on and off the ship. In contrast, when your river cruise vessel docks you simply walk up the gangway and into the town or city – in many cases the dock is located right at the heart of things. Despite these differences, however, most people who enjoy ocean cruising and the relaxing rhythm of life afloat are attracted to river cruises as well.

On board, passengers are well looked after. Most modern river cruise vessels are fully air-conditioned, with several public rooms, including a dining room, observation lounge and bar, as well as a small library. Many vessels have a sauna, solarium and a small gymnasium. There is plenty of open deck space, and the top deck – typically running almost the entire length of the vessel – will have chairs and sun loungers, a bar area and often a small plunge pool. One word of caution: River cruise companies and tour operators almost always overstate the "star" ratings they award themselves in brochures and marketing material. The first genuine five-star river cruise vessel has yet to arrive on the market. Even so, on almost any vessel, the comfort and convenience, combined with the on-shore excursions, adds up to a wonderfully relaxing, yet stimulating, holiday. ❏

Douglas Ward is the author of the annual Berlitz "Complete Guide to Cruising and Cruise Ships", which reviews more than 260 cruise ships in detail.

PRECEDING PAGES: the *Swiss Crystal* at Trier; the Seine from Pont Alexandre III in Paris; quintessential Rhine scenery at Bacharach. **LEFT:** relaxing on a private balcony.

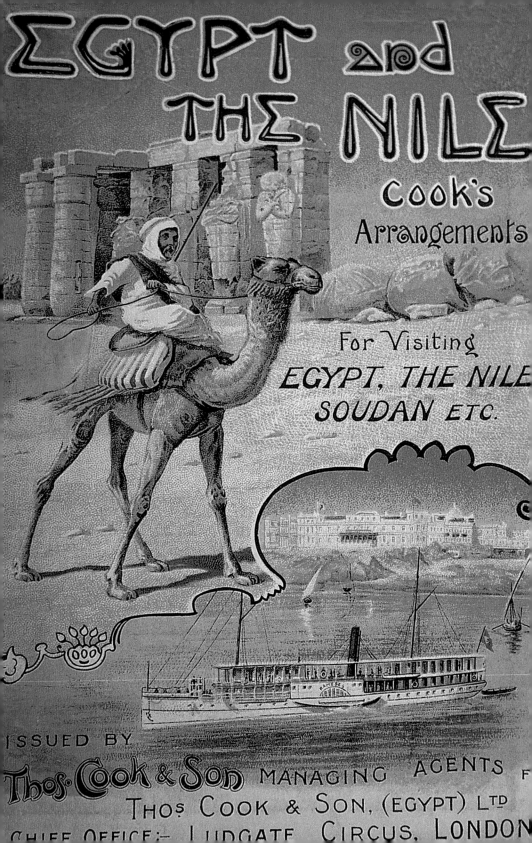

EGYPT and THE NILE

Cook's Arrangements

For Visiting
EGYPT, THE NILE
SOUDAN ETC.

ISSUED BY

Thos. Cook & Son MANAGING AGENTS F

Thos Cook & Son, (EGYPT) LTD

CHIEF OFFICE:— LUDGATE CIRCUS, LONDON

RIVER TRANSPORT AND THE GROWTH OF RIVER CRUISING

*River cruising as a commercial activity has existed only since the 1960s
in Europe, although Nile cruises have a longer pedigree*

Rivers nourish the lands through which they flow like a life vein, providing water supply, sediments to fertilise the soil and vital transportation routes as they carve their way through the landscape. Wars have been fought and kingdoms won and lost over Europe's waterways and the rights to them.

Ancient civilisations grew up around the mighty rivers of the Near East – along the Tigris and Euphrates in Mesopotamia and the Nile in Egypt, where the first urban settlements developed some 6,500 years ago. Likewise, the Danube and the Rhine in Europe, and the Volga and the Don in European Russia, each of which formed a natural route along which the population could spread, encouraged the development of settled cultures. All continue to provide an economic lifeline in modern times.

Taming the waters

Passenger-carrying vessels capable of travelling on rivers have a long history, particularly on the Nile, where exploratory expeditions were carried out by the Pharaohs more than 3,500 years ago, and on the Rhine, which has been in use for carrying cargo for over 2,000 years.

In days gone by, navigation of even the most benign-looking waterway was fraught with danger. Rivers are unpredictable, flowing at irregular speed as variations in terrain create rapids, shallows, hidden depths and treacherous whirlpools. River vessels would often have to be removed from the water and carried around the hazardous sections, or hauled upstream through a series of dams and weirs.

Throughout history, efforts have been made to tame these dangerous stretches. The first primitive locks were built in Song-dynasty China in the late 10th century, and a more advanced system was developed in medieval

Europe, albeit on a small scale. But it wasn't until the 17th and 18th centuries that major advances in technology began to make it possible for engineers to alter the course of rivers significantly. By the 1800s, canals were

being dug and larger scale locks created all over the continent, meaning that river traffic could progress safely around difficult stretches of water, avoiding being smashed on rocks.

Many people have been visionaries when it comes to rivers and canals. In 8th-century France, Charlemagne dreamed of establishing a navigable waterway between the Danube and Main rivers (at its planning stage, called the "Fossa Carolina"), although it was to remain purely a vision for the next 1,200 years. Entrepreneurial landowners saw opportunities to collect taxes from anyone navigating the Rhine, with a procession of spectacular castles built overlooking the river expressly for this

LEFT: an early Thomas Cook poster advertising cruises along the Nile.
RIGHT: cruising on the Nile at Aswan in the 1860s.

purpose. Towns and cities were built on rivers everywhere for practical and strategic (and to some degree aesthetic) purposes, and eventually, as people became more prosperous, a fledgling leisure industry began to develop.

With the rise of the concept of the holiday, and the idea of travel for leisure, it was, perhaps, inevitable that someone would chance upon the idea of offering a river cruise, with so many rivers and so many destinations to discover. Expeditions along the Nile had taken place since 1500 BC, with the ancient Egyptians making forays to the south to see what lay beyond their kingdoms. But it was the travel

company Thomas Cook that ostensibly started commercial cruises in Egypt. Thomas and John Cook had already launched a travel business in Britain, but in 1870, Khedive Ismail, viceroy of the Ottoman Empire, employed the company as an agent for Nile passenger traffic. By 1880, the Egyptian government was so pleased with business generated by the Cooks that the company was granted a monopoly on Nile cruise steamers. In those days, the fare from England to Upper Egypt was between £81 and £119, for an expedition involving considerable overland travel. Over 20 years, the Cooks reckoned to have boosted the Egyptian economy by some three to four million pounds

with their incoming business – a huge amount in those days.

The steam engine was used in river vessels from the early years of the 19th century, and over time its development and refinement provided more power and more efficiency. Around 100 years later, the advent of diesel power elevated the reliability and timekeeping of the early river cruise vessels to a new level.

River cruising in Europe

In Europe, river cruising as form of recreation only really began to catch on in the 1960s. By this time, ocean cruising was well established as a glamorous and exciting way to travel, and transatlantic voyages had been booming for decades. Rivers were less exotic; people may have travelled between two points by river as it was the quickest way to arrive, but the concept of a floating hotel on the river was very new.

Although in these early days the vessels were little more than glorified water buses, owners and operators soon started to add a variety of facilities to mirror the sophisticated scene that was already well established on the ocean-going cruises. And as the river cruise industry grew, purpose-built vessels were constructed with better equipment and comfort levels.

The Rhine and the Danube were the first European rivers to attract this kind of tourism (while the Nile continued to be more popular than either), but as demand grew, more and more rivers were introduced: the Po in Italy, the Seine and Rhône in France, the Douro in Portugal. After the fall of the Iron Curtain at the end of the 1980s, Eastern European rivers suddenly became accessible, and popular – the Elbe in the Czech Republic and Germany, and the fabled Russian waterways, the potential of which – as a convenient way of exploring the Russian countryside without the hassle associated with travelling in the former Soviet Union – was quickly realised.

Europe has certainly been spearheading the growth of the contemporary river cruise scene, with many new and innovative vessels having been built and introduced in the late 1990s. There is, however, one particular vessel that changed the thinking of river cruise operators – the *Mozart*, built in 1987 to operate on the River Danube for the Donau-Dampfschiffahrts-Gesellshaft (commonly known as DDSG), and today the flagship of upscale river cruise operator Peter Deilmann. When it was introduced, the *Mozart* was hailed as the most luxurious vessel on *any* European river at that time, with its rosewood panelling, original works of art, lavish cabins and marble bathrooms. Since then, river cruise designers and builders have been working hard to provide more and more spacious cabins, public areas, and more extensive and better dining facilities to keep up with the change in consumer tastes and demands.

The latest river cruise vessels are so much better, in so many ways, than the basic floating accommodation that they replaced, with

was finally opened to provide the means for larger craft of up to 3,300 tons to navigate all the way from the North Sea to the Black Sea, linking as it does the rivers Rhine, Main and Danube. It meant that the maritime map of Europe was completely rewritten. The canal was the culmination of many years of planning, and its construction was the largest traffic-engineering project in European history *(see page 68)*.

A chronology of river cruising

1811 Regular steamboat service starts in the USA when the stern-paddlewheel steamboat

LLOYD-MITTELMEER-ᵤₙᵈ ORIENTFAHRTEN

swimming pools, hot tubs, teak decks, libraries and skilled chefs providing lavish, multi-course dinners. For sheer opulence, some of the interiors of the Nile boats are hard to beat. Some of the cruise barges on the canals and waterways of France, too, have some delightful touches, emulating the finest of French country-house hotels, with cuisine and wines to match.

The European waterways network received a major boost in 1992, when on 25 September, the 170-km (106-mile) Main–Danube Canal

New Orleans leaves Pittsburgh. The vessel takes four months to arrive in New Orleans, but the era of the steamboats is ushered in. Although the USA is first, Europe is not far behind.

1812 In Vienna, a vessel named *Caroline* becomes the first steam-driven vessel on the Danube. Its introduction is significant, meaning that for the first time (discounting some sailing boats such as Egyptian feluccas) vessels can move upstream under their own power rather than being towed.

1826 On 11 June, members of the Cologne Chamber of Commerce advocate the founding of a steamship company: The Prussian Rhine

LEFT: sightseeing on a Rhine steamer, 1909.
ABOVE: the North German Lloyd Bremen line advertises its Nile cruise on a 1929 postcard.

Steamship Company (Donau-Dampfschif-fahrts-Gesellshaft-Köln) begins operations, and river cruise vessel trials are carried out. The company, which establishes its headquarters in Cologne, becomes commonly known as DDSG (later as the KD Rhine Line, or simply KD, standing for Köln-Düsseldorf). Thus, long-haul river cruising on the Rhine and Danube becomes a reality for many travellers.

1827 DDSG starts a scheduled service with the steamship *Concordia*, which is purchased from Baron Cotta, a friend and publisher of the philosopher and writer Goethe.

1829 The Erste Donau-Dampfschiffahrts-

changes from a cargo-passenger carrier to passenger traffic only.

1856 In the Treaty of Paris, the European Commission of the Danube is established. This body aims to make the river an international waterway with free passage for all. The countries through which the river flows are liable for its maintenance.The Russian boundary is withdrawn 20 kms (12 miles) north of the Danube.

1857 The riparian states (those states whose land includes the frontage of rivers and canals as they appear in nature) meet in Vienna to regulate the entire Danube River from Ulm in Germany (one of the highest points of the

Gesellshaft (DDSG) is founded in order to provide regular steamer service to points along the Danube. The company establishes its headquarters in Vienna.

1836 The Steamship Company for the Lower and Middle Rhine of Düsseldorf (Dampschif-fahrts-Gesellschaft für den Niede- und Mittelrhein, Düsseldorf) is created as a joint stockholding company.

1838 The first all-iron steamship, the *Graf von Paris*, is placed in service on the River Danube.

1853 A joint management company, the Rhine Steamship Company Cologne and Düsseldorf (Rhein-Dampfschiffahrt Köln und Düsseldorf) is founded. It becomes known simply as KD, and

Upper Danube) to Braila in Romania (close to the delta), where two arms of the river are joined again. However, this proves largely unsuccessful due to the dominance at the time of the Austro-Hungarian Empire.

1869 The travel company Thomas Cook starts cruises on the River Nile when Thomas Cook himself takes 30 travellers up the Nile by steamer. Together with a small party of friends, he returns in November 1869 to attend the opening of the Suez Canal.

1870 Sulina, on the Black Sea, is declared a free port, and cargo is allowed to pass upriver on the Danube without formality.

1872 Thomas Cook and Son open an office in

Cairo to provide local booking facilities for Nile cruises.

1895–9 Navigation along the treacherous Iron Gates section of the River Danube, to the east of Budapest, is improved following blasting and canal construction.

1902 The final Sulina arm cut-off is completed. This shortens the River Danube by 11 nautical miles and improves navigation and access to the Black Sea.

1913 KD Rhine Line carries approximately two million passengers in its fleet of 32 vessels.

1919 The Treaty of Versailles is signed, granting four rivers (Elbe, Danube, Oder and Vltava)

1939 At the outbreak of World War II, KD Rhine Line owns 22 steamers and six motor vessels.

1947 Recommencement of scheduled KD Rhine Line service takes place after the war.

1948 The Belgrade Convention is signed. This is established to regulate the whole navigable River Danube. It is composed only of the riparian states, except for Germany (or Austria) at first.

1960 The first properly "packaged" river cruises on the River Rhine, between Basel and Rotterdam, using new vessels of the KD Rhine Line specifically constructed for river cruises.

"international" status for the free passage of goods and passengers.

1921 The European Commission of the Danube resumes operations. A new International Commission of the Danube is set up for the "fluvial" river from Ulm to Braila. Luxury operator Hapag-Lloyd starts operation.

1927 KD Rhine Line places the first diesel-powered vessels into service on the River Danube.

1929 The last side-paddle-driven steamer, the *Mainz*, is built for the KD Rhine Line.

LEFT: the Franz Josef paddle steamer on the Danube, 1853.
ABOVE: cruising the Volga, 2005.

1964 Cruises between Koblenz and Trier are offered following the canalisation of the River Moselle.

1967 The Cologne and Düsseldorf joint-stock companies are amalgamated to become simply KD Rhine Line.

1976 Uniworld is founded by Serba Ilich in California, and becomes one of the first cruise companies to charter Russian-built river cruise vessels on the Volga and other Russian waterways specifically catering to American passengers.

1978 The tour operator Abercrombie & Kent begins offering river cruises in Europe, principally for its American clients.

1979 Construction of the new KD Rhine Line headquarters complex is begun in 1979 on Handelskai in Vienna (from which most river vessels depart). The founding stone is laid by the President of the Republic on 25 April 1979 during the celebrations of the 125th anniversary of the founding of the DDSG.

1983 Peter Deilmann River Cruises starts river cruise operations on the River Danube.

1987 Peter Deilmann launches the *Mozart*, still regarded today as one of the most luxurious river cruising vessels in the world.

1992 On 25 September, the maritime map of Europe is redrawn when the Main–Danube

Canal is finally opened, thus providing the means for larger craft (up to 3,300 tons) to navigate all the way from the North Sea to the Black Sea, linking as it does the rivers Rhine, Main and Danube. The construction of the canal is the largest traffic-engineering project in Europe and changes cargo shipping in particular.

1994 Vantage Deluxe World Tours is founded in Boston to offer river cruises in Europe exclusively for Americans.

1995 For the first time, KD Rhine Line starts to offer river cruises with selected marketing partners in several countries. Integrated holiday packages are marketed as all-inclusive

products, complete with airline or train travel, transfers and hotels included in the total price.

1996 As a result of internal reorganisation, KD River Cruises (KD Deutsche Flusskreutzfahrten GmbH) is founded, a full-service tour operator offering a range of river cruises in the worldwide marketplace.

The *River Cloud* is built for German-owned Sea Cloud Cruises, setting new standards with its opulent, 1930s-style décor.

1997 Viking River Cruises is founded by a group of investors headed by Norwegian entrepreneur Torstein Hagen (one of the original founders of the now defunct ocean-going Royal Viking Line). The new company offers river cruises aboard four Russian river cruise vessels.

1999 Following an extensive restoration project, on 26 August the original paddle steamer *Goethe* (built in 1913) re-enters service on the River Rhine in Germany for steam-powered nostalgia cruises during the summer months. The *Goethe* is the largest side-wheel paddle steamer in the world.

2000 KD River Cruises celebrates 40 years in the river cruise business, but is then partly taken over by Viking River Cruises (KD Deutsche Flusskreutzfahrt, not including the KD Rhine Line passenger ferries, scheduled services and day-excursion operations). The takeover includes the landing stages, an extremely valuable asset. The combined fleet amounts to 26 river cruise vessels accommodating a total of 4,197 passengers, and instantly becomes the largest fleet of river cruise vessels in the world.

2001 As a result of a dramatic drop in business resulting from fear of international travel generated by the terrorist attacks of 11 September, the Switzerland-based river cruise and tour company Mittelthurgau ceases operations.

The *River Cloud II* is built specifically for cruising Italy's River Po.

2002 USA-based Uniworld forms Global River Cruises to oversee its operations in Europe. Global River Cruises purchases 75 percent of Holland River Line.

2004 Peter Deilmann launches the *Heidelberg*, a new luxury ship for the Rhine. The British river cruising market expands by 23 percent, with the Rhine and the Nile the most popular rivers.

2005 Viking River Cruises launches the five-star *Viking Sun* on the Rhine. ❑

A History of Canals

5000 BC The Egyptians build the world's first canals in order to bypass the rapids on the River Nile. They have continued networking their canal and inland waterway system for transportation, irrigation and agriculture uses ever since.

1st century AD The Romans build canals in Europe in order to provide transportation routes and to secure their empire. Some of the canals in England, France and Holland date back to Roman times.

984 The first pound-lock is invented by the Chinese engineer Chiao Weo-Yo. This was to become the model by which all canal locks would be built for many centuries to come.

1500–1650 Inland waterways are revived and put to more use as high road taxes and insecure roadways make travelling by water preferable, particularly for traders. This sparks a renaissance in canal-building all over Europe, as longer and longer trade routes are established.

The ruling classes in Paris decree that more canals should be completed in order to provide better transportation for the food delicacies produced far away in the countryside. In the Upper Loire, the beautiful Canal du Briare is constructed (it is still in use today).

1681 The construction of the Canal du Midi makes the age-old dream of constructing a through waterway between the Atlantic Ocean and the Mediterranean come true. It is a mammoth project, testing the mettle of some of the best engineers of the day, including Leonardo da Vinci. The canal rises 187 metres (614 ft) in its 182-km (114-mile) course and relies on a series of 75 locks to link the waterways that course through southwestern France to the Atlantic Ocean.

1761 The opening of England's first entirely man-made waterway, The Bridgewater Canal in Lancashire. This is part of almost 4,000 miles of waterways constructed in Great Britain during the 18th century, providing a comprehensive network vital for rapid industrialisation.

LEFT: Peter Deilmann's *Mozart*. **RIGHT:** the Duke of Bridgewater, builder of England's first true canal.

1789 Canal-building in France almost comes to a stop with the French Revolution. While the northern Canal du Bourgogne (Burgundy Canal) is completed, the southern network of canals is delayed.

1800–1850 Major expansion of the network of inland waterways throughout Europe, meeting the needs of the rapidly industrialising economy.

1859 Work on the Suez Canal gets under way, but in Europe, the canal system starts falling into disrepair, having been overtaken by the advent of the locomotive and the creation of a Europe-wide railway system.

1966 A British reporter, Robert Parsons, has the idea of converting commercial barges into upmarket vessels for passenger use, and selling tours to explore the French countryside. He and his brother purchase a barge, the *Planers*, convert it into a cruise barge and operate its maiden voyage in May 1966 between Paris and Dijon – and the barge cruise industry is born.

1992 Opening of the Main–Danube Canal.

2000s More than 50 cruise barges and river cruise vessels currently operate on the canal systems of Belgium, France, Germany, Holland and the United Kingdom. ❏

EUROPEAN RIVER CRUISES: WHAT'S AVAILABLE

An overview of river cruises and river cruise companies to help you plan a trip.

Further information and contact details are in Travel Tips, pages 315–20

There is no question that Europe and Egypt are the world's most popular regions for river cruising, attracting hundreds of thousands of holidaymakers a year. From their origins as little more than waterborne bus tours, the European river cruise scene has developed into a more sophisticated type of holiday, with a variety of themes, itineraries, combinations of cruising and hotel stays, and styles of vessel. The race is now on to see who can deliver the most sophisticated ships, with larger cabins and bathrooms, private balconies, exciting facilities on board, more adventurous itineraries and a wider range of shore excursions to choose from than ever before.

Europe's heartland offers the greatest concentration of navigable waterways in the world today. The rivers – the Rhine, Danube and Elbe – offer a unique perspective on the historic landscapes through which they carve their way, passing historic cities, medieval towns and fabled villages, their courses overlooked by forbidding castles, dense forests and rolling hills. Cruising along these waterways is an ideal way to gain an insight into the cultures, heritage and traditions of these lands, and the day-to-day lives of the people who live alongside the water.

Ten countries

Part of the appeal of European river cruising is the variety of landscapes and cultures it offers in such a short time. A cruise along the full length of the Danube, for example, will take you through 10 countries, the route punctuated throughout with castles, gorges, historic cities, riverside abbeys and Roman antiquities.

Needless to say, it isn't all so picturesque – Europe's waterways also have a good deal of inland ports and heavy industry, and the river scenery can be bleakly industrial at times. Close to cities, factories and power stations along the

banks will be common sights. The most obvious exception is the Nile; the most popular stretch of the river for cruises, between Luxor and Aswan, is rural, tranquil and beautiful.

The most popular rivers in mainland Europe for cruising are the Danube and the Rhine (and its tributaries the Moselle, Main and Neckar). Less travelled are the Elbe, the Rhône/Saône and Seine in France, together with Italy's Po and Portugal's Douro, while "new" – in other words, relatively undiscovered – rivers include the Dnieper in Ukraine, the Vistula in Poland, and the Guadiana in southern Portugal. Russian river cruising, mainly between Moscow and St Petersburg, is consistently popular, and is a fantastic way to visit places that would otherwise be difficult to reach. The original cruising river, the Nile, with its magnificent sights, continues to attract large numbers of tourists.

LEFT: taking it easy on the sun deck.
RIGHT: the sumptuous interior of the River Cloud.

Standards and ratings

River cruising in Europe has reached a sophisticated level today, and cruise operators are adopting more and more of the practices of ocean-going cruise lines, as the market becomes increasingly demanding. New vessels always have cabins with private balconies, a trend which has been very strong in ocean cruising over the last decade. Luxury vessels are becoming more so, with cruise operators emphasising features such as the quality of the bed linen, the cabin amenities and the ratio of staff to passengers. Some have small spas on board. And many river cruise operators now include sporting

Types of cruise

Certain vessels cater for specific language groups and may, for example, only be sold in the USA, or to German-speakers. While anybody can book one of these cruises, everything from the food to the entertainment and the general lifestyle will be geared to a certain market. There is a clear trend for vessels aimed at Americans to have more American-style cuisine, for example, and to be entirely non-smoking (except on deck). There are several cruises sold to all markets, which means a good, international mix on board – but opportunities for culture clashes as well.

activities such as cycling and golf in addition to the traditional cultural activities.

Nonetheless, the river cruise market is confusing. There is no standard star rating, although all river cruise operators brand their vessels three-, four- or five-star. You'll never see a one- or two-star river boat! Different countries have different interpretations of this, and a Russian or Egyptian five-star vessel will not be the same as one on the Danube or the Rhine. To give a clear idea of the standards of vessels on all the routes covered in this guide, we have included the independent ratings of the Maritime Evaluations Group on pages 355–360.

Most river cruises are sold as all-inclusive packages, often including a couple of days' hotel accommodation at the beginning or end of the cruise. If you are already in Europe, many cruises can be purchased as "cruise-only" for greater flexibility, so you can add on your own hotel stays afterwards. Many cruise lines package these, for example, adding a few nights in Prague after a cruise on the Elbe, or flying into Munich and spending a weekend there before driving to Passau to join a Danube cruise.

ABOVE: river cruise vessels sit long, low and sleek in the water. **RIGHT:** the crew are well trained to assist passengers.

Excursions and themes

A whole range of optional excursions is available on river cruises, from the standard sightseeing tours to more specialised cultural tours – such as following the path of Harry Lime (from the famous 1949 film *The Third Man*) in Vienna. There are also more active pursuits on offer, such as hot-air ballooning over the Danube, or horse-riding in the countryside south of Budapest. Often, the excursions are included in the price, which makes a huge difference to the cost of the cruise. If they are not, you can either buy a separate excursion "package", or book the trips individually once on board. Sometimes, it's a mix of the two. For example, on a Nile cruise, you should expect all temple visits to be included in the cost, but things like hot-air ballooning over Luxor, or a side trip to Abu Simbel, will be extra.

Themed cruises are increasingly popular, as cruise companies compete with one another to offer more creative itineraries. Europe's rivers lend themselves to all sorts of themes, from music, art and literature in Russia to gardens along the Rhine, featuring visits to famous botanical gardens, not to mention castles and their grounds and gardens. Other special cruises involve classical and jazz music, fine food and wine-tasting, shopping, and, of course,

RIVER CRUISE TERMINOLOGY

A **river cruise vessel** or **riverboat** has a flat bottom, and is designed to cruise along shallow waterways. River cruise vessels typically travel at speeds of between 10 and 18 knots. There is a captain and crew; accommodation, all meals (three each day, plus mid-morning, mid-afternoon and late-night snacks), and some light entertainment are provided. River cruise vessels carry between 50 and 300 passengers.

Ships sail on oceans (not rivers), generally have a deep hull, and can carry between 50 and 4,000 passengers. An ocean-going **cruise ship** can carry boats (lifeboats, search and rescue boats, and shore tenders). Note therefore, that a ship can carry a boat, but a boat cannot carry a ship.

A **cruise barge** (sometimes referred to as **hotel barges** by their owners and marketers) is a flat-bottomed craft that draws a shallow draft. Most are converted from their former use as cargo-carrying craft. Cruise barges travel much more slowly than river cruise vessels, at between 3 and 10 knots. Cruise barges typically have only one deck (a few have two decks), which includes space for cabins, plus a combination dining room/lounge. Most carry between six and 12 passengers; a few can carry up to 24 passengers.

Christmas and New Year celebrations, particularly in Austria, France and Germany. Also popular in Germany is the magical Rhine in Flames festival in August; a river cruise provides a ringside seat for the spectacular fireworks displays.

Even when a cruise does not have a theme, a taste of local culture is often brought on board. Russian river cruises, for example, may have Russian lessons, vodka-tasting and tea ceremonies. In Portugal, port-tastings are laid on. The cuisine on board will often reflect the country through which the vessel is passing, unlike ocean cruises, where menus are planned from a head office, regardless of where the ship is sailing.

educational and destination lectures, and some light entertainment. You will soon realise that a river cruise can provide excellent value for money when compared to a land-based holiday. Then there's the bonus that, although you're moving, you have to pack and unpack only once.

Having said that, as with any other form of holiday, the price bands are wide and costs vary according to the standard of the vessel, the cabin and the destination. An outside twin on Peter Deilmann's *Mozart*, considered the most luxurious river vessel afloat, costs around $370 per person per night, while a suite is around $695. A

What it all costs

Typical rates for river cruises are from US$800 to over $3,000 per person for a one-week cruise, including meals, cabin with private facilities, side trips and airport/railway transfers. This may sound expensive, but all things considered, river cruises are actually very affordable. Calculate what accommodation would cost on land: it can be hard to find a small hotel room in almost any major city today for less than $100 a night – and for that you'll probably get a view of a parking lot or brick wall. Then estimate the cost of three restaurant meals a day. Add the cost of attentive, friendly service, as well as transfers, social functions,

twin on the *Viking Pakhomov* in Russia, meanwhile, costs around $229 per person per night. The daily rate on the River Elbe with Viking River Cruises is about $269. On the Nile, a luxury cruise costs around $260 per person per night in peak season ($1,800 in a suite), dropping to $160 ($1,120 in a suite) in low season (July and August). Nile prices include all shore excursions. All the above prices apply to the cruise only – airfares and other transport costs typically included in a package deal will add significantly to the total cost, particularly if you are travelling from the US.

Hotel barge cruising prices are higher than those of river cruises as there are far fewer people per vessel and a much higher level of service and food, as well as the fact that all drinks and excursions are included. A week on a privately-chartered, crewed barge with a company like Afloat in France can cost up to $5,000 per person; six nights with European Waterways in southwest France costs around $2,400. Again these prices exclude airfares (but do include the train fare from Paris).

Who takes these cruises?

River cruises appeal to those who like to travel in small numbers, but they are particularly well suited to couples – especially those over 50, senior-age honeymooners and groups of friends. Many passengers are retirees, or professionals with plenty of flexible time and disposable income. In short, they appeal to anyone who is culturally aware and wants to experience the heart of a country and its people, instead of simply travelling through it.

A cruise is actually the perfect environment for singles – safe and convivial – but cruising alone is an expensive business, as almost no vessels have dedicated cabins for singles. Although you can occupy a double cabin on your own, you'll be penalised with higher fares, a constant bugbear of the single traveller.

As for honeymooners, river cruises provide a delightful setting, although they tend to appeal more to honeymooners of senior years. Most arrangements will have been taken care of before you sail, so all you have to do is show up. Some vessels have accommodation in double-, queen- or king-sized beds, too – although in general, you'll find that the cabins (and particularly the bathrooms) are very small when compared to a typical hotel room. The other drawback is that you don't actually get that much time alone, as you eat with other people and take excursions in groups.

You will not see many children on river cruises, although a cruise does provide an educational, safe, crime-free environment. For those with young children, cots can usually be provided if you ask at the time of booking, but high chairs and children's meals will not usually be available on board. There are no children's playrooms, and babysitting is at

the discretion of the hotel manager and crew.

Chartering a hotel barge in France *(see pages 30–31 and 193–199)* is a popular option for families. Barges typically carry between six and 12, and the cruise and catering can be adapted to your needs.

When to go

Summer is the peak season for European river cruising. The weather should be good, but attractions will be crowded. If you don't enjoy the throngs of visitors that typically invade Central Europe's most historic cities, towns and villages during the height of the summer season, it would

be worth taking your river cruise during other seasons, when prices are also lower. Certain places are actually better off-season; the beautiful Wachau Valley of the Danube, for example, can rival the USA's east coast for its magnificent autumn colours.

Most river cruise vessels stop overnight, giving you the chance to take in the sights and sounds of major destinations. Going in the off-season also means there will be a better chance to obtain tickets for a concert, ballet or opera in such distinguished cities as Budapest, Prague or Vienna. The off-season for mass tourism is the on-season for many of the best cultural events in any case, particularly in winter.

LEFT: on the Elblàg Canal in Poland, boats negotiate a 100-metre (330-ft) climb via railed embankments.
RIGHT: taking it easy on a French barge cruise.

A river cruise during the Christmas season, when the sights, sounds and smells are enhanced by the month of Advent, can be magical, particularly to German-speaking destinations, which have a tradition of beautiful Christmas markets. The scents of cinnamon, gingerbread, roasting chestnuts and *Glühwein* (spiced wine) fill the air during the Christmas holiday season. Festive Christmas markets fill the squares in most cities, towns and villages along the Danube and Rhine rivers with seasonal celebratory food, handicrafts and wonderful Christmas decorations. Market artisans demonstrate traditional arts and crafts, and market stalls are all beautifully decorated to stalls provides the olde-world setting in this magical place.

CroisiEurope and Viking River Cruises are two river cruise operators that have special cruises to the Christmas markets of Europe. CroisiEurope (a French operator) typically starts and ends its Christmas cruises in Strasbourg. Viking River Cruises typically operates its Christmas cruises from Nuremberg to Vienna (or reverse).

The Nile has different cruising seasons from Europe. January to March is popular, when the weather is cooler. June to October is low season, when it's ferociously hot, although cruises

the nines. At night, the lights form a magical backdrop to the gaily decorated markets and add a jovial ambience that is difficult to find anywhere else.

Regensburg, often a starting or finishing point for several river cruise vessels, has its Christmas market in the town's charming square. Vienna has a number of Christmas markets, and the window dressing of the stores along the wide Kartnerstrasse is among the very best in the world. The most famous Christmas market is in Nuremberg, however. Located in the old walled section of the city, it is the oldest in Germany, having begun in the 17th century. Row upon row of specially constructed still operate. During these summer months, the antiquities are a lot less crowded, but shore excursions do start very, very early; most operators aim to have passengers back on board by 10am, before the heat becomes unbearable. When the vessel is moving, though, the breeze makes the climate very pleasant.

Barge cruising

Barge cruising provides a complete antidote to the pressures of life in a fast-paced world, from a life of relentless speed to a far slower one, in comfortable, very well-appointed surroundings with fine food and enjoyable company. Most cruise barges operate six-day cruises so that the seventh day can be spent in cleaning and preparing the vessel again for the next set of passengers.

Full board aboard your chosen barge cruise is included in the cruise fare, and everything is cooked to order. If the weather is fine, breakfast and lunches can, aboard some cruise barges, be taken on deck. All drinks (both alcoholic and non-alcoholic), champagne and wines with dinner are typically included.

In Europe, barge cruises can be taken in Belgium, France, Germany, and Holland, although the most popular country is undoubtedly France, where barge cruising has been

bar), bicycles, side trips, and airport/railway transfers. Typically, other activities, such as horse riding, golf, tennis or hot-air ballooning, can be arranged for you (at extra cost).

The dress code is totally casual at all times (don't even think of taking a tux, or even a tie), but at the beginning and end of the season (April–October/November), the weather can be unreliable, sometimes cold and wet, so make sure you take clothing that can be layered, including sweaters and a waterproof windbreaker. *For more on barge cruising in France see pages 193–199. For listings of cruise barge companies see pages 317–318.*

carefully packaged and practised for many years. Almost all crew aboard the barges in France speak English and French; many of them also speak German and Spanish.

Barge cruise rates typically range from US$800 to more than $3,000 per person for a six-day cruise, with considerable variation according to the season. All rates typically include a champagne reception, a cabin with private facilities, all meals, good wine with lunch and dinner, beverages (including an open

LEFT: *L'Art de Vivre* luxury barge cruises the canals of Burgundy in central France.
ABOVE: shelling walnuts at the Sarlat festival, Dordogne.

RIVER CRUISE COMPANIES

For full contact details see pages 317–320.

Abercrombie & Kent

Abercrombie & Kent was founded in 1953 in Chicago, Illinois, by the father of Geoffrey Kent, the company's current American president, and started out as an operator of African safari tours. The company has offered river cruises since 1978. Today, as part of a broad portfolio of upmarket holidays, it sells luxury barge cruises, as well as Nile cruises on the very smart *Sun Boat IV*, which the company owns. *Sun Boat* passengers enjoy a number of perks, including private docking at Luxor, Aswan and Kom Ombo.

Arosa

In 2003, the US cruise giant Carnival Corporation pulled out of the European river cruising market with the sale of four vessels under its Arosa brand (part of Seetours, in turn part of P&O Princess, which Carnival owns) to German shipowner Horst Rahe.

Arosa is now being developed as a young (relatively), active brand. The fleet of six vessels is being extended to ten, with a strong emphasis on activity, shopping, nightlife, on-board spa treatments and "experiences". The product is marketed exclusively to the German-speaking market. You can't miss the Arosa boats

to cruise the Danube. Passengers are mainly American, 55-plus, and the cruises focus strongly on "enrichment", with on-board lecturers and a comprehensive tour programme included in the price.

CroisiEurope – Alsace Croisières

Alsace Croisières was founded in 1979 in France, and merged with CroisiEurope in 1997. The company has its headquarters in Strasbourg, and has offices in Lyon and Paris. The fleet consists of 25 river cruise vessels (some owned, some chartered). CroisiEurope specialises in river cruising for French-speaking

on the Danube and the Rhône – they sport big red lips and a red rose painted on the bow.

Avalon Waterways

This is a new river cruise operator, based in Colorado and formed by coach tour giants Globus and Cosmos. The company launched in 2004 on the Danube, Rhine and Moselle rivers with one ship, the MS *Symphony*, and quickly added the *Artistry* to its fleet in May 2004. This new vessel attracted a lot of attention because of its French balconies, and "big ship" features in the bedrooms – satellite TV, large, comfortable beds, duvets and minibars. In 2005, another vessel, *Poetry*, was launched

passengers who don't particularly care to mingle with passengers of other nationalities. It has its own extensive fleet of river cruise vessels, most of which have the same layout, cabin sizes, features and facilities, and thus there is consistency across the brand.

CroisiEurope also features gastronomic theme cruises several times each year, including dinners ashore with such notable French chefs as Marc Haeberlin and Paul Bocuse.

Grand Circle Travel

Grand Circle Travel was founded in New York by Ethel Andrus, a retired schoolteacher, in 1958. She founded the American Association of Retired Persons (AARP – today a very large organisation for senior citizens) and served its members until 1982. Grand Circle Travel was purchased in 1985 by Alan Lewis and moved to Boston. Today, Grand Circle Travel serves all retired Americans, not just AARP members, and has a fleet of six vessels. The company also offers an extensive array of pre- and post-cruise optional stays and tours.

Dining is in an open-seating arrangement, and smoking is not allowed inside any of the vessels (only outside on the open decks). The vessels have a library, and four of the six have a small gym. All on-board announcements are made in English. The company has negotiated prime docking space in many cities, so that passengers from other ships do not walk through the public areas.

Noble Caledonia

Noble Caledonia was founded in London in 1991 by Christer Salen and Andrew Cochran, as an outgrowth of the very successful ocean-going expedition cruise company Salen Lindblad Cruising, of New York (presently known as Quark Expeditions). Noble Caledonia started offering river cruises in 1992.

Noble Caledonia is known for its creative packaging of hassle-free river cruises in many parts of the world, including Europe, Russia, China and Burma. The company has its own exclusive charters as well as booking into other river cruise operators' vessels, and tailors the river cruise holiday to its mainly British and North American passengers, for whom such things as transfers and baggage handling are always included in attractively packaged, good-value river cruise and land holidays.

Note that because Noble Caledonia does not directly own its own river cruise vessels, the company has to rely on the operating and product-delivery standards of those on board the vessels under charter (although the company always has one or more representatives aboard each and every sailing). All on-board announcements are typically made in English (and/or whichever language is spoken by the operating company).

LEFT: the Christmas market at Trier on the Moselle.
RIGHT: a few cruises covered in this book – such as those on the Vistula, Guadiana and some Scottish itineraries – spend some time in coastal waters.

Orient-Express

In 2004, the luxury hotel, train and cruise operator Orient-Express acquired the French canal and river cruise company Afloat in France, including five de luxe canal barges. The barges, known as *péniches*, accommodate between six and 12 passengers, and are the last word in luxury; two even have heated swimming pools.

Bicycles for guests are carried on board and excursions include wine-tasting and private chateau visits. Barge cruises can be combined with a journey on the luxurious Venice Simplon-Orient Express train from London or Venice to Paris.

Peter Deilmann River Cruises

The late Peter Deilmann was one of the true pioneers when he started his river cruise operations along Europe's rivers in 1983. In 1993, he took over Danube operator Erste Donau as well as Dresdner Kreutzfahrt.

The company, now run by Deilmann's two daughters, owns a small shipbuilding yard which builds the river cruise vessels for its fleet, thus providing consistency and control in terms of fit and finish and interior décor. There are marketing and sales offices in Alexandria (Virginia, USA) and London (UK), while the head office is located in Neustadt in Holstein, Germany. The fleet presently consists of nine river cruise vessels, seven of which are rated five-star.

The Peter Deilmann company markets extensively to North American, British and German-speaking passengers and has over 300 itineraries from which to choose. The interior décor of the vessels is elegant, even grand, like that found in small European boutique hotels, with lots of dark woods and gleaming brass, as well as a substantial amount of artwork, most chosen by Peter Deilmann himself from an extensive collection. There is a certified doctor aboard all Peter Deilmann river cruise vessels. All cruises are of seven nights or

started offering river cruises in 1991 and has both exclusive charters and allocations of cabins on other river cruise operators' vessels. Passengers are mainly German-speaking, and transfers and baggage handling are usually included in attractively packaged, good-value river cruise and land holidays.

Note that because the company does not directly own its own river cruise vessels, it therefore has to rely on the operating and product-delivery standards of those on board the vessels under charter (although Phoenix Reisen always has one or more representatives aboard each and every sailing).

longer, and several themes have recently been introduced, including music on the Danube, post-cruise golf in France and Germany, cycle tours and garden cruises.

Note that two of the vessels have interior (no view) cabins: *Danube Princess* (eight) and *Mozart* (four). All on-board announcements are typically made in English and German or in German only, depending on the passenger mix on each cruise.

Phoenix Reisen

Phoenix Reisen was founded in 1974 by Johannes Zurneiden. The company has its headquarters in Bonn, Germany. Phoenix Reisen

Cruises are packaged at a very moderate price and, although the vessels are not the best around, they are quite adequate and very comfortable. Basic-quality table wines are usually included for lunch and dinner. All on-board announcements are made in German.

Scylla Tours

Scylla Tours, a family-run business, was founded in 1973 by Andre Reitsma and is based in Basel, Switzerland. The fleet presently consists of 12 modern, comfortable river cruise vessels with fairly traditional interior design, fittings and soft furnishings. Some have balcony cabins. The deck lounge chairs are made of stainless steel or aluminium, rather than plastic, and are more elegant, practical and comfortable. Note that smoking is permitted, but only on the open deck and on one side of the lounge. All on-board announcements are typically made in German (although this depends on the vessel charterers). Scylla Tours operates on most of Europe's main rivers, including the Rhine and tributaries, the Danube, the Elbe and the Po.

Sea Cloud Cruises

Sea Cloud Cruises was founded in 1978 by a consortium of nine shipowners. The company started operating river cruises in 1996. The fleet

Transocean Tours

Transocean Tours was founded in 1954. The company is well known in Europe (particularly in Germany), and operates two fine ocean-going cruise ships *(Astor* and *Astoria)*. It started offering river cruises in 1980. The company charters several river cruise vessels in Europe and Russia, principally for its German-speaking passengers who enjoy the traditional rather than the contemporary. Table wines are usually included for lunch and dinner, and on-board announcements are typically made in German.

The company offers cruises on the Danube, Rhine and tributaries, Moldau (as the Vltava is

presently consists of two river cruise vessels, the most upscale in Europe, *River Cloud* and *River Cloud II*. Both are often under charter to various cruise/tour operators at the upper end of the market. The décor and facilties are superb, while cuisine and service on board is of an extremely high standard. While the cruises appear expensive, they are worth it (remember that, in this case, you really do get what you pay for). All on-board announcements are made in English and German.

LEFT: luxury cabin on the *Danube Princess*.
ABOVE: all river cruises include some form of on-board entertainment, usually performed by the crew.

known to German speakers) and Elbe, the Dutch waterways, the Rhône and the Douro, as well as in Russia.

Travel Renaissance

Travel Renaissance was founded in 1977 by Graham Clubb, its present owner. One of the major sellers of river cruises in the United Kingdom (for over 20 years Travel Renaissance was the general sales agent for KD River Cruises, which was acquired by Viking River Cruises in 2000), it now sells river cruises on many of the world's rivers. The company does not own or operate any vessels of its own; it therefore has to rely on the operating and product-delivery standards of those on board the vessels under charter (although the company always has one or more representatives aboard each and every sailing). The company's passengers are all English-speaking, and all on-board announcements are made in English (although this will depend on the vessel and passenger mix).

Uniworld

California-based Uniworld was founded by Yugoslavian travel entrepreneur Serba Ilich in 1976. and is now owned by The Travel Corporation. The company started offering river

cruises in 1994 (in Europe, adding China in 1996). Uniworld was also one of the first major companies to charter Russian river cruise vessels exclusively for use by American passengers. Uniworld features cruises across Europe and Russia, as well as in China (where vessels are operated by Victoria Cruises). The fleet presently consists of 21 vessels.

The company has its own wholly owned dedicated river cruise line in Europe, Global River Cruises (which owns 75 percent of Holland River Line), established as a Swiss-owned company and based in Basel, Switzerland. On the cruises, food and service are geared to American tastes, and the boats have

features like large double beds and a non-smoking policy (except on deck). All shore excursions are included in the price of the cruise, and each vessel has its own cruise manager. Announcements are made in English only.

Value World Tours

Value World Tours was founded in 1993 by Samo Toplak, and first started offering river cruises in Russia using chartered vessels and sailings. The company caters exclusively to North Americans. River cruise vessels used for its programmes are part of a fleet of 13 chartered or leased boats, none of which is owned by the company; it also books into programmes operated by other river cruise owner/operators such as Viking River Cruises, so there may be a mix of nationalities on board. The company therefore has to rely on the operating and product-delivery standards of those on board the vessels under charter (although the company always has one or more representatives aboard each and every sailing). The company specialises in river cruises to Egypt, Europe and European Russia (as well as to China). Shore excursions are included, but port and air taxes are not. All announcements are typically made in English, although this will depend on whether a vessel is under full charter or not.

Vantage Deluxe World Tours

Vantage Deluxe World Tours was founded in 1994 by Gordon Lewis, whose son, Henry, is the present president. The company has its headquarters in Boston, USA, and serves the North American market. The fleet presently consists of three vessels (the *River Explorer*, *River Navigator* and *River Odyssey*) owned by the company, as well as a variety of charter cruisers in Russia, on the Elbe and on the French waterways.

All three of the company's own vessels are relatively new and very smart. Dining is in an open-seating arrangement (there are no assigned tables). Smoking is not allowed inside any of the vessels (only outside on the open decks). Special touches like bathrobes in the cabins, feather duvets, CNN television and minibars are available, and one vessel, the *River Odyssey*, even has a walking track for exercise.

Low-salt, low-fat, gluten-free and diabetic menu selections are available. All on-board announcements are made in English.

Viking River Cruises

Viking River Cruises was founded by a group of investors headed by Torstein Hagen (formerly connected with the now defunct ocean-going Royal Viking Line) and Christer Salen (formerly connected with Salen Lindblad Cruising – the ocean-going expedition cruise company now called Quark Expeditions). The company has grown fast from small beginnings in 1997, when it started with one, then four Russian vessels. It then purchased Aqua Viva, a French operator with two vessels. In 2000, in something of a major coup in the river cruise industry, Viking River Cruises purchased KD cruise operator, with a range of itineraries all across Europe and European Russia.

Aboard some vessels, soft drinks, beer and wine are included for lunch and dinner, and food and its presentation and taste are strong points. General service levels on board (and off) are consistently excellent. The destination and itinerary literature is extensive and extremely informative.

Some vessels (typically the newest ones) cater exclusively to North Americans (marketed in the USA by California-based Viking River Cruises Inc.), while others cater to European and international passengers. On-board

River Cruises (the oldest established operator of river cruise vessels in Europe). Included in the purchase were the landing stages, an extremely valuable asset.

An aggressive new-build programme saw several new vessels built specifically for North American passengers and introduced in a period of just two years. The fleet presently consists of 24 river cruise vessels, some of which are very new, and some of which are older. Viking is now the world's largest river

LEFT: modern river cruise vessels use radar and sophisticated electronics.
ABOVE: cruising past Melk Abbey on the Danube.

announcements may be made in one, two or several languages, depending on the passenger-nationality mix. However, aboard the newer vessels dedicated to the American market, announcements are made in English only.

Voyages Jules Verne

This London-based tour operator was founded in 1977, operating exotic train journeys in Central Asia. The company expanded rapidly in the 1980s, and in 1998 was acquired by Kuoni Travel. Today, it packages a wide variety of river cruises in France, Egypt, Russia, Spain and Portugal, as well as Christmas cruises on the Danube. ❑

AN A–Z OF RIVER CRUISING

A full rundown of what to expect on board, from types of cabin, food and drink, to making the most of a day on the water. See also Travel Tips, pages 321–4

River cruise vessels may look broadly similar from the outside, but levels of comfort and equipment on board do in fact vary widely. This chapter is a comprehensive guide to what you can expect.

Accommodation (cabins)

Although most cabins are on the small side when compared to hotel rooms, with limited closet and drawer space, they should prove to be quite comfortable for a one- or two-week journey. Virtually all cabins have an outside (river-facing) view, with the exception of the *Danube Princess* and *Mozart*, which have a few interior (no view) cabins. Almost all cabins will have a private bathroom.

Generally speaking, the higher up the vessel you are, the better, roomier (and more expensive) your cabin will be. *(For information on cabin costs see page 28.)* Upper-deck cabins have larger river-view windows than cabins on the lowest deck, which usually have smaller or half-height windows or portholes. In real-estate terminology, this translates to location, location, location. However, there are generally only two decks of cabins aboard most vessels in Europe and on the Nile – only the Russian vessels typically have three or four decks of cabins. Cabin sizes vary from a dimensionally challenged 6 sq. metres (64 sq. ft) to a very expansive 45 sq. metres (484 sq. ft), depending on vessel and river. Some vessels have "suites", which are usually a much larger cabin rather than a suite of rooms in the traditional sense.

Expect bathrooms to be functional rather than sumptuous – there simply isn't room on a river cruise vessel to accommodate the luxurious touches you would find in a hotel suite, or in the top suites on board an ocean-going ship.

Romantics should note that twin beds are the norm, particularly aboard some of the older vessels; most of these are normally fixed and can seldom be pushed together. Many cabins in the latest vessels feature a personal safe, a minibar, a television and DVD, and an alarm clock/radio. The ceilings may be rather low, however

(they tend to be somewhat higher in vessels built before 1980), and the beds are typically shorter and narrower than you may be used to at home.

Perhaps the most noticeable recent design feature is one that imitates the ocean-going cruise ships, and that is the introduction of cabins with that revered bit of space – a private balcony. Sitting there sipping drinks while watching the scenery drift by really is the most delightfully decadent feeling. Having said that, not all "balconies" have any space for seating at all – some are so-called "French balconies", where the doors open but there is a railing immediately outside.

On European river cruises and cruise barges, European duvets are usually provided, rather

---

LEFT: cruising down the Elbe.
RIGHT: celebrating the start of the cruise.

than sheets and blankets. Anti-allergenic pillows may be available, although it is wise to make your request known at the time of booking.

Cuisine

Good food and service are essential elements of any successful river cruise operation. In this regard, there is a wide variation, and some operators are much better than others. All meals are included in the price of the cruise, but alcoholic drinks are almost always extra.

Although much of what is served is intended to satisfy the tastes of whichever nationality is prevalent on board *(see panel on page 42)*, river

Most vessels feature self-serve buffets for breakfast and luncheon. While buffets look fine when they are fresh, after a few minutes of attack by passengers serving themselves, they generally look quite unappetising. Aboard some vessels (particularly the better ones in Europe), the order for hot choices will be taken by your table waiter and cooked to order in the galley.

Passengers should not have to play guessing games when it comes to food, but many river cruise operators still forget to put labels on food items; this slows down any buffet operation. Labels on salad dressings, sauces and cheeses are often forgotten or slightly vague,

cruise operators do often try hard to provide cuisine that reflects the region in which they are cruising – goulash in Hungary, Middle Eastern dishes in Egypt, *blinis* in Russia, for example. Wines will also usually reflect the region in which you are cruising; in Egypt, it's a good idea to develop a taste for the local wines as all imported alcohol is very expensive on board.

On the lower-priced river cruise vessels you will inevitably get frozen food that has simply been reheated. To get fresh food (particularly fresh fish and the best cuts of meats), river cruise operators must pay significantly more, adding to the overall price of a cruise. It's certainly a case of getting what you pay for.

particularly aboard vessels with passengers of many nationalities.

All dining rooms have large river picture-view windows and typically almost all passengers, including those not seated by a window, will have a view. If the boat is docked, though, you may be moored two or three deep, in which case the curtains will be closed to prevent people on the neighbouring vessel from staring in. This can be disappointing on a sunny day, and also claustrophobic.

The principal difference in the present design of dining rooms lies in the layout of the buffet display-counter set-up. In many cases, little attention has been paid to food presentation, and little thought given to hygiene; you won't see the antiseptic wipes present on most ocean-going ships nowadays. Tables located adjacent to the doors or open entrance to the galley (kitchen) tend to be noisy, and should be avoided if possible.

Where you eat and with whom depends on the vessel and the operating company. Aboard all European vessels, for example, dining is at one seating for all meals. Aboard the German vessels of Peter Deilmann River Cruises and those operated by Viking River Cruises, two of the largest European operators, dining is at assigned tables (this means you could be seated whom you wish. Tables for two are a rarity; most tables seat four, six or eight. It is a good idea to ask to be seated at a larger table, because if you are a couple seated at a table for four and you do not get along with your table partners, there is no one else to talk to. And remember, if the ship is full, it may be difficult to change tables once the cruise has started. If you are assigned to a table with people you don't like, discreetly ask the maître d' to move you – they will try.

Dinner is normally a fully served meal (aboard some river cruise vessels, you can help yourself to salads and cheeses from the evening buffet). There will usually be a choice of only

next to or opposite strangers, who may or may not speak your language, depending on where the vessel is marketed). Aboard the vessels operated by Grand Circle Travel and Vantage Deluxe World Tours, there are no assigned or reserved tables).

Dining options

Dinner is normally a one-seating meal, with either assigned or unassigned table seating. When it is unassigned, you can sit where you want, with

LEFT: Rhine cruise ship lit up at night.
ABOVE: the evening meal is a chance to get to know your fellow passengers.

two main courses, and eating "off menu", for example, ordering a grilled steak instead of the richer fare on offer, is not standard practice as it may be in smart hotels or on board ocean-going cruise ships.

Most river cruise vessels cannot offer a real "gourmet" experience because the galley (a vessel's kitchen) may be striving to turn out up to 300 meals at the same time, from a very small and confined space. The chefs will, however, bake all bread on board and will often produce surprisingly elaborate pastries, cakes and canapés. In general you will find a good selection of palatable, pleasing and complete meals served in comfortable surroundings. Of course, river cruise vessels that have fewer passengers will be able to offer better meals.

Experienced passengers who "collect" river cruises have seen, smelt and tasted it all before: at worst, you may come across rock-hard lobster, year-old farmed and frostbitten shrimp, stringy chicken and grenade-quality meats. Not to mention processed cheese, soggy salty crackers, unripe fruits and coffee that looks (and tastes) like army surplus paint... Sadly, it is all there in the river cruise industry's global cafeteria.

Most passengers agree that river cruise coffee is generally poor, but often it is simply the chlorinated water that gives it a different taste. Euro-

peans prefer strong coffee, usually made from the coffee beans of African countries like Kenya, while North Americans usually drink coffee from Colombia or Jamaica. European tea drinkers like to drink tea out of teacups, not coffee or mugs (very few river cruise vessels know how to make a decent cup of tea, so British passengers in particular should be aware of this).

A word about wine etiquette. If you are sharing a table with strangers, do you buy your own or do you split the bill? Generally, if you all get on well and nobody is a visibly fast or heavy drinker, or is boasting about their expensive tastes, it's pleasant, and conducive to a good

NATIONALITIES AND DIETARY PREFERENCES

There are some notable differences between the different nationalities of passengers, and these are reflected in what's likely to be on offer on board. Some well-known examples:

Asian, British, French, German and other European passengers like boiled eggs served in real china eggcups for breakfast. North Americans rarely eat boiled eggs, however, and most often put the eggs into a bowl to be eaten with a fork.

German passengers enjoy a wide variety of breads (especially dark breads) and bread rolls as well as a good choice of cheeses for breakfast and lunch. They tend to

like yellow (not white) potatoes.

French passengers have a liking for soft, not flaky, croissants, and may request brioche and jam (jelly) for breakfast.

North Americans tend to drink weak coffee or iced tea with everything, often before, during and after a meal. If this is your preference, you will have to make it clear; in Europe, coffee is normally only served after the meal, not with dessert.

North Americans tend to eat fast, whereas Europeans, for example, like to dine in a more leisurely fashion, treating mealtimes as social occasions.

atmosphere, if you can take turns to buy the wine. If in doubt, simply buy your own – nobody will be offended.

Special requirements

If you are vegetarian, vegan, macrobiotic, counting calories, want a salt-free, sugar-restricted, low-fat, low-cholesterol, or any other diet, advise your travel agent at the time of booking, and get the river cruise operator to confirm that the ship can actually handle your dietary requirements. Note that food does tend to be liberally sprinkled with salt (particularly aboard the vessels operating on Russia's rivers and waterways), and vegetables are often cooked with sauces containing dairy products, salt and sugar. Chefs on board river cruise vessels may not have much experience in catering for vegetarians, so be prepared for repetitive dishes and sometimes odd combinations, such as pasta and chips...

Genetically modified food

The subject of genetically modified food continues to receive much press and attention. Most discerning river cruise operators understand that passengers may require assurances as to their position on the matter. Suffice it to say that there are some by-products of genetically modified food that are difficult to detect due to current labelling regulations. Some (but not all) river cruise operators work closely with their food suppliers to identify and remove any products that contain these ingredients.

If you are unhappy with any aspect of the dining room operation or food, the sooner you tell someone the better. Do not wait until the cruise is over to send a scathing letter to the cruise line, for then it is too late to do anything positive.

Disabled passengers

In general, most vessels lack adequate facilities for passengers with disabilities. Few have elevators, for example, although some have special chair lifts on tracks that rise with the stairs. However, it's on land where most problems occur, particularly in countries where cities are very old and public facilities for the disabled scarcely exist. Depending on the river, many landing stages are connected to steps

LEFT: luxury cabin on the *Viking Kirov*.
RIGHT: most cruises have at least one night when passengers put on a show.

leading up to a city or town. Also, in some locations, vessels are berthed side by side, and passengers may have to walk across the narrow gangways of several vessels to reach land. Think carefully before booking a river cruise if you have mobility problems. It can be done, but you will need a lot of assistance, and hardly any river cruise vessels have cabins for wheelchair users.

Wheelchair accessibility in some destinations can be frustrating, and wheelchair-accessible transportation will be limited. Also, in some destinations, vessels are often tied up alongside each other (the view from your cabin may well

be obscured). This means there could be two, three or four vessels tied up together, and anyone in a wheelchair would have to be carried across the vessels (possibly including steps) in order to be placed on the dockside.

Many riverside cities are hilly, and destinations such as Bratislava have numerous steps to negotiate between river level and street level. Also take into account the fact that many cities are very old, and many cobblestone streets, which make wheeling bone-shakingly difficult and uncomfortable. Vessels occasionally tie up at night in outlying areas, and the staff are not allowed to carry you in your wheelchair across the landing ramp.

Most coaches used for shore excursions or transfers do not have any facilities for carrying wheelchair-bound passengers (no special seats or hydraulic lowering platforms), and no storage space for wheelchairs.

The engine room

It is quite possible that you can make a visit to the engine room, if you so wish (ask at the reception desk). Note, however, that the engine room aboard almost all river cruise vessels is an extremely compact space and will inevitably be very noisy and quite dirty, due to the fact that engines are of the diesel type. You can also ask

to visit the galley and the bridge. On an ocean-going ship, these areas are strictly off-limits because of security reasons, but river cruise vessels are more relaxed and informal. The only time bridge visits are not encouraged is during complicated manoeuvres or bad weather.

Excursions ashore

Shore excursions on a river cruise are a highlight for many passengers, with everything from helicopter rides and hot-air ballooning to wine-tasting, horse riding and musical recitals in historic venues on offer. When shore excursions are included in the cruise fare it will be reflected

ENVIRONMENTAL ISSUES

The release of waste into rivers is a long-standing problem, and although many have cleaned up their act, a significant number of European waterways remain contaminated with industrial toxins, municipal waste and agricultural run-off. Within the European Union, there are strict emission controls in force, but these are not always easy to monitor effectively. In the Balkan reaches of the Danube, chemical spills have decimated fish stocks and other wildlife.

River cruise vessels typically have a waste food compressor that "juices" the waste and disposes of it in the river (and which in turn is eaten by fish). A biological sewage-treatment plant helps minimise pollution.

in the price, but this does take the pressure off holiday spending. If you are visiting new places and want the value of a good guide, it's best to choose a company where excursions are included. Normally, this will comprise full days of activities when the ship is in port and often a couple of evening events, too.

When river cruise operators plan and oversee optional excursions, they assume that passengers have not been to a place before, and aim to show them its highlights in a comfortable manner and at a reasonable price.

Buses or minibuses are usually the principal choice of transportation. This cuts costs and allows the tour operator to narrow the selection of guides to only those most competent, knowledgeable, and fluent in whatever language the majority of passengers speak, while providing some degree of security and control.

Learn to read between the lines on shore excursions: The term "visit" should be taken to mean actually entering the place or building concerned, whereas "see" should be taken to mean viewing from the outside (as from a bus, for example). Beware of excursion guides who give you a coloured disk to wear for "identification". They may be marking you as a "rich" tourist for local shopkeepers. Many cruise lines' ground handlers have the annoy-

pants, taking into account the timing of meals on board (these may be altered according to excursion times). Departure times are listed in the descriptive literature and in the daily programme (delivered to your cabin), and may or may not be announced over the vessel's public address system. There are no refunds if you miss the excursion. If you are hearing-impaired, make arrangements with the shore-excursion staff to assist you in departing for your excursions at the correct times.

City excursions for larger cities are basically superficial, although they do provide a useful introduction. To see specific sights in more

ing habit of throwing in an unannounced factory or shop visit on a shore excursion. This is inevitably a ruse for the guide and the tour operator to earn commission. It's particularly bad practice in Russia and Egypt. If you can see your guide building up to this, it's worth negotiating ten minutes in the shop instead of half an hour and adding 20 minutes instead to the local market.

Optional excursions are timed to be most convenient for the greatest number of partici-

detail, or to get to know a city in a more intimate fashion, go alone with a guidebook or with a small group and a private guide. Go by taxi or bus, or walk directly to the places that are of most interest to you.

Going solo? If you hire a taxi for sightseeing, negotiate the price in advance, and do not pay until you get back to the vessel or to your final destination. If you are with friends, hiring a taxi for a full- or half-day sightseeing trip can often work out far cheaper than renting a car, and you also avoid the hazards of driving. Naturally, prices vary according to destination, but this can be an excellent way of sightseeing, particularly if you can find a driver who speaks

FAR LEFT: service levels are high.
LEFT: some vessels have stairlifts.
ABOVE: the sun deck has many uses.

your language, and who has a comfortable, air-conditioned vehicle.

Health on board

Although first-aid kits are carried, river cruise vessels, unlike ocean-going cruise ships, don't generally have a doctor or nurse on board (with the exception of Peter Deilmann River Cruises and most Russian vessels). However, as the shore is never too far away, any necessary arrangements can be made quickly. Always take out comprehensive travel and medical insurance before travelling. It is extremely unlikely that you will get seasick unless the flat-

bottomed river cruiser crosses open water on a choppy day. This occurs at the mouth of the River Elbe, and when crossing Russia's Lake Ladoga to get to Valaam Island, as well as on the new river/ ocean cruises offered along the Algarve. On any of these, take seasickness-prevention pills as a precaution.

Information on board

If you need help or information, the reception desk is the place to start. Centrally located, this is the nerve centre of the vessel for general passenger information and problems. Opening hours are posted on the desk and given in the daily programme.which is delivered to your cabin every

evening detailing the following day's activities. A few vessels have internet access *(see page 50)*. Most river cruise vessels also have a library, offering a small selection of books, reference material and periodicals, as well as board games such as Scrabble, backgammon and chess.

Main lounge

Here, the placement of the bar is important, in that it acts as a vessel's main interior lounge, with large panoramic windows for river viewing. Ideally, sight lines should not be impeded. In other words, placing the bar at the back of the room provides more prime seating and viewing spaces in the all-important forward section (particularly when the outside weather may be chilly at the beginning and end of the cruise season in Europe).

Money and expenses on board

Full board is always included in the cruise fare or tour package price. This typically includes a self-serve buffet breakfast, self-serve lunch, afternoon coffee/tea, full-service dinner and late-night snack. In most cases, the chefs aboard river cruise vessels purchase their own food in local markets, so it's usually very fresh. Aboard some vessels and hotel barges, beer, soft drinks and wine may also be included in the fare.

There's no need to carry cash on board, although of course you will need it for any shore excursions; *see following page*. It is now the norm to cruise cash-free and to settle your account with one payment (by cash or credit card) prior to disembarking on the last day. Often this is arranged by making an imprint of a credit card when you embark, permitting you to sign for everything. Before the end of the cruise, a detailed statement is delivered to your cabin. Some cruise lines may discontinue their "cashless" system for the last day of the cruise, which can be most irritating – this means you must carry and pay with cash for all purchases.

Money on shore

Many banks, particularly in Eastern Europe, are uneasy with travellers' cheques. Not only will you need a passport to change them into the local currency, but you may also end up paying a commission to convert them.

It would be better to carry a major credit/debit card. You will get a better rate when you use these cards at one of the international cashpoint network operators than from most high-street outlets, or bureaux de change. A credit card will be useful if you are, for example, taking a River Danube cruise, which traverses several countries.

Overall, it is best to diversify your funds, use a combination of payment methods, and *always* have some back-up cash (euros or dollars) to hand. Most travel insurance policies will cover money stolen from a credit card – typically up to US$300.

Of the countries included in this book, Austria, Belgium, France, Germany, Holland, Italy, Portugal and Spain all use euros. Those countries which became EU member states in 2004

Other facilities

Some of the larger vessels may also have a small pool, sauna, massage room, library area and, occasionally, internet access *(see page 50)*. More upmarket vessels have a small hairdressing salon, a proper shore excursion office, a laundry for passengers' use, and sometimes a doctor on board (not a legal requirement for a river cruise in Europe). The *Mozart*, the height of luxury, has a fitness centre and coffee shop.

Some additional features may be less obvious. More recent vessels may have stair lifts. Some have cabin windows that open fully, or French balconies, or hotel-style beds rather than

(including the Czech Republic, Slovakia, Hungary and Poland) may switch to the euro by 2007 or 2008 (the Balkan countries still use their own currencies, but euros – or dollars – are generally accepted on the tourist trail). The currency in Russia is the rouble, and in Egypt the Egyptian pound. If you are taking a Russian or Nile cruise, it's best to purchase local currency when you arrive (exchange rates are better than you will find if you purchase currency in the UK or US before departure).

LEFT: the reception area displays arrival and departure times.
ABOVE: the lounge bar on Peter Deilmann's *Cezanne*.

single beds arranged in an L-shape (common on older vessels).

On-board bookings

It's advisable to make appointments as soon after boarding as possible (particularly on short cruises) for things like the on-board spa and hairdresser, if there is one. Charges are comparable to those ashore. It is also essential that you advise the cruise operator at the time of booking of any special dietary requirements.

On deck

Most vessels have a decent amount of outdoor deck space, and the atmosphere on deck is usually convivial – it's a great place to sit, relax and watch the scenery drift by. Many of the older vessels (pre-1990) also have a small, sheltered, aft viewing deck.

The top deck is the most important area for many passengers. It is typically an open deck, and runs almost the full length of the vessel. In the front will be the navigation bridge (pilot house), which, on some vessels, will have been cleverly constructed so that it can be lowered hydraulically into the deck below to avoid low bridges – particularly on parts of the Danube, the Elbe and the Po. Any other canopies and side railings are also designed so that they can

Safety on the river

Within the European Union, travel companies and tour operators that sell river cruises have to adhere to certain rules regarding fire, food preparation and water quality. On cruises in Egypt and Russia, safety may be more variable. A good Egyptian cruise vessel hotel manager will proudly show guests the kitchen and the water-purification equipment (stomach upsets are a big issue among travellers to Egypt). If he or she won't, you should be suspicious and exercise extreme caution when eating salad from the buffet or ordering ice in drinks.

be folded down (some vessels have canopies for deck buffets), while chairs and sun loungers will remain on deck.

Many vessels will have a life-size chess game or a sunken small pool – a plunge pool rather than somewhere to swim. When the top deck is in use, it is a wonderful vantage point for the ease of river life, for watching the scenery constantly unfolding before you. Every second is different, and this is where there is a vast difference between ocean-going and river cruising – the proximity of the shore from a river vessel makes it all come alive. The top deck is also a very social place, where you'll meet others, have light meals and simply sit and talk.

There will always be some basic safety and life-saving equipment on board, but the crew are not obliged to carry out lifeboat drill as they are on an ocean-going vessel.

When it comes to fire precautions, the age of the vessel does count as well; most older vessels don't have sprinkler systems, for example. On some rivers, cruises are seasonal; so, too, are the staff, which means that safety training may not be as good as it should be. Always familiarise yourself with the nearest exit and the location of life jackets as a precaution.

There have, fortunately, been very few incidents involving river cruise vessels in trouble over the past ten years. The good thing is that you're never too far from a river bank.

Perhaps the most suspect when it comes to safety are the older vessels on the Nile, where safety standards are extremely basic. Navigation is by vision only, in daylight hours, with boats operating a system of flashes of a mirror, toots on the horn or, in an emergency, radio contact, to avoid traffic coming in the opposite direction. There are no depth sounders on board. If you visit the bridge on a Nile cruiser, you'll be astonished at how basic it is. In Europe, most vessels operating on the Danube adhere to strict safety standards set by the German and Swiss classification societies. Unless the captain holds licences for the various sections of the Danube, there may be a river pilot aboard for most of the time. Radar and echo sounders form part of the navigation equipment.

Security has become an issue on board river and ocean-going vessels since 9/11. While ocean-going ships will scan luggage and operate a swipe-card system with photo ID for everyone boarding the ship, river cruise operators are a lot more relaxed. Luggage is not X-rayed. Photo ID cards are not usually issued. The newer river cruise vessels do have entryway doors that are secured by a code that can be changed during the cruise, or, indeed, at any time. Many of the older vessels (typically those built before 2000) do not have entryway doors with codes, although all vessels normally have one member of the crew on gangway access duty in all ports and destinations.

In Egypt, the situation is different. People and bags are scanned before boarding any vessel and, indeed, before entering any hotel or temple ashore. There are armed guards everywhere – on the bridge of every Nile cruiser, at major antiquities and temples, on tourist buses and generally patrolling the streets. Strangely, this is not intimidating; their presence is more benign and reassuring, and, despite the recent tragedies it has endured, Egypt is still a welcoming, relatively easy place in which to travel once you've learned to deal with the enthusiasm of the local traders.

LEFT: the top deck should be a place to sit and relax, watch the scenery drift by and, sometimes, be entertained.
RIGHT: a promenade deck runs right around river cruise vessels.

Sailing times

In each destination, the vessel's sailing time will be posted at the gangway (this is usually in the main lobby/reception desk). Note that river cruise vessels do not usually wait for individual passengers who are delayed. Don't miss the boat! If you do, then you will have to catch up with it at the next port of call.

Smoking policy

In continental Europe, Russia and Egypt, a lot of people still smoke, and on a cruise of mixed nationalities there are likely to be smokers who will light up in the bar and possibly in

the restaurant. Smoke can sometimes permeate the corridors of river cruisers, too. In general, aboard most vessels smoking is not permitted in any cabin, although this depends in part on the operator and, in part, on the mix of nationalities on board. People will still smoke on their private balconies.

If you feel really strongly about smoking, you're best advised to look for a vessel marketed to North American passengers. These are the only ones to enforce a total smoking ban inside – people can still smoke on the open decks. Incidentally, Italy now has a complete ban on smoking in public places, which includes river cruise vessels.

Telephones and the internet

Most river cruise vessels (but not cruise barges) have a direct-dial satellite telephone system. You can call from your cabin to anywhere in the world, and calls are completed instantly. Satellite calls are incredibly expensive, though, and you would be better advised to take a cell-phone along instead to stay in touch with home. There is a signal throughout most of Europe and all the way along the Nile from Aswan to Luxor, provided your phone is set up for roaming.

A few vessels have internet/email access, although only the very latest ones; the *MS Amadagio*, for example, brand new in 2006 and cruising the Danube, will have internet access in every cabin. Several of the more luxurious Nile cruisers have a computer terminal in the library with internet access. On most European vessels, though, passengers will only be able to receive emails via the reception desk. Messages will be printed off and delivered to cabins. If internet access is important, it's better to rely on cyber cafés along the way (almost all of the larger ports of call will have these).

What to wear

River cruise vessels tend to have a more relaxed attitude to dress code than ocean-going vessels,

RIVER GENDERS

Whether a river is known as a he or a she depends on its behaviour. Take the River Rhône, for example – almost always referred to in the masculine because the waters can be turbulent, bothersome and rough at times. The Saône, on the other hand, is a gentler kind of river – more beautiful, more tranquil – and is thus referred to as "she", as is the "beautiful" Blue Danube (although Napoleon described the Danube as the "king of the rivers of Europe"). The Rhine is male, always referred to as "Father Rhine". The Nile is also deemed a masculine river. The River Volga is always referred to as the "dear little mother" (even though it is the mightiest river in Europe).

the more traditional of which have a dress code for dinner every night. The best bet is to go for smart-casual in the evenings, and practical during the day. Sturdy, comfortable footwear is essential for walking around medieval towns, with their cobbled streets.

On one evening, there is usually a special captain's dinner, when it's advisable to dress up a bit more, but no more formal than jacket and tie for men and cocktail dresses for women.

Sometimes there will be a fancy-dress evening. These are purely optional, but you'll find, particularly on the Nile, where an Egyptian evening is inevitable, that people do make an effort. ❑

A Day on Board

Life on a river cruise tends to start early in the morning, as most days include fairly intensive sightseeing. Waking up to the sound of birdsong is a wonderful way to start the day, and early morning is a great time to be up on deck with a cup of coffee, communing with nature in the fresh, damp air.

Breakfast is a hearty affair, usually with a hot and cold buffet and, on more luxurious vessels, an omelette station. A lot of European vessels have German-influenced breakfasts, with cheeses and cold cuts. If the vessel is sailing, everybody will be up on deck soon after breakfast, sunbathing, reading and watching the scenery drift by. If there's something of note to see, the on-board lecturer will often provide running commentary. Some vessels have binoculars and birdwatching books in the library, too. A day on the river has a dreamy quality, and after a few hours, it's easy to appreciate why people find river cruising so relaxing.

On days in port, you'll see coaches lined up on the quayside, and most passengers will disappear on excursions soon after breakfast (sometimes as early as 8am). There won't be anything laid on for those who choose to stay behind, although lunch will, of course, be served. In Europe, a lot of tours involve walking, as medieval town centres were not built for buses, so those with walking difficulties should be careful about which cruise they book. Also, bear in mind that a lot of the docks are a long way from the town, so independent sightseeing can be tricky and involve long walks or cab journeys. The Nile is an exception; Nile cruisers almost always dock in the middle of Luxor or Aswan.

Lunch is always a buffet. There will be a good choice of fresh green salad items, although dressings may be standard and unimaginative. In continental Europe, low-calorie, low-fat, low-salt and low-cholesterol salad dressings are often difficult to find.

Sometimes the vessel will stay in port all day and sometimes it will move at lunchtime to the next port of call, and there will be another short excursion before dinner. People usually gather in the bar before dinner, and sometimes there is a talk from the on-board guide about the following day's excursions.

LEFT: facilities on luxury vessels such as the *Sea Cloud* includes fitness equipment and saunas.
RIGHT: all vessels have plenty of outdoor space in which to sit and read or watch the scenery slowly drift by.

Dinner will typically consist of a choice of a hot or cold appetiser, choice of two entrées (one fish, one meat), and dessert. Some vessels provide lavish, seven-course meals, which are impressive but not good for the waistline (take some exercise by walking around the deck a few times, and/or walk as much as possible on shore excursions). Vegetarians can be catered for but the food may be a little stodgy or unimaginative.

Typically, you'll share a table with other passengers, usually speaking your language. This can be a great way to make new friends, but if it doesn't work out, it is perfectly acceptable to ask to be moved.

After dinner, there may be entertainment in the

bar in the form of a local dance troupe, or a talk on the following day's excursions. Often, there will be an evening excursion ashore, for example, to the ballet in Moscow, or to a Johann Strauss recital in Vienna. These are usually great fun and a good break from the routine of life on board. Otherwise, people tend to gather in the bar, or, on hot nights, on deck with a *digestif*. The bar usually stays open until the last person leaves. River cruising does not, however, involve wild nightlife; people tend to go to bed fairly early. If the vessel is in port all night, though, there's nothing to stop you sampling the local scene. You can return to the vessel whenever you like, provided you have taken your key and ID with you. ❑

PLACES

*A guide to the river cruise routes and ports of
Europe and the Nile, accompanied by diagrammatic maps.
Major ports of call are described in photo essays*

European river cruises cover a wide area and a great variety of destinations, west to east from the green Atlantic fringes of Scotland and Ireland to the steppes of Russia and Ukraine, south to north from the terracotta-hued warmth of Portugal and Italy to the dark, cool forests of Poland and Germany.

It is the heart of the European continent, though, that is in most people's minds when they consider a river cruise. The earliest European river cruises were on the Rhine, and later the Danube, and it isn't hard to see why. Accessible and wonderfully scenic, a trip on these great waterways instantly transports the passenger into old Europe, providing a constantly changing perspective on its history and landscapes.

The Rhine is justly famous for the fabulous scenery along its middle course between the German cities of Mainz and Koblenz, an utterly romantic riverscape of brooding castles perched atop steep hills covered in vineyards. Its major tributaries – the Moselle, Neckar and Main – are also well-established cruise rivers. Most Danube cruises concentrate on the stretch between Passau on the German/Austrian border via Vienna and Bratislava to the Hungarian capital, Budapest – although there is also plenty of interest along the upper course in southern Germany (now linked to the Rhine via the Main–Danube Canal), as well as the lesser-known lower reaches which traverse the Balkans en route to the Black Sea. The Elbe, running from the Czech Republic through eastern Germany to the North Sea, is the other popular river of Central Europe; itineraries explore the beautiful cities of Prague and Dresden.

The second major region for European cruises is Russia. These have proved consistently popular over the years, providing an ideal way to experience a part of the world that was, until recent years, largely off-limits to tourists. Moscow to St Petersburg is by far the most travelled route, offering two fascinating cities and a wealth of interest in between.

It is, however, beyond Europe – on the exotic Nile – that river cruising began. Caesar and Cleopatra are said to have enjoyed a romantic sojourn on its waters, while Thomas Cook set up a cruise business in Egypt in the 1800s – and the river has lost none of its considerable allure. A Nile cruise is simply the best way, bar none, to witness the extraordinary sights of Upper Egypt.

Away from these major cruise rivers, there is a variety of lesser-known waterways to explore. Some, such as the Vistula in Poland and the Guadiana in Portugal, are newcomers to the industry. Others – notably the Douro in northern Portugal, the Po in Italy, and the Rhône and Seine in France – are well established. A wide range of barge cruises and other trips are also possible, mainly in France, the United Kingdom, Ireland and the Low Countries. ❏

PRECEDING PAGES: Reichsburg Castle towers above the Moselle town of Cochem; cruising along the Nile; passing through a lock on the Moscow–Volga Canal.
LEFT: the Chain Bridge, Budapest, illuminated at night.

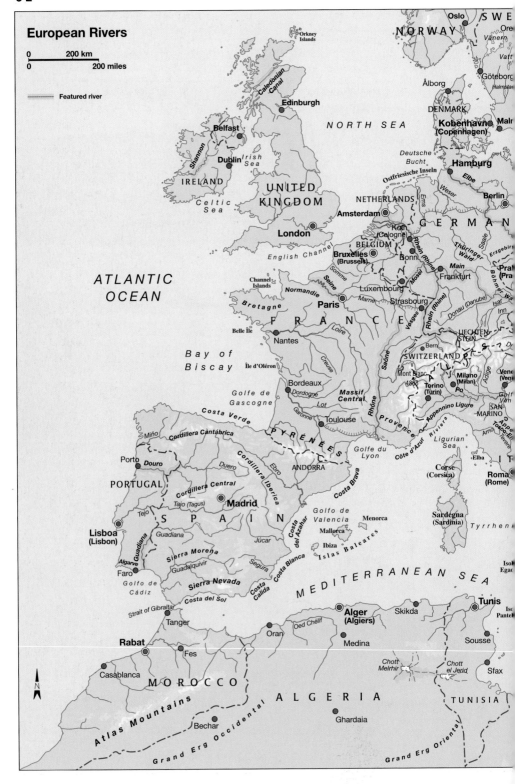

European Rivers

0	200 km
0	200 miles

——— Featured river

ATLANTIC OCEAN

NORTH SEA

NORWAY

SWE

Oslo

Ore

Vänern

Vätt

Ålborg

Göteborg

Halmsta

DENMARK

København
(Copenhagen)

Malr

Deutsche
Bucht

Hamburg

Ostfriesische Inseln

Elbe

Berlin

Weser

G E R M A N

Ems

Saale

Thüringer
Wald

Erzgebir

Köln
(Cologne)

Rhein (Rhine)

Pra
(Pra

Böhm

NETHERLANDS

Amsterdam

Bonn

Main

Frankfurt

Mosel

Isar

Wa

BELGIUM

Bruxelles
(Brussels)

Luxembourg

Strasbourg

Rhein (Rhine)

Donau (Danube)

Inn

Orkney
Islands

Edinburgh

Belfast

Dublin

Irish
Sea

Shannon

IRELAND

Celtic
Sea

UNITED
KINGDOM

London

English Channel

Channel
Islands

Somme

Seine

Normandie

Paris

Bretagne

Marne

Vosges

LIECHTEN-
STEIN

Bern

SWITZERLAND

Adige

Ven
(Ven

Belle Île

Nantes

Loire

Creuse

Mont Blanc
4808

Torino
(Turin)

Milano
(Milan)

Po

SAN
MARINO

Golf
Ven

Bay of
Biscay

Île d'Oléron

Bordeaux

Dordogne

Lot

Massif
Central

Rhône

Saône

Provence

Appennino Ligure

Arno

App

Golfe de
Gascogne

Garonne

Toulouse

Côte d'Azur

Riviera

Ligurian
Sea

Elba

I T

Costa Verde

Miño

Cordillera Cantábrica

PYRÉNÉES

Ebro

ANDORRA

Golfe du
Lyon

Corse
(Corsica)

Roma
(Rome)

Porto

Douro

Duero

Cordillera Ibérica

Costa Brava

PORTUGAL

Cordillera Central

Tejo

Madrid

Tajo (Tagus)

Golfo de
Valencia

Menorca

Sardegna
(Sardinia)

Tyrrhen

Lisboa
(Lisbon)

Guadiana

S P A I N

Júcar

Mallorca

Islas Baleares

Ibiza

Iso
Egac

Algarve

Faro

Sierra Morena

Guadalquivir

Segura

Costa del Azahar

Costa Blanca

MEDITERRANEAN SEA

Golfo de
Cádiz

Sierra Nevada

Costa Calida

Tunis

Iso
Pantel

Costa del Sol

Alger
(Algiers)

Skikda

Strait of Gibraltar

Tanger

Sousse

Rabat

Oran

Oed Chélif

Medina

Sfax

Fes

Chott
Melrhir

Chott
el Jerid

Casablanca

M O R O C C O

A L G E R I A

TUNISIA

Atlas Mountains

Bechar

Grand Erg Occidental

Ghardaia

Grand Erg Orienta

N

THE DANUBE

Winding its way east and south from the foothills of the Alps to the distant shores of the Black Sea, this majestic waterway is a perennial favourite for river cruises

Maps on pages 70, 80, 97

T he Danube has shaped the history of Central Europe over many centuries, as an important transportation route and economic lifeline between the heart of Europe and the Balkans, although, commercially, it is less busy than the Rhine. It has halted armies at its banks and been the inspiration for musical serenades, interludes and waltzes. Yet despite Strauss's famous *Blue Danube Waltz*, the river, its bed thick with sediment, is actually a murky brown, not blue – although some claim that it can have an azure sheen in the spring and autumn sunshine.

Europe's second-longest river after the Volga, the Danube flows through a range of scenery on the long journey from its source in the Black Forest to the vast delta on the Black Sea, cutting through the wooded hills of Bavaria to the steep terraces and castles of the wine-growing country of Lower Austria, then on to the edge of the Hungarian steppes and into the Balkans. The river has carved deep gorges across ancient mountain ranges, while in other places, meanders across broad, marshy plains. Sightseeing opportunities are numerous, from medieval monasteries to castles, fabulous museums and unspoilt national parks.

Towns and cities of particular interest include Regensburg and Passau in Germany; Linz and Vienna in Austria; Bratislava in Slovakia; Budapest in Hungary, and Vidin in Bulgaria. Other highlights include Dürnstein and Melk in Austria's alluring Wachau Valley, and historic Esztergom in Hungary. Most cruises spend at least one night in Vienna and Budapest.

Visitors have a huge choice of itineraries, but the most rewarding is to cruise the river's entire length. There's something fascinating and addictive about the Danube, a promise of discovery and mystery as it flows eastwards through ever-more exotic lands. For many passengers, it is a first and exciting foray into the former Eastern Bloc. Take a shorter voyage as far as Budapest, and you'll find yourself looking longingly at the barges and cruise vessels continuing their journey through the Balkans towards the Black Sea, and vowing to come back and explore Serbia, Romania and Bulgaria, countries where tourism is still very much in its infancy.

The course of the Danube

The source of the mighty Danube is marked by an ornate fountain and ornamental pool in the gardens of the Furstenburg Palace at Donaueschingen in the hills of the Black Forest in southwestern Germany, where the two source streams, the Breg and the Brigach, unite. From here to its marshy delta on the distant Black Sea coast of Romania, the river flows through six countries and forms the border with three

PRECEDING PAGES: a misty morning on the river.
LEFT: passing vineyards on the Danube at Dürnstein, Austria.
BELOW: the grey heron is a common species along much of the river.

A kilometre marker:
along the Danube,
distances are
measured not from the
source to the estuary,
as is customary in
Europe, but from the
estuary to the source.

BELOW: In Habsburg
times, Bratislava –
then called Pozsony
(or Pressburg to
Germans) – was
largely Hungarian.

more, covering a distance of some 2,888 km (1,794 miles). Along the way, some 300 tributaries join the river to bolster its flow. This lengthy course can be divided up into three sections.

The Upper Danube runs for approximately 1,000 km (620 miles), stretching from its source to the "Hungarian Gate", the point near the Slovakian border at which the river crosses into the wide Carpathian Basin. Along this section of the river there is considerable inclination of the river bed, and a rapid current. The first navigable point is at Regensburg.

The **Middle Danube** is approximately 940 km (580 miles) long. From the Hungarian Gate it courses east across the plain until, at the Great Bend, it runs into the hard granite of the Börzsöny and Cserhát Hills, and swings suddenly south to Budapest. The Danube then meanders across the Great Hungarian Plain, clipping the northeastern corner of Croatia before surging across the plains of Vojvodina in northern Serbia to reach the dramatic Iron Gates gorge on the Serbia–Romania border. Here, the river cuts through the southern spur of the crescent-shaped Carpathian mountain range.

The **Lower Danube** is approximately 950 km (590 miles) long. The river here is broad, shallow and marshy as it forges across the Wallachian Plain (forming the border of Romania and Bulgaria) to the large delta by the Black Sea.

Historic boundary

As with many of the world's major rivers, the Danube has historically marked a dividing line between peoples, cultures and empires. Its waters formed the northern boundary of the Roman Empire in southeastern Europe for centuries, and in later times eased the path of the Crusaders to the Near East and then the

Turks into the European heartland. The river still acts as a divide between several countries today, forming a long section of the borders between Slovakia and Hungary, Croatia and Serbia-Montenegro, Romania and Bulgaria, as well as shorter frontiers between Austria and Slovakia, Romania and Ukraine.

Of course, the Danube has also long been an important transport link through Europe's heartlands. For the Romans, it formed a natural barrier against the barbarian world – as on the Rhine, fortifications along its length protected the empire against attack from Germanic and Slavic tribes; several of these early strongholds evolved into towns and cities (Vienna, Budapest and Belgrade all developed close to the former Roman defences). The Crusaders used the Danube to travel to Byzantium, and the Ottomans advanced along the river into Central Europe.

Maps on pages 70, 80, 97

In the 19th century, when most of the Danubian lands lay within the Austro-Hungarian (Habsburg) Empire, the river became a vital link between the industrial centres of Germany and the farmlands of the Balkans.

The effect of the world wars

World War I completely changed the political map of Europe, sweeping away the vast Habsburg Empire through which the Danube had flowed for much of its course. Suddenly there were a host of new independent states, and the river had truly become an international waterway, to be supervised by a European commission. Later, after the next cataclysmic war had further shattered the region, the Belgrade Convention was signed by the 11 member states of the Danube Commission in 1948, forming an agreement for free navigation on the river and an undertaking that each member state would maintain its section of the waterway in a navigable condition.

BELOW: Castle Devin near the Hungarian Gate, traditional divide between the Upper and Middle Danube.

During these immediate post-war years Europe was in the process of being split into East and West, and the Danube subsequently crossed right through the heart of the divided continent, forming sections of the borders between Austria in the West, Hungary and what was then Czechoslovakia in the East. Commercial shipping continued through those years, of course, but only since 1990 has river tourism come into its own between the cities of Vienna, Bratislava and Budapest.

During the 1999 war with Milosevic's Yugoslavia, NATO bombed strategic bridges across the Danube in Serbian territory, and left the river filled with unexploded ordnance and dangerous underwater debris. In 2002, the Danube Commission officially declared the river safe again, following a huge clean-up operation.

The evolution of river cruising

Metals, salt, fur and amber were transported along the Danube all the way back to prehistoric times. The Romans set up garrisons along the river (one of which was eventually to become Vienna), and civilian settlements grew up around these. As the Roman roads fell into decline, the river became the most efficient east–west transport route, and by the Middle Ages it had become a major artery for long-distance trade with Greece and India. Wooden ships and drafts would drift downstream, discharge their cargo and then be broken up and sold. Larger boats would be hauled upstream again, with barges often in long chains, towed by horses.

By 1812, the Habsburg government had introduced steam-powered vessels to the Danube, and in 1830 the steamship *Franz I* began a scheduled service between

Until relatively recently, the Danube and its valley provided a rich habitat for an abundance of birdlife, amphibians and fish. Since the 1950s, the construction of hydroelectric dams and a huge increase in pollution (including some major chemical spills) has had a profound impact on the environment. Nonetheless, some stretches are still relatively wild by European standards.

BELOW:
the Main–Danube Canal.

Vienna and Budapest. The boat was operated by Donau-Dampfschiffahrts-Gesellschaft, Erste (DDSG), which within 50 years became the world's largest inland-navigation company, with 201 steamships and 750 towed barges. Further services were rapidly launched to Linz and Ulm, and in 1834 the first steamship travelled downstream from the Iron Gates to the delta.

Conditions were, however, still very basic. C.W. Vane, the Marquess of Londonderry, travelled across Europe along the Rhine and Danube, and wrote about her experiences in a book, *A Steam Voyage to Constantinople, by the Rhine and Danube in 1840–1841*. There were no railways connecting Central Europe with the Balkans, and the "roads" were primitive cart tracks. These were dangerous times, with the threat of armed robbery by brigands – notorious in the Balkans – and sporadic local riots and small wars. Travelling by horse and carriage would have been almost impossible, so the river was an important thoroughfare.

The military legacy

During the two world wars, parts of the Danube were closed to navigation, and the DDSG company was forced to sell off around half its fleet as civilian river transport fell into decline. New boats were being constructed for military use – tankers, tugs and cargo vessels. Some of these are still in use today.

Passenger traffic on the river resumed in the mid-1940s and throughout the 1950s, and river trade on the Danube thrived. Steam-driven vessels with side-paddlewheel propulsion still existed on the river well into the 1960s. Occasionally today, one of the well-preserved examples (such as the 1926-built *De Majestiet*) can be seen at one of Europe's big steam festivals.

Throughout the 1970s, Danube pleasure cruises grew in popularity, steam

THE MAIN–DANUBE CANAL

In 793, Charlemagne had the vision of establishing a navigable waterway between the Danube and Main rivers, to be called the "Fossa Carolina". Thousands of Charlemagne's workers began to dig a navigable trench between the Rezat and Altmühl rivers. But the project failed due to incessant rain and the resulting "invasion" of water. One section, now called the Karlsgraben, still exists today.

Charlemagne's vision was finally realised on 25 September 1992, when the 170-km (106-mile) Main–Danube Canal was finally opened, providing the means for larger craft of up to 3,300 tons to navigate all the way from the North Sea to the Black Sea. The construction of the canal, linking the rivers Rhine, Main and Danube, is one of Europe's largest transport-engineering projects.

Costing 4.7 billion German marks to build, the canal runs through rural Bavaria and rises 406 metres (1,332 ft) via 16 locks, with up to 24 metres (78 ft) lifting height. It was cleverly constructed to blend with the surrounding landscape, and it looks more like a river than a canal. Some 75 million marks were invested in nature reserves and conservation projects. The canal is 55 metres (180 ft) wide and 4 metres (13 ft) deep, and flows into the Danube at Kelheim in Germany.

power having given way to diesel. German shipping operator Peter Deilmann was founded in 1968 and was the first to introduce boats to the Danube with similar service levels to ocean-going cruise liners. Although many other companies operate on the river today, including Bulgarian, Hungarian and Romanian cruise boats, Peter Deilmann continues to win awards for its luxurious vessels.

What to expect

There are many permutations of river cruise on the Danube and many tour operators selling them, although most of these tend to use the large, well-appointed fleet of Viking River Cruises, which has five boats operating specifically for the English-speaking market and several more for other markets. Peter Deilmann has two luxury vessels and Austria Travel two more, while Blue Water Holidays has four. *For contact details of all cruise operators, see pages 317–318.*

The majority of Danube cruises last for a week to ten days, almost always with a day or two in both Vienna and Budapest. Seven-night cruises from Passau (on the German-Austrian border) sail as far as Budapest, then turn round and return to Passau, taking in Dürnstein, Vienna, Esztergom, Bratislava, Melk and Grein. Other cruises on this stretch of the river start and finish in Regensburg, or operate one-way between Regensburg and Budapest. Some Danube cruises start in Vienna or Budapest, usually spending at least one night in the city before departing. Typical itineraries include Vienna or Budapest to Nuremberg (cruising on a section of the Main–Danube Canal at the end).

Longer itineraries merge a Danube cruise with a Rhine cruise; the whole distance between the North Sea and the Black Sea is, after all, navigable. Blue Water Holidays has a 24-day itinerary from Amsterdam to the Black Sea, taking

Maps on pages 70, 80, 97

TIP

There are regular hydrofoil services between Vienna, Bratislava and Budapest. These are a convenient way of continuing your river voyage if you have left the cruise and want to explore the three cities in further depth.

BELOW: river dancing at Dürnstein.

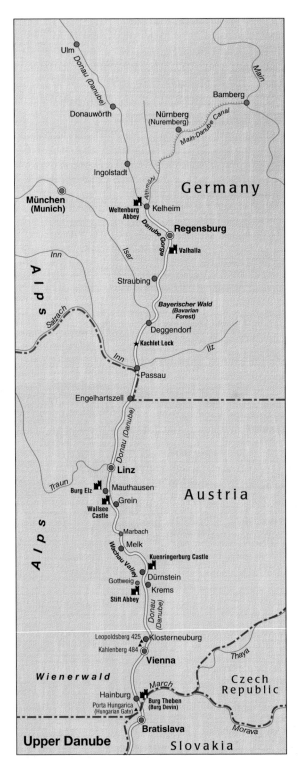

in Cologne, Koblenz, Rudesheim, Heidelberg, Wurzburg, Bamberg, Nuremberg, Kelheim, Regensburg, Passau, Melk, Vienna, Bratislava, Budapest, Kalocsa, Belgrade, the Iron Gates, Rousse and Constanta, with two days in Bucharest at the end. Others operate Vienna (or Budapest) to Amsterdam cruises lasting 10 to 14 days.

Overnight stops

Cruises which take in the longest section of the Danube itself (as opposed to the Danube combined with another river or canal) operate between Passau and Constanta, a voyage of 10 or 12 nights. There's usually an overnight in both Vienna and Budapest, and other ports of call include, in addition to those mentioned above, Kalocsa, Mohacs, Belgrade, Turnu Severin, Vidin, Russe and Oltenitza. These cruises also pass through the spectacular Iron Gate Gorge. Other versions taking in the lower course of the river sail from Budapest to Bucharest.

There are, however, many more combinations on offer on this most popular of rivers. Some tour operators include two days in Prague before travelling by coach to meet the boat at Nuremberg, or a stay in Salzburg before boarding at Passau; some offer Christmas and New Year cruises from Vienna; others feature winter shopping cruises, visiting the traditional Christmas markets in Vienna and Nuremberg and sometimes Prague. Themed classical music cruises are also arranged by the big river cruise operators such as Viking and Peter Deilmann.

DESTINATION HIGHLIGHTS

The navigable upper stretch of the Danube, and the adjoining Main–Danube Canal, wend their way through the eastern half of Bavaria, one of Germany's least populated areas, with wide expanses of rolling countryside sloping gradually upwards to the wild Bavarian Forest along the Czech border. Historic Nuremberg (Nürnberg) and Regensburg are the only large cities in this conservative Catholic region, quite distinct from other parts of Germany in its dialect and culture.

Along the Main–Danube Canal
● **Km 0.** This marks the beginning of the Main–Danube Canal, a vital link in the chain of waterways linking the Rhine Delta on the Dutch coast to the Danube Delta. The canal cuts across the rolling hills of central northern Bavaria, linking the River Main with the Danube at Kelheim.

● **Bamberg, Germany (Km 3–6.4; Main–Danube Canal)**
Known for its symphony orchestra and tasty smoked beer *(Rauchbier)*, this medieval city's narrow, winding streets are lined with Baroque patrician houses. The old town, the 11th-century cathedral and the Bamberg Reiter (Bamberg Horseman) statue were declared a World Heritage Site by UNESCO in 1993. The river Regnitz runs through the middle of the city, joining up with the Main 3 km (2 miles) downstream.

The tombs of the Holy Roman Emperor Heinrich II and Pope Clement II are housed in the magnificent cathedral. The old **Town Hall**, or Rathaus, sits in the middle of a twin-arched bridge over the river and is a most impressive sight, and old fishermen's cottages can be seen close by on the river bank. In Schillerplatz, you can see **Hoffmann's House** (open May–Oct Tues–Fri 4pm–6pm, Sat–Sun 10–12am), dedicated to the poet, musician and caricaturist, author of *The Tales of Hoffmann*. Bamberg is also known as the home of several well-known breweries.

The scenery as you head south towards Nuremberg is craggy and forested, giving the area the name 'Frankische Schweiz' (Franconia's Switzerland).

● **Nuremberg, Germany (Km 67.8–72; Main–Danube Canal)**
Half-timbered houses, cobbled streets and Gothic churches with intricate spires

Map on page 70

The Main–Danube Canal and the Danube itself are marked along the entire length of their courses by kilometre boards, large signs along the banks with black lettering (see picture on page 66). The kilometre indicators are a useful way of locating points of interest along the way.

BELOW: Bamberg's old Town Hall on the River Regnitz.

From 1927 to 1935 Nuremberg's huge Zeppelinfeld Arena staged Hitler's Nazi rallies that were immortalized by Leni Riefenstahl in Triumph des Willens (Triumph of the Wills).

and grand gateways are all part of the architectural heritage of Bavaria's second-largest city, as is the almost intact 5-km (3-mile) city wall with its 80 defensive watchtowers. Most of the sights are contained within the walls and are easy to find on foot, although you'll need to take a taxi, public transport or the ship's shuttle service for the 15-minute drive from the suburban dock to the old town.

One of the best views of the city and surroundings can be had from the medieval **Kaiserburg** (Imperial Castle), an imperial residence for 500 years (open daily Apr–Sept 9am–6pm; Oct–Mar 10am–4pm). The famed post-World War II trials of Nuremberg took place at the Palace of Justice.

Peter Henlein invented the world's first pocket watch in Nuremberg in 1510, and the world's first globe was also made here. You can see examples of early watches on display at the **German National Museum of Art and Culture** (Germanisches Nationalmuseum; open Tues–Sun 10am–6pm, Wed until 9pm), the largest museum of its kind in the German-speaking world. Another highlight is the **Albrecht Dürer House** (open Fri–Wed 10am–5pm, Thurs until 8pm) with its multimedia show depicting the life of the German painter, printmaker, draughtsman and art theorist, generally regarded as the greatest German Renaissance artist.

It's also worth paying a visit to the **Schöner Brunnen Fountain** in the Hauptmarkt. This towering, ornamented treasure was carefully covered during World War II to protect it from Allied bombing. A wrought-iron fence encloses it, and there is a bronze ring looped around one part of the fence. Turning this ring three times is supposed to grant the turner's wish. Needless to say, there is usually a line of visitors waiting to be photographed doing just that.

BELOW: Weltenburg Abbey at Kelheim.

SCENIC CRUISING – NUREMBERG TO KELHEIM

Sometimes it is difficult to tell you are cruising a man-made waterway along this southern section of the Main–Danube Canal, as you pass steep, thickly wooded hills topped with castles and stately residences. Look out for Hirschberg Palace, a former bishop's hunting lodge, above the village of Beilgriess, and the three castles towering above Riedenburg: Rosenburg, Rabenstein and Tachenstein along a stretch known as the Altmühtal.

Also keep an eye out for nearby Prunn Castle, spectaculaly perched on a steep limestone spur of rock protruding from a cliff outside the village of Nusshausen. The castle was first mentioned in 1037, and it is thanks to Ludwig I that it is so well preserved – he made it a historic monument in 1827. A previously unknown manuscript of the *Song of the Nibelungs* was found here in 1576; it is now in the Bavarian State Library in Munich.

● **Kelheim, Germany (Km 2,415)**

Positioned at the confluence of the River Danube and the Main–Danube Canal, Kelheim is the gateway to the dramatic scenery of the Danube Gorge. Typically, you disembark the vessel and take a bus and boat tour that includes a visit to the famed **Weltenburg Abbey**, founded in AD 610 on a much-flooded spur of land. The monks here have brewed dark ale since 1050, and their haunting Gregorian chants can often be heard. In Kelheim itself, the **Archaeological Museum** (Archaeologisches Museum; open Apr–Oct Tues–Sun 10am–4pm) has numerous exhibits relating to Neanderthal remains unearthed during the construction of the canal.

Just beyond Kelheim is the magnificent **Danube Gorge**, which was declared a European Area of Outstanding Natural Beauty in 1978. The scenery is quite spectacular and because the Danube has forced itself through mountains of Jurassic chalk and limestone, it has produced some superb cliff formations that are reminiscent of the Norwegian fjords, with names like 'The Beehive', 'The Mitre' and 'The Bavarian Lion'. Most excursions include a tour of the city of Kelheim before rejoining the boat, moored up in the centre. The end of the Main–Danube Canal is at Km 2,411. From here, the cruise along the River Danube proper begins.

The Upper Danube from Ingolstadt to Passau

● **Ingolstadt, Germany (Km 2,460)**

The old university town of Ingolstadt, between Ulm and Kelheim, rests among idyllic green meadows and is dominated by St Mary's Minster (Maria-de-Victoria-Kirche). It is offered as a side trip from Kelheim. Perhaps the most famous building is the **Bavarian Army Museum** (Bayerisches Armeemuseum;

Map on page 70

BELOW: Thuringian sausages are sold at stalls all over the region.

Traditional Bavarian lederhosen are still worn, and have remained a symbol of regional pride.

BELOW: Valhalla, the 19th-century temple near Regensburg.

open Tues–Sun 8.45am–4.30pm), which is housed in the huge chambers of a 15th-century fortress. The museum has a collection of some 17,000 model soldiers depicting the battle of Leuthen and displayed in a diorama, as well as a large number of firearms that trace the history and evolution of weaponry. On the opposite bank of the Danube, a subsidiary fortification (known as Reduit Tilly and also used for open-air concerts in summer) has an exhibition about World War I on display.

● **Regensburg, Germany (Km 2,381–2,377)**

Founded by Marcus Aurelius over 2,000 years ago, Regensburg is one of the best-preserved of all European medieval cities, having escaped the bombing of World War II, and is the oldest city on the entire length of the Danube; the first Roman camp here has been dated by historians to AD 70, and parts of the original Roman wall can still be seen. The city's 12th–14th-century **Patricians' Houses** are architecturally fascinating, and are reminiscent of the medieval tower-houses of San Gimignano in Tuscany. Riverboats dock close to the centre, within walking distance of the main sights, and tours are usually a half-day, with free time afterwards.

Visit the **Stone Bridge**, built between 1135 and 1146 and, with 16 arches, a masterpiece of medieval engineering. The **Cathedral**, regarded as the best example of Gothic architecture in Bavaria, has some superb stained-glass windows in its twin towers, which were added between 1859 and 1861 at the request of King Ludwig I of Bavaria, and a tranquil 15th-century cloister.

The heart of the city is **Neupfarrplatz**, which presents Regensburg's history in microcosm. Over the years it has been the home of Roman officers, the

Jewish quarter, the marketplace, the scene of riots and protests, and of the mass burning of books by the Nazis. Between 1995 and 1998, massive excavations revealed Gothic and Romanesque synagogues, remains of the old Jewish houses and a treasure trove of gold coins. Guided tours and a multimedia presentation operate (Thurs, Fri and Sat at 2.30pm; also Sun and Mon in July and Aug).

Some 11 km (7 miles) downstream from Regensburg, just outside Donaustauf, look out for a white classical temple with Doric columns on the hillside, approached by a grand staircase. This is **Valhalla** (Walhalla), home of the gods in German mythology – in this case, built by Ludwig I in the 1830s as a kind of Teutonic Hall of Fame, and a copy of the Parthenon in Athens.

● Deggendorf, Germany (Km 2,286–2,284)

Leaving behind the stately mansions lining the banks in Regensburg, the river flows southeast through the dense Bavarian Forest, criss-crossed with walking and cycling trails and, in winter, a popular cross-country skiing area. Deggendorf, surrounded by woods, developed early as a commercial centre, the first settlements being recorded in AD 750. A number of river cruise vessels are built here, located as it is directly on the bank of the river; vessels can be launched sideways into the water – a technique that was also used infrequently for ocean-going cruise ships (nowadays, ships are built in dry docks which are then flooded so that the finished ship can sail or be towed out).

One of the finest examples of Baroque architecture in Bavaria can be seen in the towers of the parish church of the Assumption of the Virgin Mary.

● Passau, Germany (Km 2,210)

En route to Passau, the river flows past pretty Bavarian villages and cuts through rolling hills, many of them topped with the ruins of medieval castles. At Km 2,231, boats pass through the Kachlet Lock, built in 1927. Look out for the fish ladder to the left of the lock; the series of ascending pools allows fish to swim past the obstruction caused by the lock.

The starting point for many cruises on the Danube, Passau, located 290 metres (950 ft) above sea level, marks the border between Germany and Austria. Ships dock right in the centre. Somewhat fancifully dubbed "the Venice of the Danube" because of the three rivers that converge here (it is also sometimes called Dreiflüssestadt – the city of three rivers) and the Italianate style of the architecture, Passau has been a bishopric for 1,200 years. **St Stephan's** magnificent Baroque-style cathedral, north of the Alps, houses Europe's largest pipe organ; it has 17,774 pipes in three banks, and 233 registers, or stops. Liszt wrote his *Hungarian Coronation Mass* for this cathedral in 1857. There are daily organ recitals at midday from May to October.

Passau's location as the confluence of the three rivers, the Danube, Ilz and Inn, means it often suffers from flooding, the most recent being the devastating floods of the summer of 2002, after which national emergency funds were required to dig the old town out of the mud. The tower of the town hall shows the

Map on page 70

The Danube valley at Regensburg was inhabited long before the arrival of the Romans. A Celtic settlement on the same spot where the Romans founded their city was called Radabona.

BELOW: half-timbered buildings at Nuremberg.

Johann Strauss the Younger composed the famous Blue Danube Waltz *in 1867. The full name of the composition is* An der Schönen Blauen Donau (By the Beautiful Blue Danube).

BELOW: Passau, meeting point of three rivers and two nations.

high-water marks, the highest recorded being in 1501, 1595 and 1954. The three rivers are, in fact, different colours; on a sunny day at Dreiflüsseck ("Three Rivers Corner"), a well-known lookout point where they converge, you can clearly see the milky-green water of the Inn merging with the swirling, dark, peaty Ilz and the brown Danube. The Inn is considerably larger than the other two rivers when it reaches Passau – technically, the Danube should be called the Inn downstream from this point.

Passau is a good place for shopping. There's an open-air market on Tuesdays and Fridays in front of the cathedral, and local arts and crafts can be found along Höllgasse, the main shopping street. There are numerous cafés, pubs and bars with waterfront locations, making the most of the watery location.

● **Km 2,201.** This marks the border between the state of Bavaria, Germany, and the state of Upper Austria, Austria.

Passau to Vienna

Between Passau and Linz, the Danube flows through the heart of Upper Austria (Oberösterreich), a quiet region of wooded hills, small villages and photogenic Baroque abbeys. Beyond Linz, Austria's largest province – Lower Austria (Niederösterreich) – extends eastwards to Vienna through a subtle rolling landscape of verdant vineyards peppered with monasteries and castles. The highlight lies between Krems and Melk, a region known as the Wachau Valley, famed for its beautiful scenery, fine wines and apricot brandy. Vines were first planted by the Celts, but it was the Romans who turned viticulture into a real art. By the time of the Renaissance, 31 monasteries in the valley were

producing significant quantities of wine. October is an especially good time to cruise the Wachau, when the leaves turn dazzling shades of yellow, red and fiery orange.

Map on page 70

● Linz, Austria (Km 2,138)

Although the Renaissance and Baroque centre of the city, which is the provincial capital of Upper Austria, is attractive, Linz is a steel-and-iron town through and through. Walk from the mooring at the Nibelung Bridge to the Old Town, or take Europe's steepest adhesion railway up to the summit of Postlingberg to the pilgrimage church of the **Seven Pains of Maria** (open daily May–Oct 7am–8pm; Nov–Apr 8am–6pm). The classic Linzer Torte, with a pastry base, redcurrant jam filling and criss-cross pattern on the almond-encrusted top, was invented here. You can taste the real thing in one of the many street cafés.

At Km 2,202, the Jochenstein Rock rises out of the river. Legend has it that this is the home of Isa, a water nymph, sister of the Rhine's famous Lorelei who lured sailors to their deaths with her beautiful voice.

● Mauthausen, Austria (Km 2,112)

Although the sleepy town of Mauthausen is not on the itineraries of many river cruises, some vessels do stop here. It is of interest principally to those wanting to take a tour to one of the World War II concentration camps. Over 122,000 people died at Mauthausen and its 49 subsidiary camps. One of the buildings is now a museum, and you can still see some of the huts and rooms in which prisoners suffered and died. It's a haunting, sobering place.

Today, the houses of this little town come almost down to the water's edge. From Mauthausen, you can take a tour to the castle of **Burg Elz**, nestled in romantic woodland setting a few kilometres from the riverfront.

The river flows past several imposing castles between Mauthausen and Melk, the next major attraction. Sturdy-looking **Wallsee Castle** at Km 2,093 was built over 1,000 years ago on the walls of a Roman fortification. The village of **Grein**, meanwhile, is dominated by a hulking castle on a small hill. The castle now houses the **Museum of Shipping** (open Tues–Sun, June–Sept 10am–6pm; May and Oct 10am–noon, 1–5pm), commemorating what was once one of the most dangerous stretches of the Danube, with rapids and vortices. At **Marbach**, the 17th-century Maria Taferl church, a famous pilgrimage destination, looks down on the little village from a steep hill.

BELOW: white storks on their chimney-top nest.

● Melk, Austria (Km 2,019)

The graceful, ochre-coloured **Benedictine Abbey** of Melk (open daily 9am–5pm; one-hour guided tour in English at 2.55pm daily Apr–Oct), perched on a steep hill overlooking the river, is the reason many people choose a Danube cruise. The Baroque church towers are visible from some distance away against a background of wooded hills as you approach on the water. Melk Abbey was founded in the year 1089 by Leopold II and dominates the little town, though at the same time blending in beautifully with the surrounding landscape.

It was completely reconstructed in Baroque style in the early 18th century by the architect Jakob Prandtauer, who died before its completion. The imposing abbey was completed by Prandtauer's nephew and assistant, Joseph Munggenast.

The imperial rooms of the abbey once accommodated such renowned figures as Emperor Charles VI and Maria Theresa, Pope Pius VI and Napoleon – all presently immortalised in a permanent wax museum. Paul Troger frescos can be found in the library, which houses over 85,000 leatherbound volumes. A Gutenberg Bible was on display here for many years but has since been sold, and can be viewed at Yale Library in Boston, Massachusetts.

The balconies command sweeping views of the Danube. A short organ concert is typically held for anyone on a shore excursion. This venerable instrument, played by Mozart in 1767, built by Gregor Hradetzky of Krems, has three keyboards, 45 registers (stops) and 3,553 pipes. The imperial rooms are currently home to the most modern abbey museum in Austria. A mixture of light, sound and new media depicts the story of the monastery's treasures over the last 910 years.

All river cruise operators include Melk as a shore excursion, but you can also visit independently. The visit takes about two hours.

● Dürnstein, Austria (Km 2,008)

Beyond Melk, the Danube carves its way through the beautiful **Wachau Valley**, a 30-km (18-mile) section of steep, terraced slopes of vineyards and forested hills, which turn incredible shades of red and gold in the autumn. It is regarded by many as one of the most scenic stretches of the river. In its midst is Dürnstein, discernible from some distance away because of the jagged outline of the ruined castle on the hilltop, and the unusual sky-blue Baroque church tower squatting like a giant pepperpot on the river bank.

A steep one-hour walk/climb from the charming, if touristy, little town (boats

The 1986 film version of Umberto Eco's novel The Name of the Rose, *starring Sean Connery, was partly shot in the great monastery at Melk.*

BELOW: the lavish interior of Melk Abbey.
RIGHT: the west façade of Melk Abbey, which faces the river.

dock close to the centre) leads to the Babenberg Duke Leopold's **Kuenringerburg Castle**. Richard the Lionheart was incarcerated here for more than a year in the 12th century for swindling the Babenberg family by selling the island of Cyprus, which belonged to some of their relatives, to some Maltese knights. He was released after paying an incredible 100,000 marks – truly a king's ransom in those days. There's not much of the castle to see nowadays, but the views along the Wachau Valley and over the town below are breathtaking.

The other main sight of Dürnstein is the elaborate **Baroque Monastery** (open daily Apr–Oct 9am–6pm) that hosts concerts and exhibitions. Its distinctive powder-blue-and-white tower is best viewed from the river.

If you don't want to climb all the way up to the castle for a view, an alternative can be had from the Danube Terrace of the smart Hotel Schloss Dürnstein, in a peaceful setting at one end of the town's main cobblestone street. Inside the Baroque church there are beautiful stucco reliefs, altarpieces and an impressive, decoratively carved pulpit and choir stalls.

Dürnstein also has several *Heurige* – wine taverns where wine is sold direct from the vineyards. These have complicated opening times, but a good indication is a bunch of evergreen boughs hung over the doorway, which means there is wine in the house. The main season is during the summer, when you can usually find a cool garden in which to sit and sample the local produce.

● Krems, Austria (Km 2,002)

This university town, together with its former sister town of Stein at the eastern end of the Wachau wine-growing district, grew wealthy from the 12th century onwards as a result of trade in iron, grain, wine and salt. The scenery is still hilly,

Map on page 70

Dürnstein is one of the most picturesque towns along the Austrian Danube.

BELOW: the verdant Wachau Valley.

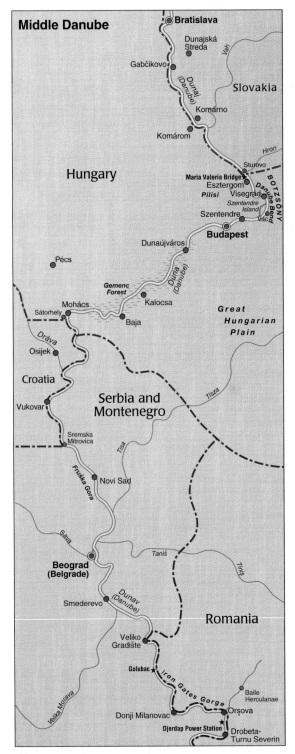

Middle Danube

with steeply terraced vineyards positioned to catch every ray of sunshine. The town of Krems is a particularly important example of successful restoration work, and the centre has been a UNESCO World Heritage Site since 2000. Krems was the home of the painter Martin Johann ("Kremser") Schmidt, who created many great works in the churches of Austria.

One of the nearby attractions, and also a World Heritage Site, is the lovely **Stift Abbey Gottweig** (open daily June–Sept 9am–6pm; Oct–May 10am–6pm), set on the side of a hill. Its kitsch Benedictine architecture – corner towers, onion domes and a pale-pink façade – has earned it the title of "Austria's Monte Cassino", after the Italian abbey where the Benedictine Order first became established.

● **Klosterneuburg, Austria (Km 1,139.5)**

Just before reaching Vienna, as the river curves gently around to the south, is Klosterneuburg with its imposing 12th-century **Augustinian Monastery**, topped by a dome in the form of the Imperial Crown (monastery open Mon–Fri 9am–6pm, Sat–Sun 10am–5pm; museum open May–Nov Tues–Sun same hours). The highlight is the magnificent enamel-and-gilt Verdun altar. The picturesque road between Klosterneuburg and Hütteldorf is known as the Vienna High Road; it leads back along the upper slopes of the Kahlenberg and the Leopoldsberg on the edge of the Vienna Woods (Wienerwald), both of which have cafés and panoramic terraces with sweeping views of Vienna, the Danube and the lowlands of the Marchfeld stretching to the Slovak border beyond.

● **Vienna, Austria (Km 1,928)**

Once the Danube has passed Kahlenberg and Leopoldsberg, the scenery begins to flatten out. The river has now reached the edges of the Pannonian (Hungarian) Plain. Vienna itself is located 170 metres (560 ft) above sea level, and is built in a highly strategic location, at the junction of routes going east to west from Hungary to the Alps, and north to south from the North Sea to the Adriatic.

Vienna was, for centuries, the seat of the mighty Habsburg dynasty, and is also the birthplace of Schubert, and of the music of Mozart (he composed his greatest operas and symphonies here), Beethoven and Strauss. The city exudes romance at any time of year, with its beautiful parks and Baroque palaces, elegant shops and legendary coffee houses. Most cruises spend at least one night here, giving plenty of opportunity to see the sights, attend a performance at the opera (in June and September), listen to the Vienna Boys' Choir, or admire the white Lipizzaner horses at the Spanish Riding School. *For details on what to see in Vienna, see pages 82–85.*

Map on page 80

The Middle Danube: from the Hungarian Gate to Budapest

Beyond Vienna the river enters Burgenland, Austria's easternmost province, a relatively flat region with a more Hungarian feel than the rest of the country and a thriving wine-growing industry. This part of Austria was once occupied by the Ottoman Turks, and traces of their presence still remain, for example in the walls and gates of Purbach, on the western shores of Neusiedler See.

Vienna's passion for coffee dates back to 1683, when it is said the defeated Turks left sacks of coffee beans behind as they beat a hasty retreat.

● The Hungarian Gate (Km 1,880)

The scenery east of Vienna is flat, as the river flows slowly through broad meadows lined with birch and alder trees before approaching the low hills of the Little Carpathians. The hill known as Porta Hungarica, or the Hungarian Gate (also the Deviner Tor or Pressburg Gate) marks the end of the upper course of the Danube and the river's entry into the Carpathian Basin and the former Eastern Bloc. **Burg Theben**, a castle which resisted the Turkish invasion of 1683 but was destroyed by the French in 1809, overlooks the Danube from the 500-metre (1,640-ft) summit of Thebener Kogels. Shortly beyond here, at Km 1872.7, is the the border between Austria and Slovakia.

BELOW: a Turk's head hangs on a wall in St Margarethen.

At one point, travellers might have felt a thrill of excitement, passing from the West into the mysterious territory of the Eastern Bloc, but today, there is little noticeable difference. The villages along the river are slightly shabbier and there are still some old-fashioned Russian- and East German-built cars around, but these days the towns along the river have internet cafés, lively bars and mobile-phone masts just like those upstream.

The area that is now Slovakia was part of the powerful Habsburg Empire for centuries, ruled by Hungary (much of southern Slovakia still has a sizeable Hungarian population), until the uncomfortable union of the Czech and Slovak republics following the demise of the empire at the end of World War I. In 1939, under Hitler, the Germans created a protectorate known as the Slovakian Republic, but by 1945, the Slovaks were once again united with the Czechs. Czechoslovakia emerged from four decades of communism in 1989 following the Velvet Revolution, before the Velvet Divorce of 1993 split it into two.

The new Slovak Republic struggled at first, plunging headlong into economic depression, but has seen a remarkable reversal of fortune and, in 2004, joined both NATO and the EU. After centuries of domination by their neighbours, Slovaks can now celebrate their national pride, their heritage and their language. ➤ *page 86*

PORTS OF CALL: VIENNA

Vienna's compact historic centre is a treasure trove of secular and sacred gems, from the famous coffee houses and grand Habsburg palaces to the magnificent Gothic cathedral at its heart. For centuries, all manner of ideas were fomented and flourished among the city's palaces and cafés. Art and music, theatre, medicine and psychology found the ideal climate in which to grow. Vienna has music in its blood. It is a city where the music never stops and has been home to some of the great composers, including Mozart, Haydn and Beethoven; and to some equally great architects from the historicist Heinrich von Ferstel to Otto Wagner, founder of the Viennese *Jugendstil* (art nouveau) movement.

TOP CITY SIGHTS

ORIENTATION

The Danube does not pass through the centre of Vienna – instead it runs through the northeast part of the city. Most river cruise vessels stop at the Vienna Shipping Centre (Schiffahrtszentrum), about 3km (2 miles) from the old centre. Others, however, dock at the pretty wine-growing suburb of Nussdorf to the north of the city, easily reached by taxi or public transport (20 minutes by tram). The whole centre is encircled by the Ringstrasse, inside which most of the main sights are located. Walking tours, cycling tours and even Segway Human Transporter tours operate regularly.

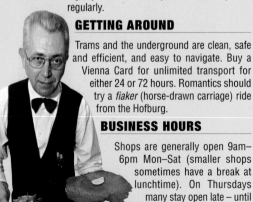

GETTING AROUND

Trams and the underground are clean, safe and efficient, and easy to navigate. Buy a Vienna Card for unlimited transport for either 24 or 72 hours. Romantics should try a *fiaker* (horse-drawn carriage) ride from the Hofburg.

BUSINESS HOURS

Shops are generally open 9am–6pm Mon–Sat (smaller shops sometimes have a break at lunchtime). On Thursdays many stay open late – until 8pm. Some larger shops open on Sundays.

▲ SCHÖNBRUNN PALACE
A short distance from the inner city lies the Schönbrunn Palace (open daily Apr–Jun and Sept–Oct 8.30am–5pm, Jul–Aug 8.30am–6pm, Nov–Mar 8.30am–4.30pm), the imperial summer residence. Leopold I wished to build a palace to rival Versailles but financial difficulties stalled his plans. It was not until 1743 that Empress Maria Theresa employed Nikolaus Pacassi to build the fabulous palace we see today. In the formal grounds are the Baroque zoo, the Palm House and the graceful Gloriette, a neoclassical colonnade perched on the crest of a hill.

▶ STEPHANSDOM
St Stephen's Cathedral (open daily 6am–10pm except during services), with its distinctive roof, is one of Vienna's most famous landmarks and one of the greatest Gothic structures in Europe. The interior is rich in woodcarvings, altars and paintings. Climb the steps of the south tower for a breathtaking view of the city.

EXCURSIONS

To the west and southwest of the city lie the beautiful **Vienna Woods** (Wienerwald). The northern section of the woods is easily accessible by public transport from the city centre – take a picnic and enjoy the sweeping views across the city. Pass the evening in a *Heurige* (wine tavern) in one of the wine-growing villages, such as **Grinzing** or **Nussdorf**. The Burgenland region to the southeast of Vienna is the setting for one of the largest lakes in Europe, Lake Neusiedler. Take a day trip to its capital, **Eisenstadt**, burial place of Haydn. Some excellent wine is grown here and it's a popular weekend getaway for the Viennese.

► MUSEUM QUARTER
The Museums Quartier (visitor and ticket centre open Sat–Wed 10am–7pm, Thur–Fri 10am–9pm) is a giant cultural complex which includes the Museum of Modern Art (MUMOK) and the Leopold Museum, with its wonderful collection of 19th and 20th century art, including Schiele's *Moa the Dancer (pictured right)*. At the centre of the complex, the Kunsthalle holds temporary exhibitions.

▼ STAATSOPER
Vienna's magnificent opera house was constructed in the 1860s, and rebuilt in

1945 after suffering a direct hit in a bombing raid. It was inaugurated in 1869 with Mozart's *Don Giovanni*. The main façade is elaborately decorated with frescos

depicting The Magic Flute. Once a year the stage and orchestra stalls turn into a giant dance floor for the Vienna Opera Ball.

▲ PRATER
The Prater (open Mar–Oct daily 10am–midnight), an open fairground and amusement park, is a favourite place of relaxation for the Viennese. Its main attraction is the Riesenrad, the giant Ferris wheel which was immortalised in the 1949 film *The Third Man*. This extensive stretch of parkland and woodland extends for almost 5km (3 miles).

Gustav Klimt designed the *Beethoven Frieze*, on display on the lower floor, a visual interpretation of Beethoven's Ninth Symphony. The cubic foyer is crowned by a dome of 3,000 gilt laurel leaves. Over the entrance is the motto "To Each Time its Art, to Art its Freedom", a riposte from the Secession artists to the conservative Academy of Fine Arts.

▲ KUNSTHISTORISCHES MUSEUM

Several famous artists helped create the interior of the Kunsthistorisches Museum (open Tues–Sun 10am–6pm, Thurs 10am–9pm). A huge number of art treasures amassed by the Habsburgs are on display, including a fine collection of ancient Egyptian and Greek Art, and works by many of the great European masters.

▼ BELVEDERE

The Belvedere (open Tues–Sun 10am–6pm), a palace of sumptuous

▲ COFFEE HOUSES

The Viennese coffee-house tradition is deeply rooted in the country's culture and history, dating back over 300 years. Gentry and intellectuals mingled in the shady and fashionable Kaffeehaus. People take their coffee seriously here and there are names for every shade, from black to white. Coffee is served in a wide variety of ways, often with the addition of alcohol or whipped cream, though always with an obligatory glass of water.

◄ KARLSPLATZ

Otto Wagner's two wonderfully elegant entrance pavilions for the Stadtbahn on Karlsplatz date from 1894 and are prime examples of *Jugendstil* (art nouveau). For the designs of the pavilions, he combined a green iron framework with marble slabs and gilded sunflower decoration, and pioneered a new form of architecture in which functionality and simplicity of ornament were the priority.

◄ SECESSION BUILDING

The Secession Building (open Tues–Sun 10am–6pm, Thurs 10am–8pm) was built as a "temple of art" to plans by Joseph Maria Olbrich in 1897.

proportions, was built between 1714 and 1723 for Prince Eugene of Savoy. It is in fact two palaces, the Upper and Lower Belvedere, joined by terraced gardens. Today it houses three museums containing works of Austrian and European art and sculpture.

▶ **HOFBURG**

The Hofburg was the winter residence of the ruling Habsburgs. Within the confines of this vast and impressive Imperial Palace are the Spanish Riding School and the sleek Lipizzaner horses, and the Burgkapelle, where the Vienna Boys' Choir sing Sunday Mass. Notable collections housed here are the Collection of Court Porcelain and Silver and the Imperial Treasury, containing crown jewels and ecclesiastical treasures. The palatial National Library, also in the complex, contains more than 2 million manuscripts, printed books, maps and musical scores.

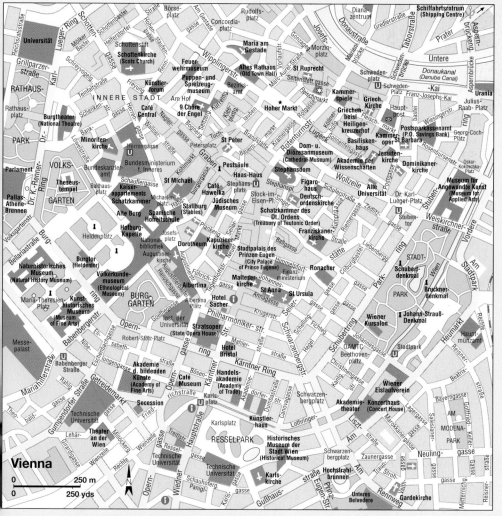

Vienna

0 — 250 m
0 — 250 yds

Esztergom Cathedral contains the remains of Cardinal Mindszenty, a fierce opponent of Communist Party rule. During the 1956 uprising he sought refuge in the US embassy, where he lived for 15 years.

RIGHT: waltzing at Vienna's Opernball.

● **Bratislava, Slovakia (Km 1,869)**

As the boat approaches Bratislava, two landmarks stand out: the castle on the left bank, high and mighty above the town, and the communist-era bridge with its revolving restaurant. After passing underneath the concrete span, the boat moors on the left, conveniently close to the lovely old town.

Most vessels spend half a day at the Slovak capital, sufficient time to visit the reconstructed 9th-century castle and stroll around the largely pedestrianised old town. As well as various historical buildings, Bratislava is noted for its wines, grown on the sunny slopes of the Little Carpathians which run in a long line to the north of the city, and its eclectic cuisine – a mixture of Austrian, Hungarian, Jewish and Czech. *For details on what to see in Bratislava, see pages 88–89.*

From Bratislava, the river flows southeast then east towards Esztergom in Hungary, forming a natural border between Hungary, on the right bank, and Slovakia, on the left. At **Gabcikovo** (Km 1,819) the river descends through one of its deepest locks, with a drop of 18 metres (60 ft). The double lock is an important source of hydroelectric power, and it's worth being on deck for the transit, if only to experience the sinking feeling as the vessel is rapidly dropped down into the lock basin. Beyond this point the river widens, with dense forests along its banks. Deposits of silt along the banks has built them up, so that the surrounding countryside feels lower than the river.

● **Esztergom, Hungary (Km 1,718)**

Formerly the Roman settlement of Gran, Esztergom is located in the foothills of the Pilis Mountains, right on the border with Slovakia; a ferry makes the

VIENNA AND THE DANUBE

Until the 19th century, Vienna was not located on the Danube at all. The river meandered through the wetlands east of the old city, flooding frequently, and even houses within the city boundary suffered inundation from the rising water-table. The route of the river bed today was created between 1870 and 1875. The banks were strengthened and the Danube Canal created (not technically a canal but a flowing section of the river), around which the city has grown up.

The long, thin Donauinsel, or Danube Island, was finished as recently as the late 1980s as a flood-protection zone and a recreational area for the city. It was created by construction of the New Danube (Neu Donau), a discharge channel parallel to the island's left bank. The city is now in theory protected from major floods. The best view of the river is from the Leopoldsberg in the Vienna Woods.

short hop across the river to the Slovakian resort town of Sturovo, next to where the river cruise boats moor up. The two countries are also linked by the green iron Maria Valeria Bridge, blown up by the Germans in World War II and reconstructed, finally, in 2001.

Map on page 80

Esztergom is famous for its vast, neoclassical **Cathedral**, flanked by a redbrick castle, which towers over the city. The giant dome is one of the world's largest and can be seen for miles around. The castle itself was the seat of government for Hungary's kings and queens for more than 300 years when the Hungarian lands further south were held by the Ottoman Turks, while the town was the centre of the Catholic Church in Hungary, which flourished during the reign of Louis I (1342–82), a role it retains today. The cathedral was built in the 19th century to replace its predecessor, ransacked by the Turks in 1543 after they pushed northwards, although the red-marble Bakócz Chapel inside survived.

The **Treasury** (open daily 9am–5pm in summer; 11am–4pm at other times of year; closed Jan and Feb) is absolutely breathtaking, containing jewels, gold and ceremonial robes of fabulous richness. The crypt holds the vaults of the cathedral's prelates, but more impressive is the scale of the building's foundations, with walls 17 metres (56 ft) thick.

While the cathedral is the main attraction, the **Castle Museum** (open Tues–Sun 10am–6pm; 9am–5pm in winter) is of interest to anyone keen on weapons, old coins and pottery. The **Christian Museum** (open Tues–Sun 10am–5pm; closed Jan and Feb) has Hungary's largest collection of medieval art outside the National Gallery in Budapest.

● Danube Bend, Hungary (Km 1,694)

After leaving Esztergom, the scenery becomes more interesting as the river enters the stretch known as the **Danube Bend**. This continues as far as Szentendre and is regarded as the most beautiful part of the Danube within Hungary. Small farming communities and clusters of holiday homes are dotted along the banks. The hills, topped by ruined castles, once served as royal hunting grounds, and affluent tourists still come to shoot deer and wild boar. The most spectacular section is the approach to Visegrád, where the steep, forested hills of the Börzsöny and Pilis ranges force the river into a majestic gorge.

● Visegrád, Hungary (Km 1,694)

Usually visited as part of a tour from Esztergom, Visegrád's strikingly sited **citadel** (open mid-Mar–mid-Oct daily 9.30am–5.30pm, weekends only rest of the year) sits high on a crag overlooking the Danube. It has been steadily restored since the 19th century, and contains displays on Visegrád's history and the Angevin kings who started using the town as a royal residence from the 14th century. The structure itself dates from 1259, when it was built to guard against the Mongol threat. Later, a **royal palace** was constructed next to the river, and by the late 15th century, Visegrád was one of the most celebrated courts in Europe. Both the palace and the citadel were destroyed by the Turks, with the former only ➤ *page 90*

BELOW: detail from the palace at Visegrád.

PORTS OF CALL: BRATISLAVA

Located right at the heart of central Europe close to Slovakia's borders with Austria and Hungary, Bratislava has changed its identity, and its name, more times than it cares to remember. In Habsburg times, the city was Pressburg to the Germans and Pozsony to the Magyars. Renamed Bratislava after the creation of Czechoslovakia following World War I, it emerged from the communist years to become capital of the new state of Slovakia in 1993. An ambitious rebuilding and restoration programme has transformed the city. The picturesque old town is clustered around a low hill on the left bank of a broad stretch of the river.

ORIENTATION

The pier is just outside the Old Town (staré mesto), at the foot of the castle hill on Fajndrovo Naba street. The whole waterfront is currently being renovated so there may be building work.

GETTING AROUND

Almost all of the compact centre is pedestrianised, so the best way to explore is on foot – although there are buses, trolleybuses and trams around the city. Buy a ticket before boarding. Taxis can be hailed on the street.

BUSINESS HOURS

Shops are open 8am–6pm Monday–Friday and 9am–noon Saturdays, with larger department stores and malls usually open until 8pm. Very few shops – mainly convenience stores – are open on Sundays. Things to buy include Tokay wines from Hungary, Modra ceramics and Bohemian crystal.

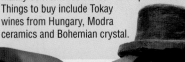

TOP CITY SIGHTS

▲ **CASTLE (HRAD)**
The great bulk of Bratislava castle (open daily Apr–Sept 9am–8pm, Oct–Mar 9am–6pm), visible from afar and looking not dissimilar to an upturned table, was built in the 16th century on top of earlier fortifications. Visit the **Treasury** and the **Slovak National Museum** (Slovenské Národné Múzeum; open Tues–Sun 9am–5pm) with displays of weaponry, folk art and furniture.

▼ **THE OLD TOWN**
Perfect for exploring on foot, Bratislava's Old Town (Staré mesto) has been magnificently restored in recent years. The whole area is picturesque, but highlights include the leafy Hlavné and Frantiskánske squares, and Michalská and Ventúrska streets – which run into each other– and are lined with fabulous Baroque palaces.

▲ **ST MICHAEL'S GATE**
The 14th-century St Michael's Gate (Michalská Veža; open Tues–Fri 10am–5pm, Sat–Sun

Pálffyho Palace (open Tues–Fri 10am–6pm Sat–Sun 10am–5pm). This distinguished building now houses the Academy of Fine Arts. There is a collection of Gothic paintings and sculpture and a selection of early 19th century works by Hungarian and Slovak artists. Temporary exhibitions are held on the ground floor.

▶ ST MARTIN'S CATHEDRAL

Bratislava was an important Hungarian city for hundreds of years, and the 15th-century St Martin's Cathedral (Dóm sv Martina open daily except during services) was the venue of Hungarian coronations for over 250 years until 1830. Rebuilt with Baroque exuberance in the 18th century, the unusual spire is topped by a tiny Hungarian crown. The interior is dominated by Gothic fan vaulting.

EXCURSIONS

The slopes of the **Little Carpathians**, rising steeply from the northern suburbs of Bratislava, are a premier wine-growing region. Wine tastings are available almost everywhere. Picturesque villages include Jur and Modra.

11am–6pm) is the only medieval town gateway still standing. The tower, which was given its baroque cupola in the 18th century, is surmounted by a statue of the archangel, St Michael. Climb to the top of the tower for a panoramic view of the Old Town.

▲ CLOCK MUSEUM

The House of the Good Shepherd is a delicate-looking house with a fine yellow stucco facade which was built in 1760 in pure Rococo style. Each storey consists of a single room. It houses the Clock Museum (Múzeum Hodín; open Tues–Fri 10am–5pm Sat–Sun 11am–6pm), which has a collection of Baroque and Empire clocks.

PÁLFFYHO PALACE

In 1762, the six-year old Wolfgang Amadeus Mozart gave a performance in the

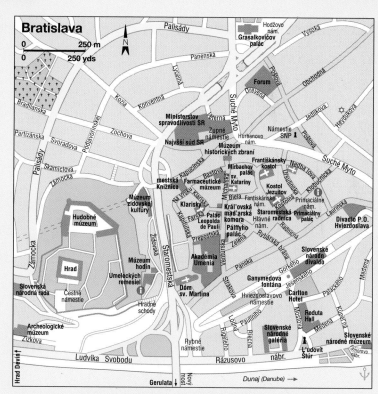

Visegrád's citadel towers over the waters of the Danube Bend.

BELOW: the Danube Bend is a highlight of any Danube cruise.

unearthed by archaeologists in the 1930s. The hexagonal keep of **Solomon's Tower** (open May–Sept Tues–Sun 9am–4.30pm), whose main purpose was to levy tolls on passing river traffic, lies at the water's edge north of the palace.

Heading downstream, river vessels sail to the left of **Szentendre Island**, which extends for some 38 km (24 miles) and is 3 km (2 miles) wide; city-dwellers from Budapest come here at weekends for the fishing and the sandy beaches. The easterly channel misses Szentendre, though it can be an excursion from Budapest, visited for its picturesque lanes of colour-washed Baroque houses rising up to hilltop churches. The little town of **Vác** near by was once a Roman fortress, but was badly plundered over the centuries by the Mongols and Turks. Its fortunes revived in the 18th century with a flurry of house construction in Baroque style and the building of one of the country's finest neoclassical edifices, the **Cathedral**. The point where the two branches of the Danube which had parted to flow round Szentendre meet again marks the northern city limits of Budapest.

● **Budapest, Hungary (Km 1,647)**

Be sure to be on deck as your vessel enters the Hungarian capital, as the view from the water is stunning by day or night, with the old town of Buda clinging to a steep hillside on the right and the graceful, neo-Gothic Parliament Building lining the flat left bank (Pest). At night, the eight bridges which link the once-separate cities are strung with twinkling fairy lights, while coloured lasers and dramatic floodlights play on the old castle walls of Buda.

The city also marks the starting point for the second half of river cruises (typically of 14 days or more) that can go all the way to the Black Sea. *For details on what to see in Budapest, see pages 92–95.*

Map on page 80

● Kalocsa, Hungary (Km 1,515)

From Budapest the Danube continues south towards Kalocsa, the next port of call, across a broad plain, dotted with oxbow lakes (small bodies of water left behind when a river changes its course) and tributaries. Before dams upstream regulated the flow, this area often flooded, and, as a result, has never been significantly developed and has a fairly bleak appearance. You will, however, see a lot of river traffic, particularly Russian, Romanian and Bulgarian passenger ships making their way upstream to Budapest, and barges transporting freight to and from the oil refinery at Százhalombatta.

Kalocsa is a pretty town in the middle of the Puszta region, located on a terrace overlooking the Danube, 10 km (6 miles) from the river itself (passengers are taken by coach) and famous for growing the paprika that gives Hungarian *goulash* its distinctive flavour. It's an important agricultural and tourism centre, surrounded by pepper fields, and the shops are packed with paprika souvenirs, from painted eggs to colourful pottery and embroidered linen. Some of the houses are painted with bright murals depicting floral motifs interwoven with splashes of scarlet pepper.

Some 1,000 years ago, Kalocsa was the seat of the archdiocese, and the **Archbishop's Palace**, whose permanent exhibition of ecclesiastical relics and treasure is open to the public (Tues–Sun Apr–Oct 9am–5pm, by appointment in winter). The **House of Folk Art Museum** and the **Karoly Visky Museum** feature the colourful local painting for which the region is famous (open Apr–Oct daily 9am–5pm), while for something different, the world's only **Paprika Museum** documents the history of paprika production in Hungary, from growing to different pepper types and the processing technique (open Apr–Oct daily 9am–5pm). ➤ *page 96*

The Archbishop's Palace in Kalocsa has a remarkable library with 120,000 volumes, including a Bible signed by Luther.

BELOW:
paprika peppers hanging up to dry.

KALOCSA'S HARVEST

For three to four weeks in the autumn, starting in September, some 3,200 hectares (8,000 acres) of fields around Kalocsa are packed with farm workers picking the "red gold" for which the town is famous: paprika peppers. All over the town, long strings of scarlet peppers festoon balconies and windows, where they will hang for two to three weeks to develop in the autumn sunshine. Then they are washed, dried and ground into paprika powder.

Meanwhile, the town celebrates the harvest with an exuberant Paprika Festival, including sporting events, a fish-soup cooking contest (with paprika an important ingredient, of course), a paprika harvest parade and a lavish paprika harvest ball.

Hungary shares with Spain the claim to growing the largest crops of paprika in Europe, though both countries grow milder species than the South American types.

PORTS OF CALL: BUDAPEST

There is something satisfying about Budapest which goes beyond the attractions of its fabulous, romantic riverine setting. It is the cultural heart of the nation and a city of international standing, yet it still possesses some of its late 19th-century flair and romance. Nostalgia can be found in the sumptuous spas offering the simple pleasure of bathing in thermal waters, and in the grand old coffee houses, still frequented by artists of all backgrounds and interests.

As the grime of 40 years of neglect is removed from one monument after another, the great city of former days continues to re-emerge.

ORIENTATION

Budapest is the perfect destination for river cruises, because the Danube flows right through the heart of the city, and river cruise vessels subsequently dock in a superbly convenient (and also picturesque) location. This is a major river port, so the exact location of your dock could be anywhere between Elizabeth (Erzsébet híd) and Freedom (Szabadság híd) bridges, but always on the Pest (east) side.

GETTING AROUND

Public transport in Budapest is efficient and cheap. An integrated network of trams and buses, the underground and suburban railway provide access to all parts of the city, but all forms of transport shut down at 11.30pm.

BUSINESS HOURS

Most shops and department stores open Mon–Fri 10am–6pm and Sat 9am–1pm. Shops stay open until 8pm on Thursday. Some of the new hypermarkets are open 24 hours.

TOP CITY SIGHTS

▲ PARLIAMENT BUILDING

Strongly reminiscent of the Palace of Westminster in London, the Parliament Building (Országház) is one of Budapest's most famous sights. There are guided tours in English at 10am, noon, 2pm and 5pm. The neo-Gothic pile, which was completed in 1902, extends along the Danube for some 268 metres (292 yards).

▼ CHAIN BRIDGE

When it was completed in 1849, the Chain Bridge (Széchenyi Lánchíd) linked the two halves of the city, Buda and Pest, for the first time (there are now eight Danube bridges in the Hungarian capital, as well as more on the outskirts). Count Istvan Széchenyi, the 19th-century reformer and innovator, brought in engineers from Great Britain

'turns' once a year to send the sand running anew.

VÁCI UTCA

Long, narrow and pedestrianised for much of its length, Váci Utca (pronounced *vah-tsee ooh-tsa*) is a busy and fashionable shopping street which also flaunts a range of bars, cafés and restaurants. At its northern end is the square of Vörösmarty tér. At No. 7 is one of the city's main meeting places and home to Gerbeaud, doyen of the city's prosperous café society since 1884 and a major tourist attraction in itself.

EXCURSIONS

A short distance upstream from Budapest, the Danube dramatically alters its easterly course for a southern tack. The name of this region is the Danube Bend and there are delightful historic towns to explore. In summer, boats make a five-hour journey from Budapest to **Ezstergom**, stopping en route at **Szentendre** and **Visegrád**. An alternative is a 25-minute helicopter trip over the area.

to construct the graceful span, which is beautifully floodlit at night.

▶ **GELLÉRT HILL**
Rising steeply from the Buda riverfront, the craggy, wooded heights of Gellért Hill (Gellért hegy) can be seen from almost anywhere in the city (not least from the river cruise vessel dock). Naturally, the views are tremendous, extending as far as the distant Matra mountains on the Slovak border on a clear day.

▶ **HEROES' SQUARE**
At the end of Andrassy utca, one of Pest's major thoroughfares, is the wide open space of Heroes' Square (Hœ sök tere), with its 36-metre (118-ft) Millennium Monument, erected in 1896 to mark 1,000 years of the Magyar state. The square is flanked by the Palace of Art and Museum of Fine Arts *(see*

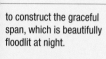

▲ **MUSEUM OF FINE ARTS**
Hungary's pre-eminent art gallery, the Museum of Fine Arts (Szépmüvészeti Múzeum; open Tues–Sun 10am–5.30pm) has a huge collection. The main focus is European art from 1300–1800, notably works by the Spanish school including El Greco, Goya and Velázquez.

right), and behind the former is the world's largest hourglass, unveiled in May 2004 to mark Hungary's admission into the European Union. Some 8 metres (26 ft) in diameter, the structure

▶ **MÁTYÁS CHURCH**
The focal point of the old town of Buda, high above the river, the Mátyás Church (Mátyás templom; church open daily 6am–8pm; free; exhibition rooms open daily 9.30am–5.30pm) is named after Hungary's most popular medieval king, Mátyás Corvinus Hunyadi (1458–90). The Habsburg emperor Franz Josef I was crowned king of Hungary here in 1867. The unusual geometric patterns on the roof, the stained-glass windows and other details date from the 19th century, but parts of the building are far older. Outside the

church in Trinity Square (Szentháromság tér) is the mighty equestrian statue of St Stephen.

▲ **FISHERMAN'S BASTION**
Overlooking the Danube and just in front of the Mátyás Church, the fairy-tale spires and turrets of the Fisherman's Bastion (Halászbástya) afford the classic view of Budapest

(see the main picture on previous page). Built onto the castle walls in the early 20th century purely for ornamental reasons, the monument's name is a reference to the fishermen who heroically defended the ramparts here against invaders in the 18th century.

▼ **THE HUNGARIAN NATIONAL MUSEUM**
The large Hungarian National Museum (Magyar Nemzeti múzeum; open May–Oct Tues–Sun 10am–6pm; Nov–Apr 10am–5pm) is the most important museum in the city. St Stephen's Crown, the symbol of Hungarian sovereignty, was returned here in 1978, having been stolen by the Wehrmacht in World War II. Inside, amid monumental architectural and ornamental details, the whole story of Hungary unfolds – from prehistory right up to the 21st century. On display are prehistoric remains, ancient jewellery and tools, Roman mosaics, a 17th-century Turkish tent fitted out with grand carpets, and a Baroque library. There is some notable royal regalia, although the crown, orb, sceptre and sword have been moved to the Parliament Building.

▼ CENTRAL MARKET HALL

One of the best places for souvenirs in the city is the upstairs section of the cavernous Central Market Hall (Nagy Vásárcsarnok; open Mon–Fri 6am–6pm, Sat 6am–2pm) at the Pest side of Freedom Bridge.

▶ GELLÉRT BATHS

At the southern edge of Gellérthegy, the Gellért

Baths (Gellért gyógfürdő; open daily 6am–7pm, later at weekends June–Sept) comprise medicinal baths as well as regular swimming pools, all decorated in opulent art nouveau style. The unisex indoor pool has a vaulted glass ceiling and Roman-style carved columns, while the thermal baths (segregated by sex) feature marble statues, fine mosaics and glazed tiles.

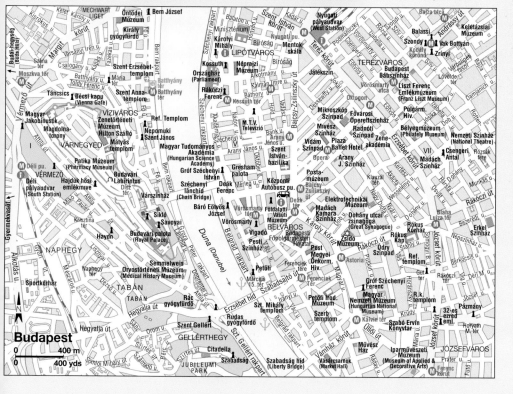

Map on opposite page

Some cruise companies operate tours from Mohács to the pleasant Hungarian city of Pécs, known for its Islamic monuments, museums and university.

From Kalocsa river flows past the **Gemenc Forest**, which extends for 25 km (15 miles) along its right bank and forms part of the Danube-Drave National Park. The landscape is a mixture of lakes with reed beds and shady woodlands of willows, poplars, oaks and rowans, the habitat of red deer and wild boar. The town of **Baja** lies in a restful setting on the banks of the Sugovica, a tributary of the Danube. The main square, Szentháromság tér, opens out onto the river.

● Mohács (Km 1,447)

Mohács is the last town in Hungary past which the river flows before meeting the Croatia–Serbia border. It was the setting for one of Hungary's greatest catastrophes, when in 1526, the Turks destroyed the Hungarian cavalry and with it most of the country's leaders. After this, the Turks occupied Austria and Hungary until 1687, when Karl von Lothringen and Ludwig von Baden defeated the Ottoman troops on Harsany Mountain. The 1526 massacre is commemorated at Sátorhely, 7 km (4 miles) southwest of the town, where a **memorial park** (open Apr–Oct daily 9am–5pm) displays items discovered on the site of the battle.

● Croatia–Serbia border (Km 1,433)

This marker indicates the "T-junction" border between Hungary, Croatia and Serbia. Flowing south, the Danube forms the Croatia–Serbia border for a few kilometres before looping into Croatia proper for a short distance. It then re-joins the border, which is followed all the way to Bačka Palanka, 45 km (28 miles) west of Novi Sad.

Croatia and Serbia formed the bulk of the Yugoslav Federation, which was ripped apart in the war of 1991–5. Croatia is now on the road to EU membership,

BELOW: detail from the battle of Mohács as depicted by Seyyid Lokman of the Ottoman court.

and has seen a revival of tourism on its scenic Adriatic coast. Serbia is now the senior partner in a loose commonwealth known officially as the State Union of Serbia and Montenegro. The actual Serbian state dates back to the 9th century, although the Kingdom of Serbia was not established until the 11th century. In 1918, the country became part of Yugoslavia, along with Slovenia and Croatia.

After the death of Tito in 1980, the delicate balance betweeen the republics began to break down. Serbian leader Slobodan Miloševic exploited tensions, as Croats and others began to resent Serb political dominance to an ever greater degree. The culmination was the bloody civil war which lasted from 1991 to 1995. Later, Miloševic removed the autonomy of Kosovo, which led to conflict between the Kosovan Albanians and the Serbian military, the displacement of thousands of Kosovans and further horrific brutality. NATO intervened in 1999 to try to stop the escalating humanitarian crisis in Kosovo, during which time several bridges along the Danube were bombed, closing this section of the river to commercial traffic. What was left of Yugoslavia (after the independence of Slovenia, Croatia, Bosnia Hercegovina and Macedonia in the mid-1990s) was renamed Serbia and Montenegro in 2003. Kosovo remains under United Nations adminstration. In 2000, the Danube Commission began a 26 million clean-up of the river, with EU funding, and in 2002, the river was opened again to shipping along its entire length.

At Km 1,335 the Croatian town of **Vukovar** appears on the right bank. This was the scene of some of the most ferocious fighting between Croats and Serbs during the war.

● Novi Sad, Serbia (Km 1,255)

As the Danube flows towards Novi Sad, the valley is wide and the river itself dotted with islands. The humid climate has enabled thick, jungly vegetation to thrive, and the area has rich birdlife.

Novi Sad, an important transit port to the northwest of Belgrade, is located on the left bank of the Danube in the

Lower Danube

Republic Square in Belgrade is a popular meeting-place.

BELOW: drinks on deck.

ethnically mixed region of Vojvodina, populated by Serbs, Hungarians, Yugoslavs, Slovaks, Croats and Montenegrins. It is surrounded by fertile plains, farms and vineyards, with mountains in the distance to the south.

This university city has developed around the settlement which was founded by Serbs in the late 17th century – the original town was on the right bank, around the huge **Petrovaradin Fortress**. This is one of the largest fortifications in Europe, often dubbed "Gibraltar on the Danube", and was rebuilt by the Austrians into the present huge structure after 1699 as part of the military frontier with the Ottoman Empire, having being destroyed by the Turks when they occupied Hungary. Today, the fortress houses an art academy, various museums, cafés and artists' studios. You can explore the 16 km (10 miles) of catacombs under the fortress on a guided walk. Tours (Tues–Sun 10am–4pm) start from the museum. In July every year, the fortress at Novi Sad hosts Exit, the largest rock music festival of its kind in south-eastern Europe.

Novi Sad was a major target in the NATO bombing campaign in 1999, which destroyed the city's three main bridges, Sloboda Bridge, opened in 1981; Zezeli Bridge (formerly called Marshal Tito Bridge), completed in 1961; and the Petrovaradin Rail Bridge, built in 1946. Rebuilding has since taken place, and the river was again opened to through navigation in 2001 following the removal of mines and other ordnance debris.

● Belgrade, Serbia (Km 1,170)

Belgrade, capital of Serbia (and of the former Yugoslavia), is strategically located on the southern edge of the great Carpathian Basin, at the confluence of the River Danube and River Sava, and has a turbulent history. It is one of the oldest cities in Europe and nowadays forms the largest urban area in southeastern Europe after Athens. The ravages of communism and damage from the war in 1999 are still visible, and the city is noticeably less colourful (and wealthy) than Budapest, but vibrant nonetheless, with a busy, pedestrianised centre.

The best way to take in the sights is on a guided tour, as the city is sprawling and English isn't widely spoken. River cruise passenger tours include the **Belgrade Fortress**, once the city's military stronghold but today surrounded by the elegant, 19th-century parkland of the **Kalemegdan Citadel**, housing Orthodox churches, Turkish baths, Muslim tombs and the military museum. Elsewhere, there are some beautiful buildings, old and new, in eclectic styles, from the mock-Renaissance National Theatre, designed in the style of Milan's La Scala, to postmodern glass towers.

From Belgrade the river flows east to meet the Romanian border some 90 km (56 miles) downstream; the landscape becomes hilly from this point onwards. Many cruises will make a stop at the Serbian town of **Veliko Gradište**, 115 km (70 miles) downriver from Belgrade, set in hilly scenery within the 650-sq.-km (250-sq.-mile) **Djerdap National Park**. The river widens here into the Srebrno Jezero (Silver Lake), which leads into the magnificent Iron Gates section of the river, nearly 100 km (60 miles) in length.

● Iron Gates (Serbian–Romanian border; Km 1,059–942)

River cruisers spend a whole day cruising the Iron Gates (Porțile de Fier), one of the highlights of any Danube itinerary. The river cuts through the southern spur of the Carpathian Mountains where they meet the northern foothills of the Balkan ranges, forming an emphatic natural boundary between Serbia and Romania. The "true" Iron Gates is in fact a single narrow gorge, which boats enter at Km 949, but the name is generally given to the entire stretch of river between Km 1,059 and Km 942 – a series of gorges linked by wider stretches of river. There are towering cliffs on either side, although these are less impressive than they were before the river level was raised in the 1970s *(see below)*. Parts of the river bed here are among the world's deepest, with depths up to 60 metres (196 ft).

At the eastern end of the Iron Gates, at Km 942, is the enormous **Djerdap Hydro-electric power station** complex. There are actually two power stations (one belonging to Serbia and the other belonging to Romania), two double-level locks, and a barrage supporting a railway and road bridge. The whole project involved much resiting of infrastructure, the reconstruction of 13 river harbours and the relocation of many inhabitants (8,400 within Serbia and 14,500 within Romania) at the time of its construction, which, when completed in 1972, had cost an estimated $500 million. The dam has raised the Danube's water level by some 33 metres (100 ft), and removed the treacherous currents and whirlpools at a stroke. On the negative side, the higher water has hugely diminished the grandeur of the landscape, obliterated a number of historic towns and villages (notably the Turkish island enclave of Ada Kaleh, a short distance downstream from Orşova; *see margin note, page 100)*, and the river's diminished flow is no longer sufficient to flush pollution – chemical toxins and other waste – downriver and out to sea.

Map on page 97

TIP

Some river cruises offer excursions to Băile Herculane, a pleasant spa resort in the mountains north of Orşova. The spa was founded by the Romans, and the legend is that Hercules himself bathed here.

BELOW: barges pass through the Iron Gates Gorge.

Some 3 km (2 miles) downstream from Orşova, the island of Ada Kaleh, completely submerged since the completion of the Djerdap dam, was once a prized asset. Fortified in the 17th century by the Habsburgs, it later fell to the Turks. After their empire shrank, the island was left as an outpost of the Turkish sultan; absorbed into Romania from 1923, it remained a Turkish community until finally abandoned to the river in 1971.

BELOW: the Tabula Traiana.

The first gorge is the **Golubac**, 14 km (9 miles) in length. The town of Golubac was flooded by the power-station project, but nine massive towers – the ruins of a castle that was, for more than two and a half centuries, a base for the Turks for their raids to the north and west until they left in 1688 – can still be seen on the Serbian side. After a broader section, the second gorge – the **Gospodin Vir** – extends for a further 15 km (10 miles). Beyond is the famous **Kazan gorge**, 19 km (13 miles) long, where the river flows between towering cliffs soaring 700 metres (2,300 ft) through a chasm only 150 metres (492 ft) across. The **Tabula Traiana** plaque *(see panel below)* is on the right bank at Km 964. On the Romanian side, an image of the Dacian chief Decebalus is carved into the rock.

The old town of Orşova, at Km 951, was flooded by the rise in water levels, and largely rebuilt higher up the hill. From here to the dam, 10 km (6 miles) downstream, is the "true" **Iron Gates**, once the most dangerous stretch for shipping. In AD 103, Trajan ordered a **bridge** to be built here to facilitate his army's march into Wallachia. For its time, the bridge was an engineering masterpiece (there is still some some uncertainty about how its construction was actually achieved in such a short time), spanning over 1 km (⅔ mile) across the raging torrent. A few of the old pillars have been preserved by the water's edge.

● Turnu Severin/Drobeta, Romania (Km 930)

Drobeta, the former Dacian and Roman city (today's Turnu Severin), was completely rebuilt in 1829, following the signing of the peace treaty of Adrianopol. The Roman Emperor Trajan had his headquarters here, and it was the starting point for his campaigns to northern Europe. Turnu Severin is sometimes referred

TABULA TRAIANA

The Tabula Traiana (Trajan's Tablet), at Km 964, is a monument from Roman times that was laid to commemorate the construction of the Roman military road to the colony of Dacia.

Trajan led two campaigns (in AD 101–2 and 105–6) to conquer Dacia. The stone plaque, which is on the Serbian side of the river, marks the place where he began to construct his 40-km (25-mile) road around the treacherous cliffs of the Danube, a few miles upstream from the point where work on the remarkable bridge *(see main text, above)* commenced in AD 103. Both served as a vital link during the second campaign.

Before the gorge was flooded with the creation of the massive Djerdap hydro-electric plant, the plaque was actually located 40 metres (130 ft) lower. Today, it is set in a rocky cliff, just above the water level of the Danube. The original inscription can still be seen, although the words "Tabula Traiana" are a more recent addition.

to as the "town of the roses" because of its many rose gardens (it is also an important wood and food-processing centre). Look out for bottles of pure essential rose oil in the shops, normally one of the world's most expensive perfume ingredients and available here at bargain prices.

Map on page 97

From here onwards, the Danube enters it **Lower Course**, forming the border between Bulgaria to the south and Romania to the north, with sightseeing stops on either side. This southern region of Romania, Wallachia, set between the Danube and the Carpathian Mountains, was a principality from the late Middle Ages to the mid-19th century. The area came under threat from Ottoman invaders in the 14th century, but was successfully defended to prevent the expansion of the Ottoman Empire into Central Europe. Wallachia remained autonomous throughout three centuries of Turkish rule from the mid-15th century, but voted to unite with Moldavia in 1859 to create the state of Romania.

Rulers of Wallachia included Vlad the Impaler, son of Vlad Dracul, inspiration for Bram Stoker's novel, *Dracula*. Vlad Tepeş (which means "impaler") was famed for his gruesome way of executing his enemies – sticking them through the middle on a sharp stake, hoisting it upright and watching while gravity caused them to slide slowly and agonisingly downwards.

Wallachia today is a more peaceful place. As in most of Romania, the rural areas are beautiful, with the snowy Carpathian Mountains as a backdrop, and small, traditional farmhouses along the river banks.

Bulgaria is one of Europe's poorest countries, although probable EU membership in 2007 may bring prosperity.

● Vidin, Bulgaria (Km 790)

Vidin, on the Bulgarian side of the river, occupies the site of an old Celtic settlement and is one of the country's oldest towns, dating back to Roman times. The dramatic **fortress of Baba Vida**, (open daily, summer 8.30am–5pm; winter 10am–5pm) built in the 14th century, is the best-preserved example of medieval architecture in the country and looms impressively on the bank of the Danube as you approach. In fact, the whole town used to be famous for its fairy-tale minarets, towers and domes, although its skyline suffered from the building of ugly concrete apartment blocks during the communist era. Most tours combine Baba Vida with a visit to the amazing village of Belogradschik, cut directly into sandstone rock.

BELOW: Vidin's historical museum.

● Orehovo, Bulgaria (Km 678)

The river broadens out considerably as it makes its way along the Bulgarian–Romanian border. Vineyards and fruit plantations line the slowly rising banks, and the small town of Orehovo makes for a picturesque sight from the top deck. This is an important trading point for wine, grapes and grain. Less romantically, it's also a loading point for coal onto river barges, and sometimes gets covered in an unsightly layer of black dust.

● Rousse, Bulgaria (Km 495)

Rousse is the largest and most important river port in Bulgaria, set in gorgeous, rolling countryside brilliant with sunflowers in summer and golden wheatfields in autumn. The city itself was once the garrison of the Roman Danube fleets and was known as Sexaginta

Bran Castle in southern Transylvania, marketed to tourists as the home of Vlad the Impaler, the 15th-century prince whose gory acts inspired Bram Stoker to create Count Dracula.

BELOW: Bulgarian yoghurt salad served in a *mehana*.

Prista – "Sixty Ships". Today, it's an industrial centre, and across the river you can see the grim-looking factories of Giurgiu in Romania.

Most of the attractions are outside the centre. A short drive away is the **Rusenski Lom National Park**, where a tributary of the Danube has carved a sheer-sided gorge through the uplifted limestone. Here, you can visit the **Rock Monasteries of Ivanovo**, where hermit monks hollowed cells, churches and chapels out of the rock between the 11th and 14th centuries. Tours also include a visit to **Cerven**, a pretty medieval hilltop town overlooking the Chemi Lom River and surrounded by fortified walls. Within the walls are several fine examples of medieval architecture and 14th-century wall-paintings. Nearby is the imposing **Basarbovo Monastery**, sprawling across a steep hilltop.

● Giurgiu, Romania (Km 493)

Not a port of call as such, but vessels pass the industrial sprawl of Giurgiu, some 65 km (40 miles) south of Bucharest. Romanian crude oil is loaded here for shipping, via a pipeline that connects it with the oilfields of Ploiești. A two-level, combined highway and railway bridge, the Friendship Bridge, 2,224 metres (7,296 ft) long, is one of the longest in in Europe, opened in 1954 to connect Romania with Bulgaria. This is the first bridge across the river since Vidin, 300 km (200 miles) to the west.

From here onwards, the Danube slowly broadens as it nears the Black Sea. The river banks are incredibly fertile, with cereals, vines and cotton growing in the fields. At Km 375, Bratul Ostrov, you'll leave Bulgaria behind. Silistra, on the right bank, is close to the **Srebâna National Park**, the lake of which attracts large numbers of wading birds as well as Dalmatian pelicans.

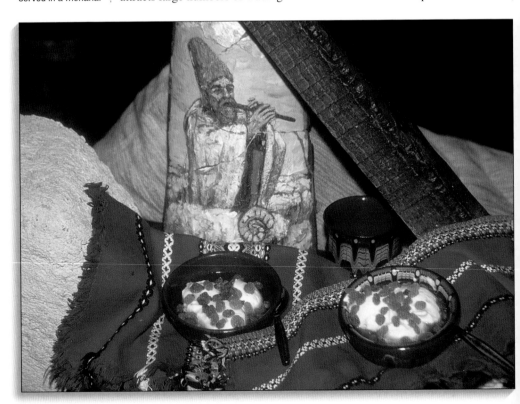

The Danube twists around to the north before Constanta *(see page 104)*, a big port city on the Black Sea. River cruises which end here complete their journey on the Danube–Black Sea Canal, although others continue north to the mighty Danube Delta, where the river splits into three arms and drains into the sea.

Most river cruisers don't stop on this final stretch north of Constanta, although there are still things to see. At Km 171, **Braila** on the left bank has an almost Italian look, with grand monumental buildings. This agricultural port town was once known as the gypsy capital of Europe; both Romania and Bulgaria still have large gypsy populations, with their inherent problems of racism from non-gypsies, and high unemployment. **Galati**, at Km 151, is a major river port, rebuilt in 1960 after bombing in World War II, and now an important and relatively prosperous centre of iron and steel production.

● Bucharest, Romania

The Romanian capital is located an hour by coach from Giurgiu. It holds a certain fascination for most people, mainly due to the legacy of the hated dictator, Nicolae Ceauşescu, who did his best to destroy the elegant, French-style boulevards and replace them with brutalist communist architecture. Elements of both remain today. A visit to his monstrous **Parliament Palace**, the second-largest building in the world after the Pentagon, should not be missed; seven of the 3,000 rooms can be visited (open daily 10am–4pm, until 6pm in summer; Fri, Sat and Sun only when Parliament is in session). Look out for the 24-carat gold ceilings. Also visit the Royal Palace Square, where the famous riots started that led to the collapse of the communist dictatorship in December 1989.

Other attractions include the **Biserica Stavropoleos**, a lovely 18th-century

One of the areas of Bucharest to have survived Ceauşescu's destruction is the historic quarter known as the Lipscani area. There is much to be enjoyed here – old churches, inns, shops and cobbled alleyways.

BELOW: the gigantic Parliament Palace, Bucharest.

church in the unique Brancovenese architectural style, using stone and wood and blending Renaissance with Byzantine design. **Muzeul Satului** is an outdoor "village museum'" within the city, giving a good insight into Romanian arts and crafts (open daily 10am–7pm).

● Izmail, Ukraine (Km 90)

Izmail is an important shipment and trans-shipment port for cargo, and is located about 80 km (50 miles) from the Black Sea. Coal and iron ore for Austria are typically shipped through here, and you'll see busy river traffic day and night. It is here that most river cruise vessels end their Danube voyage. Many of them, particularly those belonging to Russian companies, were built here at the Korneuburg shipyard.

● Constanta, Romania (Km 0)

Constanta is the capital of southeastern Romania, the country's principal seaport and its most important commercial centre, founded in the 7th century BC. There are several interesting excursions from here, not least the remains of **Histria**, the oldest Romanian town, founded by the Greeks 2,500 years ago to the north of Constanta among the saltwater lagoons of the delta. Histria was a trading post on the lagoon of Sinoe and remained active until the 6th century AD. You can walk around and see the old walls, public buildings, baths and an impressive array of archaeological finds in the on-site museum.

In the city, the excellent **National History and Archaeological Museum** features stunning Roman statuettes, glass vessels from the 1st century, gold and silver coins and a magnificent slab of mosaic flooring (open daily 9am–8pm).

Romania has a breeding programme of various types of sturgeon in the Danube Delta and is a growing exporter of caviar, even more so now that stocks of sturgeon in the Caspian Sea are severely depleted. You can buy it in Constanta, but do your bit for conservation and avoid anything on the black market.

BELOW:
Constanta beach.

Alternatively, many people choose to relax on the wide, sandy Black Sea beaches after the long river voyage, and explore the string of holiday resorts that lie on the same latitude as Venice and the Côte d'Azur.

● The Danube Delta

The delta proper of the Danube begins at Km 79.6, and the river, which flows not into the Black Sea as such, but into the delta, divides into three large "arms": the Kilia Arm, the Sulina Arm, and the St George's Arm.

The Kilia Arm is 120 km (74½ miles) long, forms the border between Romania and the Ukraine, and drains about 63 percent of the Danube's water. St George's Arm is 105 km (65 miles) long, and drains about 30 percent of the Danube's water. It turns into the Duna Vatu Canal after flowing through the Macin Mountains, and then flows into the 394-sq.km (152-sq. mile) Lake Razelm. Sfintu Gheorghe (St George) is a fishing centre, and is the last village before the waters empty into the Black Sea. Romanian black caviar is processed here, and you'll see fishermen in black punts transporting their valuable cargo.

Fishing from a ferry in the Danube Delta. Huge carp are the prime attraction here.

The Sulina Arm is 72 km (45 miles) long, but drains off between only 7–14 percent of the Danube's water. Constant digging is a consequence of the low water levels along this stretch. **Sulina** itself (Km 0) is located at the official mouth of the Danube, and has "moles" that stretch out into the sea in order to prevent the build up of silt in the harbour. You can see an old lighthouse marking the former edge of the delta, some distance from the estuary, an indication of how much the delta has grown. Here, the river blends almost imperceptibly with the Black Sea after a voyage of 2,888 km (1,794 miles). ❏

BELOW: a nesting colony of white pelicans.

A HAVEN FOR WILDLIFE

The Danube Delta, a UNESCO Natural World Heritage Site, covers an area of 4,500 sq. km (1,750 sq. miles), most of which is in Romania, with the remainder in Ukraine. Some 20 percent is land, covered by marsh poplars, oak forests, desert dunes and pasture; the rest is water, reeds and quagmire – the largest area of continuous marshland in Europe. Over 35 species of freshwater fish, including the endangered caviar-bearing sturgeon, live in the brackish water, and there are more than 300 species of birds, making this one of the world's largest and most important bird reserves.

The region's official symbol is a pelican; it is the last natural habitat of the white pelican and Dalmatian pelican in Europe, and there are only an estimated 25–40 breeding pairs of Dalmatian pelican left, representing 5 percent of the entire world's population. Mammals include otter, stoat, mink and wildcat, and there are several rare snakes in the forested areas. There are also some 800 plant families, making this an incredibly diverse area.

You'll see plenty of floating hotels and paddle boats, but it is possible to escape into the tranquil labyrinth of the water channels with an experienced local fisherman who knows his way through the maze.

THE RHINE AND TRIBUTARIES

The Rhine is a magnificent river for cruising, with its vineyard-clad slopes and romantic castles. The Moselle, Neckar and Main tributaries hold plenty of interest, too

Map on page 114

Old Father Rhine, as the Germans lovingly call it, is Europe's most important commercial waterway, flowing for some 1,320 km (820 miles) from source to estuary. The Rhine has long been Europe's busiest river, with some of the densest shipping traffic in the world, yet its waters and turbulent past have inspired poets and romantics for centuries. The mystery of the river comes alive in the folklore tales of Lorelei and the Nibelung, the music of Wagner and Beethoven, and in the countless legends surrounding the fairy-tale castles and fortresses that line its banks.

Although it is essentially seen as a German river, the Rhine crosses several international boundaries, passing through no fewer than six countries – Austria, Liechtenstein, Switzerland, Germany and the Netherlands – on its journey from the Alps to the North Sea. Although the stretch known as the Middle Rhine, or the Romantic Rhine, with its towering cliffs, castles and vineyards and dense forests, is the best-known, the river has many other faces as it flows along the German–French border, or cuts a course across the flat, agricultural landscapes of the Netherlands in the final stages of its journey north.

Together with Lake Constance, the Rhine forms a reservoir of drinking water for approximately 30 million Germans. It irrigates mile upon mile of vineyards. It has been an essential transport route through Europe since prehistoric times and has given rise to a string of prosperous towns and cities along its banks. A cruise on the Rhine is rarely without something to draw the eye. Heavily laden barges chug their way north or south, pleasure cruisers ply the waters from one beauty spot to the next, and hikers, swimmers and cyclists enjoy the river's banks and beaches. In parts, there is abundant birdlife to spot, spectacular castles to identify and bridges, statues and monuments all charting the river's history.

PRECEDING PAGES: sailing past Lorelei rocks on the Rhine. **LEFT:** vineyards at Rüdesheim. **BELOW:** tasting the fruits of the Moselle.

The course of the Rhine

The source of the Rhine is a mountain brook that trickles out from the craggy Gotthard Massif in south-eastern Switzerland. This is where two small streams, the Hinterrhein and Vorderrhein, unite to form the Alpine Rhine (Alpernrhein). The waters then flow along the borders of Liechtenstein and Austria and into the beautiful sweep of Lake Constance (Bodensee), emerging from the other side of the lake to tumble over the Rhine Falls, Europe's biggest waterfall, near Schaffhausen in Switzerland, where the river plunges 21 metres (69 ft). The river is joined here by the Aar, doubling its volume.

The next stretch, known as the High Rhine (Hochrhein), forms the Swiss–German frontier. At Basel, the river executes a sharp right turn, the "Rhine

*The Celts called the
Rhine "Renos". To
the Romans, it was
"Rhenus". Rhein,
Rhin and Rijn (the
modern German,
French and Dutch
names) are
derivatives of both.*

Knee", to head northwards, cutting a course through a broad valley along the Franco-German border. Close to the city of Karlsruhe, the French border is left behind and the river enters its German heartland. After holding a northerly course for some distance, it twists to the west between Mainz and Bingen, an area known as the Rheingau, before forcing its way through the Binger Loch (Hole of Bingen), a steep gorge which marks the beginning of the Middle Rhine, or Romantic Rhine. The river then flows northwest through the Uplands (Rheinisches Schiefergebirge) along its most scenic stretch with steep vine-clad slopes, deep gorges and dramatic castles towering over the water.

Below Bonn the river becomes the Lower Rhine (Niederrhein). It then travels through the flat territory of Germany's heavily industrialised Westphalia and the neighbouring Netherlands, where it divides into a number of delta arms, the principal ones being the Lek and the Waal, before finally disgorging into the North Sea.

The Rhine is fed by a number of tributaries, the most important being major rivers in their own right, such as the Main and the Moselle. River cruises operate on both of these, usually in conjunction with the Middle Rhine, and also on the pretty Neckar, which flows through one of Germany's biggest tourist attractions, the city of Heidelberg.

The evolution of river cruising

Much of the length of the Rhine was once dotted with Roman settlements and encampments, temples, villas and amphitheatres. As with parts of the Danube, the river marked the boundary of the empire for centuries. Caesar's armies reached its banks in 58–51 BC, and the first bridge was constructed near what is now Koblenz, giving the Romans access to and control over the right bank,

BELOW: an early advertisement for a Thomas Cook tour.

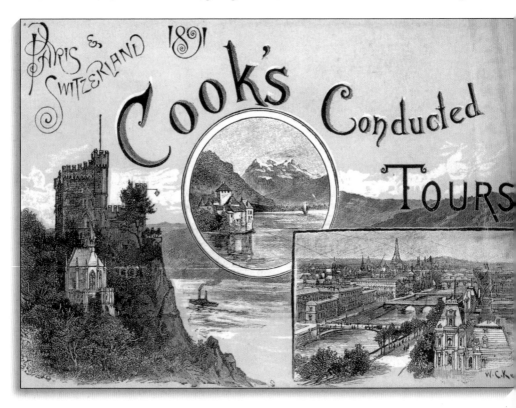

which in their opinion was the outermost border of civilisation, beyond which savage, hostile Germanic tribes lurked. To protect themselves, the Romans built a 550-km (344-mile) boundary wall, the *Limes*, its length interspersed with camps and watchtowers, the foundations of which are often still visible today.

The Rhine has been a vital transport artery through the middle of Europe for thousands of years, although the passage of river boats has often been fraught with difficulty, danger – and expense. In the Middle Ages, castles guarded each bend in the river, and ships' captains would have to pay to get past. Avaricious guilds in the various towns, and in the Middle Ages some 62 customs stations, added to the difficulty, and anybody who couldn't pay, or didn't want to pay, was most likely to be slung into a grim dungeon.

As recently as the mid-19th century, eight cities between Basel and Dordrecht still had what was known as "staple rights", which meant ships could be forced to unload their cargo on the spot and offer it for sale. In 1831, however, the Rhine Shipping Act was signed as a first step towards making the Rhine an international waterway. This was rewritten in 1868 as the Mannheim Rhine Shipping Act, ratified by Belgium, France, Germany, the Netherlands, Belgium, Switzerland and Great Britain, and is still enforced today.

The eclipse of paddle steamers

Scheduled services on passenger paddle steamers began in 1826, operated by Preussisch-Rheinischen-Dampfschiffahrts-Gesellschaft of Cologne (Köln) and were later augmented in 1836 by Dampfschiffahrts-Gesellschaft für den Nieder und Mittelrhein of Düsseldorf. By 1853, much cargo and passenger traffic had been lost to the railway, and the two companies merged to form K (for Köln) D (for Düsseldorf) German Rhine Lines. Over the next few years, KD absorbed several competitors, and, by the outbreak of World War I, was operating 38 paddle steamers along the river. Some 20 of these were still in action by the outbreak of World War II, although the fleet sustained heavy losses. After the war, many of the vessels were repaired and put back into scheduled service, although by the 1960s, when the first hotel boats for longer river cruises began to emerge, only six paddle steamers were left. One of them, the *Goethe*, built in 1913, still operates today.

River cruising grew throughout the 1970s and 1980s, but KD was suffering financially by the 1990s, and in 2000, a majority share was taken by Premicom AG, which sold off the long-haul operation to Viking River Cruises, established in 1997 by a Scandinavian and Dutch consortium. KD now operates day trips and party cruises on 14 vessels, while Viking has gone on to become the world's largest river cruise company, with 25 vessels, several of which are based on the Rhine. Peter Deilmann also offers cruises on the Rhine and its tributaries, as does American operator Uniworld.

What to expect

There are four principal routes for river cruises on the Rhine and its major tributaries – the Main, Moselle and Neckar – although there are endless permutations of cruise and stay, short cruises, longer cruises and

Map on page 114

Tke stone kilometre markers along the Rhine are shown as black numbers on a white background except in the Netherlands, where they are white on black. Half-kilometre signs on busy stretches of the river are indicated as a cross.

BELOW: all hands on deck.

even combined cruises taking in the whole of the Rhine and the entire length of the Danube. Ships can sail at night, so it is possible to cover great distances in a short space of time.

The most popular section of the Rhine itself is between Cologne and Mainz. Moselle cruises operate between Koblenz and Trier, while the main route along the Neckar is between Mannheim and Stuttgart. Voyage time depends on the number of stops but surprisingly great distances can be covered on the Rhine in a short time as vessels sail through the night. A classic Rhine cruise from Düsseldorf to Basel and back, for example, takes between five and seven days, spending time in the beautiful Rhine Gorge and visiting Rüdesheim, Braubach, Cochem and Koblenz. "Taster" cruises are also available, operating between Basel and Düsseldorf, a voyage of three nights/four days. Amsterdam to Basel usually takes eight days. A cruise on the Main, meanwhile, might actually start on the Danube, sailing from Passau, up the Main-Danube Canal to the Main and as far as Frankfurt, a voyage of seven days.

An emphasis on culture

Expect a culture-intensive holiday on any of these cruises. Most fellow passengers will have an interest in European history, and there are many castles, cathedrals and Roman antiquities to visit. In the Rhine Gorge and other wine-growing areas, there are plenty of opportunities to taste and buy wine. Most days and some evenings are spent in port, with the ship sailing at night. In the Rhine Gorge itself, you will be able to lounge on deck and admire the scenery, but on most other days, the ship will be docked. Many of the tours are guided city walks, as it's difficult to get a coach around Germany's medieval town

centres. This fact, and the uneven cobbled streets, can present a problem for anybody not steady on their feet, and access for wheelchairs is usually restricted.

Some cruise lines bring lecturers on board and hold cultural talks, musical evenings and wine-tasting. Theme cruises operate, too, focusing on activities such as cycling (there are often cycle paths alongside the river), golf, or visiting gardens. There are also several wine cruises, not surprisingly, taking in the wines of Alsace and the Rheingau, and cruises to see the annual Rhine in Flames festival in summer. Expect the standard of accommodation and food on board to be high; both Peter Deilmann and Viking River Cruises operate some of their finest ships on these waters.

Map on page 114

DESTINATION HIGHLIGHTS ON THE RHINE

● **Basel, Switzerland (Km 165–169)**

Basel, the navigable limit of the Rhine, is the starting point for many cruises. The city has grown up either side of the river, with the industrial Kleinbasel section to the north and the lovely old part, Grossbasel, on the south bank. Basel has a real international flavour; it is, after all, where three countries – France, Germany and Switzerland – meet. Situated at the "knee" of the Rhine, it is the location of the oldest university in Switzerland, together with some 30 museums and an inviting old town – a jumble of medieval buildings along the hilly river bank (a short walk from the cruise boat landing stage). Basel is also steeped in Roman history.

The focal point of the city is the **Rathaus** (Town Hall) and marketplace, around which are several late Gothic, Renaissance and Baroque guildhalls. The 13th-century Romanesque **Münster** (Cathedral) is an unusual shade of red, its slender towers built from sandstone quarried from the nearby Vosges Mountains.

Holbein's portrait of Dorothea Kannengeisser in Basel's Kunstmuseum.

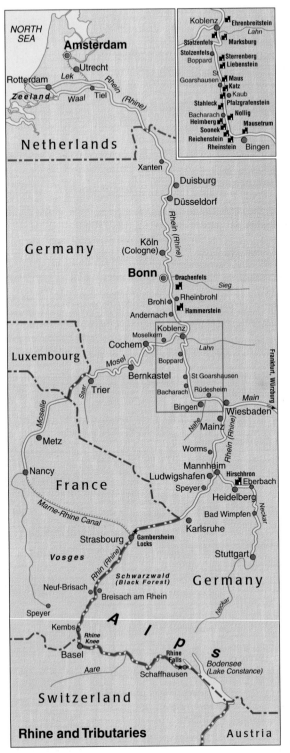

Rhine and Tributaries

Three of the original city gates survive, too, including the 12th-century **Gallus Gate**, its roof adorned with colourful glazed tiles.

There are several museums worth visiting, including a good modern art establishment, the **Kunstmuseum** (open Tues–Sun 10am–5pm), where you can view two Picasso paintings (*The Seated Harlequin* and *Two Brothers*), purchased by the people of the city in 1967, together with four others the artist donated. The museum has an outstanding collection of 15th- and 16th-century Flemish art, including the world's largest collection of Holbeins.

The best way to explore Basel is to wander the narrow streets, many of which, particularly around the university, are not wide enough to accommodate a car. Take a stroll along the river bank, too, on the north bank, facing the old city.

Basel is famous for its music festivals and industrial trade fairs, the most famous being the **Autumn Fair**, which has been held each and every year since 1471. The **Fasnacht Festival** is a three-day masked carnival held on the Monday following Ash Wednesday.

● **Breisach, Germany (Km 226)**

Forming a natural border between France and Germany, the Rhine flows north from Basel and immediately descends through a series of locks – ten in total – on the way north to Karlsruhe in Germany. The oldest lock is at Kembs, which can boast a control tower designed by Le Corbusier.

The town of Breisach clings to a basalt rock outcrop opposite its French counterpart, Neuf-Brisach. Boats moor on the German side for a swift visit to the Romanesque-Gothic **St Stephan Cathedral**, built between the 12th and 13th centuries.

The river is now flowing through the pleasant wine country of Alsace, with the Black Forest on one side and the imposing Vosges Mountains on the other, vineyards sloping gently down to the river. Pretty villages are dotted along the banks, and you can often see storks nesting on top of the chimneystacks of the houses.

● **Strasbourg, France (Km 294.3)**

The delightful medieval city of Strasbourg is the seat of the Council of Europe, the European Commission on Human Rights and the European Science Foundation, and is also capital and cultural centre of the Alsace region of France. The port is the largest on the Upper Rhine, and a large network of docks provides freight and other services.

Map on page 114

Strasbourg's centre is surrounded by the River Ill, and is mainly pedestrianised, particularly the area known as **Petite France**, where the river splits into a number of canals. At the end of Petite France, look out for the **Ponts Couverts**, a series of wooden footbridges dating back to the 13th century (but no longer covered).

The focal point of it all is **Place Gutenberg**, named after Johannes Gutenberg, the inventor of the printing press *(see panel on page 118)*, who lived here during the 15th century and whose statue stands at the centre of the square. A highlight of any visit is the massive hulk of the **Cathédrale de Notre Dame**, the tallest medieval building in Europe, its viewing platform reached by a wearying 332 steps up inside the tower. It's worth the climb for the vista of the Black Forest (and, in the other direction, the Vosges Mountains) beyond the colourful roofs of the old town. At noon, crowds are drawn to the astronomical clock inside the cathedral, adorned with a **Parade of the Apostles** which dates from 1838. Alsatian café culture plays a large part in the day-to-day life of the city, the experience enhanced by attractive squares surrounded by pretty, half-timbered houses. Most cafés sell a fabulous array of cakes and pattisseries.

Many river cruises start and end in Strasbourg, and the Gare Fluviale is located adjacent to the rue du Havre, a short walk from the heart of the city on an arm of the Ill.

It was in Strasbourg that the song to be later known as the Marseillaise *was composed. It was written overnight on 24–25 April 1792 by a soldier named Rouget de Lisle, who called it* War Song for the Rhine Army.

BELOW: café culture in Strasbourg.

*Taking part in the
Fasnacht
celebrations in Basel.*

BELOW:
the Nibelung
Bridge at Worms.

● Gambersheim Locks, France (Km 309)

Just outside Strasbourg, the Gambersheim Locks are a recent construction, put into operation in 1974. They are the largest inland waterway locks in France. There are two chambers, each with a length of 270 metres (885 ft), and the locks are in operation 24 hours a day, all year round (it takes about 15 minutes to pass through). About 20 million tons of freight pass through the locks each year, as well as numerous river cruise vessels, and being on deck as the ship goes through the lock, often in the company of cargo vessels, is fascinating.

● Speyer, Germany (Km 400)

After parting company with the French-German border and the northern fringes of the Black Forest, the Rhine passes the large city of Karlsruhe and then meanders through gentle hills. The town of Speyer is typically used as a short stop so that passengers can leave the vessel to take a tour to nearby Heidelberg (*see page 138*), although Speyer itself has a few noteworthy sights.

The city, which started as a Celtic settlement and then around 100 BC became a Roman trading post, was burnt down on the order of Louis XIV in 1689. After it was returned to Germany in 1816, it became the government seat of Bavaria Palatinate (a palatinate being a historic state of the Holy Roman Empire) until 1845. Eight German emperors and kings and three empresses are buried in the crypt of the **Cathedral**, which was founded in 1030. Close to the cathedral is the **Historisches Museum der Pfalz** (Museum of Palatinate History; open Tues–Sun 10am–6pm), which includes a history of wine, among other exhibits. The 12th-century subterranean **Jewish Baths**, part of an old synagogue, also make for an interesting visit.

● Mannheim, Germany (Km 415–425)

A short sail up the river from Speyer is Mannheim, on the right bank, opposite the industrial city of Ludwigshafen. Mannheim was founded in 1606 in a circular layout that covered the peninsula between the Neckar and the Rhine. The city has grown into a modern finance and insurance centre but has some attractive old parts, including the elegant **Mannheim Palace**, which is now the university, and the art deco architecture around **Friedrichsplatz**.

● Ludwigshafen, Germany (Km 424.7)

Ludwigshafen, on the left bank as you cruise north, is not usually a port of call, but is of interest nonetheless. Ludwigshafen (which translates as "Ludwig's Harbour") was originally constructed in 1607 as a military stronghold for Mannheim on the opposite bank. The harbour was constructed at the beginning of the 19th century, and the town became an independent community in the middle of the 19th century. The land was sold to Bavaria, and its king, Ludwig I, had the town renamed Ludwigshafen. Today, it has a strong industrial economic base and is home to the chemical giant BASF, the manufacturing complex of which fronts the river. The main attraction here is the shopping and the 10-metre (33-ft) mural painted by Joan Miró on the front of the Wilhelm Hack Museum.

Just beyond Ludwigshafen is the mouth of the River Neckar, which flows into the Rhine and swells it considerably. Cruises calling at Heidelberg *(see page 138)* will take a detour from the Rhine into the Neckar at this point.

Map on page 114

● Worms, Germany (Km 443.2)

Sunny vineyards now slope gently down to the river banks (this is recorded as being the warmest spot in Germany) as the Rhine lazily carves its way north to the Celtic settlement of Worms. Evidence of human habitation dating back 6,000 years has been found here.

In more recent times, Worms was an imperial residence on the banks of the Rhine and the centre of the Burgundian Empire that was destroyed by the Huns in AD 437, an event which gave rise to the legendary *Nibelungen Saga*, a much-loved keystone of Germany's literary heritage. Today, Worms is best known as a wine-trading centre. The vineyards surrounding the city produce the grapes used for making Liebfraumilch, a much-maligned semi-sweet white wine which is none the less popular with both the German and export markets.

Worms is normally one of several possible jumping-off points for tours to Heidelberg, but if you stay in the city (boats usually moor near the centre), visit the chunky sandstone **Peter and Paul Cathedral** in the centre, with six round Romanesque towers and a magnificent rose window. Some 45 imperial parliaments were held here at a time when Worms was a powerful regional city.

The city also has Europe's largest **Jewish Cemetery**, with some of the graves dating back over 1,000 years. The cemetery was desecrated by the Nazis but has been restored. Also look out for the **Nibelung Bridge** and its bronze statue of Hagen (the villain of the saga) throwing the treasure of the Nibelungs into the

One of the seminal moments of the Reformation took place in Worms in 1521 when Luther met the elected Emperor of the German States and Cities at the Diet of Worms. Luther refused to recant his theses, but threats from his supporters allowed him to escape to the safety of Wartburg Castle.

BELOW: the Jewish cemetery at Worms.

The Rheingau area may be famous for its wine, but – of course – German beer isn't bad either.

BELOW: Johannes Gutenberg.

water. Every August, there's a **Nibelungen Festival**, which takes place in the cathedral. Less romantically, as you leave the city you'll see a vast nuclear power station on the banks at Biblis.

● **Mainz, Germany (Km 498.5)**

Wine-growing villages come thick and fast now as the river winds it way north, and where one region ends, cultivation of the next grape variety begins. Asparagus, revered as a delicacy, is also grown in this area, and if you're cruising in May or June, you'll see *spargel* menus in all the restaurants, with asparagus served in every course.

Mainz, strategically located on the west bank of the Rhine opposite the mouth of the River Main *(see page 134)*, is over 2,000 years old, having been founded as the Roman camp Moguntiacum. It is the capital city of the Rhineland-Palatinate and has a history as seat of electors and bishops. Much of the city was devastated by bombing in World War II and has been rebuilt. In the Old Town, visit the six-towered Cathedral, originally constructed in AD 975 and a highlight of ecclesiastical architecture in the Upper Rhine region.

Mainz is also home to the **Gutenberg Museum** (open Tues–Sat 9am–5pm, Sun 11am–3pm), which tells the history of printing. The city is also one of the main centres of the Rhine wine trade. There are several museums and palaces to explore, but one sight not to miss is **St Stephen's Church**, with its stunning stained-glass windows by the French painter Marc Chagall.

● **Wiesbaden, Germany (Km 503)**

The capital of Hesse, located on the opposite bank from Mainz, has been dated

JOHANNES GUTENBERG

The most famous son of Mainz is Johannes Gutenberg (*c.*1397–1468), the inventor of movable type and book printing. He moved to Strasbourg in 1434, where he invented the revolutionary system of printing with moveable letters. Ten years later he returned to Mainz and won the patronage of Johann Fust, a local tradesman and wealthy burgher who provided Gutenberg with the funds to print the 42-line Gutenberg Bibles, 48 copies of which are still in existence. The university, founded in the 15th century, was named after him, and there's also a memorial to the great man in Gutenbergplatz.

The partnership with Fust ended with legal action to recover the money advanced to Gutenberg. Unable to repay the debt, Gutenberg had no option but to pass ownership of the press to Fust, so it was he and a new partner, Peter Schöffer, who published the Psalter in 1457. Little is known about Gutenberg's later years, though it is recorded that he was taken into the court of Archbishop Adolf of Nassau in 1465. He died two years later, although the church in Mainz where he is thought to have been buried no longer exists.

Gutenberg's invention spread so rapidly that the names of over 1,000 fonts, mostly German, have come down to us from the 15th century.

back to the Stone Age, although the town was essentially developed by the Romans, who were attracted to the thermal springs. Today, the city has 28 of these, as well as many spas and patrician houses, built in the 19th century when wealthy visitors came from all over Europe to take the waters. Johann Wolfgang von Goethe, the grandfather of German Romanticism, was among the privileged who came here to relax. Wiesbaden is not normally a port of call, but you'll see the city spread out along the river banks as you pass.

● **Rüdesheim, Germany (Km 526.7)**

The Rhine is now entering its most beautiful stretch, carving a deep valley between the Hunsrück Mountains on the west bank and the Taunus on the east. You'll see strings of pleasure boats on day trips, as well as the faintly incongruous sight of heavily laden industrial barges ploughing through the water past quaint little villages with ornate weathercocks and graceful church spires, scarlet geraniums cascading from balconies on the immaculate old houses.

Rüdesheim, in the heart of the Rheingau wine-growing area, was the terminal point of the old Merchant Road that originated in Lohr and circumvented the waterfalls that once made this stretch of the river treacherous. Boats dock in the centre, which is easily walkable, the uneven cobbled streets aside. The town is famous for the wine estates on the surrounding hills, the products of which are celebrated in the famous **Drosselgasse**, a pretty, narrow street absolutely packed with bars and wine taverns (and, in high season, tourists). Near the town, a cable car will take you to the top of the Rheingau hills to see the famous **Niederwald Denkmal Monument** – a fussy bronze statue of Germania built to commemorate the founding of the German Empire in 1871.

While in Rüdesheim, visit the Rheingau and Weinmuseum housed in Brömserburg, where you can learn more about the region and its wine production.

LEFT: before...
BELOW: ...and after.

Four castles were built to protect this important merchant centre and trading route, one of which, **Brömserburg**, belonged for a while to the Knights of Rüdesheim and is today a wine museum. The castle was built in the 9th century and is the oldest on the Rhine. It once served as a customs station; the waters were so dangerous here that ships had to unload their cargoes and transport them by land, avoiding the infamous "Hole of Bingen" with its reefs and swirls.

There's more to Rüdesheim than wine, though. **Siegfried's Mechanisches Musikkabinett** (Siegfried's Mechanical Music Cabinet; open Mar–Dec daily 10am–6pm), a highly unusual museum located in the Brömserhof (parts of which date back to the 15th century) and opened in 1969, is famous for its outstanding collection of priceless mechanical musical instruments. All 250 of the instruments have been collected from the period spanning 150 years prior to 1930, and all have been restored. Siegfried Wendel, the museum's owner, is always on hand, and frequently plays some of the instruments for visitors. On a more gruesome note, visit the **Medieval Torture Museum** (open Apr–Nov daily 10am–6pm), depicting the history of torture throughout the Middle Ages, and the practice of witch-hunting.

From this point onwards it is worth staying on deck, as the vessel passes through some the most alluring and romantic countryside in Europe, with amazing towers and castles perched on impossible rock outcrops overlooking the narrow, swirling waters of the Rhine.

● Mauseturm, Germany (Km 529)

Below the mouth of the Nahe, close to Rüdesheim and Bingen, a slender red-and-yellow tower looking like something out of a Disney cartoon perches on a small island. The legend relates how the original tower was built by the evil, hard-hearted Archbishop Hatto of Mainz in 1208 as a reinforcement for the customs castle, Ehrenfels, which stands in ruinous state on the opposite hillside. The tower's strategic position allowed the archbishop to fleece passing traffic on the Rhine. To bolster his income, peasants were levied a corn tithe, which he collected in a large barn in Mainz. After a bad harvest, the hungry populace went to Mainz and asked for grain. Archbishop Hatto, having promised to help, then proceeded to lock them up in his tithe barn and set fire to it.

Everyone inside perished, but the story goes that some mice escaped. The archbishop departed to his castle on the island by boat from Bingen, opposite Rüdesheim, but the mice followed him… and then ate him alive, even though he had had his bed suspended by chains from the ceiling, so that it was well above the floor.

The castle thus became known as the Mice Castle (Mauseturm), although its actual title was once Mautturm (Customs Tower). Under France's King Louis XIV, the castle was burnt down, although fortunately it was restored by the King of Prussia in 1855 and used as a signal tower for shipping, to warn ships of the treacherous whirlpools and rocks of the Hole of Bingen. It remained in this manner until 1974, when the channel was deepened, and, since then it has been inhabited only by bats, and the ghost of the evil archbishop.

● Rheinstein Castle, Germany (Km 533)

Rheinstein, on the west bank, was originally constructed as an imperial castle for the purpose of exercising customs rights and toll collections, and to protect the surrounding estates. It is one of the oldest castle buildings on the Rhine, and has an astounding position; the steely-grey castle actually appears as though it's part of a huge, jagged slab of rock, high on the hillside.

Rheinstein reputedly dates back to the 9th century, although its exact year of construction is unknown. It belonged to the archbishops of Mainz, who named it after the city's patron saint, Bonifatius, although its original name was Vogtberg. From the 16th century, it fell into ruin. In 1823, Prince Friedrich of Prussia bought what was left for 100 reichsmarks. His great-granddaughter sold it in 1975, in an advanced state of dilapidation, to a Tirolese singer. It is now preserved thanks to a society founded by the singer, donations from tourists and income from its rental for private parties.

● Reichenstein Castle, Germany (Km 534.4)

Confusingly, Reichenstein is right next to Rheinstein, although it is in a rather better state of repair. In the 19th century, this solid-looking fortress was called Falkenburg Castle. It was erected to protect the property of Cornelimunster Abbey near Aachen in the 11th century, although subsequent owners eventually resorted to extortion to earn a living. The castle has been destroyed and rebuilt several times, the last time in 1899, when several neo-Gothic touches were added. Today it functions as a hotel.

From here, the river sweeps round a curve to the left, passing several more impressive castles: **Burg Sooneck**, the privately owned **Heimburg** and, on the

Map on page 114

BELOW:
Pfalzgrafenstein
Castle.

TIP

The Rhine in Flames celebration takes place in August each year. An 80-strong flotilla of brightly decorated ships, barges and boats sails along the Rhine, as tremendous firework displays are launched from the vessels, stately buildings and from around the surrounding countryside.

RIGHT: medieval armour for a virtuous knight.

right bank, the ruined **Nollig Castle**, little more than a keep nowadays. Almost directly opposite is the crumbling remain of **Burg Furstenberg**, gradually disintegrating into the vineyards over which it stands. Just beyond the medieval village of Bacharach is **Burg Stahleck**, a smartly renovated castle which now houses a youth hostel.

● **Pfalzgrafenstein Castle, Germany (Km 545)**

This is undoubtedly one of the most curious castle creations in the world, a six-storey tower clinging to a tiny island in the middle of the swirling waters and resembling a ship. The castle was erected in 1326 by King Ludwig I of Bavaria purely for collecting customs duties from passing vessels on the Rhine. Anyone who couldn't pay would be sent down a rope to the "dungeon" – a platform floating at the bottom of a deep well. Since 1946 it has been the property of the state of the Rhineland Palatinate. Although it has been repaired and restored, purely for tourism purposes, the castle was in use as a signal point for Rhine shipping until the 1960s. Opposite stands the small town of Kaub.

● **Lorelei, St Goarshausen, Germany (Km 554.6)**

Nobody can pass through the medieval wine-growing village of St Goarshausen without learning the legend of the Lorelei. Here, the river carves its way through a steep, narrow gorge, with its bed descending down to 25 metres (82 ft) in places, winding around jagged rocks and creating powerful whirlpools which have sucked many a ship below the surface. The gorge, with its 132-metre (433-ft) cliffs, is so narrow that the railway line which runs alongside the river has been cut into rock tunnels. A bronze statue of the maiden Lorelei looks down on

BURG RHEINFELS

N ear St Goar on the west bank is the vast fortress of Burg Rheinfels (Km 557), which was built from 1245 by Count Dieter V of Katzenelnbogen and became the largest on the Rhine. Like many Rhine castles, it was built to support the extraction of tolls from river traffic. During the 16th and 17th centuries the Hessian landgraves (German count) adapted the castle to become a comfortable residence as well as a stronghold. About 500 people lived here in peacetime, though the numbers would be swelled by a further 3,500 during hostilities. Though the castle withstood the assault of 28,000 of Louis XIV's troops, it finally fell in 1797 to the French, who left it a romantic ruin. It was used for much of the 19th century as a quarry. Nonetheless there is much to see, including a labyrinth of tunnels.

A watercolour of the castle *c.* 1844 by J.M.W. Turner hangs at Norwich City Art Gallery in England.

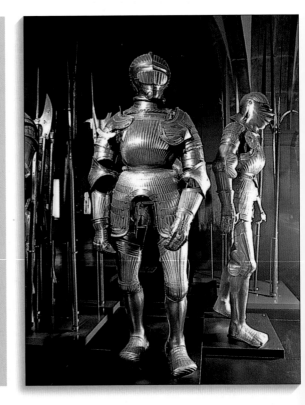

the river from where, as related by the famous poem written by Heinrich Heine in 1824, the mysterious nymph would once appear, captivating sailors with her beauty and her hypnotic singing before luring them onto the rocks to their death. The poem *Die Lorelei*, set to music in 1837, is seen as the epitome of Rhine Romanticism.

● Liebenstein Castle and Sterrenberg Castle, Germany (Km 566.5)

Just past St Goarshausen, look out for the wittily-named Katz and Maus castles on the right bank. The names are actually coincidental; Katz belonged to the Dukes of Katzenelnbogen, while Maus comes from "Maut", or toll. Further on, the castle on the left, Rheinfels *(see also panel opposite)*, is an enormous hulk of a building, and was once the most important castle on the Rhine, belonging to the dukes of Katzenelnbogen. The French army partially destroyed it in 1797 and took much of the stone to Koblenz to build Ehrenbreitstein Fortress, although plenty was left behind. The castle today has been partly repaired and houses an exclusive hotel. This is the location of part of the famous September firework festival, the Rhine in Flames.

As the boat nears Boppard, you'll see ruins of two 12th-century castles, Sterrenberg and Liebenstein, built close together. These were inhabited by two brothers who hated each other so much that they erected a wall between the castles. The story goes that they made up their differences, and for fun, decided to wake each other with an arrow shot every morning. Inevitably, one killed the other by mistake with a badly aimed arrow.

● Boppard, Germany (Km 570.5)

The river now curves round in a wide loop, with picturesque wine-growing villages clustered on its banks at the foot of the vineyards. The attractive little town of Boppard, founded by the Celts and later fortified by the Romans, is a popular call for most river cruise vessels, which tie up right in front of the centre. Eight of the original 28 Roman towers are still standing, as well as the medieval town gates and many old, half-timbered houses. Grapes (mostly Riesling) are grown on slopes that are among the steepest in all of Germany's vineyards, used by the 14 full-time cooperatives that obtain more than 500,000 litres (approximately 109 imperial gallons) from the cultivation. Needless to say, there are plenty of opportunities to taste and buy the wine, and the town often has a festive air, with bands playing in the various sunny gardens of the many wine taverns.

The Gothic church has some lovely old wall-paintings and intriguing tombs, while the castle on the river bank is now a museum housing some of the work of furniture-maker Michel Thonet, who developed the technique of bending wood, and was famous for creating chairs for the coffee houses of Vienna. You can also take a cable car to **Gedeons Eck** to capture the view of the Rhine's tight, meandering course, so much so that it looks like four separate lakes, giving the viewing spot the name Vier-Seen-Blick (Four Lakes view).

Map on page 114

The story of the Lorelei may be fiction, but the reality of boats sinking in the whirlpools or being smashed against the rocks of the fearsome gorge is not. Things have improved, however: the channel has been dredged, and signal masts have been erected to keep boatmen on course.

BELOW: the legendary Lorelei.

Die Loreley.

Die schönste Jungfrau sitzet / Dort oben wunderbar, / Ihr goldnes Geschmeide blitzet, / Sie kämmt ihr goldenes Haar.

Sie kämmt es mit goldenem Kamm / Und singt ein Lied dabei / Das hat eine wundersame, / Gewaltige Melodei.

Board games are provided in the library. Some vessels also offer DVDs; internet access, however, is still a rarity.

BELOW:
an aerial view of Stolzenfels Castle.

● Marksburg Castle, Germany (Km 580)

This beautiful, mystical castle is the only one in the entire Rhine Valley never to have been destroyed, and is easily the most visited, as it gives the best insight into medieval life. It dates all the way back to 1150, towering majestically 170 metres (557 ft) above the town of Braubach. The original founder, one of the nobles of Braubach, named it after St Mark. A successor, Eberhard von Eppstein, had the castle extended and further fortified in 1219, and it was occupied after 1220 by vassals of the Counts Palatine. In 1283, the castle was acquired by the counts of Katzenelnbogen.

At the end of the 19th century it passed to the German Castles Association, which has its headquarters and archives here. The library houses over 12,000 volumes. A tour of the castle will take you through not only the citadel itself, but also the impressive kitchens in the Gothic Hall building. There is a gruesome torture chamber in the cellar of the older hall building, where a great assortment of grisly instruments of torture can be viewed.

A complete replica of the castle can be seen today in an amusement park in Japan. It appears that the Japanese offered to buy the original ruin, have it dismantled and shipped to Japan, for 250 million marks, but were refused by the German Castles Association – hence the replica.

● Stolzenfels Castle, Germany (Km 585.2)

Located just south of Koblenz and surrounded by thick forest, this handsome, imperial yellow castle was originally built in the 13th century to defend the nearby silver mines. The castle was destroyed by the French but rebuilt in 1852 by the Prussian Crown Prince Friedrich-Wilhelm IV, in neo-Gothic style. In

the castle's chapel, important works from the period of High Romanticism can be found in the wall murals. It is one of the best-known castles along the Rhine.

Map on page 114

● Koblenz, Germany (Km 591.5 Rhine/Km 0.30 Moselle)

The river broadens at Koblenz, a bustling regional garrison town and a former Roman trading settlement that grew up at the point where the Rhine meets the Moselle *(see page 135)*. The town lies on the massif of the Middle Rhine Highlands, bordered by North Rhine-Westphalia to the north, Hesse to the east and Saarland to the south. The Rhine bisects it diagonally from southeast to northwest. Boats dock right next to the old town, which is easy to explore on foot.

Koblenz is a typical old German country town, with wood-beamed houses, cobbled strets and dazzling displays of blooms in every balcony. A giant equestrian statue of Prince William I stands at the confluence point of the rivers, called **Deutsches Eck** (German Corner). You can climb the 107 steps for an outstanding view of the town from the gallery at the base of the statue. This is where the Teutonic Knights established their first base, in 1216. The Romanesque church of **St Castor** is the city's oldest building, dating from 836. It is significant in that the decision to carve up Charlemagne's empire was taken here.

● Ehrenbreitstein Castle, Germany (Km 592.3)

Located opposite the mouth of the Moselle, where it flows into the Rhine at Koblenz, this squat, solid-looking fortress was built around 1100 on a site that is 116 metres (380 ft) above the water, with incredible views over both rivers, the Eifel Hills and the city of Koblenz. It was acquired in 1152 by the Electorate

LEFT: film poster for *The Bridge At Remagen* (1969).

REMAGEN BRIDGE

Just outside Rolandseck, look for the stubby bridge towers on either side of the river. They were once joined by a steel railway bridge which, for reasons unknown, the Germans were unable to destroy during World War II. In March 1945, the bridge was captured by American soldiers, General Eisenhower remarking that "the bridge was worth its weight in gold". Hitler court-martialled the soldiers who failed to blow it up and had four of them shot, but inexplicably the bridge collapsed ten days after its capture, killing 28 Americans.

The bridge was the setting for a 1969 film entiled *The Bridge at Remagen*, starring George Segal and Robert Vaughn. However, the storyline was largely fictitious and it was shot in Czechoslovakia.

The surviving towers are now a museum dedicated to peace. A room in one of the towers shows a documentary about the bridge made by the Royal Military Academy at Sandhurst, England.

of Trier and expanded, becoming a fortress around 1500 with the addition of more fortifications. By 1750, after several breaches by the French, the fortress was made impregnable by the brilliant architect Balthasar Neumann. Today, the castle houses the **National Collection of Monuments to Technology**, and also serves as a youth hostel. Ehrenbreitstein Castle is also one of the sites for the annual Rhine in Flames celebration, usually in August, when the castle is drenched in red light with smoke billowing from all sections.

● Andernach, Germany (Km 613.3)

From Koblenz, most river cruises head straight for Cologne (on northbound itineraries), bypassing the increasingly industrialised towns dotted along the banks. Andernach is not a stop as such, but has an interesting past and can trace its history back further than almost any other German town. Traces of early Stone Age and Bronze Age settlements have been unearthed.

● Rolandseck Castle, Germany (Km 640)

The river is now passing the northernmost vineyards of one of Germany's main red-wine-growing districts. Despite the diminishing hills and increasing urbanisation, the banks are still lined with castles: the ruined Hammerstein, and Rheineck, which was rebuilt in rather grand style by a family of rich German bankers. At Rheinbrohl and its counterpart, Brohl, on the opposite bank, the **Limes Tower** is a replica of the original Roman construction of a barrier, which extended from here to the Danube, marking the northern boundary of the Roman Empire.

Like many other Rhine castles, Rolandseck was originally a fortress that also served as a customs station. It is now in ruins, but old archways can still be

BELOW: Siegfried slays the dragon.

THE NIBELUNG LEGENDS

What the *Iliad* and the *Odyssey* are to Greece and the Arthurian legends are to Britain, the *Nibelungen Saga* is to Germany: a statement of an archetypal myth that has remained an enduring element of the national identity.

The Nibelung legends are a blend of fact and fiction, recounting the history of the Burgundian (Nibelung) court, whose capital was at Worms, until its downfall at the hands of Attila the Hun (or "Etzel"). There are records of Attila defeating a Burgundian tribe in AD 437, and also documentation of Queen Brunhild, although no evidence has been found of an invincible Siegfried brought down by intrigue and betrayal.

One main source of the legends is the *Nibelungenlied*, penned by anonymous authors around 1200, probably drawing on the tales of wandering bards. The first half deals with the life and death of Siegfried, the second with the Nibelungs' total defeat by Attila. Another villain is the scheming courtier Hagen, who at one point throws the Nibelung treasure into the Rhine: there's a statue of him caught in the act by today's Nibelung Bridge in Worms.

Richard Wagner used the concept of "Rheingold" in his opera cycle *Der Ring des Nibelungen*. Fritz Lang's masterful silent film adaptation is a more literal rendering of the saga.

found on the grounds, the principal one being Rolandsbogen (Roland's Arch). The Rolandsbogen got its name from the legend of the young knight Roland, who is said to have looked yearningly down from this window at the cloister Nonnenwerth, on an island in the middle of the Rhine, where his beloved was incarcerated. She had taken her vows because she had believed that he would not return from the Crusades. He did come home, but she was not allowed to leave the nunnery, and the couple died apart, their love unfulfilled. It is said that a tunnel led from the castle to the cloister Nonnenwerth, but the castle was destroyed in the 17th century, and the last remaining archway of the ruin collapsed in 1839. The poet Ferdinand Freilligrath had the idea that the Rolandsbogen should be restored – and it was, in 1840. It now rests some 150 metres (500 ft) above the Rhine, covered in a thick growth of ivy.

Map on page 114

The Romans built wooden watchtowers at various points along the Rhine. These were part of a long line of fortifications known as the limes.

BELOW:
prize exhibit.

● Drachenfels Castle, Germany (Km 643.7)

According to legend, it was at the foot of the sheer Drachenfels (Dragon's Rock) cliff that Siegfried, the hero of the *Nibelungen Saga*, slew the dragon and then bathed in its blood in order to render himself invulnerable. The castle guarding the clifftop is now a ruin, and can be reached by funicular from Bad Godesburg. Once there, you'll have a magnificent view of the Seven Mountains, the gateway to Germany's picturesque wine-growing area. (There are actually over 40 peaks in the "Seven Mountains": the German name is *Siebengebirge* – *sieben* meaning seven – but it is probably a corruption of *siefen*, which means "mountain stream".) On the way up to the castle is **Drachenburg**, a neo-Gothic red-brick 19th-century folly, built by a rich stockbroker on top of a much older fortress, started by the Cologne Archbishop Arnold I in 1140.

● Bonn, Germany (Km 655)

The Rhine now flows through the suburbs of Bonn, the former German capital. The Romans named Bonn Castra Bonnensia 2,000 years ago, when it formed part of their Rhine Valley defences, although meaningful development did not begin until the Middle Ages. The city became the residence of the electors and archbishops of Cologne in the 17th century, and was the capital of West Germany before reunification and the eventual reinstatement of Berlin as the home of government in 1999. Today, Bonn is a university town, and has several museums on the bank of the Rhine in the "Museum Mile", including the **Kunst- und Ausstellungshalle** (Art and Exhibition Hall; open Tues–Wed 10am–9pm, Thur–Sun 10am–7pm) with exhibitions of art, technology, history and architecture; and the **Kunstmuseum** (Museum of Art; open Tues–Sun 10am–6pm, Wed till 5pm).

Beethoven was born here in a house that, since 1890, has been a **museum** (Beethovenhaus; open Apr–Sept Mon–Sat 10am–6pm, Sun 11am–4pm; Mar–Oct Mon–Sat 10am–5pm, Sun 1–4pm); you can see original handwritten manuscripts, his instruments (including a piano complete with amplified sound to allow for his deafness), listening horns and life and death masks. There is a colourful market every ➤ *page 130*

PORTS OF CALL: COLOGNE

Cologne is a busy modern city with a strong sense of historical heritage. Already established as an important centre in Roman times and resurgent in the Middle Ages, today's city centre is still dominated by its glorious twin-towered Cathedral. Repeatedly bombed in World War II, Cologne preserved its historic street pattern when it was rebuilt and, although most buildings are modern, much of its traditional atmosphere survives. It's a lively place, best experienced for those with stamina during the merry-making of *Karneval* time. The historic core of Cologne is large, bounded by the semi-circular boulevard of the Ring running along the line of the old city walls, although the epicentre of city life is to be found in the busy squares around the Cathedral.

ORIENTATION

River cruise vessels dock conveniently at the Rheingarten / Frankenwerft on the left bank, right in the heart of things and close to the Cathedral.

GETTING AROUND

Cologne's excellent public transport system is made up of buses, trams and an S-Bahn and U-Bahn (underground) train system that covers the city and suburbs. Investing in a 24-hour ticket or three-day pass will make getting around less expensive. The city centre is easily explored on foot as many tourist areas are pedestrianised. With wide cycling paths flanking both sides of the river, hiring a bike is a good option.

BUSINESS HOURS

Most shops in the city centre open between 9am and 10am, and close between 6pm and 8pm. On Thursday, shops are usually open until 7.30–8pm, Saturday until 4pm. Banks are open weekdays 9am–4pm but large cities are expanding their services. Most multi-storey car parks in the city centre are open 24 hours a day.

TOP CITY SIGHTS

▲ ▼ COLOGNE CATHEDRAL
With its awesome dimensions, the Cathedral (Dom; open daily 6am–7.30pm) is the unmistakable landmark of the city, its two mighty towers the defining symbol of Cologne's skyline. Construction began in 1248 and resumed in 1880, the final result remaining true to the original plans. A winding staircase of 509 steps leads to a viewing platform 95 metres (312ft) up in the south tower, where the view amply rewards your efforts.

▲ FISCHMARKT
There are few reminders today that the people of Cologne once bought and sold fish, but adjacent to the river is the city's old harbour area and the former fish market. The late-Gothic

▶ MUSEUM RÖMISCH-GERMANISCHES

Containing treasures from over 2,000 years ago after the Romans had established their camp of *Colonia* here, the museum was built over the famous Dionysus Mosaic. (Open Tues–Sun 10am–5pm, Wed until 7pm.)

WALLRAF-RICHARTZ MUSEUM

This is Cologne's oldest museum (open Tues

10am–8pm, Wed–Fri 10am–6pm, Sat–Sun 11am–6pm), showing art from AD 1300–1900. The collection represents every period and school, from Dutch and Flemish masters to French Impressionists, with works by Dürer, Rembrandt, Rubens, Degas and Cézanne, among many others.

◀ ST GEREON CHURCH CUPOLA

This medieval church is known for its intricate floor mosaic of David and Goliath and its unique decagon-shaped dome. It contains the tomb of St Gereon and other martyrs.

buildings surrounding the square, now lined with bars and restaurants, have been preserved in their distinct, original style.

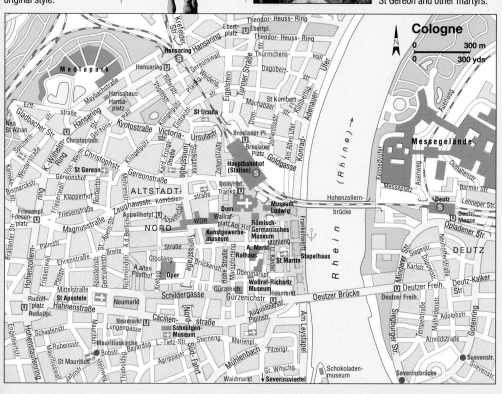

Cologne

0 ——— 300 m
0 ——— 300 yds

Beyond Bonn, look for a dramatic circular tower on the hilltop at Godesburg. This is Godesburg Castle, built in 1210 by the Archbishop of Cologne. Only the round tower and parts of the walls remain today.

weekday near the Baroque town hall. The city also has some interesting architecture, much of which escaped World War II unscathed. The university is housed in a former palace, construction of which started in 1697. **Poppelsdorf Palace** was built in the same era, and has a lush botanical garden.

● Cologne, Germany (Km 688)

Heading downstream towards Cologne, the passing landscape is flat and industrial, but not entirely without interest, particularly at weekends, when the whole city appears to take to the river banks for dog-walking, rollerblading, cycling and jogging.

Both Düsseldorf and Cologne (Köln in German) suffered terrible damage in World War II from Allied bombing, but Cologne's best-loved feature, the soaring Gothic cathedral, thankfully survived. Shoppers will enjoy walking the Hohe-Strasse, close to the docking area. Needless to say, you'll see countless establishments offering eau de Cologne, the city's most famous product. Its brand name is actually 4711, which was the former street number of the perfumery. *For details on what to see in Cologne, see pages 128–129.*

● Düsseldorf, Germany (Km 744.2)

The capital of North Rhine-Westphalia, Düsseldorf was also once best-known for its iron and steel production, although nowadays it is an important centre for banking. It is also famous for its beer, with a number of microbreweries and some 260 pubs operating in the atmospheric **Altstadt** (Old Town), and for its shopping, particularly along the Königsallee.

Although it is surrounded by heavy industry, Düsseldorf is also known as a

BELOW:
the Arithmeum
Museum in Bonn.

Map on page 114

lively cultural centre. The Bolkerstrasse, one of the city's most attractive streets, was the birthplace of the celebrated German poet Heinrich Heine, author of *Die Lorelei (see page 123)*. The **Fine Arts Museum** is worth a visit, as is the **Ceramic Museum**, and the **Lambertus Basilica**, begun in 1288 and best-known for the unusual sight of its twisted spire. The **Castle Tower**, meanwhile, houses a museum of navigation. But most visitors choose to spend their day either shopping or sampling the smooth, dark "Alt" beer, served chilled, in an ancient pub or a riverside beer garden.

The Romantic composer Schumann (1810–56) attempted to drown himself in the Rhine in 1854 during a bout of depression. He lived in the city of Düsseldorf for four years, and had been appointed conductor of the municipal orchestra in 1850.

Most river cruisers head along the Rhine at speed at this point, cutting quickly through Germany's heavily industrialised northwest towards Amsterdam. Passing **Duisberg**, look out for the world's largest inland harbour, stretching 30 km (19 miles) along the river bank; Duisberg is an important centre of steel production and coal mining. This was not always the case; although the town was wealthy and an early member of the Hanseatic League, the river changed its course in the 14th century, and the harbour dried up. It was only when a new harbour was built in the 19th century that Duisberg was once again connected to the river and began to regain its former wealth.

● Xanten, Germany (Km 824)

Founded by the Romans as a military camp around AD 100, Xanten was a prosperous trading centre during the Middle Ages until the 16th century, when it met the same unthinkable fate as Duisberg. The Rhine altered its course, and the city suddenly found itself no longer on the water. Xanten was badly damaged by bombs in World War II, although it is now regarded as a model city for the impressive reconstruction work that has since been carried out.

BELOW: Düsseldorf waterfront architecture, designed by Frank Gehry.

Things to see include the medieval **City Walls**, the elaborate **Gothic Cathedral**, which has an intricately carved altar, and the **Archaeological Park** with its impressive Roman remains (open daily Mar–Oct 9am–6pm, Nov 9am–5pm, Dec–Feb 10am–4pm). River cruise vessels moor out of town, and a coach is usually supplied to reach the centre.

● Utrecht, Holland (Km 31, Amsterdam-Rhine Canal)

Northwest of Xanten the Rhine enters the Netherlands and splits into two; the Waal to the south, the Lek to the north. At Tiel, Amsterdam-bound river cruise vessels enter the Amsterdam–Rhine Canal, opened in 1952 and 72 km (45 miles) long, via the Prins Bernardsluis lock, Europe's largest inland lock. Considered to be the most heavily used canal in Europe, the Amsterdam–Rhine Canal is constantly bustling with commercial traffic and, in summer, cruise vessels.

You'll pass through flat, agricultural countryside, with typical, picture-postcard Dutch scenes – Freisian cows grazing in the fields, windmills dotted along the horizon and ranks of tall poplars lining the banks. The first major city is the university town of Utrecht, the fourth-largest settlement of the Netherlands, and the capital of Utrecht Province. Magnificent churches proliferate here (Michael's Cathedral, St Jacobskerk, St Janskerk and St Pieterskerk). There's a large student population with its attendant ➤ *page 134*

PORTS OF CALL: AMSTERDAM

Cosmopolitan Amsterdam, with its laid-back atmosphere, its centuries-old canals, flower markets and ubiquitous bicycles, is one of Europe's most enjoyable destinations, unique in many ways – not least for its balance of past and present. Perhaps no community has ever had such a glorious explosion of wealth and culture as Amsterdam during the 17th century, the city's Golden Age, yet this is a place that has always looked forward rather than back. The modern city is exuberant, with a tremendous range of cultural life from world-class art galleries to wacky street theatre.

ORIENTATION

Most river cruise vessels dock close to the city centre, between the Centraal railway station at the Passagiers Terminal (up to about 800 yards to the east of the station).

GETTING AROUND

The centre of Amsterdam is compact, and most places can easily be reached on foot. When crossing the road, watch out for bicycles, which can appear out of nowhere. Trams and taxis are plentiful. Canal tours are an essential part of any visit to the city; there are several companies in front of Centraal Station, with departures from here, along Rokin, by the Rijksmuseum and Heineken Brewery further south.

BUSINESS HOURS

Shops open 8.30 or 9am–6pm, Mon–Fri. Most shops close at 5pm on Saturday. Late-night shopping is Thursday until 9pm. Most banks and government offices are open Mon–Fri 9am–5pm.

TOP CITY SIGHTS

▲ CANAL RING
Amsterdam's horseshoe-shaped network of canals is the city's most distinctive feature and a must-see for visitors – lined with tall, elegant mansions from the 17th and 18th centuries. The canal ring *(grachtengordel)* encompassing the three parallel waterways of Herengracht, Keizersgracht and Prinsengracht is the most scenic stretch.

▲ MARITIME MUSEUM
Documenting and celebrating Amsterdam's illustrious maritime history, the Maritime Museum (Scheepvaartmuseum; open Tues–Sun 10am–5pm, daily during school holidays) assembles some fascinating material and is recommended.

▶ RIJKSMUSEUM
Somewhat diminished by major renovation work which will continue until 2008, Amsterdam's most famous art gallery is still worth a few hours of your time. Rembrandt's group portrait, *The Night Watch* is the most famous work of the fabulous collection, which includes a comprehensive range of 15th-century Dutch art. Open daily 10am–6pm.

10am–5pm, daily during school holidays) assembles some fascinating material and is recommended.

▶ **RIJKSMUSEUM**
Somewhat diminished by major renovation work which will continue until 2008, Amsterdam's most famous art gallery is still worth a few hours of your time. Rembrandt's group portrait, *The Night Watch* is the most famous work of the fabulous collection, which includes a comprehensive range of 15th-century Dutch art. Open daily 10am–6pm.

Herengracht, Keizersgracht and Prinsengracht is the most scenic stretch.

▲ **MARITIME MUSEUM**
Documenting and celebrating Amsterdam's illustrious maritime history, the Maritime Museum (Scheepvaart-museum; open Tues–Sun

▲ **DE LOOIER ANTIQUES MARKET** A vast indoor antiques market (open daily except Friday) selling anything from memorabilia

▲ **CANAL RING**
Amsterdam's horseshoe-shaped network of canals is the city's most distinctive feature and a must-see for visitors – lined with tall, elegant mansions from the 17th and 18th centuries. The canal ring *(grachtengordel)* encompassing the three parallel waterways of

Amsterdam

The Dutch love their tulips, whether real or woodcarved.

bars and cafés; the city's university, founded in 1636, is the largest of the Netherlands' state universities.

● **Amsterdam, Holland (Km 0, Amsterdam-Rhine Canal)**

Compact, cosmopolitan Amsterdam actually consists of about 90 islands connected by about 400 stone bridges, and over 100 km (62 miles) of man-made canals. The city lies near the sea on the narrow land strips between Lake Isjeel and the North Sea, with the River Amstel cutting through the centre. It is the largest diamond-trading centre in Europe and home to art treasures in the **Vincent van Gogh Museum** and the **Rijksmuseum**, and historic sites like the **Anne Frank House**, although it's equally pleasant to explore on a self-guided walking tour; with the canals laid out in concentric circles and the streets like spokes on a bicycle wheel, it's difficult to get lost. There are "brown cafes" (so-called because of the tobacco stains on the ceilings) everywhere, as well as pleasant outdoor pubs. *For details on what to see in Amsterdam, see pages 132–133.*

THE MAIN

The Main, one of the Rhine's most significant tributaries, is 524 km (325 miles) long, and starts at Kulmbach in Germany from the confluence of the brooks known as the White and Red Main, which have their sources in the Fichtel Mountains and the Franconian Alb respectively. The river flows through Bavaria, Baden-Württemberg and Hessen. River cruise vessels typically sail on the section between Frankfurt and Würzburg, passing forested hills, lush meadows and historic towns. The river was once used for transporting wood on huge rafts downstream to the Rhine. Today, it flows through an amazing 34 locks between Bamberg *(see page 71)*, from where it becomes navigable, to the mouth at Mainz, by which time it's a formidable body of water. Since the 1992 completion of the Main–Danube Canal *(see page 68)*, which starts at Bamberg on the Main, the breadth of continental Europe is navigable from the mouth of the Rhine in the west to the mouth of the Danube in the east.

BELOW: herring consumption, the traditional way.

Destination highlights

● **Frankfurt-am-Main, Germany**

Frankfurt-am-Main is often used as a starting point for cruising the Middle Rhine. A busy, modern, industrial city with a famously Manhattan-like skyline (dubbed "Mainhattan"), Frankfurt has something of a reputation for being dull, but in fact is easily worth a day or two of your time. The most beautiful part is unquestionably the **Roemerberg** (Roman Hill), where 11 magnificent patrician houses have been joined together to create the **Rathaus** (Town Hall), now a popular gathering place. Opposite is the **Historische Ostzeile**, a row of medieval, half-timbered houses (rebuilt) on an elegant, cobbled square, full of pubs and restaurants. There are several good museums in the vicinity: the **Museum für Moderne Kunst** (Museum of Modern Art; open Tues–Sun 10am–5pm, until 8pm on Thurs) includes work by Roy Lichtenstein and Andy Warhol. The **Zeil**, Germany's longest shopping street, starts at the historic Hauptwache, once a police station and now a café, and nearby is **Fressgass** (Glutton's Lane), a whole street lined with restaurants and cafés, buzzing with life on a summer lunchtime or evening.

Along the Rhine embankment, known as **Museumsufer** (Museum Bank), are nine museums covering art, film, architecture, ethnology, communications and icons. Just to the southeast of here is **Sachsenhausen**, a pretty district packed with outdoor pubs, where large crowds gather on summer nights and drink *Ebbelwoi*, a kind of apple wine, in great quantity.

● **Würzburg, Germany**

Between Frankfurt and Würzburg, the river meanders in wide loops through gently undulating countryside, passing historic cities such as **Seiligenstadt**, where the Roman Emperor Trajan had a fort constructed that later became a royal Franconian court. Further on, set amidst rich agricultural countryside, is Aschaffenburg, where you'll see the very grand Renaissance **Johannisburg Palace**, a square, red-sandstone structure built in 1605 on the river bank for an archbishop, and now housing a museum and art gallery.

Würzburg itself is a majestic-looking city, all the more fascinating because it has been almost completely rebuilt after one devastating bombing raid at the end of World War II, when the entire town took shelter in the Marienburg Fortress on a hillside, avoiding the damage. Some 85 percent of the city was ruined but has been painstakingly reconstructed.

Würzburg today is a wine-making centre and prestigious university city. It was here, in the late 19th century, that Wilhelm Conrad Rontgen discovered the X-ray. Things to see include the **Residenz** (open daily April–Oct 9am–6pm; Nov–Mar 10am–4pm), one of Europe's most impressive Baroque palaces, built between 1719 and 1744 by Balthasar Neumann. The palace contains lavish staircases and fabulous ceiling frescos, and a beautiful garden of ornate statues. Miraculously, most of the treasures survived the bombing.

Tours also include a visit to the **Festung Marien-berg**, a solid rectangular fortress founded in 1201, with various wings added over the following five centuries, during which it was occupied by bishops.

THE MOSELLE (MOSEL)

The Moselle (or Mosel, to use the German spelling), which is, at 535 km (332 miles), the longest of the Rhine's tributaries, is narrower and, some say, prettier than the Rhine. It rises in the Vosges Mountains at some 735 metres (2,410 ft) above sea level. Moselle means "little Maas" in French, a reference to the fact that, in prehistoric times, its bed joined that of the Maas. The river was only developed into a navigable waterway as recently as 1964, an event made possible by the signing of a contract between France, Germany and Luxembourg, following which a system of 14 locks was constructed.

The Moselle itself twists and turns in a series of sharp

Map on page 114

Germany's most famous novelist and playwright, Johann Wolfgang von Goethe, was born in Frankfurt in 1749. The house at Grosser Hirschgraben 23–25 is now a museum.

BELOW: decorations at a Christmas market in Frankfurt.

The central wine cellars of Bernkastel-Kues hold over 65 million litres (14 million gallons) of wine, the produce of more than 5,000 wine-growers.

bends as it cuts its way through a deep valley, the sides lined with steeply terraced vineyards, before merging with the Rhine at Koblenz *(see page 125)*, at an altitude some 676 metres (2,218 ft) lower than its source. On its journey it forms the border between Luxembourg and Germany for a distance of 36 km (22 miles). The Moselle is navigable from Thionville in France to Koblenz, a distance of 270 km (165 miles).

Destination highlights

● Moselkern, Germany (Km 34)

This small, sleepy hamlet provides a stopping point for boats, so that passengers can take a tour to **Burg Eltz**, set not on a hillside but deep in the forest, and belonging to the family of the Count of Elce. The castle is unusual in that it is really a collection of three houses; like many German castles, it resembles something out of a children's fantasy story, intricate and asymmetrical, in a fairy-tale woodland setting. A drawbridge-like entrance from a steep winding forest road just adds to the atmosphere. Inside, you can see the treasures collected by the counts who have lived in the castle since 1150, including several valuable paintings and weapons.

● Cochem, Germany (Km 51.3)

One of the loveliest and most picturesque of all the towns along the Moselle, Cochem is located at the beginning of a sweeping 20-km (13-mile) bend in the river. The walled **Old Town** is laced with narrow alleys, and the skyline is dominated by the **Imperial Castle**, which has a rectangular keep (*donjon*) and numerous small towers. Worth a look is the **Capuchin Monastery**, built in 1623 and

BELOW: cruising down the Moselle at Cochem.

restored for use today as a cultural centre. The Baroque **Town Hall** is also of note, as are the old gabled houses overlooking the Market Fountain. The Moselle Wine Week takes place here in mid-June each year, although the wine taverns along the riverfront have "green wine" (very young wine) available all year round.

● **Bernkastel, Germany (Km 129.4)**

The river continues to carve its way through the gentle hills in wide arcs, past castles, vineyards and magnificent country houses. The popular summer resort town of Bernkastel is second only to Trier as the best-known town on the Middle Moselle. It straddles the river at the confluence of the Tiefenbach stream, opposite the town of Kues. The ruins of the **Landshut Fortress** dominate the town, which is filled with gorgeous half-timbered houses.

The **Middle Moselle Wine Festival** is staged during the first week in September, a time of much merriment, although wine is a year-round theme here. In Kues on the opposite bank, there's a famous hospital, St Nikolaus, established by the theologist and philosopher Nikolaus of Kues in 1458 and donated to the town. Today the hospital is a home for the elderly, but has a valuable scientific library and its own vineyards. The **Moselwein Museum** (open daily 10am–5pm, winter 2–5pm) is part of the complex, and for a small fee, you can taste over 100 fine regional wines and buy them at lowered prices.

The bridge on a typical river cruise vessel features hi-tech navigational equipment.

● **Trier, Germany (Km 181.5–191.4)**

Trier is the principal city of the Moselle Valley and the oldest in Germany; growing up around a ford used by the Germanic-Celtic tribe Treveri tribe before being officially founded in 16 BC by the Roman Emperor Caesar Augustus, who named it Augusta Treverorum. Trier, which lies in the Middle Rhine Highlands, is bordered by Luxembourg and Belgium to the west, North Rhine-Westphalia to the north and Saarland to the south.

BELOW: half-timbered buildings of Bernkastel.

One of the best-preserved and most important Roman edifices in Germany is the 2nd-century, four-storey **Porta Nigra** (Town Gate), built of sandstone (originally without mortar) and today protected as a UNESCO World Heritage Site. You can visit the **Constantine Baths**, and other remaining Roman relics such as a 20,000-seat **Amphitheatre** and Roman bridge. A cross dating from AD 958 can be found in the market square, while close by is the Petrus Fountain, constructed in 1595.

Trier is also famous as the birthplace of **Karl Marx**, in 1818. His house still stands in Bruckenstrasse and is open to the public (Nov–March, Mon 2–5pm, Tues–Sun 10am–1pm and 3pm–6pm; Apr–Oct, Monday 1–6pm, Tues–Sun 10am–6pm).

THE NECKAR

The Neckar is one of the longest tributaries to flow into the Rhine. Its source is in the Baar in a region between the Black Forest and the Swabian Alb (the region in which the Danube also has its source), to the east of the Rhine in Baden-Württemberg, north of Lake Constance. The river is 367 km (228 miles) long and navigable for 203 km (126 miles), although some

Every vessel has a traditional ship's bell.

stretches have canals that enable cargo vessels to make their way through the 26 sets of locks as far upstream as Plochingen.

The Neckar flows through some of Germany's most beautiful countryside, castles guarding every curve of the river, and vines and forests sloping right down to the banks. The whole valley is one of Germany's great summer playgrounds, with pleasure boats, canoes, punts and dinghies out on the water, and cyclists and hikers enjoying the scene from the banks.

After a journey of 367 km (228 miles) past great towns and cities including Stuttgart and Heidelberg, the river cuts briefly across the flatter, more industrialised Rhine plain and disgorges its contents into the major river at the city of Mannheim.

Destination highlights

● Heidelberg, Germany (Km 22.7)

Heidelberg, located just over 20 km (13 miles) upstream on the Neckar from Mannheim, is the epitome of German Romanticism, nestling on the south side of the river and set against the forested hills of Oldenwald, and dominated by a sprawling red-sandstone castle complex. This venerable city is the old capital of the Electorate of the Palatinate, although its history goes back a good deal further than that – some 600,000 years, in fact: The jawbone of *Homo heidelbergiensis*, the oldest human remains discovered in Europe, was found near here. Thousands of years later, Celts and Romans settled the area. Count Palatine Ruprecht I founded Germany's oldest university here in 1386, and for 500 years the Electoral College, which was responsible for electing the German kings, was based in the city. **Heidelberg Castle** (open daily 8am–5.30pm;

Map on page 114

guided tours only), constructed with a moat and several keeps, is considered to be the most magnificent castle ruin in all of Germany, and attracts several million visitors a year.

The castle took 400 years to build and encompasses many different architectural styles. It was destroyed by the French during the Wars of Succession between 1689 and 1693, then subsequently rebuilt only to be destroyed again in 1764 when freak lightning struck and burnt it to the ground. Today, some parts lie in ruins, while other sections have been restored to be used for concerts and banquets or to house museums. The whole complex can be reached on foot by steps and walkways that lead up to it from the city, spread along the river below, or via a funicular railway. Highlights include the Friedrich Wing, with impressive statues of the German kings, and the Heidelberg Tun, one of the world's largest wine vats.

Heidelberg is famous not only for its castle and university but also its printing machines, which are exported all over the world.

Within the castle complex, the **Otto Henry Palace** is a richly decorated Renaissance building constructed in 1556. Although only the façade remains, it is a splendid reminder that this was the first such Renaissance building to be built in northern Europe. Inside is the **Deutsches Apothekenmuseum** (open daily 10am–5.30pm), containing old medical instruments and medicine bottles.

The city below is full of wonderful Baroque and Renaissance buildings, and remains an important university town, its population swelled by 28,000 students, so there's always a lively buzz during term-time. Other things to see include the **Heilggeistkirche** (Church of the Holy Ghost), the wonderful Renaissance façade of the **Hotel Ritter** and the **Old Bridge** (the Karl Theodore Brücke) over the Neckar, which Goethe believed to be one of the wonders of the world, thanks to its breathtaking view. For more views, head off along the

BELOW: the Old Bridge at Heidelberg.

Philosphenweg (Philosopher's Path) up the Heiligenberg, leaving behind the bustle of the town and turning back to look down at the barges and pleasure boats chugging along the river below, and your cruise boat, docked right next to the old town.

● **Eberbach, Germany (Km 57.4)**

Beyond Heidelberg, the river twists and turns as it forces its way through the sandstone hills of the Oberwald, past pretty villages and medieval castles; **Hirschhorn** is especially memorable, perched high on a hilltop overlooking a small, red-roofed town.

Eberbach is a small market town, overlooked by the craggy towers of the ruined Staufer Castle. Here, one of one of the best-kept medieval monasterial establishments in all of Germany, the **Eberbach Cloister**, was built in the 12th century, in two stages; the first from 1145 to 1160, and the second from 1170 to 1186. Architectural scholars will enjoy the remarkable monks' dormitory. It was built as a double-naved, rib-vaulted room with a slightly rising floor; columns were shortened accordingly, and the finished article provides the illusion that it is much longer than it really is (approximately 85 metres/279 ft). Nowadays, the cloister is used as a hotel and conference centre. You can still see the interior, although it's unlikely to be included on a shore excursion.

● **Bad Wimpfen, Germany (Km 100)**

BELOW:
Heidelberg Castle.

The river now flows past wooded hills, each seemingly with its own castle – Zwingenberg, Neuburg, Hornberg, Horneck and the still-intact Guttenberg.

THE WINTER QUEEN

The Englischebau section on the west side of Heidelberg Castle was constructed by the Elector Frederick V in honour of his wife, Elizabeth Stuart (1596–1662), the daughter of James I of England who became grandmother of the future George I. The plain square-window façade of the "English building" is completely different in style compared to the more opulent architecture of the rest of the castle.

Born at Falkland Palace in Scotland, Elizabeth was Queen of Bohemia for only a year, before being forced to flee with the defeat of the Elector's forces by the Habsburg Emperor. Her brief reign in the winter of 1619–20 led to her being referred to as the "Winter Queen" and Frederick as the "Winter King".

They were forced into exile in Holland, enduring considerable privations before Frederick's death in 1632. Elizabeth then returned to England and lived at Ashdown House in Oxfordshire, England.

Located at the mouth of the River Jagst, the former imperial town of Bad Wimpfen is a saline health spa that is extremely popular with Germans looking for a cure (taking the waters in a spa is commonplace in Germany). From the river, there is a superb view of the old **Staufer Palace**, with its red-and-blue towers and Romanesque arcades. The town itself is extremely pretty, with richly decorated half-timbered houses and narrow streets.

Map on page 114

● Stuttgart, Germany (Km 179–189)

Wealthy in financial and cultural terms, Stuttgart is the capital city of Baden-Württemberg. While it is on the Neckar, it's most likely to be somewhere you would visit before or after a cruise, as most Neckar cruises call only at Heidelberg. Stuttgart is known as the spiritual home of Mercedes-Benz, building of which was started here by two remarkable pioneers, Gottfried Daimler (1834–1900) and Carl Benz (1844–1929). At night, the famous trademark of Mercedes – a three-pointed star within a circle – can be seen illuminated high above the city.

Statue of Goethe and the writer and poet Friedrich Schiller on Weimar's Theaterplatz.

Definitely worth a visit for automobile-lovers is the **Daimler-Benz Museum** (open Tues–Sun 9am–5pm), with over 100 vintage and veteran cars on display. If that's not enough, visit the **Porsche Museum** (open Mon–Fri 9am–4pm, Sat and Sun 9am–5pm, to see a display of 50 vintage cars. Also worth seeing is the **Linden Museum** (open Tues–Sun 10am–7pm), with its many sections displaying ethnological collection from around the world and the **Staatsgalerie** (open Tues–Sun 10am–6pm, Thurs 10am–9pm), one of Germany's finest art collections. The city itself has a handsome centre with many 16th-century buildings, including two palaces, one of which houses the ministries of culture and finance. ❏

BELOW: looking down at Boppard on the Rhine.

Benelux Waterways

Many of the waterways of the Netherlands and Belgium are actually branches of the Rhine, which breaks up into several arms as it nears the North Sea. An intricate network of canals and channels links these rivers to the Maas (the Meuse), the other important commercial waterway to cross the Low Countries.

Several river cruise vessels operate in this compact region in spring and summer, taking in the pastoral scenery, the bulb fields of the Netherlands, medieval towns and villages and important centres like Antwerp and Rotterdam. Distances are short, so these cruises offer plenty of opportunity for sightseeing and evenings ashore. Other cruises call at some Dutch and Belgian ports before heading south on the Rhine.

Bruges

The historic town of Bruges is one of the most beautiful – and visited – in Europe, its medieval architecture astonishingly well preserved, with narrow, cobbled streets and gabled houses overlooking a network of canals. Visit the many ancient churches, the 13th-century market hall, with a famous 47-bell carillon in the belfry, the town hall and the museums. Bruges is famous for its lacemakers and its chocolate shops, and also has excellent restaurants and a lively café culture.

Ghent

Like Bruges, but far less well known, Ghent is a superbly preserved medieval town, with so many bridges, gabled houses and old mansions that it feels like walking through a film set. The town was once the centre of Belgium's textile industry, and is still an important commercial port. It's also well known for its floral displays, which adorn many of the houses. Visit the 12th-century Gothic Cathedral of St Bavon and Gravenseteen Castle, as well as the ruined 7th-century St. Bavon's Abbey and the remains of the Cistercian Abbey of Byloke.

Antwerp

Antwerp is a pleasant, bustling city, although it lacks the historic charm of Bruges and Ghent, having been heavily bombed during the war, when it was occupied by the Germans. Today, it is an important diamond-cutting centre, and if you're in the market for some jewels, this is the place to be. Visits here invariably involve a tour of a diamond workshop, which is fascinating.

Antwerp also has the largest church in Belgium, the magnificent Gothic cathedral of Notre Dame, which contains paintings by Peter Paul Rubens, who lived in in Antwerp. Despite the mainly modern look of the city, some beautiful medieval guild houses still line the marketplace.

Middleburg

Another lovely old medieval town, Middleberg found riches through trading wine and cloth in the Middle Ages. Notable buildings include the 16th-century town hall, the Abbey of St. Nicholas, founded in 1150, and the 16th-century New Church. As you walk around the town, you'll see several of the old gates, which are still intact.

Dordrecht

Dordrecht, in southern Holland, is located on no fewer than four rivers, the Merwede, Noord, Oude Maas (Old Meuse) and Dordtse Kil. In medieval times it was a prosperous port, and many of the old buildings, quays and canals are still present. The 14th-century Grote Kerk (Church of Our Lady) is impressive, with a huge tower and intricately carved choir stalls.

Rotterdam

Located on the Maas and linked to the Rhine by canal, Rotterdam is one of the world's busiest seaports. Much of the city was destroyed by bombing in World War II, but the fabulous art collection of the Boijmans-van Beuningen Museum and the Blijdorp Zoological Garden, with its wonderful setting and collection of exotic birds, are both regulars on river cruise itineraries.

Gouda

Gouda needs little introduction as the home of the yellow cheese with the orange rind. Thursday is the best day to visit, when the cheese market is held in front of the Waag, a 17th-century weighing house, where cheese is still weighed in the traditional fashion. It's one of the most authentic and impressive cheese markets, with plenty of opportunity for tasting. There's a cheesemaking exhibition here, as well as demonstrations of other Dutch crafts, like pottery and clog-making.

Maastricht

Maastricht, in the far south of the Netherlands, is a picturesque old university town, the Maas River flowing slowly through its centre. It is known to most as the setting for the signing of the European Union's Maastricht Treaty in 1991, but is of significant historic interest as well. Underneath the city, you can tour the man-made St Pietersburg Caves and some of the 20,000 passages hollowed out of the rock in Roman times and used over the centuries to hide from marauding armies. ❏

LEFT: enjoying a canal tour through the picturesque city of Bruges.
RIGHT: tulips in full bloom.

THE ELBE AND VISTULA

From the Czech Republic to Germany's sandy North Sea coast, an Elbe cruise offers a range of landscapes and some fascinating cities. Poland's Vistula is a lesser-known cruise river

Maps on pages 148, 167

The Elbe and Vistula rivers drain a large proportion of the North European Plain as they wend their way from the Central European heartlands to the sandy shores of the North and Baltic seas, each passing a series of venerable cities en route. The Elbe has long been popular for river tourism, whereas cruises on the Vistula are a recent phenomenon.

THE ELBE

The River Elbe runs for 1,165 km (725 miles) from its source in the Czech Republic to the North Sea coast of Germany, passing through a wide range of scenery en route. From the highlands of Bohemia it curves west then north to the dramatic sandstone massif south of Dresden, continuing through the hills and vineyards of Saxony to reach the marshy woodlands of the Lüneburg Heath and the flatlands of the North European Plain. The history of the river is inextricably linked with division. In earlier days, it divided the Slavs and the Germans; later, a stretch of the river separated the former East and West Germany. From the Czech border to beyond Wittenberg the Elbe flows through the heart of the erstwhile German Democratic Republic (East Germany), its towns and villages still perceptibly less prosperous than those further west.

Great cities have grown up along its banks, including beautiful, Baroque Dresden, and Hamburg, Germany's most important sea and river port. An Elbe cruise also travels a short distance along the Vltava River to the fairy-tale Czech capital, Prague, and much further north, along the Havel tributary to Berlin, until 1990 the city divided between East and West and now the united country's cosmopolitan capital. Fascinating historic towns along the river's course include Wittenberg, where Dr Martin Luther began the Protestant Reformation, Dessau, heart of the Bauhaus movement, and Meissen, world-famous for its fine porcelain.

Elbe cruises are available in a variety of permutations, usually between Berlin and Prague. Some continue north all the way to Hamburg; some even take in the coast and islands of the North Sea. All offer an opportunity to spend a couple of days in both Berlin and Prague, which are highly recommended.

The course of the river

The Elbe rises on the southern side of Krkonoše (Giant) Mountains of Bohemia, on the border of the Czech Republic and Poland, at an altitude of 1,500 metres (4,920 ft), and, fed by a number of small streams, tumbles several hundred metres through dramatic, rugged scenery, eventually flowing in a sweeping curve in a northwesterly direction through the heart of the Czech lowlands. At Melnik, its volume is

PRECEDING PAGES: river cruise vessels lined up at Dresden. **LEFT:** Charles Bridge in Prague. **BELOW:** Dresden's new Frauenkirche.

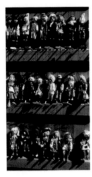

Wooden marionettes depict hundreds of different characters. Prague is full of stalls selling traditional wooden toys such as these.

more than doubled by the Vltava, which has wound its way northwards through Bohemia and the city of Prague. It is here that the Czech measurement of the river in kilometres starts; Melnik is marked as Km 0, despite the fact that the river is already some 260 km (162 miles) from its source.

The Elbe swells further at Litoměřice, where the reddish-brown Ohre joins it to create a waterway 140 metres (459 ft) wide. The river then forces its way through the basaltic mass of the Ceské Stredohori, carving a deep, narrow, rock-strewn gorge known as the Porta Bohemica before crossing the frontier into Germany.

Here, the Elbe forges a course through the Sandstone Mountains, known locally as the Saxon Alps, or Saxonian Switzerland, a name given by two home-sick Swiss painters in Dresden in the 18th century. The passage through the verdant Elbesandstein Mountains is especially beautiful, with high cliffs eroded into strange shapes, thick forests and ruined castles along the banks.

The Elbe then passes Dresden and Meissen, where it cuts through the Meissen Massif, and sets a course northwest for the North Sea across the expansive North German Plain, passing gently rolling hills, sloping vineyards and rich agricultural land. After Magdeburg, the woods give way to meadows and undulating plains, and, as the river heads further north, the climate becomes cooler and the landscape flatter. Beyond the mighty port city of Hamburg, fed by several tributaries along the way, the waters flow out into the North Sea at Cuxhaven.

At Brunsbüttel, near the estuary, the Elbe passes the mouth of the Kiel Canal (also known as the Kaiser Wilhelm Canal), a 98-km (60-mile) man-made waterway connecting the North and Baltic seas. It was constructed by the German government in the late 19th century across the northwest of the state of Schleswig-Holstein, from Brunbüttelkoog to Holenau, on the Kieler Bucht of the Baltic Sea, and became an international waterway following the signing of the Treaty of Versailles in 1919.

The **Vltava** (known to Germans as the Moldau) is a Czech tributary of the Elbe, although its source actually lies in the Bohemian Forest in Germany. It is 440 km (273 miles) long, and joins the Elbe at Melnik, a short distance north of Prague, having run right through the middle of the Czech capital.

The other major tributary is the Havel, some 350 km (215 miles) long, which rises in the Mecklenburg Lakes in northern Germany. It flows through Berlin to Potsdam and Brandenburg and enters the Elbe near Havelberg. Cruises which visit Berlin either sail up the Havel as far as Potsdam, or stop at Magdeburg on the Elbe and take passengers to the capital by coach.

Evolution of river cruising

The Elbe has had an influence on European geography since the time of the Romans, who knew it as the Albis. The legions attempted to extend their empire east from the Rhine to the Elbe,

Elbe, Vltava and Oder

but were forced to retreat in the battle of the Teutoburg Forest in AD 9. By the Middle Ages, the river formed the eastern limit of the empire of Charlemagne. By now, both the Elbe and the Vltava were important navigation routes for the transport of timber northwards from the Bohemian forests, and there were large, prosperous settlements along both rivers. Trade along the river grew in the late Middle Ages as the Hanseatic League cities became more powerful. By the middle of the 16th century, it was being used to transport salt.

With the lack of motive power, boats had to be towed upstream again by horses or teams of men once the cargo had been discharged. This was a tough job, with the journey upstream from Hamburg to Dresden taking an average of six weeks. Eventually the vessels were replaced by lighter rafts, easier to move upriver but unfortunately very difficult to steer – chaos would ensue when one coming upstream met one going downstream. Yet the last raft was retired only in 1948.

Sorting out the system

A later method – made possible by the shallowness of the Elbe – involved hauling vessels along a chain, moved by a heavy winch powered by a steam engine; this chain was 730 km (456 miles) long, extending from Hamburg to Melnik in today's Czech Republic (shorter versions were used on the Volga, Seine and Meuse). Germany only abandoned the Elbe chain system in 1943, by which time paddle steamers were powerful enough to make the journey unaided.

With the construction of locks and canals upstream, the Elbe and Vltava have been navigable for commercial vessels as far as Prague since 1842. Groynes had to be constructed to prevent entire sections of bank being washed away in floods, and some of the most winding sections were straightened.

Map on page 148

The Czechs call the Elbe the Labe, and the Romans knew it as the Albis, but all three names stem from the Indo-Germanic albi or the Latin albus, which means "white" or "shining".

BELOW: viewing Dresden from the Elbe.

In 1945, as World War II was drawing to a close, Nazi forces were trapped between the advancing Allies, coming from the west, and the Soviet troops moving in from the east. The troops actually met at the river near Torgau on 25 April 1945, now known as Elbe Day because of its significance in bringing the war to an end. It was here, on the river, that the Allied and Soviet leaders reaffirmed in a blaze of publicity their commitment to put an end to the Third Reich.

After the war, a section of the Elbe from Schnackenburg to Lauenburg became the border between East and West Germany. The river was used for commercial shipping, but leisure cruising did not start until the late 1980s, apart from day trips from Dresden, where a number of vintage paddle steamers are still in service. The East German government actually ordered a ship called the *Dresden*, cruises on which were to be sold purely to Americans (and not to West Germans) to bring in much-needed hard currency. After the fall of the regime, a quango was set up to sell off former government assets, and the vessel was acquired in 1991 by Peter Deilmann and refitted. It is still in service today.

Although the Elbe is increasingly popular, river cruises will always be limited by the size of vessel that can ply its often shallow waters, low bridges and narrow course. Peter Deilmann has added two luxury boats in recent years, and Viking operates a small fleet. There are also a few smaller operators, but small boats equal high per-person costs, putting a natural limit on the size of the market.

What to expect

Most Elbe cruises take in Berlin at one end (with the boat staying at Potsdam, the most convenient port on the River Havel to the German capital) and Prague at the other, having left the Elbe at Melnik and travelled a short distance to the south along the Vltava. Typical ports of call include Postdam, Magdeburg, Wittenberg, Meissen, Dresden, Königstein and Prague.

Many bridges across the River Elbe are extremely low, so river cruise vessels have had to be built specially for this river, only two decks high, giving them a curiously squat appearance. This construction does mean public rooms are compromised somewhat, but there are still some very luxurious vessels on the river, including the three five-star-rated boats operated by Peter Deilmann. Two of these, the *Frederic Chopin* and the *Katharina von Bora* (named after Martin Luther's wife) have spacious cabins with French balconies and lavishly appointed lounges and dining rooms.

A cruise on the Elbe is destination-intensive, often with more than one stop each day. There will be some scenic cruising in the early morning and late afternoon, but the boat is usually moored up for sightseeing trips. Some cruise lines include all of these in the price, while others charge extra. Either way, the moorings are often in the centre of town, making it easy to explore independently.

Fellow passengers on the Elbe will be an international mix. This cruise has particular appeal to Germans who lived in the former West Germany, rediscovering parts of their own country with which they had lost touch, as well as Americans and British passengers.

While a cruise on the Elbe is better suited to those with mobility difficulties than some other rivers, it's still

Traffic has been banned from Prague's Charles Bridge, making it an oasis of pedestrian calm. Begun in 1357, it forms the central part of the "Royal Way" along which medieval kings walked to their coronation.

BELOW: lunch is served.

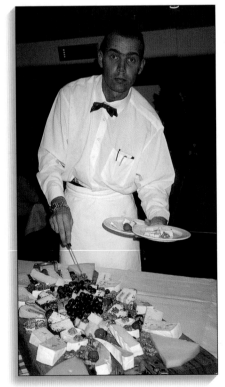

not an easy journey. Facilities are limited; Peter Deilmann's five-star *Dresden* has one cabin adapted for wheelchair use, while Viking River Cruises' *Viking Fontane* has a stair lift. Many of the tours are by modern coach, but they do visit old towns with cobbled streets, and castles with steps and uneven pathways. Before booking, take advice from the cruise line.

Destination highlights

● Prague, Czech Republic (Vltava, Km 45–55)

Starting or finishing point for most Elbe/Vltava cruises (although the vessel actually docks at Ústi, 70 km/43 miles to the north, or at Děčin, even further out), the romantic, fairy-tale city of Prague is located on a curve of the winding Vltava River, a tributary of the Elbe, and known to Germans as the Moldau. Graceful bridges span the river, including the famous **Charles Bridge**, the Lesser Quarter clinging to one side and the Old Town to the other, surveyed from above by the 10th-century **Hradčany** (Prague Castle). The city has inspired composers including Mozart, Smetana and Dvořák, as well as poets, writers, revolutionaries and intellectuals. It's still a great university city and seat of learning, with nightlife to match in the legendary bars and pubs. *For details on what to see in Prague, see pages 152–155.*

● Litoměřice, Czech Republic (Elbe, Km 45)

Known by the Germans as Leitmeritz, this former royal city is dubbed the "Garden of Bohemia", thanks to the surrounding fields of corn, hops, grapes and other fruits. The town itself has many Baroque and Renaissance buildings, and its centre is dominated by the large **Katedrála Sv Štěpána** ➤ *page 156*

Map on page 148

Josef Lada's image of the Good Soldier Švejk, the eponymous character of Jaroslav Hašek's novel, is often thought of as representing the Czech national character.

BELOW: the Vltava river runs through the heart of Prague.

PORTS OF CALL: PRAGUE

Prague is one of Europe's top tourist destinations, and it's not hard to see why. The city today is a living documentary of its past, from its Romanesque beginnings to Gothic churches and monasteries, and fine Baroque palaces. More recent are magnificent Art Nouveau boulevards from the 19th century. Dozens of gilded spires and towers pierce the skyline, and the cobbled streets of the old town are packed with beautiful old houses, their façades ornately decorated.

TOP CITY SIGHTS

ORIENTATION

Prague has a magnificent setting, surrounded by wooded hills with the River Vltava running right through the heart of the city. To get to and from the centre of Prague, buses are provided from the river cruise vessels, which are usually berthed upstream in Ústi. Ústi itself is a busy industrial coal town on the Elbe, around 70km (43 miles) north of Prague and close to the confluence of the Elbe and the Vltava. Some vessels dock at Děčin, a further 25km (14 miles) north of Ústi.

GETTING AROUND

The various means of public transport are cheap, clean, efficient and well-integrated. The network includes trams and buses, the Metro and the funicular up the Petrín Hill.

BUSINESS HOURS

Most shops in Prague are open weekdays 9am–6pm or 7pm, with smaller speciality stores typically open from 10am–6pm. City centre shops (especially around Wenceslas Square and Na příkopě), department stores and malls are generally open 10am–6pm on Saturdays, and some keep similar hours on Sundays, too. Smaller shops may close their doors for a couple of hours during lunchtime. Away from the city centre, most shops close at 1pm on Saturday and remain shut on Sunday.

▲ CHARLES BRIDGE (KARLŮV MOST)

Slightly curved and spanning the Vltava River between the Old Town and the hill leading up to the castle, Charles Bridge is a Gothic masterpiece, with the added impact of some fine baroque sculpture. The first stone bridge was constructed here during the second half of the 12th century, in place of the wooden structure that was situated further to the north. The 30 statues adorning the bridge were added over a period of 250 years. The oldest and most significant statue is that of St John of Nepomuk, which was installed in 1683. Many are now replicas and the valuable originals can be seen in the Lapidarium of the National Museum.

The bridge is usually very crowded with sightseers; for a more atmospheric experience visit early in the morning or late at night.

▲ PRAGUE CASTLE (HRAD)

With its commanding position high above the river, the castle (open Apr–Oct daily 9am–5pm; Nov–Mar 9am–4pm) has been key to every epoch in the city's history. It is the most extensive complex of buildings in the city,

containing St Vitus
Cathedral, the Royal
Palace and many other
monuments. It also serves
as the seat of the president
of the republic.

▼ ST VITUS CATHEDRAL (KATEDRÁLA SV. VÍTA)

Prague's magnificent Gothic
cathedral contains not only
chapels and tombs, but also
some fine stained glass,
including the window
designed by art nouveau
artist Alphons Mucha
(pictured below). The main
attraction inside the
cathedral is St Wenceslas's

Chapel,
built by Petr Parler in which
the national saint Wenceslas
was interred. The saint's
sacred place is exceptionally
ornate; walls are decorated
with polished jasper,
amethysts, agate and
emeralds, as well as fine
gilding and frescos.

▼ JEWISH QUARTER (JOSEFOV)

The Jews of Prague suffered
persecution from the Middle
Ages, but found some
freedom in their ghetto, now
preserved as the Jewish
Quarter and a memorial to
their tenacity. The earliest
mention of Prague's Jewish
community comes from a
document by the Jewish
merchant Abraham ben
Jakob, dated 965. The
ghetto, built in about 1100
and surrounded by a wall,
soon became one of the
largest Jewish communities
in Europe. Major sites
include the **Old-New
Synagogue** (open
Sun–Thurs 9.30am–6pm,
Fri 9.30am–5pm), the oldest
remaining synagogue in
Europe in which services
are still held. Nearby,
the **Old Jewish
Cemetery** is both a
moving and
fascinating place
and was the last
resting place for
Jews between the
15th and 18th
centuries. The number
of graves is much greater
than the 12,000
gravestones would sugges –
this was the only place
where Jews could be
buried, so graves were
layered one above the other.
The Jewish community was
destroyed in World War II,
when thousands were sent
to their deaths. Today there
are around 1,500 people of
Jewish descent in Prague.

▶ LORETO CHURCH

The Loreto Church (open
Tues–Sun 9am–12.15pm,
1–4.30pm) is dedicated to
the Virgin Mary and is the
most famous pilgrimage
church in Prague. The ornate
facade and frescos in the
cloister date from the 18th

EXCURSIONS

Some 30 km (19 miles) south-west
of Prague is the biggest attraction in
the region, **Karlstejn Castle** (open
Mar–Jan Tues–Sun 9am–3pm, till
6pm in summer). Some of the
world's finest frescos can be seen in
the Chapel of the Holy Cross. The
castle is reached by train from
Prague's Smíchov station (Metro
line B), calling at Karlstejn station.
From Karlstejn village the way to the
castle leads steeply uphill for 1.5 km
(1 mile). Horse-drawn carriages
make the climb easier. The castle
can only be viewed
as part of a
conducted
tour.

century. In the tower is a
glockenspiel of 27 bells,
which play a Czech hymn to
the Virgin Mary every hour.
The highlight is the Treasure
Chamber which contains the
remarkable Diamond
Monstrance, a gift from a
Bohemian nobleman. It was
made in 1699 by Baptist
Kanischbauer and Matthias
Stegner of Vienna and is
studded with over 6,000
diamonds.

12 months of the year, painted by Josef Manés (these have now been replaced with replicas). The performance of the upper part of the clock is what draws the hordes of tourists. On the hour the figures play the same scene: Death rings the death knell and turns an hourglass upside down. The 12 Apostles proceed along the little windows which open before the chimes, and a cockerel flaps its wings and crows.

▼ NATIONAL GALLERY (NÁRODNÍ GALERIE)

In Sternberg Palace, within the castle complex, is the National Gallery (open Tues–Sun 10am–6pm), which houses a fine collection of European art. There are three levels; the ground floor houses German and Austrian art from the 15th to the 18th centuries; the first floor comprises the art of antiquity, icons and the art of the Netherlands and Italy of the 14th–16th centuries; the second floor has Italian, Spanish, French,

▲ OLD TOWN SQUARE (STAROMESTSKÉ NÁMESTÍ)

Prague's picturesque Old Town Square is the natural mid-point of the Old Town, and the heart of Prague. Memorial tablets on the Town Hall Tower are reminders of various important events that have taken place here over the centuries. In the 12th century the Old Town Square was a central market place and a major crossroads on central European merchant routes. Over the next few centuries many

buildings of Romanesque, Baroque and Gothic styles were erected.

The Jan Hus monument in the centre of the square is in honour of the 15th-century reformer who stood up against the corrupt practices of the Catholic Church.

▲ TYN CHURCH

The landmark pointed towers of the Týn Church (open for mass Mon–Fri

9am–midday, 1–2pm) are one of the icons of Prague, looming 80 metres (260 ft) above the Old Town. The building was erected between 1365 and 1511, and features many noteworthy Bohemian Baroque works of art and the oldest baptismal font (1414) in Prague. To the right of the high altar is the tombstone of the famous Danish astronomer Tycho Brahe, who worked at the court of Rudolf II. The church is a source of great national pride, and the facade, particularly when floodlit at night, is one of the finest sights in the Old Town.

▶ ASTRONOMICAL CLOCK

The astronomical clock on the Town Hall Tower dates from 1410. It consists of three parts. In the middle is the actual clock, which also shows the movement of the sun and moon through the zodiac. Underneath is the calendar, with scenes from country life symbolising the

Dutch and Flemish art of the 16th–18th centuries. Albrecht Dürer's large-scale *Feast of the Rosary (pictured above)* is perhaps the most famous exhibit.

▼ **WENCESLAS SQUARE (VÁCLAVSKÉ NÁMĚSTÍ)**
Nearly a kilometre (two-thirds of a mile) long, Wenceslas Square is not really a square at all, but a wide boulevard. Nowadays, the former horse market is dominated by hotels, bars, restaurants, cafes, banks and department stores. It is a busy area, along which half of Prague seem to stroll. The historic square is crowned by the giant equestrian statue of St Wenceslas, erected by Josef Myslbek in 1912 after taking 30 years to plan and design.

▶ **NATIONAL THEATRE (NÁRODNÍ DIVADLO)**
This is the city's main cultural venue and a potent symbol of the Czech spirit. In 1845 the ruling Habsburgs turned down the request for a Czech theatre. In response, money was collected on a voluntary basis, and the building of a Czech theatre was declared a national duty. Built in an Italian Renaissance style in 1881, the theatre was destroyed in a fire just before it was due to open. Under Josef Schulz's direction, using many notable artists including Vojtech Hynais, it was quickly rebuilt with the aid of endowments and donations and opened in 1883. The auditorium is only open to the public during performances.

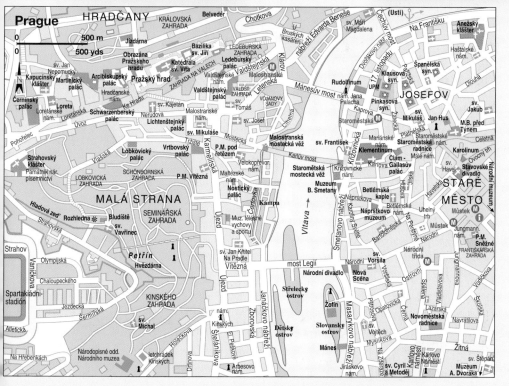

No visit to northern Bohemia would be complete without sampling the local beer. The region is the cradle of hop-growing, and the area around Zatec produces a hop with a pleasant aroma and a spicy, resinous quality.

BELOW:
Bohemian Crystal.

(St Stephen's Cathedral) and the town hall, originally Gothic, but rebuilt in the Renaissance style. The old **Market Square** is the largest in northern Bohemia, surrounded by pretty townhouses from just about all architectural styles and periods – Gothic, Renaissance, Baroque and Biedermeier. River cruises calling here spend half a day and offer a guided walking tour, mooring near the town centre.

● **Děčín, Czech Republic (Elbe, Km 95)**

Some cruise lines use Děčín as the jumping-off point for Prague, despite its considerable distance from the capital. Around here, craggy cliffs form the river banks, with a railway line running parallel to the river and, in towns like Děčín and Ústí, busy docks along the banks. If you're moored in Děčín, the likelihood is that you will spend most of your time exploring Prague (a bus transfer is usually provided), although the town has some attractive old patrician houses, a Baroque church and an imposing castle.

● **Bad Schandau, Germany (Elbe, Km 10)**

The river kilometre-markers get confusing around the Czech–German border. Just when you've come to terms with the fact that you're no longer looking at Vltava river-kilometre signs but those applying to the Elbe, the markers change from Km 109 (the distance from the confluence with the Vltava) to Km 3 (the German measurement of kilometres from the border).

The scenery around Bad Schandau is gorgeous. Known as the "Region of the Rocks", forested table mountains, rock columns and dark caves loom over the river banks. The boat is now entering the beautiful Elbe Sandstone Moun-

BOHEMIAN GLASS

Bohemian Crystal remains an exclusive brand name, despite having factories scattered throughout the country. Lead crystal ranges in lead content from 14 percent to 24 percent and comes in myriad shapes and patterns. New items from major manufacturers are usually good buys: traditional decanters, vases, bowls and glasses, with patterns cut by hand, make pretty souvenirs or gifts, and are to be had at roughly half the price of that in other European countries – although now it's almost impossible to find a good deal in antique shops. More modern designs in glasswear are also popular, from large, decorative sculptures to vases. Bunches of large glass flowers mimic the shape of fresh blooms.

There is a long and venerable history of glass manufacture in Bohemia. There is evidence that the Bronze Age settlers of the region manufactured glass in the form of beads for necklaces and bracelets, and during the Middle Ages the first glass drinking vessels, window panes and wall mosaics were produced. The classic form of the Bohemian Baroque wineglass with a cut pedestal foot dates back many centuries. Various forms, including chandeliers, mirrors and tableware, have been exported to the courts of the King of France, the Tsar and other royalty across Europe.

Map on page 148

tains, their flanks guarded by romantic-looking castles. Tiny villages huddle on the banks and the hillsides, and life appears to move at a slower pace.

Bad Schandau itself is a spa town, developed in the mid-18th century when health-giving springs were discovered. A cure centre and hotels were quick to follow. The parish church dates back to 1704. Its altar and pulpit are carved from local sandstone, and the altar is set with precious stones.

The town lies at the heart of walking and climbing country, so you'll see a lot of hikers and climbers. During the days of the Third Reich, some climbers would help refugees over the secret mountain passes and across the border into Czechoslovakia. Nowadays, there are walking trails or, as an alternative way up the mountains, the Kirnitzschtal Railway, built in the 1920s, which leads to the Lichtenhainer Waterfalls.

Erosion has carved the Sandstone Mountains around Königstein into odd-looking rock formations. They have been given nicknames such as Catapult, Sofa, Monk, Locomotive, Wolf's Ravine and Swine's Bottom.

● Königstein, Germany (Km 17)

From Bad Schandau, it's worth being on deck to watch the spectacular scenery slip by as the river continues to carve its way through the sandstone, the cliffs towering above the water with overhangs, canyons, weird rock towers and precarious-looking pinnacles. Once you've passed the spa town of Rathen, set against a natural amphitheatre of cliffs, the dramatic medieval **Königstein Fortress** (open daily, summer 9am–8pm; winter 9am–6pm) comes into view, 360 metres (1,180 ft) above the river. Cruise ships usually stop here for a brief visit, taking passengers by coach to the fortress. Königstein has been rebuilt and strengthened several times, and in its day was considered impregnable; a well was dug 150 metres (490 ft) into the rock in case of siege. Inside, you can see the living quarters and workshop of Friedrich Böttger, the alchemist who discovered the secret of making

BELOW: the rugged crags of the Elbe Sandstone Mountains.

Accordion-playing street musicians are seen all over Central Europe.

BELOW: Dresden's stunning new Frauenkirche.

true porcelain in 1709 *(see page 160)*. Prior to this, Böttger was incarcerated here from 1706–7 when the castle served as a jail – the Elector of Saxony, Augustus the Strong, had held him in "protective custody" in order to be the beneficiary of the alchemist's quest to manufacture gold. Other prominent prisoners included the social democrat August Bebel and the poet Frank Wedekind.

From Königstein, the river snakes its way in a wide arc around Lillenstein, a hulking monolith with sheer cliffs 80 metres (260 ft) high. Shortly after this point, the boat passes the pretty town of **Pirna**, considered the northern gateway to Saxon Switzerland. This place has been inhabited for over 6,000 years, as it's an easy point at which to cross the river, and was a major trading centre in the Middle Ages.

● Dresden, Germany (Km 50–61)

The Elbe runs for 25 km (15 miles) right through the middle of this venerable German city, the capital of Saxony once again since 1990 and world-renowned for its fabulous art treasures, which have given it the epithet "Florence on the Elbe". There are water meadows and green parks close to the centre giving a marvellous feeling of open space. The river cruise landing stage is right in the centre of the city, and most boats spend the night here, a good opportunity to see the beautiful sandstone buildings illuminated by dramatic floodlights.

Dresden will always be remembered for the devastating bombing in 1945 which flattened the city centre and cost some 35,000 people their lives. For years, the **Frauenkirche** (Church of Our Lady) was left ruined, as a reminder of the destruction, but it has now been rebuilt as an exact replica of its former self. The city centre is now a protected UNESCO site and has almost been fully restored, thanks to a 50-year rebuilding project.

Map on page 148

Dresden is a very attractive city and, for many, is a highlight of an Elbe cruise. The **Town Hall Tower**, standing at 100 metres (330 ft), will always by law be the tallest building. The 13th-century **Kreuzkirche**, meanwhile, rebuilt in 1764 after the Seven Years War, is said to contain a fragment of the Holy Cross, and is a wonderful example of Baroque architecture.

Another beautiful Baroque building is the meticulously restored 18th-century **Zwinger Palace** (open Tues–Sun 10am–6pm), a superb collection of graceful pavilions on the south bank of the Elbe, known for its superb art collection of Old Masters, including pieces by Raphael and Rembrandt. Music-lovers should see the incredible **Semper Opera House**, in which performances are given from September to May. On the opposite side of the river (the left bank) is the quadrilateral **Japanese Palace**, built to display August the Strong's superb collection of Meissen porcelain and tableware. Do not miss an opportunity to visit the **castle** (open Wed–Mon 10am–6pm), built in 1547 and under restoration since 1960. Some of the original treasures are still there, and the Green Vault is top of the list to see, containing the breathtaking treasures of the Saxon princes – precious stones, jewellery, ivory, pearls, coral and crystal.

The crossed blue swords that are the symbol of the Meissen State Porcelain Factory were taken from the Elector of Saxony's coat of arms, and were the world's first trademark.

● **Meissen, Germany (Km 80–83)**

Between Dresden and Meissen, the river passes hills and vineyards, woodlands and villages, the hills more gentle than the dramatic sandstone formations upriver. Meissen is a lovely old town, dominated by the slender Gothic spires of the **Cathedral** and the hulking **Albrechtsburg Castle**, built in 1525. There has been a settlement since AD 968, but the town really rose to fame in 1710 with the advent of porcelain manufacture.

LEFT evening light at Dresden.

DRESDEN PADDLERS

Dresden has the largest fleet of paddle steamers in the world, and can also claim to have the paddle steamer with the oldest working engine: the *Diesbar*, though built in 1884, has an oscillating twin-cylinder steam engine that dates from 1841. She is also the only coal-fired paddler in the fleet.

The royal assent to inaugurate steam navigation on the Elbe was given on 8 July 1836, and the first vessel began services between Dresden and Rathen the following year. By 1911, the fleet numbered 33, but at the end of World War II it had dropped to ten Today there are nine of these paddlers cruising the river between Meissen and Děčin in the Czech Republic. The oldest ship is the *Stadt Wehlen* (1879) and the youngest is the *Leipzig* (1929). The fleet has been restored to preserve their character, and meals are served on some cruises, which include evening jazz and Dixieland excursions.

Augustus the Strong, Elector of Saxony (where he was known as Frederick Augustus I) from 1694 to 1733, had earlier employed the renegade alchemist Friedrich Böttger to make gold, partly in order to raise much-needed funds for the state, and partly (of course) out of personal greed. Not surprisingly, this scheme had failed, but in 1709 Böttger realised that valuable white porcelain could be made from nacrite, of which there were large deposits near by, and the castle was quickly turned into a factory. The famous blue-glaze technique was discovered in 1740, and the porcelain soon became known all over the world. The castle houses an art collection today, with a number of early Meissen pieces (open daily, summer 10am–6pm; winter 10am–5pm). There's also a porcelain workshop in the town, **Meissen Porzellan Manufaktur** (open daily, summer 9am–6pm; winter 9am–5pm).

● Torgau (Km 154)

The countryside now flattens out as the river crosses a broad plain, with abundant birdlife. The town of Torgau is overlooked by **Hartenfels Castle**, the name of which means "hard rock". The castle was built in the 15th and 16th centuries and is considered the most important early Renaissance palace in Germany. Its chapel was consecrated by Martin Luther in 1544, and the castle played an important role in the Reformation thereafter.

Take time to walk around the old centre, the streets lined with wonderful old patrician houses from the 16th and 17th centuries. Look out for the oldest pharmacy in Saxony and the oldest toy shop in the whole of Germany. You will also see the house where Martin Luther's wife, Katharina von Bora, died of injuries sustained in an accident while trying to flee the plague.

BELOW: Meissen.

● Wittenberg, Germany (Km 215)

Wittenberg is a sleepy town, brought to life by hordes of visitors who come here to see where the Protestant Reformation began. The mooring is some distance from the town, so it's best to take a coach tour.

Dr Martin Luther, an Augustine monk and university lecturer, famously nailed 95 theses to the door of the Palace Church on 31 October 1517, an act which is defined by historians as beginning the Reformation. Three years later, Luther was excommunicated by the Pope. In honour of his memory, the first line of his hymn "A Strong Fortress is Our God" was inlaid in mosaics around the top of the church tower. **Luther's house** can also be visited, as can **St Marien's Church**, where he preached. An oak tree marks the spot where he burnt the papal bull condemning his doctrines. Near by is **Luther Hall**, a museum dedicated to the Reformation (open Apr–Oct daily 9am–6pm, Nov–Mar Tues–Sun 10am–5pm).

● Dessau, Germany (River Mulde, no km marker)

The stretch of the river approaching Dessau (which is actually located on the Mulde, a tributary of the Elbe) is not the most scenic, although it is ecologically very important. Both rivers meander their way across a wide, marshy floodplain, through boggy woodland which, although not especially attractive, is part of an important biosphere reserve. Look out for the varied birdlife – herons, storks and crows along the river and red kites wheeling overhead. You may even spot beavers, although most of them build their dams on the small streams which flow into the main river.

If a stop is made at Dessau, a short drive from the river, it's a brief one, mainly to see the Bauhaus architecture for which the town is famous. The

Map on page 148

Dr Martin Luther (1483–1546), painted by Lucas Cranach the Elder in 1529 (Uffizi Museum, Florence).

BELOW:
the Wittenberg Bible, 1534, translated into German by Luther.

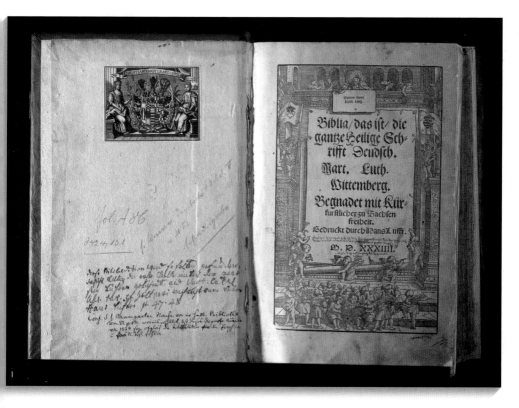

Bauhaus Building itself is a steel, glass and concrete structure remarkably avant-garde in style for 1925, when it was built by Walter Gropius, who had moved the Bauhaus school from Weimar to Dessau. The Bauhaus movement was banned by the Nazis in 1933, and the building was opened in 1977 as a museum, although it's a design centre today with no access to the public. There are a few more examples of Bauhaus architecture around the town, including an estate of 16 houses in the Toerten district.

● **Magdeburg, Germany (Km 326–333)**

Located about midway along the Elbe on the river's vast, fertile flood plain southwest of Berlin, Magdeburg sits at a natural crossroads and lies at the junction of six railway lines and seven arterial roads. The city is linked with Berlin and the lower River Oder by a system of canals, and to the River Rhine by the Mittelland Canal. This is the starting (or finishing) point for Elbe cruises which don't sail all the way up to Potsdam. Boats moor in the centre, a few blocks from the Altstadt (Old Town) and the cathedral.

Magdeburg was almost destroyed in 1945; some 80 percent of the town was reduced to rubble. Now, it's a superb example of a traditional German town, albeit a reconstructed one. In fact, it has been in existence since AD 937, when a settlement grew up around a monastery founded by Otto I to carry out Slavic missionary work. After this, Magdeburg did not take long to become an influential imperial city. The town's museum houses the Magdeburg Rider, Germany's oldest equestrian statue, created in 1240. There is a replica of it in front of the town hall.

BELOW: Bauhaus architecture at Dessau.

Amazingly, many of the Romanesque buildings survived the wartime bombing; the **Kloster Unseren Lieben Frauen** (Monastery of Our Lady) was built

in 1064, and is one of Germany's most important buildings from that era. The **Cathedral**, where Emperor Otto is buried, dates from AD 955, although it was rebuilt after a fire in 1209. Inside, there's a sculpture by Ernst Barlach in remembrance of men who died in World War I. The sculpture was banned by the Nazis in 1937 as "decadent" but was returned to the cathedral in 1956.

Map on page 148

● Tangermunde, Germany (Km 388)

Cruises travelling all the way north to Hamburg call at Tangermunde, a former Hanseatic League town with many fine examples remaining of Gothic brick architecture and half-timbered houses. The surrounding countryside is flat and marshy, although outside the town, the river banks are steep, with meadows beyond. Most cruise companies offer a walking tour of the centre, a protected historic area with medieval fortifications.

● Potsdam, Germany (River Havel, no km marker)

For centuries an insignificant Slavic fishing town on the Havel, Potsdam was "discovered" by Friedrich Wilhelm, the Great Elector, who enjoyed hunting in the lakeside woodlands. He built a castle here in 1662, and a further 16 castles, palaces and opulently landscaped parks were added by subsequent royal inhabitants. In the 17th century, Potsdam was also something of a multicultural community after the Tolerance Edict of 1665 offered asylum to refugees from France, and many Huguenots settled here.

The most famous of Potsdam's palaces is the astonishing **Sanssouci**, a short drive from where the boat is moored, built for Friedrich II (open Apr–Oct Tues–Sun 9am–5pm; Nov–Mar Tues–Sun 9am–4pm). The bijou ➤ *page 166*

BELOW: across the river to Tangermunde.

PORTS OF CALL: BERLIN

Berlin is an exciting place to visit. In recent years, the newly revived capital has expanded at a rapid pace, and the city almost feels like a living art gallery. Signs of change are everywhere, but despite its stone, steel and glass, Berlin is the greenest metropolis in Europe, with more than 40 percent of its area covered by lakes and rivers, parkland and woods. It is also possible to escape the bustle very quickly; the city has a fine recreational zone right on its doorstep.

TOP CITY SIGHTS

ORIENTATION

Cruises which visit Berlin either sail up the Havel as far as Potsdam, or stop at Magdeburg on the Elbe and take passengers to the capital by coach.

GETTING AROUND

The quickest way of getting around this large, sprawling city is by the integrated public-transport system (BVG). An interconnected three-zone system (A, B, and C) requires only one ticket and allows you to use the bus, underground (U-Bahn), overground rail (S-Bahn) and tram. Free coloured maps of Berlin's *Schnellbahnnetz* (the entire network of S-Bahn, U-Bahn and mainline trains) are obtained from kiosks on station platforms. Tickets are available from the orange-coloured machines at the entrances to all U- and S-Bahn stations. Public transport runs from 4.30am to 12.30am. The flat terrain and network of bicycle paths make cycling around the city a pleasure, and there are numerous bicycle-hire outlets.

BUSINESS HOURS

Shops in Berlin are generally open Mon–Sat from 8 or 9am until 6 or 6.30pm, but some close earlier on Saturdays. Shopping malls are open Mon–Sat from 9 or 10am until 8pm. Most are closed on Sundays. Banks open Mon–Fri 9am–4pm.

▲ BRANDENBURG GATE

The Brandenburg Gate has played varying roles in the history of Berlin. Napoleon marched through here on his triumphant way to Russia, and when the Berlin Wall fell in 1989, the gates came to symbolise freedom and unity. The sandstone structure is based on the gateway to the Acropolis in Athens.

▼ CHECKPOINT CHARLIE

From 1961 until 1990, Checkpoint Charlie was the only crossing point between East and West Berlin. Today the former border crossing has become a shrine to the Berlin Wall's memory. Nothing remains of the actual military installation today, although a small guardhouse *(pictured)* was rebuilt in the middle of the street. For more information on the general history of the Wall, visit the nearby Museum Haus am Checkpoint Charlie 5 (open daily 9am–10pm) at Friedrichstrasse 44.

parliamentary proceedings from above. Open daily 8am–midnight.

MUSEUM ISLAND

Between the River Spree and Kupfergraben lies Museum Island, which ranks as one of the world's finest museum complexes and is a UNESCO World Heritage Site. The stunning diversity of displays includes everything from ancient archaeological artefacts to early 20th-century German and European art. All five museums are open Tues–Sun 10am–6pm, Thurs 10am–10pm.

KURFÜRSTENDAMM

Inspired by the Champs-Elysées in Paris, Ku'damm (as it's usually known) is the most popular boulevard in Berlin, and is flanked by a

EXCURSIONS

Schloss Sanssouci (Potsdam) was commissioned by Frederick the Great and designed by von Knobelsdorff in 1744. Open Tues–Sun 9am–5pm, 4pm in winter. Take a Regional Express train from Bahnhof Zoo to Potsdam Hauptbahnhof.

series of exclusive hotels, department stores and cafés. In the 1920s it became the meeting-place for Berlin's intellectuals.

◀ **REICHSTAG BUILDING**
The Reichstag, restored to prominence with the return of the goverment to Berlin in 1999 and crowned by a spectacular glass dome

designed by Sir Norman Foster, was originally built in the late 19th century in Italian Renaissance style. A broad spiral ramp enables visitors to watch

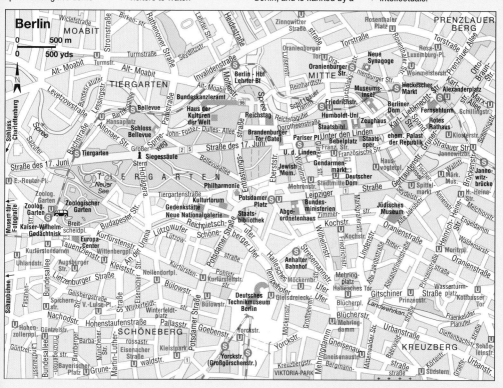

palace, with just 12 eclectically decorated rooms open to the public, is perhaps most famous for its dramatic terraced gardens, with sweeping flights of steps leading up from the lake to the building's ochre-coloured rococo façade. There are many more attractions in the surrounding park, including the Chinese Tea House, the Neues Palais (built for royal staff and guests), the Charlottenhof Palace, Roman-style baths and the Italian Renaissance Orangery.

Another attraction of Potsdam is the **Babelsberg Film Studios**, famous in the 1920s and revived in 1992 as an international media- and film-centre. There's a studio tour with various interactive components, and a stunt show (open daily 10am–6pm, until 8pm on Thurs).

Beaches have been created at various points on Berlin's 180 km (112 miles) of waterway, complete with beach bars and umbrellas.

● Berlin, Germany (River Havel, no km marker)

Germany's capital actually lies on the River Havel, which passes through a complex system of lakes and locks, so river cruisers usually moor up at Potsdam and passengers are brought by coach to the city centre. Berlin has metamorphosed since the fall of the Wall in 1990 into a buzzing, thriving metropolis, drawing artists and entrepreneurs, movers and shakers into its midst. Innovative architecture, ultra-chic shopping along the Kurfürstendamm, grand boulevards and lavish monuments collectively create one of Europe's most exciting capitals – and the nightlife is legendary, too.

Most cruise itineraries allow a couple of days in Berlin, to take in the beautiful neoclassical buildings along Unter den Linden, the Brandenburg Gate and the Reichstag, the Museuminsel (Museum Island), now a UNESCO World Heritage Site. Slightly more off the beaten track are some of the multicultural suburbs like Kreuzberg or the patrician Charlottenburg, or the nearby lakes and forests.

For details on what to see in Berlin, see pages 164–5.

BELOW: the IMAX cinema at Berlin's Potsdamer Platz.

● Hamburg, Germany (Km 623)

A handful of cruises on the Elbe continue up to Hamburg, where the river is wide and sluggish, meandering across flat marshland. On the way there, as you pass Lauenburg, look out for the old half-timbered sailors' houses on the river bank. Some cruises stop at Lauenburg to visit the Elbtalaue Nature Reserve, which is done in a most civilised fashion, by horse drawn carriage. Look out for cranes and storks, glossy-leaved water lilies, orchids, sundew and marsh marigolds as you clip-clop through the watery woodlands.

Best-known, somewhat unfairly, for its raunchy nightlife, Hamburg is actually a very dignified and elegant city, the notorious Reeperbahn red-light district aside. It is the heart of Germany's publishing industry, the city is also Germany's main seaport, despite the fact that it is some 110 km (70 miles) inland, on the right bank of the Elbe where it meets the River Alster.

The city is criss-crossed by canals and has numerous green squares and corners, with lively street cafés. Exploring the canals and waterfront on a boat tour is one of the most restful ways to get around. Otherwise, things to see include the **Rathaus** (Town Hall), built in neo-Renaissance style in 1887 and set in one corner of the Binnenalster, an inland lake. On Sunday mornings, head for the **Fischmarkt**, a noisy, atmospheric marketplace where everything from fish to household clutter is sold. The city has numerous museums, including the **Kunsthalle** (open Tues–Sun 10am–6pm, until 9pm on Thurs), one of Germany's finest collections of art, with exhibits from the 13th to the 20th centuries. Hamburg is also good for shopping; there are a lot of high-quality boutique shops, while the major department stores are located in Jungfernsteig, Monckebergstrasse and Spitalerstrasse.

Maps on pages 148, 167

THE ODER

The Oder is a little-cruised river, known as a sanctuary for birdlife, that forms the border between Poland and Germany for a distance of 186 km (116 miles). This isolated river valley is green and lush, lined with meadows and ancient forests, as well as expanses of grass and moorland. Apart from the occasional sleepy hamlet, the only signs of human life are cyclists and hikers. But this was also the region in which the Russians broke through the German lines in World War II to commence their final assault on Berlin, and it is rich in history.

When cruises operate on the Oder, they usually start in Berlin, travel east along the Havel to join the Oder, and then sail either south to Wroclaw (Breslau) or north to Szczecin, close to the river's mouth on the Baltic Sea.

THE VISTULA

Poland's longest river carves its way for 1,050 km (650 miles) through a landscape of forests and meadows, castles and medieval towns. Vistula cruises are few and far between, but are a fascinating way to explore the north of the country, which has a proud and intriguing history as well as areas of great natural beauty. Cruises tend to start in Gdańsk and head only a little way inland (the river is navigable for

More than 75,000 people were imprisoned for trying to escape across Berlin's infamous Wall. Some 239 people were killed in the attempt, but 5,043 made it across.

BELOW: on the banks of the Vistula.

Baltic amber, formed from the resin of decayed evergreens, has been Poland's gold for centuries, and is still in demand for contemporary jewellery.

BELOW: St Mary's astrological clock, Gdańsk.

barges and most other vessels only as far as Bydgoszcz, 30 km/20 miles downstream from Toruń), instead traversing the network of canals and minor rivers around the delta and offering excursions as far afield as the Kaliningrad enclave of Russia (between Poland and Lithuania).

The course and history of the river

The Vistula (Wisła in Polish) rises in the Beskid Mountains in Poland's deep south, close to the Czech and Slovak borders. It flows through the historic city of Kraków before descending in a long, lazy "S" across wide plains and passing major cities including the capital Warsaw, Płock, Toruń and Gdańsk. The waters eventually empty into the Vistula Lagoon on the Baltic Sea.

The estuary is a labyrinth of sandbars, dunes, spits and beaches, as well as water meadows, and changes constantly, partly due to the build-up of silt and partly due to human intervention – the river has to be dredged from time to time. The area attracts some 250 species of waterfowl, 61 of which breed here.

Tribes have lived along the Vistula, certainly around the delta, for at least 2,000 years. The river has historically formed part of an important trade route extending from the Baltic to the Black Sea, linking with the Dnieper (now in neighbouring Ukraine but once flowing through part of a larger Poland). The trade route was known as the Amber Road, along which amber and other items from northern Europe were transported to Greece, Egypt and further afield.

What to expect

This really is the cutting edge of river cruising, and the areas visited are a lot less developed (and consequently less spoilt) than the rest of Europe. There are few

tourists around and a lot of fascinating places to see, from medieval castles to amber deposits and elk reserves. Expect some long coach journeys – although the river weaves through many of Poland's major cities, river cruise vessels generally remain in the north of the country. Cruise vessels also sail on the northern coastal lagoons, and through the complex canal network up to the Russian border.

Map on page 167

Destination highlights

● Gdańsk

Gdańsk, which is Poland's oldest city, is known to many for its role as the base of the Solidarity movement in 1980, a protest which sent shock waves across the Eastern Bloc. The town is 1,000 years old, and has been occupied by countless invading forces, from Teutonic Knights to Prussians and Nazis. This was the place where the first shots of World War II were fired.

Gdańsk was badly damaged in the war, but has been sensitively restored, with old gateways, towers and cobbled streets. City tours include the **shipyards**, where Solidarity was started by Lech Wałęsa, the **Maritime Museum** (open Tues–Sun 10am–5pm), **Neptune's Fountain** and the **Church of the Virgin Mary** (the largest in Poland), which is adorned by a large, 15th-century **Astrological Clock**, showing the moon phases and the positions of the zodiac signs. Amazingly, the clock is still in working order. The hinterland of Gdańsk is subtly beautiful, with rolling hills, peaceful lakes and long, sandy beaches.

● Toruń

The lovely medieval city of Toruń, a UNESCO World Heritage Site, is visited either on a long coach tour from a northern port or as a port of call on a river cruise. The

BELOW: Gdańsk townhouses.

TIP

On the outskirts of
Warsaw, Wilanów
Palace (open
Wed–Mon 9.30am–
2.30pm, until 5.30pm
on Wed and Sun in
summer) is considered
by many to be
Poland's most
beautiful secular
Baroque building. It
has retained the
grandeur of a royal
palace, and is set in a
magnificent park.

town was once a wealthy Hanseatic port, despite being a long distance inland, and was the birthplace of the astronomer Copernicus in 1473. His former home is now a **museum** (open Tues–Sun 10am–4pm, until 6pm on Wed, Fri and Sat May–Aug). The whole town is like something out of a film set or a fairy-tale, with defensive walls, towers, Gothic squares, crooked medieval houses and churches. There's always a lively buzz, as Toruń is a big university town.

● **Warsaw (Warszawa)**

The Polish capital lies some 390 km (240 miles) south of Gdańsk and is usually offered as a coach tour. The city today is a thriving commercial centre with smart hotels and designer shops, a far cry from the days of communist rule. Despite being the scene of many battles, Warsaw (Warszawa; pronounced *var-shava)* has been painstakingly restored several times, and many of the historic buildings look exactly as they would have originally, particularly around the **Old Town Market Square** (Rynek Starego Miasta), which is surrounded by burghers' houses dating from the 15th to 19th centuries. Other highlights include the Gothic **Cathedral of St John** and the imposing **Royal Castle** on Zamkowy Square, the rebulding of which took 20 years from 1971 (open Tues–Sat 10am–6pm, Sun 11am–6pm). Also well worth seeing is the **Łazienkowski Palace and Park**, a romantic place with its grand architecture and landscaped gardens (palace open Tues–Sun 9am–4pm, park open daylight hours).

● **Elblàg**

Elblàg is actually on the Elblàg River, 60 km (37 miles) southeast of Gdańsk, reached on a river cruise via the Vistula Delta. It used to be an important seaport

BELOW:
the Church of the
Holy Spirit at Toruń.

until the lagoon became silted up. The old town has many Gothic, Renaissance and Baroque houses, several of which have been restored, including **St Nicolas's Cathedral**, the 14th-century **City Gate** and **St Mary's Church**.

Another reason for visiting Elblàg is to join the 81-km (51-mile) **Elblàg Canal**, which connects the Vistula Estuary to Ostróda in the scenic Mazurian lake district to the south. Traversing the canal is a unique experience; there is a height difference of 100 metres (330 ft) to navigate, so vessels travel through two sets of locks and along five inclined planes, which involves them actually leaving the water and being carried on railed trolleys *(see picture on page 28)*.

Maps on pages 167, 170

● **Frombork**

Frombork, formerly Frauenberg, is a short distance across the Vistula Lagoon from Elblàg, and is located close to the Russian border. The main reason for visiting is to see the **Nicolaus Copernicus Museum** (open daily 9.30am–5pm), housed in a former 14th-century palace which was rebuilt in the 18th century. The astronomer, who determined that the planets circle the sun, lived here for many years until his death in 1543.

● **The Curonian Spit**

This is a rare chance to visit (by coach) this narrow strip of sand separating a huge lagoon from the Baltic Sea, and belonging partly to Russia and partly to Lithuania. It is almost 100 km (60 miles) in length, but at one point only 400 metres (435 yds) wide. The dunes are among Europe's highest, and the area has been declared a UNESCO site of outstanding natural interest. The tour usually includes a trip to the amber mines, too; you'll see amber on sale everywhere. ❏

Copernicus statue at Toruń, the town of his birth.

BELOW: timeless Polish countryside.

FRANCE: RHÔNE AND SEINE

These two rivers offer very different views of France, southern and northern, yet the appeal of fine food, wine and beautiful scenery both rural and urban, is a constant

Map on page 176

The French enjoy their rivers. Throughout the country, languid watercourses thread their way through an ensemble of rural landscapes rich in natural beauty, past ancient towns and villages, campsites and bathing beaches. The Rhône (sometimes combined with the Saône) and the Seine are the major waterways for river cruising, and each has its own distinctive appeal. The Rhône Valley south of Lyon is representative of the warm, terracotta-roofed southern half of France, while a Seine cruise brings a new perspective to the green north, as well as being an excellent way to see Paris. French waterways are also very popular for barge cruising *(see pages 193–199)*.

THE RHÔNE (AND SAÔNE)

The evocative names of Burgundy, Avignon, Lyon and Mâcon conjure up all kinds of delicious images, from fields of yellow sunflowers and purple lavender to ruby-red wines, truffles, rich cheeses and plates of charcuterie, not to mention magnificent Roman antiquities and colourful market towns. The Rhône flows through the gastronomic heart of France, carving its way across some of the most beautiful wine-growing country, as well as handsome, historic cities such as Avignon and Arles. A cruise on this river awakens all the senses.

PRECEDING PAGES: a traditional French market. **LEFT:** Avignon's Pont St Bénézet. **BELOW:** haute cuisine on the river bank.

The course of the river

The Rhône starts its 812-km (505-mile) journey deep in the Swiss Alps. The swift-flowing river descends west through a long valley before turning sharply north at Martigny towards Lake Geneva. It emerges from the western end of this large lake to force its way through the Jura Mountains into the Rhône-Alpes region of France, meandering south and west to Lyon where it is joined by the Saône. Now wide and strong, the river courses straight south to Avignon, Arles and the Camargue delta region. The stretch between Lyon and Arles is the true Rhône Valley, with sunny banks lined with vineyards against a backdrop of hills and mountains.

The Rhône Valley represents a northward extension of the Mediterranean climate, at least as far as Valence, with hotter and drier summers than in adjacent regions. It also acts as a conduit for the gusty winds of the *mistral*, when cold air from the north is funnelled down through the valley to chill the Camargue, Marseilles and the Riviera. The *mistral* can blow at any time of year, but is more prevalent during winter and spring.

The delta begins at Arles and extends for approximately 40 km (25 miles) to the sea in two arms with the romantic, starkly beautiful salt-marshes and lagoons of La Camargue between them.

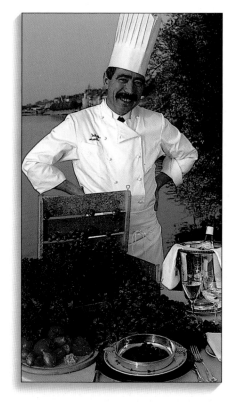

Fresh bread, in pain
or baguette *form, one
of the many
pleasures on a
French river cruise.*

The evolution of river cruising

The Rhône has always been an important trade route, linking northern Europe to the Mediterranean and forming a means for armies from the south to move north through the continent. It is, in fact, the only large river to run south into the Mediterranean Sea – Europe's only other significant Mediterranean rivers are the Po in northern Italy *(see page 203)* and the Ebro in Spain.

To the east of the Rhône Delta, the city of Marseilles was founded by the Greeks in 600 BC, and was later used by the Romans as a base from which to head upriver, planting vines as they travelled – most of the major vineyards along the river's course date back to this time. In time, the Rhône became a key link between the Greek and Roman traders and the Celtic kingdoms of the north, who traded tin and amber for salt from the south. Roman settlements sprang up along the river, aided by the construction of roads and aqueducts.

The Middle Ages, turbulent centuries of religious wars in southern France, saw the strengthening of French royal authority over the Rhône Valley. Lyon, the

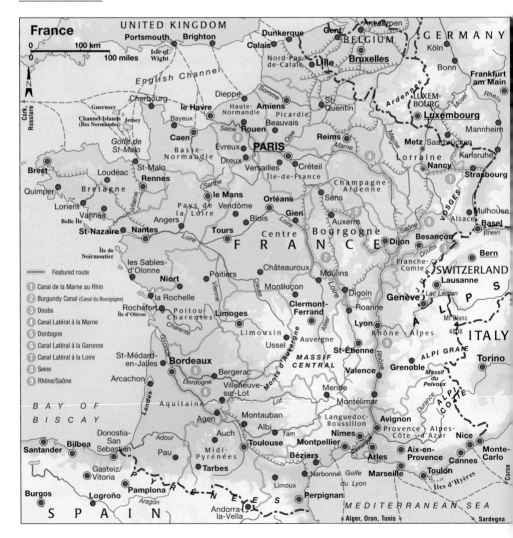

major city of the region, underwent major economic expansion and became known for its fiercely independent spirit, resisting the forces of the French Revolution in the late 18th century and an important centre of the World War II Resistance.

Until the 1830s, vessels on the Rhône were mainly wooden barges, drifting downstream with the current and being towed upstream by horses. Iron barges and paddle steamers were gradually introduced, reducing the cost of haulage significantly. Later, mechanical towage using cables attached to the river's bed or banks became the favoured method of travelling upstream, but this was expensive; more powerful tugs were gradually introduced and, later still, stronger self-propelled barges.

What to expect

Most cruises operate round trips from Lyon, heading south as far as Arles with a chance to visit the Camargue Delta. Cruises also head north along the Saône, the Rhône's main tributary. Others operate south–north, from Avignon to Chalon-sur-Saône; as train travel is so easy in France thanks to the high speed TGV network, it's relatively simple to use, say, Paris as a gateway and travel to one port for embarkation, disembark at another and get back to Paris by train.

A Rhône/Saône cruise will involve numerous opportunities to taste and buy wine, as well as sightseeing. There may be a chance to dine ashore, particularly in Lyon, home to some of the most spectacular restaurants in France. The cruising season operates from March to November. Pleasure barging *(see pages 193–199)* – either "bareboat" or crewed – remains an important part of Rhône tourism, although several companies also operate long-haul river cruise vessels, among them Viking River Cruises and Peter Deilmann Cruises.

Map on page 176

The name of the Rhône comes from the Latin Rhodanus. The river level depends partly on snow melt, with the highest levels (and fastest flow) in spring and early summer. Copious rainfall brings a secondary high level in November and December.

BELOW: scenery near Vienne.

In the centre of Chalon-sur-Saône is an obelisk erected to mark the completion of the Canal du Centre, a 118-km (73-mile) link between the Saône and the Loire. Built between 1783 and 1802, it constituted the final link in the waterway between the English Channel and the Mediterranean.

BELOW:
a bridge at Mâcon.

Destination Highlights

● Chalon-sur-Saône

This inland port lies in the very heart of Burgundy at the confluence of the Saône and the Canal du Centre, around 120 km (75 miles) north of Lyon. Chalon is often is the start for excursions to Dijon, the capital of Burgundy, which many consider to be underrated.

The heart of the town is the **Place St Vincent,** with its colourful half-timbered houses and its cathedral, the oldest parts of which date from the 11th century. It is also the birthplace of Nicéphore Niépce (1765–1833), the rather neglected inventor of photography. There is a **museum** in the town dedicated to his work and to the history of photography (open daily Wed–Mon, June–Sept 9.30am–6pm; Oct–May 9.30am–11.45am and 2pm–5.45pm).

● Mâcon

Nestled neatly into the west bank of the River Saône at the end of a 14th-century bridge (Pont St Laurent), Mâcon is located at the southern end of the Burgundy wine region and essentially forms a frontier between northern and southern France; southwards from here, the architecture becomes increasingly dominated by Romanesque, and rounded terracotta tiles replace the northern slate. Mâcon is surrounded by chestnut and pine forests and the rolling Beaujolais vineyards; any visit inevitably includes a tasting of the smoky, dry white Burgundy wines.

The 10th-century Benedictine abbey of **Cluny**, once extremely powerful, is 25 km (15 miles) northwest of Mâcon and a highlight of the trip; it can be visited by bicycle if preferred, as it's a picturesque ride through the vineyards.

● Lyon

Lyon, the gastronomic capital of France, actually lies on a little peninsula between the Rhône and Saône rivers. It was founded more than 2,000 years ago and is today the second-largest city in the country, and its most important educational centre outside Paris. The city's reputation for wonderful food is completely deserved and there are countless local specialities to try, among them *quenelles de brochet* (mousse of pike), the world-famous *coq au vin* made with the local *poulet de Bresse*, and a huge array of magnificent charcuterie.

There's also an eclectic collection of museums in the city, including the **Musée Historique des Tissus et des Arts Décoratifs** (open Tues–Sun 10am–5.30pm) – a wonderful textile museum with some rare exhibits, and the **Musée des Beaux Arts** (open Wed–Sun 10am–6pm), its collection ranked second in France only to that of the Louvre.

A visit to Lyon also usually includes a trip up Fourvière Hill, either a clamber up steep steps or a funicular ride. At the top, you can visit the **Basilique de Notre Dame** and gaze out over the city's rooftops, past the two rivers to the vineyards beyond.

● Vienne

The Rhône is wide and fast-flowing as it reaches Vienne, where it's joined by another tributary, the Gère. For once, this excursion is a break from food and wine, focusing more on the town's amazing Roman heritage; Vienne has one of the best-preserved **Roman amphitheatres** in France, on the slopes of nearby Mont Pipet, seating 13,000 and still used for theatrical performances. The **Temple d'Auguste et de Livie** in the town itself is also an arresting example of

Map below

Lyon is constantly upgrading its river banks, giving the city back to pedestrians and cyclists. You can hire out a cyclopolitain (a high-tech rickshaw propelled by both pedals and an electric motor) to take you around the city centre for just €1 per kilometre.

BELOW: the view over Lyon from the Basilique de Notre Dame.

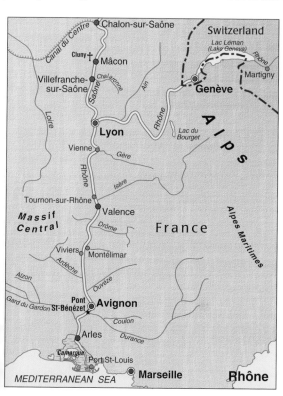

BELOW:
the Palais des
Papes in Avignon.

1st-century Roman architecture, and there are further antiquities to admire across the river at the suburb of St Roman-en-Gal, an excavation of villas, marketplaces, baths and mosaics. Vienne is well known for its **jazz festival**, which normally takes place in July.

● Tournon-sur-Rhône

The scenery as the river carves its way south is rugged and mountainous, dotted with castles and jagged rock outcrops, although vineyards are still the main feature along the banks.

Tournon is one of the region's most attractive cities, nestling on the bank of the river and overlooked by its 10th-century **castle**, built into a rock. An excursion from here enjoyed by many river cruise passengers is a ride on a nostalgic steam-hauled train *(see margin, left)* to the Ardèche region, a wild, limestone upland of craggy cliffs, gorges and caves, with red wine and lavender its main products. There are also excursions by coach to the Gorge de l'Ardèche; a road runs along the top of the red-rock gorge, the river a silvery ribbon hundreds of feet below, and there are various lookout points and peculiar rock formations.

Between Tournon and the city of Valence, the Rhône is reinforced by the turbulent waters of the Isère, flowing in from the Alps to the northeast.

● Viviers

This sleepy town dates back to the 5th century, when it was an episcopal seat. It retains much of its olde-world charm today, with medieval houses and an impressive cathedral. Ardèche excursions *(see above)* also operate from here.

● Avignon

The river is broadening out now as it enters Provence and nears the Mediterranean, although the scenery is still undulating and rich with colour – yellow sunflowers all summer long, and ranks of purple lavender spread across the hilltops, scenting the air.

The beautiful university city of Avignon is totally encircled by medieval walls and known as the "City of Popes"; in the 14th century, this was the residence of the papacy for 70 years. The ravishingly handsome medieval **Palais des Papes** at the centre is one of the great wonders of France, and was once considered to be the heart of the Christian world. Near by, look at the remains of the famous **Pont St Bénézet**, which juts out across a branch of the river, and is the subject of one of the most famous French nursery rhymes, *Sur le Pont d'Avignon*. The city has a terrific buzz on warm summer nights, with outdoor cafés and bars lining the streets and free entertainment provided by buskers and street artists, especially during the Theatre Festival in July.

● Arles and the Camargue

There's an exciting and romantic edge to the Roman city of Arles, gateway to the salt-lagoons, rice fields and cowboy country of the wild Camargue beyond. Gypsies from the surrounding villages still gather here to keep their traditions alive, and the town has a magnificent artistic heritage; it's here that Vincent Van Gogh began to lose his sanity, capturing the dazzling colours of the Provençal countryside on canvas in hallucinogenic swirls.

Arles boasts many Gallo-Roman ruins, including the famous **Amphitheatre**. Called Les Arénes, it is still used for bullfights and other performances, and can seat 20,000; this part of France continues the tradition of bullfighting like Spain, despite growing opposition. A visit to the animated **Place du Forum**, in the very heart of town, is a must; here you'll see a statue of Frédéric Mistral, the poet responsible for reviving the Provençal language in the early 20th century.

Arles is the starting point for excursions into the **Camargue**, the delta of the River Rhône and one of Europe's finest nature reserves, with its unspoilt landscape and wildlife, including pink flamingos, black bulls reared in the saltmarshes and bred for the ring, and fabulous white horses. The best way to see the delta is still on horseback; experienced riders can go out with the *gardians*, modern-day Camargue cowboys who tend the bulls.

THE SEINE

From the romantic French capital to Honfleur, one of the most picturesque of all French ports, the Seine has been witness to some remarkable characters throughout history: Joan of Arc, Van Gogh, Seurat and Claude Monet, possibly the most famous of the Impressionist painters. A cruise along this slow-flowing river is a gentle voyage through some of France's most mellow countryside, of farmland and meadows, historic towns and sleepy villages. It is also a gastronomic adventure, in the land of creamy Brie and Camembert cheeses, Calvados liqueur and Normandy cider. ➤ *page 186*

Maps on pages 179, 186

Les Arénes, the Roman amphitheatre at Arles, is still used for bullfights and other performances.

BELOW:
Joan of Arc statue on the Place des Pyramides in Paris.

PORTS OF CALL: PARIS

Paris is a city of landscapes, cut through the middle by the slowly meandering River Seine and edged with gentle hills. The Seine is the capital's widest avenue; it is spanned by a total of 37 bridges which provide some of the loveliest views of Paris.

The fascination of the French capital is eternal and has long been a magnet to artists, writers, philosophers and composers. Its grand architecture, fine cuisine and haute couture combine to make Paris one of the most glamorous European capitals.

ORIENTATION

Embarkation point for river cruise vessels heading down the Seine to Rouen and the English Channel is at the Quai Grenelle, a short distance downriver from the Eiffel Tower (Métro Bir Hakeim).

GETTING AROUND

The Paris Métro is quick and efficient. The first train runs at 5.30am, the last leaves around 12.30am. Those travelling a lot, but only in Paris for a few days, should buy a tourist ticket *(Paris-Visite)*, valid for one, three or five days on the Métro, bus and RER and SNFC trains. Buses run from 6.30am to 8.30pm, with some lines running until 12.30am.

BUSINESS HOURS

Banks open Mon–Fri 9am–5.30pm and are closed Sat and Sun. Food shops, especially bakers, tend to open early. Most department stores open from 9am until 7pm or 8pm. Most shops close on Sunday, although bakers and patisseries are usually open in the morning.

TOP CITY SIGHTS

▲ **THE LOUVRE** One of the largest palaces in Europe has assembled an incomparable collection of Old Masters, sculptures and antiquities, housing 35,000 works. It has three wings, and the superb collections are divided up into seven different sections, each assigned its own colour to help you find your way around. Highlights include Leonardo da Vinci's *Mona Lisa*. Open 9am–6pm Sat–Mon and Thur, until 9.45pm Wed and Fri.

▼ **EIFFEL TOWER** No visit to Paris would be complete without a trip to the Eiffel Tower, symbol of the city and of France herself. The metal giant looms over the area southwest of the centre. This icon of iron girders was chosen as the centrepiece to the World Fair of 1889. The first two floors are negotiated on foot or by

▼ **ARC DE TRIOMPHE** Built between 1806 and 1836, this triumphal arch is the epitome of French grandeur. The many statues on the main façade glorify the insurrection of 1792 and Napoleon's major victories.

EXCURSIONS

VERSAILLES Southwest of Paris lies the grand Palace of Versailles. Take the RER line C5 which will drop you a short distance away. Allow a full day to visit the chateau and its magnificent formal gardens. Open Oct–Apr Tues–Sun 9am– 5.30pm, May–Sept until 6.30pm.

◄ **PLACE DES VOSGES** Initially called the Place Royale, this enchanting 17th-century square, with a garden surrounded by 36 arcaded residences, was constructed by Henri IV as a showcase for his court. Today, this is the most beautiful square in Paris, and one of the capital's most sought-after addresses. The arcades house chic boutiques and cafés, and in summer plays host to classical concerts.

► **POMPIDOU CENTRE** Made entirely of glass and surrounded by a white steel grid, the Pompidou Centre is the main showcase for modern and contemporary art in Paris. Now a much-loved city icon, the "inside-out" design was controversial when it was unveiled in 1977. Open Wed–Mon 11am–10pm.

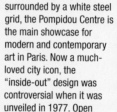
la cité des enfants

◄ **PARIS FOR FAMILIES** On the Right Bank the **Jardin des Tuileries** has pony rides, toy boats, cafés and children's trampolines, and a giant Ferris wheel at

lift, and then another lift goes up to the top. From here you will see a spectacular city panorama, best viewed one hour before sunset. Open Sept–mid-June daily 9.30am–11pm, July–Aug until midnight.

► **MÉTRO** Métro stations abound in the city, and some entrances retain their elegant art nouveau features, designed by the late-19th-century architect Hector Guimard. Two notable entrances that are still covered by his beautiful cast-iron-and-glass pavilions are at the stations of Porte Dauphine and Abbesses.

Christmas and Easter-time. To the west of Paris is the Parisian's favourite Sunday afternoon playground, the **Bois de Boulogne**, with woods and gardens, lakes and cycling tracks. On the Left Bank is the **Jardin du Luxembourg**, offering puppet shows and tennis courts.

▶ SACRÉ COEUR

Set in Monmartre is the virginal-white Basilique du Sacré Coeur. Perched on a hill, its Byzantine cupolas are as much a part of the city skyline as the Eiffel Tower; when the lights are turned on at night, the Sacré Coeur resembles a lit wedding cake. It can be reached by walking up 250 steps or by taking a funicular cable car. Open summer 9.30am–7pm, winter 10am–5.30pm.

▼ MUSÉE D'ORSAY

France's national museum of 19th-century art is housed in the former Gare d'Orsay, an ornate Beaux-Arts train station, opened in 1900 to serve passengers to the World Fair. It's an immensely dramatic setting, worth visiting for its own sake. But the museum's contents are unmissable too: there is a major collection of paintings by the Impressionists, plus works by Delacroix and Ingres. Open Tues, Wed, Fri and Sat 10am–6pm, Thur 10am–9.45pm; from 9am all days mid-June–mid-Sept.

▶ RODIN MUSEUM

Housed in the Hotel Biron is the Rodin Museum. Auguste Rodin came to live here in 1908 and stayed until his death in 1917. Here you can admire Rodin's famous works, *The Kiss* and *The*

Thinker, reputedly based on Dante contemplating the Inferno. Open Apr–Sat Tues–Sun 9.30am–5.45pm, Oct–Mar until 4.45pm.

LE PENSEVR

◀ GALERIE VIVIENNE

The area between the Palais Royal and rue du Faubourg-Montmartre is laced with picturesque shopping arcades. In the early 19th century they became the places to discover the latest fashions. The best-preserved of these latter-day shopping malls is Galerie Vivienne, which has a fine mosaic floor, intricate brass lamps and graceful glass canopies.

▼ SAINTE-CHAPELLE

This is a masterpiece of Parisian Gothic Rayonnant architecture on the Île de la Cité. The beautiful 13th-century stained glass, magnificently displayed in 85 major panels, is without equal anywhere in Paris. Open daily summer 9.30am–6pm, winter 9am–5pm.

▼ ST-GERMAIN

Here lies the historical heart of literary Paris. Its elegant streets house chic boutiques, yet it still retains a sense of animation, with crowded cafés spilling out onto the pavements. In the 1950s the area became a fertile breeding ground for literature and ideas. Existentialists, led by Jean-Paul Sartre and Albert Camus, lived in cheap hotels and gathered in local cafés

such as Café Flore and Les Deux Magots.

▶ NOTRE DAME

The cathedral's position on the banks of the Seine is an unforgettable setting. Just as Gothic cathedrals were considered symbols of paradise, so the entrance façade, with its series of sculptures, was considered to be the gateway to heaven. The stories of the Bible are depicted in the portals, paintings and stained glass of the cathedral. The scale exceeded all earlier churches – Paris became the capital only a few years

before the foundation stone was laid, and the building was designed to reflect the power of the state and its

church. Construction work on the cathedral began in 1163 and was finished around 1240. The

exquisite 13th-century north and south rose windows are star attractions. Open daily 7.45am–6.45pm.

▼ FONTAINE DE STRAVINSKI modern art in Beauborg by Niki de Saint-Phalle and Jean Tinguely.

Some of the leading Impressionists drew inspiration from scenes along the Seine. Monet's house at Giverny was close to the river, between Paris and Rouen. In 1858, the teenage Eugène Boudin met Monet in Honfleur; Monet gave him some paints and taught him how to observe the changing lights on the Seine Estuary. Edouard Manet also painted the Seine with Claude Monet and, under his influence, took to working in the open air.

The course of the river

The River Seine has its source in the Côte d'Or region of Burgundy, and is 780 km (485 miles) long. It is, in fact, the longest navigable waterway in France, and carries more commercial traffic and freight than any other French river or canal (it is linked by canals to the Loire, Rhine and Rhône).

Navigation benefits from its gentle current. The river flows to the northwest of Dijon in Burgundy, through the dry chalk plateau of Champagne to the Île de France and Paris, then loops westwards through Rouen and across Normandy before emptying into the English Channel. The estuary is wide and extends for 26 km (16 miles) between Tancarville and Le Havre. Despite the fact that it rises much further south, the Seine is measured in river kilometres from Paris, with the Île St-Louis in the heart of the city marking 0, the beginning.

The evolution of river cruising

The Seine has been navigable since 200 BC, when the Parisii tribe set up camp on what is now the Île de la Cité in the French capital. Since then, the river has been used as a route for invasions, raids, traders and tourists. Early invasions were staggering in their scale: in AD 885, 30,000 Norman pirates in 700 ships sailed up the Seine, only to find it vigorously defended by Comte Eudes, later crowned King of France.

Within Paris, the Seine has been used for sightseeing since the late 19th century, when the famous *bateaux mouches* were introduced to Paris, with their shallow hulls and (in modern times) clear perspex tops. These days the Seine is thick with boats every day and night, their multilingual commentary echoing across the water. Longer cruises operate from Paris to Honfleur and back again, calling at major sights like Giverny and Rouen, and usually taking seven nights. Operators on the river include Peter Deilmann and Viking River Cruises.

What to expect

This is a fairly intensive cruise, with sometimes more than one stop in a day. Almost all cruises, however, spend at least one night in Paris, with a chance to see the city by night. There are also excursions further afield from the boat, to sights such as the Normandy beaches.

As with most European river cruises, the Seine itineraries include towns with narrow, cobbled streets, steps and uneven ground, and are not really suitable for anybody with mobility difficulties. The river cruise vessels on the Seine do not have cabins adapted to wheelchair users.

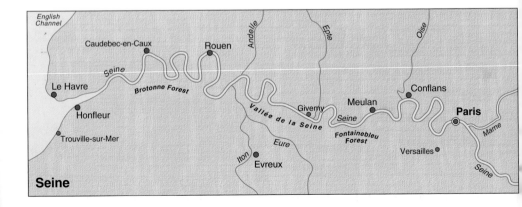

Destination Highlights

● Paris (Km 0)

The graceful, romantic French capital needs little introduction. The Eiffel Tower, Montmartre, the Louvre, Notre Dame, the designer stores and markets could easily keep visitors occupied for a week. River cruisers usually dock in the city centre, so you can enjoy the beautiful spectacle of the monuments and buildings along the Seine floodlit at night. *For details on what to see in Paris, see pages 182–185.*

● Conflans-Sainte-Honorine (Km 68)

The meandering course of the Seine means that it takes a long time for river cruise vessels to leave Paris behind. Conflans, in the northwestern suburbs, lies almost 70 km downstream from central Paris, but less than half that distance by road. Positioned at the confluence of the Oise and the Seine, this was an important shipping centre from 1855 onwards, when a chain was laid along the bed of the Seine allowing barges to be hauled upstream to the capital. As a result, Conflans has a great shipping heritage, brought to life in the **Musée de la Batellerie** (open Mon 1.30–6pm; Wed–Fri 9am–12pm and 1.30–6pm; Sat–Sun 3–6pm), with scale models of some 250 boats, as well as working models of locks and weirs. The 11th-century **Montjoie Tower** and **Saint-Maciou Church** are also worth a visit.

● Giverny (Km 147)

World-famous as the setting for the water-lily pond and graceful arched bridge immortalised by Claude Monet, who lived here for 43 years, Giverny is one of France's most visited sights, receiving 500,000 tourists a year, many of them clutching easels and paint, hoping to recreate the master's work.

Map on page 186

River cruises through the heart of Paris have been popular since the 19th century.

BELOW: scene in rural Normandy.

During the visit, you will see Monet's green-shuttered house and inspiring garden with its water-lily pond and elegant arched bridge near Vernon. His house contains the much-loved Japanese engravings as well as other memorabilia. Close by, the **Musée d'Art Americain Giverny** (open Apr–Oct daily 10am–6pm) showcases the work of US-born Impressionists who were inspired by Monet, despite the fact that he called many of them "a nuisance" when they flocked to Giverny. If you want to see work by Monet, though, you need to go to the **Musée de Vernon** (open Tues–Fri 10.30am–12.30pm and 2–6pm, weekends 2–6pm) near by, which has a couple of Monet works, some canvases by his stepdaughter and several paintings by various followers.

● **Rouen (Km 238–245)**

Rouen is known as the "City of 100 Spires", and you can see its graceful skyline as you approach along the river. Until the 17th century, it was the second largest city in France, and is still important today as France's fourth-largest port. Although badly damaged during World War II, the city has been extensively restored – in particular the 700 or so half-timber-framed buildings on the right bank of the river in the old quarter. The spot everybody wants to see, though, is the marker on the pavement in the **Place du Vieux Marché**, where Joan of Arc was burnt at the stake as a witch in 1431.

Other sights include the magnificent **Cathédrale de Notre Dame**, the western façade of which was painted by Monet (the work is housed in the city's Musée des Beaux Arts), and the medieval **Eglise St Maclou**, which contains some superb wood carvings. Also look out for the **Gros Horloge**, a splendid, gold-faced clock mounted on a building which creates a bridge across one of the narrow streets.

BELOW: Rouen's majestic cathedral.

Map on page 186

● Caudebec-en-Caux (Km 309.5)

The medieval town of Caudebec-en-Caux is only a short cruise downstream from Rouen, through pretty Normandy scenery of woods, orchards and fields. The **Eglise de Notre Dame** is the main attraction, started by the English when they had conquered the town in the 14th century, but completed by the French in 1439 after they had won the town back. The church is in Flamboyant Gothic style, with intricate stone carvings, flying buttresses and graceful spires. Tours of the town also include a visit to **Jumièges Abbey**, which was consecrated in 1067 in the presence of William the Conqueror.

● Honfleur (Km 355)

The Seine broadens out into a wide estuary as it approaches the coast, and is busy with commercial traffic. Honfleur is a charming old port city on the southern shore of the Seine Estuary, opposite the port of Le Havre; most cruises turn around here and head back to Paris.

It was from Honfleur that French settlers set out for the new lands of Canada in the 16th century. The town really is the stuff of picture postcards, particularly around the inner harbour, the **Vieux Bassin**, where narrow medieval houses overlook a colourful yacht and fishing harbour.

It's no surprise that the light, the space, the old coloured buildings and the boats have attracted artists for years, including Boudin and many of the Impressionists. You can see their work in the **Musée Eugène Boudin** (open Wed–Mon 10am–noon and 2pm–6pm), which has an ethnographic section detailing the history of the town as well as several rooms containing paintings, mainly 19th-century, of the town, including some work by Monet. ❑

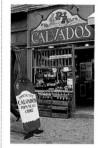

Calvados apple brandy, traditionally drunk in small quantities between each course of a long meal to stimulate appetite.

BELOW: Honfleur harbour.

BARGE CRUISING IN FRANCE

Map on page 176

A barge holiday in France is a wonderful opportunity to sample life in the slow lane in beautiful surroundings – on-board and off

A French barge cruise is a chance to de-stress completely. It's a more intimate experience than a normal river cruise, on a much smaller vessel, usually taking no more than 12 passengers. This really is life in the slow lane, on board your own luxurious, if compact, floating country house, tucked away in some forgotten corner surrounded by vineyards, ancient villages and sleepy châteaux.

Barges chug along France's more peaceful and beautiful canals, providing a method of effortless discovery, and a real change of pace to cruising aboard the larger and faster river cruise vessels which ply Europe's waterways. You can get off and walk or cycle on the towpath, and every day is a chance to explore the countryside, shop in local markets and relax on deck. Food on a good French barge holiday should be superb, comparable to the standard you would expect in a luxury ski chalet or a smart boutique hotel, with lots of local ingredients, personal tastes catered to, and fine wines.

The most popular barging regions in France include the Champagne district, northern and southern Burgundy and Lorraine, as well as the Dordogne and Garonne in the southwest.

PRECEDING PAGES: peace and quiet on the Burgundy Canal. **LEFT AND BELOW:** eating – and drinking – well is a big part of the appeal of a French barge holiday.

What to expect

There are many variations on the style of barge, although they're all comfortable. One of the first things you'll notice about your cruise barge is the glowing assortment of flowers and flower boxes that adorn the uppermost decks. Cruise barge owners appear to delight in trying to outdo each other in their displays.

Although there are some cruises of between three and 13 days, the "standard" cruise is of six days' duration, and each cruise barge operates on fixed itineraries. The barge will moor up early each evening, giving you time to pay a visit to a local village and then get a restful night's sleep. Shopping opportunities are limited to local stores, and evening entertainment is almost non-existent, and always impromptu (actually, dining is *the* entertainment).

Each vessel normally takes up to 12 people, although some take 24, and one or two take 50, making them more like small, slow-moving river cruise vessels. There are also many self-drive barges on French waterways, usually sleeping four, six or eight.

Whichever you choose, you can expect to eat and drink extremely well. Cruise barges have a deservedly fine reputation for excellent food and wine. Locally grown, fresh foods are usually purchased and prepared each day, allowing you to live well and feel like a house guest. There is no mass dining here – just the celebration of good living – a marriage that is typical

Cycling is a great way to experience the quiet French countryside, and bikes are almost always provided.

and traditional in France. All drinks (both alcoholic and non-alcoholic), champagne and wines with dinner are usually included, so there's no extras bill to worry about at the end of the vacation.

A cruise barge can either be taken exclusively by a small group, or you can book as an individual. If so, bear in mind that you will live in very close proximity to the other passengers, so a tolerant and flexible attitude is important. Think of it as an extended house party with (usually) interesting and like-minded people – Francophiles, lovers of good food and wine, anybody wanting a different pace of life. A barge cruise is actually an ideal holiday for singles, although sadly, you will have to pay the cost of a double cabin, as few barges have single rooms.

The barges are typically between 30 and 50 metres (100 and 165 ft) in length, with a beam of between 5 and 7.3 metres (16½ and 24 ft), although their actual size depends on the area of operation and the ability to manoeuvre in the many locks that line the canals. They almost always have a steel hull, with a flat bottom.

Most have been skilfully converted from cargo- or munitions-carrying barges, many of which were built in the Netherlands or Scotland, while a handful of new cruise barges have been constructed in the past few years. The overall effect is akin to the timeless appeal of a tiny country house or inn. Most are beautifully appointed inside, although the décor, amenities and appointments are typically based on the tastes of the owner/operator. Some cruise barges have air-conditioning, while most have some form of heating. Most have some form of canopied sun deck. Interiors tend to have plenty of cosy cushions on their lounge seats and armchairs. The majority will carry bicycles and some have their own minibus that follows the canal, ready to take you on excursions (all included in the cruise fare).

RIGHT: sumptuous furnishings aboard the *L'Art de Vivre*.

DISTINCTIVE DÉCOR

Many barges have special touches, reflecting the tastes and eccentricities of the owner. *Anacolouthe*, for example, has a baby grand piano in its lounge, which has rich wood panelling and a red colour theme. *Anjodi* has a hot tub and a skylight in the salon, while *Elisabeth* has a split-level dining room with oak hatch-beam ceiling. *Fleur de Lys* has a grand piano in its lounge and some rare vintage wines in the cellar, while the bathrooms have two washbasins, as well as romantic canopied beds. There's even a heated swimming pool. *Horizon II* is a split-level design with beautifully panelled interiors, also found on the *L'Art de Vivre*. *L'Impressioniste* has an exercise room and spa tub. *La Belle Epoque* also has richly panelled interiors, as well as a fitness studio, hot tub and even a sauna. *La Nouvelle Etoile* has internet access in all cabins, tiled bathrooms and an elevator (the only cruise barge to have one). *Napoléon* has one bedroom with a large, marble-clad bathroom that reminds one a little of some of the bathrooms in the Hotel Danielli in Venice (the vessel's sun deck also boast 75 sq. metres/800 sq. feet of space). *Sérénité* has lovely scrolled armrests on the dining room chairs, and the dining room is itself very spacious, with large, wood-trimmed picture windows.

Excursions form a highlight for many canal barge cruise passengers, with everything from hot-air ballooning over the vineyards to wine-tasting to horse-back riding forming part of the offerings. Most cruise barges carry bicycles, so you can do your own touring – or just potter into the nearest village for a morning *café au lait*.

You can walk (probably faster than the barge can chug along), enjoy guided tours (to cultural and historic sites of the region, private gardens, museums and vineyards), go cycling (almost all barges have bicycles), hill climbing, hot-air ballooning or horse riding, play golf or tennis. Or go shopping for food with the chef, and taste some of those wonderful French cheeses that can only be found locally.

Cruising the French canals

In France, by far the most popular barging destination in Europe, there are about 8,500 km (5,280 miles) of navigable canals and waterways, and the river and barge operators have placed their vessels in the best stretches, both for scenic beauty and architectural interest, as well as for ease of getting to and from your chosen cruise. The canals and waterways really do offer beauty, tranquility and a diversity of interests, and barge cruising is an excellent way of exploring areas not previously visited.

Although the canals and locks were constructed for pragmatic purposes and not to be aesthetically pleasing, they have, over time, become more and more attractive, surrounded by planted flowers and orchards. Many canals are lined with trees, originally planted so that their roots would help prevent erosion of the canal banks. They also provided shade for the horses (or men) that towed the early barges along the towpath. Most of the canals are over two centuries old.

Cruise barging in France means going through a constant succession of locks, each one of which takes no more than about 20 minutes to transit unless you moor up for lunch or stop to chat with the lock-keeper. Between Dijon and Mâcon in Burgundy, a cruise barge can negotiate as many as 54 locks during a six-day cruise.

The hours of operation are civilised, too. The locks in France are only allowed to operate between 8.30am and 6.30pm, with an hour off for lunch. If they are of the hand-cranked type, you can lend a hand to open or close the lock gates – it is good exercise, and you'll get to meet the lock-keepers. Some of them grow vegetables (for sale to the cruise barges) and raise flower gardens.

In addition to the locks, the French waterways also cross over some remarkable aqueducts, with fabulous views. If you haven't done this before, it is quite an experience, crossing a bridge on the water and gazing down on the scenery below. Better still, the Canal de la Marne au Rhin has a unique feature which is an amazing feat of engineering – the Arzviller Barge Lift, which moves boats lock, stock and barrel down the mountainside *(pictured on page 196)*.

The best weather in France is often in the late spring or early autumn, although each season has its own

Map on page 176

BELOW: canal locks provide an opportunity for some socialising.

attractions and appeal. The long, hot summers are more likely to see you lazing on deck or fishing from the barge than hiking along the towpath, but the warm weather does mean plenty of chance for alfresco dining. It's unlikely that you will be able to swim in the canals, though. Some barges have a small pool, but otherwise, it's a bicycle ride to the nearest lake to cool off. There are no barge cruises in winter.

Canal de la Marne au Rhin

Linking the Rhine with the Marne, this canal flows through steeply wooded valleys, past half-timbered houses and sleepy, flower-filled villages, with plenty of *auberges* along the way in which to sample quiche Lorraine as it should be, juicy sausages and Pinot gris. There are several permutations of itinerary between Strasbourg and the village of Lagarde, to the east of Nancy, the capital of Lorraine.

This canal has practically continuous locks, although almost all of these are automatic and easy to operate. A more exciting feature is the **Arzviller Barge Lift**, a fantastic creation which actually lifts barges down a mountainside, bypassing a section of the canal containing 17 locks.

Other highlights along the route include the red-sandstone **Rohan Palace** at Saverne (and the brightly painted shops in the town), and **Sarrabourg**, where the beautiful stained-glass window in the Cordeliers Chapel is by Chagall. You can also sail right into the middle of **Strasbourg** *(see page 115)*, passing the European Parliament. The whole route, though, is more about walking, cycling and munching fresh baguettes from the village *boulangerie* on deck at breakfast time than about intensive sightseeing.

BELOW: the Arzviller Barge Lift.

Burgundy Canal (Canal de Bourgogne)

Linking the Saône and the Yonne between Dijon and Migennes, the Burgundy Canal was planned in the 17th century and built in the 18th. There are 176 locks, so any barge cruise is a case of constantly hopping on and off the boat to operate them. The scenery along the route is beautiful, quintessential France – rolling hills covered with oak and maple forest, agricultural plains and plenty of vineyards. You can cycle along the towpath, or take a hot-air balloon at dawn, drifting over the hills and the Saône Valley. Keen fishermen will be able to catch pike, perch and carp, and there are several trout streams along the way.

Wine-tasting is an inevitable part of any cruise on the canal, as the route goes close to Meursault and Beaune, the wine capital of Burgundy, presenting a great chance to stock up. Other highlights include **Pont d'Ouche**, a tiny village with several moorings in a lovely setting, from where you may spot deer and wild boar in the early mornings. At **La Bussière**, visit the abbey (a short walk from the mooring) and look at the old canalside houses in the village. From **Vandenesse en Auxois**, visit the medieval hilltop village of Châteauneuf and further afield, the 15th-century Château du Commarin, with its collection of heraldic tapestries.

The Doubs

The Doubs is actually a river, although sections of it are heavily canalised, which rises in the Jura Mountains of eastern France, flows northeast along the French–Swiss border, then loops back into Switzerland and once more into France, emptying into the Saône. Some 144 locks have to be operated during the river's 236-km (148-mile) course, as it winds through the foothills of the Jura and past the vineyards of eastern Burgundy. Highlights include **Besançon**, the

Map on page 176

BELOW: Dijon rooftops.

historic capital of Franche-Comté; **Arc-et-Senans**, where an impressive 18th-century salt works has been designated a UNESCO World Heritage Site; **Dole**, the birthplace of Louis Pasteur, as well as **Dijon** and **Beaune**.

Canal Latéral à la Marne

A canal latéral is a waterway which closely follows the course of the river after which it is named – the Marne in this case. Shorter hotel barge cruises of just three nights operate along this canal, which, conveniently, passes through the heart of Champagne, with a chance to visit several of the big growers. Vineyards stretch as far as the eye can see, interspersed with the occasional château, and the countryside is green and gently rolling. **Epernay**, the capital of the champagne trade, is just south of the canal and is usually included as a tour, to see the Moët et Chandon estate and cellars, which were founded in 1743. **Reims**, to the north, is a large regional city with a magnificent cathedral, regarded as one of the most beautiful Gothic buildings in the world. Go for an evening in summer and the entire façade is floodlit, creating a magical atmosphere in the town centre.

A perennial favourite excursion, hot-air ballooning.

The Champagne region is very close to Paris, and a short cruise on this canal can easily be combined with a few days in the French capital *(see page 182)*.

Dordogne and Garonne

The waterways in western France are among the most famous in the world among wine-lovers, passing through countryside with mouth-watering appellations including Saint-Emilion, Bordeaux and Sauternes. Cruises in this beautiful part of France travel along the tidal Garonne, the Dordogne and the Canal Latéral à la Garonne, passing honey-coloured châteaux and hillside upon hillside of vines.

BELOW: shady mooring for lunch.

Bordeaux itself is underrated, with elegant 18th-century houses lining the river bank and colourful markets to explore. Other excursions include **Saint-Emilion**, an opportunity to buy seriously good red wines for laying down. **Pauillac**, a village on the broad, muddy Garonne Estuary, is another good place to buy, in the heart of the Médoc. Shakespeare fans, meanwhile, will be keen to see the village of **Nérac**; the château here was supposed to be the inspiration and setting for *Love's Labours Lost*.

Map on page 176

Canal Latéral à la Loire

This popular canal links four others to form the Canal du Centre, which joins the Saône in eastern France to the Seine in the north. The Canal Latéral à la Loire runs roughly parallel to the upper Loire River, itself not navigable, as it flows north towards Paris across gently rolling countryside of vineyards, châteaux and country villages. It is 197 km (123 miles) long and has 38 locks. Do not confuse this part of the Loire with the more famous (but mostly unavigable) Loire Valley to the southwest of Paris – it's a different part of the same, very long, river.

Highlights along include the spectacular **Briare Aqueduct**, which spans 663 metres (2,175 ft) and crosses over the Loire River, with breathtaking views of the countryside. The ornate and impressive aqueduct was built by Eiffel and almost resembles a grand Parisian boulevard for boats.

The village of Sancerre lies on the canal and is usually a port of call for wine-tasting and buying. The Parc Floral d'Apremont is another popular stop, at a pretty medieval village with glorious gardens. Also pay a visit to Nevers, a fortified city with its 14th-century gates still intact and a magnificent cathedral, and to Chavignol, where France's best goat's cheese is produced. ❏

BELOW: the Dordogne winds through some of the most picturesque scenery in France, such as here at Château Beynac.

THE PO

A cruise on the Po is a great way to see some of Italy's most breathtaking cities, sample the regional cuisine and explore the little-known delta region

Map on page 204

T he Po is Italy's longest river, and its large triangular flood plain is at the heart of the prosperous, populous and richly fertile regions of Lombardy and Veneto. Italians speak with reverence of the Po's fiery red sunsets, the tranquillity of its huge delta and the beauty of the historic cities dotted about the plain, yet the Po is not entirely benign – it is prone to flooding on an alarmingly regular basis after the late-autumn rains, inundating valuable farmland and swamping small agricultural towns.

Many of Italy's most magnificent historic cities are located in the Po Valley, including Bologna, Verona, Cremona, Mantua and Ferrara, as well as the urban sprawls of Milan and Turin further north and west. All have long, dramatic and romantic histories, filled with feuding dynasties, ferocious battles and the cultural and artistic legacies of the Renaissance era.

The prize for most people, though, is Venice, the base for Po river cruises, which typically spend a couple of days moored in the heart of the city before sailing inland as far as Cremona. An added pleasure of cruising from Venice is the chance to explore the islands of the lagoon, famous for their glass and lace-making.

PRECEDING PAGES:
Venetian backwaters.
LEFT: fishing nets in the lagoon.
BELOW: vessels are equipped with radar.

The course of the river

The River Po is 670 km (415 miles) long. It rises in the mountainous northwest of the country near the border with France, on the slopes of the pyramid-shaped Monte Viso at the southern end of the craggy Cottian Alps. For much of its course, the river flows in an easterly direction through the agricultural and industrial heartland of northern Italy, across lush, fertile plains – the Val Padana – Italy's only extensive flatlands, which encompass the northern provinces of Lombardy, Emilia-Romagna and Venetia. The Po's silty waters, fed by 141 tributaries, drain a catchment basin of 70,000 sq. km (27,000 sq. miles). The river empties into the Adriatic Sea to the south of Venice via hundreds of smaller channels, its vast, marshy delta a haven for wild birds and, at Commachio, eels, which are a prized delicacy.

The Po Valley is densely populated, the most important industrial and agricultural region of Italy. Grains (including rice), sugar beet, livestock and fruits are raised, but the intensive farming has, predictably, brought environmental problems. Around a quarter of the land along the river's banks has been denuded of natural vegetation to make way for sterile plantations of poplars harvested for cellulose. Worse, the river has been dammed for hydroelectric power and pumped full of agricultural and industrial chemicals. Until recently Milan was the largest city in the EU without proper

sewage treatment facilities, pumping effluent daily into two of the Po's tributaries.

Some of the river's natural meandering curves have been straightened, and around 23 million cubic metres (33 million cubic yds) of sand and gravel are illegally gouged out from its bed every year for the construction industry, further disturbing the natural ecosystem. Because of the danger of flooding, half the river's total length has been bolstered up by man-made earthen embankments called *argini*, which do not make for particularly scenic cruising; a voyage on the Po should be seen more as an opportunity for visiting wonderful historic cities than soaking up the scenery.

The evolution of river cruising

Etruscan migrants arrived in the Po Valley in the 12th century BC, forming settlements around Bologna. Further waves of settlers founded other cities along the Po; Milan's origins may date to Celtic tribes who arrived in the 7th century BC.

The Romans, who knew the river as Padus, ruled the region for many centuries; during this time centres of population grew along the coast and around the river delta, where settlers built dykes to protect their crops from the invading seawater. After the fall of the Roman Empire in the 5th century, many communities moved inland, away from the delta. Great family dynasties ruled the plains and cities of the north throughout the Middle Ages and the Renaissance, during which times the river was used as a main transport route to Venice, now grown fabulously rich on the profits of trade from the east.

The river's course has changed over the centuries. After the delta's natural lagoons began to fill with silt at the end of the 15th century, Venetian engineers, convinced that Po sediments would eventually clog up the inlets of their city, managed to divert the river towards the southeast. This intervention, known as the Taglio di Porto Viro (Porto Viro Cut), was completed in 1604 and was the trigger for the natural formation of the modern delta, which continues to evolve as it expands eastwards into the Adriatic.

The problem of bridges

The river has long functioned as an important transport route. Cremona is a busy industrial port, from which slag, cast iron and industrial products are ferried by barge to the coast. Boats with a very low draught are required, as the river is extremely shallow in places. River vessels also have to be very flat in shape, to get under the bridges; sometimes, if the river is high, they will tie up before a bridge and use the boat as a floating but stationary hotel, shuttling passengers backwards and forwards on excursions by coach. You will, however, see plenty of pleasure craft and self-drive barges along the river and around the Venice Lagoon.

In 2000, some 43,000 people were evacuated in Italy following flooding from heavy rains in the western and central plains of the River Po. A state of emergency was declared when the floods submerged Cremona and Mantua, two of the towns visited by passengers on River Po cruises, causing considerable damage.

The worst floods in recent memory were the torrents of November 1951, which inundated more than 450 sq. miles and displaced some 200,000 people.

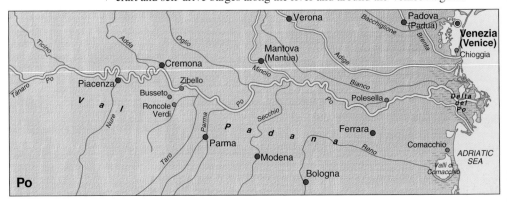

Po

Map on page 204

What to expect

Given the historical riches of the region, it may seem surprising that there aren't more river cruises on the Po. There are reasons for this, however: the Po is not an easy river for larger boats to navigate, as its depth changes constantly; capacity is therefore limited to smaller vessels. Another problem is that there are inadequate mooring facilities at many points along the river (river boats often tie up to trees at night, when sailing is forbidden). Most of the beautiful old towns that make this such a rich itinerary are located away from the river, so do not book a Po cruise with visions of prowling the lovely old cobbled streets after dark and wandering back to the boat at your leisure. Fortunately, most cruise lines offer a shuttle service into the nearby towns, so passengers are not forced to book shore excursions.

The majority of passengers stay on in Venice after a cruise, and some travel on to the Italian Lakes, south to Florence or Rome, or back to Bologna and Verona to revisit the sights in more depth. Several cruise operators can help with arrangements for passengers wishing to do this. Another option is to hire your own self-drive cruiser and potter around the Venetian Lagoon, a 51-km (32-mile) expanse created by the estuaries of three rivers, the Adige, Brenta and Po, and protected from the Adriatic Sea by a row of sandbars.

Most Po cruises operate a long summer season, from late March to early November. Spring is a wonderful time to visit, before the cities get too crowded and Venice becomes clogged with tourists and, more to the point, its canals begin to smell less than fragrant. October is also a good month, as the trees begin to turn, a gentle mist hangs over the fields at sunrise, the searing heat of the days lessens and the long lines of tour buses thin out.

BELOW: typical scenery near the Po Delta.

In February, it's Carnival in Venice, a glamorous and frenetic annual festivity that typically lasts for about two weeks. River cruise companies usually operate special Venice and lagoon cruises during this period.

There's not a huge choice of river cruise vessels on the Po, but those that do operate tend to be at the upmarket end of the spectrum. Peter Deilmann's 96-passenger *Casanova* is a smart, modern ship with a strong German following, while *Michelangelo*, owned by CroisiEurope, takes 160 passengers, many of them French. Cruises on the older and more basic *Venezia*, which takes 100 and is owned by Viking River Cruises, are sold to Americans and British passengers. For a really luxurious cruise, the sumptuous *River Cloud II* (owned by Sea Cloud Cruises) takes up to 88 passengers in some style, with large, wood-panelled cabins, candlelit dinners, a sauna and a teak sun deck with traditional wooden steamer chairs. All of these vessels operate similar itineraries, from Venice to Cremona, one way or round trip.

Scientists at the Mario Negri Institute for Pharmacological Research in Milan discovered in 2004 that nearly 4.5 kg (10 lbs) of cocaine residues flow into the Po every day.

Destination highlights

There are no kilometre markers along the Po. Cruising distances are short, and most of the time is spent sightseeing away from the boat.

● Venice

Beautiful, dreamy, romantic Venice, straddling 118 islands on the edge of the Venice Lagoon, has inspired poets, artists, musicians and lovers, and brings endless superlatives to the lips of visitors today. No matter that is it sinking at an alarming rate, floods frequently, smells of drains in the hot summer months and the canals are as clogged with traffic, albeit waterborne, as the streets of Rome. Venice is on every cruise passenger's must-see list. *For details on what to see in Venice, see pages 208–211.*

BELOW: gondolas lined up in the inner harbour of Venice.

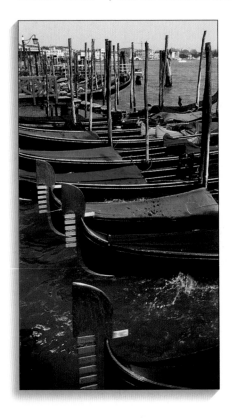

● Chioggia and Padua

The old university town of Padua is usually offered as a half-day trip from Chioggia, a busy fishing port at the southern end of the Venice Lagoon. Chioggia itself has a small, medieval centre, although most of it was destroyed in the late 14th century during a bloody and violent battle with Genoa (which the Genoese lost). The most notable buildings are the 11th-century **Cathedral**, the 14th-century **Church of San Martino** and the 14th-century **Church of San Domenico**, all of which house important paintings.

Padua lies inland on the River Bacchiglione, west of Venice. It's a lively university town (Galileo was professor of mathematics here in 1592) with some pretty squares and arcaded streets, although most people visit for the art treasures of the **Basilica del Santo**, a huge church started in 1232 for the sole purpose of housing the body of St Anthony, the patron of the town. The high altar is decorated with fabulous bronzes by Donatello, and outside in the piazza is a 15th-century statue of a Venetian count, *Gattamelata*, also by Donatello.

Art-lovers will also enjoy the magnificent **Capella degli Scrovegni** (open Tues–Sun 9am–6pm; visits restricted to 30 minutes in busy times), containing 39 frescos by Giotto. The chapel itself was commissioned in 1303 by Enrico Scrovegni as a burial place for his father. **Orto Botanica**, the oldest botanical garden in Europe, is near by.

Also visit the fabulously abundant **Mercato delle Erbe** (Market of the Herbs), a heaven for gastronomes. A huge range of regional products can be found on the colourful stalls, and there are many great photo opportunities which vary according to the season – cheese, cured hams, truffles, great piles of wild mushrooms, citrus fruits and watermelons.

Map on page 204

● Ferrara

On cruises from Venice, the boat enters the Po through its huge and complicated delta, the wide river cutting through vast expanses of uninhabited wetland. Trips to Ferrara are made from the mooring at the small town of Polesella. Both towns are prone to fog and damp in the winter, but on a sunny day Ferrara is a splendid sight, surrounded by massive ramparts with a large castle at its pleasingly peaceful centre, where there are more bicycles than cars.

Known in Renaissance times as the capital of the wealthy Este family, who flourished from the 13th to the 15th centuries, Ferrara is famous for its wide streets and lavish palaces. The family left conflicting legacies of betrayals, plots and murders, and of art and scholarship. The House of Este collapsed in 1598, after which the city fell into decline. It was badly damaged in World War II, but has since been painstakingly repaired using government funds.

The imposing **Castello Estense** (open Tues–Sun 9.30am–5.30pm) in the heart of town was once the home of the Este dynasties and is now used as government offices. Some rooms are open to the public, and you can also take ➤ *page 212*

BELOW: rice has been a major crop in the Po Valley since it was introduced in the 15th century.

PO DELTA

The peaceful marshlands and reed beds of the Po Delta are a place to escape the cities and contemplate the horizon, with only seabirds for company. You can travel for miles – walking or cycling along the high banks of the Valli, or quiet fishing lagoons – without seeing another person apart from the occasional city-dweller who has come here to fish. Take a boat trip through the reed beds and learn about the exiles and robbers who hid out here.

As well as salt pans, shimmering in the summer heat, there are acid-green rice paddies where the famed Arborio rice is cultivated. October and November is the season when the eels in the lagoon are caught in reed traps. Being on a major bird-migration route, the area is a protected nature reserve. Look out for oystercatchers, black-winged stilts, grey herons, snipe and marsh falcons, as well as more exotic species such as spoonbills and pink flamingos, all en route between Europe and Africa.

PORTS OF CALL: VENICE

More like a stage set than a city, Venice has captivated, enchanted and seduced visitors for centuries and has been endlessly portrayed by writers, painters and philosophers. Venice offers a kaleidoscope of images, from romantic gondolas to crumbling palaces on the Grand Canal. From a distance the city is a fantasy of sumptuous buildings that seem to float on the surface of the Adriatic. While most other great cities have been scarred with main roads and high-rise blocks, Venice remains unsullied by modernity, looking virtually as it did in its heyday, three centuries ago.

ORIENTATION

River cruise vessels moor along the Giudecca Canal, between the ocean cruise terminal and the entrance of the Grand Canal. You can walk from the mooring points to St Mark's Square in 20 minutes.

GETTING AROUND

The best way to get around far-flung parts of the city is by boat. It is worth buying a one-day, three-day or weekly travel pass which will allow you to travel on water buses (vaporetti), including those that go to the islands. The traghetto is a small gondola ferry that crosses the Grand Canal at certain points. Most of the time you will probably be walking, which is the most practical way to see the city centre.

BUSINESS HOURS

Shops are usually open from 9am–12.30pm or 1pm and again from 3pm or 3.30pm–7.30pm. Most of them, apart from those aimed mainly at tourists, are closed on Sunday. Churches tend to be open from 7.30am–noon, and then from 3.30pm or 4pm–6.30pm or 7pm. Office hours are normally 7.30am–12.30pm and 3.30pm–6.30pm. Museums are often closed on Monday.

TOP CITY SIGHTS

▲ **RIALTO BRIDGE**
This famous bridge crosses the Grand Canal at what used to be the busiest trading centre in the city – the Rialto market district. Two rows of shops lie within the solid, closed arches – the feature which gives it its unique appearance. This is a great place to pause and watch the river traffic, and admire the majestic sweep of palaces and warehouses swinging away to La Volta del Canal, the great elbow-like bend in the canal.

▼ **ST MARK'S BASILICA**
This is the centrepiece of St Mark's Square and is the most famous of the churches in Venice, a place the aesthete John Ruskin called "a treasure heap, a confusion of delight". Best visited in the morning, the Basilica (open Mon–Sat

EXCURSIONS

The Venetian islands make for enjoyable day trips. **BURANO** is like a mini Venice with its own canals and unique architecture. The island once produced the world's finest lace. The No. 12 ferry service to Burano leaves once an hour from Venice's

Fondamente Nuove. In 1291 Venice moved its glass-making centre to the island of **MURANO**, whose **Museo Vetrario di Murano** documents the history of the famed Venetian glass industry.

9.30am–5pm, Sun 2–4pm; daily from 7am for worshippers; leave all bags in the Ateno San Basso on Piazzetta dei Leoncini), which was modelled on Byzantine churches in Constantinople, remains a glorious confusion. Despite the sloping irregular floors, an eclectic mix of styles both inside and out, the five low domes of unequal proportions and some 500 non-matching columns, St Marks still manages to convey a sense of grandeur as well as jewel-like delicacy.

▶ SAN ROCCO

The area of San Polo that lies within the bend of the Grand Canal is home to the Scuola Grande di San Rocco, famous for its paintings by Jacopo Tintoretto (open 9am–5.30pm). His magnificent works adorn every surface: the images are larger than life, full of

chiaroscuro effects and floating, plunging figures in dramatic poses. One of the best-known is *The Glorification of St Roch* (pictured below).

▲ SCALA DE BOVOLO

The Palazzo Contarini has an outstanding external spiral staircase in its interior courtyard, the Scala Contarini del Bovolo (daily 10am–6pm), a Lombardesque work dating from 1499. *Bovolo* translates as "snailshell" in Venetian dialect.

▼ ST MARK'S MUSEUM

The museum (open same hours as the Basilica) houses some of St Mark's finest treasures. The star attraction is the world's only surviving ancient *quadriga* (four horses abreast), known as the Cavalli di San Marco (The Horses of St Mark).

These are the gilded bronze originals believed to have crowned Trajan's Arch in Rome, but later moved to Constantinople, where Doge Dandolo claimed them as spoils of war, bringing them back to Venice. Replicas adorn the façade in order to protect the originals from corrosion.

▶ GRAND CANAL

A trip along the Grand Canal, Venice's fabulous highway, is an unforgettable experience. Along certain sections of the canal the gondolas still function as *traghetti* (ferries) and, from the station to St Mark's Square, the banks are lined with ornate palaces and grand houses, mostly built between the 14th and 18th centuries. While some have been restored, others have a neglected air, awaiting their turn for renovation. Must-sees include the Ca'Grande, the Ca'Foscari, the Ca'd'Oro and the Guggenheim. As well as providing a cavalcade of pageantry, the canal offers a slice of local daily life, welcoming simpler craft such as gondolas and garbage barges.

▼ COFFEE BREAK

Before braving the hordes in the Basilica, retreat to one of the grand cafés on the

square. The most Venetian is Caffè Florian, under the arcades of the Procuratie Nuove, or the Caffè Quadri, in the Procuratie Vecchie. Prices are high, but worth it for the setting.

ST MARK'S LION *(picture on previous page)*
The winged lion represents St Mark, the patron saint of Venice, and adorns buildings, bridges and doorways. Whereas the seated lion represents the majesty of state, the walking lion symbolises sovereignty over its dominions. A golden winged lion of St Mark still adorns the city standard, and remains the symbol of the Veneto.

▶ THE ACCADEMIA

Housed in a former convent since 1807, the Accademia (open Mon 8.30am–2pm, Tues–Sun 8.30am–7pm) displays the most complete collection of 14th–18th century Venetian painting in existence. This outstanding gallery is arranged chronologically in 24 rooms, and includes works by Titian, Canaletto, Bellini and Carpaccio. Jacopo Tintoretto's dazzling St Mark's paintings, notably the haunting *Transport of the Body of St Mark*, are also here. Since the gallery is illuminated by natural light, choose a bright day to explore.

▶ DOGE'S PALACE

For nine centuries, the magnificent Doge's Palace (open daily Apr–Oct 9am–7pm; Nov–Mar 9am–5pm) was the seat of the Republic, serving as a council chamber, law court and prison, as well as the residence of most of Venice's doges. The architects of this massive structure, with peach-and-white patternings in its distinctive brick facade, achieved an incredible delicacy by balancing the bulk of the building above two floors of Istrian stone arcades.

CANNAREGIO CANAL

This faded, northerly district, once the most fashionable in Venice, was the site of the world's first Jewish ghetto. Before the advent of the causeway, the Canale di Cannaregio was the city's main entry point; it is fitting that the district remains a bridge between Venice and the mainland, between the historic and the modern.

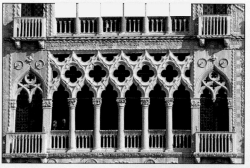

Franciscan centre is the largest and greatest of all the Venetian Gothic churches, founded in the 13th century and rebuilt in the 14th and 15th centuries. The adjoining cloisters house the state archives. The church's greatest treasure is Titian's *Assumption*, his masterpiece, hanging above the high altar. The great painter is buried here.

mythological beasts were originally picked out in gold. The restored and modernised interior now features the Galleria Franchetti, which houses numerous Renaissance bronzes and sculptures.

▶ THE FRARI
Officially known as Santa Maria Gloriosa dei Frari (open Mon–Sat 9am–6pm, Sun 1–6pm), this austere

▼ CA D'ORO
The 15th-century Ca D'Oro (open Mon 8.15am–2pm, Tues–Sun 8.15am–7.15pm) is the city's most magnificent Gothic palace. On the façade, the friezes of interlaced foliage and

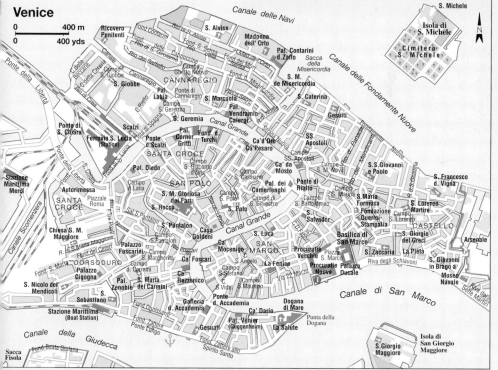

Venice

0 ___ 400 m
0 ___ 400 yds

TIP

The best way to explore the remarkable defensive walls that ring Ferrara for almost 9 km (6 miles) is to hire a bike. The walls were built between the late 15th and early 17th centuries, and are mostly constructed of red brick, punctuated by city gates, bastions and towers.

BELOW:
view of Mantua across the Mincio, a tributary of the Po.

a chilling tour of the dungeon, where various unfortunates met a grisly end.

The **Cathedral**, renovated in the 1990s, has a beautiful Romanesque-Gothic façade and an impressive museum (open daily 10am–noon, 3pm–5pm) with a collection of Renaissance pieces by Jacopo della Quercia and others. The real highlight, though, is **Palazzo Schifanoia** (open daily 9am–7pm), another spectacular residence of the Este clan, containing marvellous Renaissance frescos by Francesco del Cossa.

A maze of narrow lanes surrounds the main piazza, mainly pedestrianised, with plenty of small restaurants in which to try the local speciality, *cappelacci di zucca*, a small pasta filled with pumpkin.

● **Bologna**

Although some distance from the river (around 45 km/28 miles south), the city of Bologna is included on most itineraries, usually being offered as a full-day trip from the mooring at Polesella. The city is of great historical interest and has excellent shopping, particularly for food.

Located to the north of Florence, Bologna is the principal city of the Emilia-Romagna region and lies at the foot of the northern Apennine mountain range, some 55 metres (180 ft) above sea level. In 1088, the first university in Europe was established here; by the 12th century, many wealthy families were resident in the city. In the competitive spirit of the age, each family attempted to outdo their neighbours by building a large tower on their properties – needless to say, the bigger the tower, the more important the family. At one point there were 180 of these medieval skyscrapers looming over the city, fifteen of which still stand.

Highlights include the **Piazza Maggiore** and the neighbouring **Piazza Nettuno**, both in the heart of the city, surrounded by graceful Renaissance and medieval buildings. Both piazzas are great gathering-places, full of outdoor cafés and street artists, and buzzing with life. Between the two squares is a huge bronze of Neptune by the French sculptor Giambologna.

Bologna's beautiful **Basilica di San Petronio** is one of the largest churches in the world. Look out for the carvings depicting scenes from the New Testament by Jacopo della Quercia, and frescos by Giovanni da Modena. Within walking distance from here is the **Pinacoteca Nazionale** (open Tues–Sat 9am–2pm, Sun 9am–1pm), in the old university quarter, with works by Giotto, Raphael's *Ecstasy of St Cecilia* and some minor El Grecos and Titians.

● **Verona**

The Romanesque city that inspired Shakespeare's *Romeo and Juliet* (and *The Two Gentlemen of Verona)* is offered as a half- or full-day tour and, during the Opera Festival season of July and August, as an evening event.

Verona lies on the winding Adige River, which descends from the Italian Alps to run parallel with the Po before emptying into the Adriatic just to the north of the Po Delta, on a plain at the foot of the Lessini Mountains, approximately 105 km (65 miles) west of Venice. The compact medieval centre lends itself to slow wandering, its shopping streets lavishly paved with smooth marble, and some of the 600-year-old façades decorated with intricate frescos.

The city was the seat of the Scaligeri family, one of northern Italy's most important dynasties, throughout the medieval period. Their ruthless tactics earned them the nicknames of *Mastino* (Mastiff) and *Can Grande* (Big Dog), but

Map on page 204

Don't miss the amazing equestrian statue of Cangrande, lord of Verona between 1311 and 1329, which stands in the courtyard of Castelvecchio. It was originally on the pediment of his tomb until struck down by a storm.

BELOW: the Renaissance splendour of downtown Bologna.

A Vespa scooter is an icon of Italian design, and became the symbol of freedom for the post-war generation.

BELOW: an old postcard showing Verona's magnificent Arena.

the Scaligeris are also credited with bringing peace to a city which had long been the battleground for rival dynasties. Towards the end of their rule, the family built **Castelvecchio**, a solid-looking fortress, damaged in World War II but subsequently restored. The castle is used as a museum today (open Tues–Sun 8am–6.30pm), housing a permanent collection of Veronese art, frescos, jewellery and artefacts from the 14th to 18th century.

The **Roman Arena**, a stunning creation in rose-coloured marble on the Piazza Bra, dates to the 1st century AD and is the third-largest Roman amphitheatre in existence (open Mon 1.45–7.30pm, Tues–Sun 8.30am–7.30pm; on performance days sightseeing visits are restricted to 8.30am–3pm). If you get a chance to go to the opera, take it; the atmosphere inside is amazing and the evening really is a special occasion, with well-known Italian operas performed under the stars and fans flocking from all over the world.

An even bigger lure for most, though, is **Casa di Giulietta** (Juliet's House; open daily 7.30am–6.30pm) on Via Cappello, just off Via Mazzini, the main shopping street. The star-crossed lovers are fictional, although they are based on real families, the Cappello and the Montecchi. Whether these families were actually feuding, however, is questionable. You can see the famous balcony and recite the immortal lines, but the chances of photographing the old house without a coach party in front of it are slim.

Verona is well endowed with beautiful piazzas, with the **Piazza delle Erbe**, once the Roman Forum and surrounded by 14th-century palaces, probably the best of all. Through the Arco della Costa is the **Piazza Dei Signori**, where the Scaligeri's elaborate tombs are located. The city is also known for its regional wines, Bardolino, Recioto, Soave and Valpolicella, and has a good supply of

outdoor cafés where you can sit with a chilled Soave and a plate of antipasti, read the paper and watch the world go by.

● Mantua

The journey along the Po, with its swirling khaki waters and high, featureless banks, continues towards Mantua, again not on the Po itself but on the River Mincio, which has created three lakes that surround the city. The old centre perches serenely on a peninsula that juts out into the lakes. Sadly, the nearby petrochemical plants have polluted the water badly, but the setting is nonetheless picturesque. The city itself has ancient stone churches, small shops, lovely squares and pavement cafés. The three most impressive squares are the **Piazza dell'Erbe** with its marketplace, the medieval **Piazza del Broletto**, and the attractive, cobbled Piazza Sordello.

Mantua is the home town of the poet Virgil and was the seat of the powerful Gonzagas dynasty in the 14th century, when this was a flourishing centre for the arts. The 500-room **Palazzo Ducale** compound (open Tues–Sun 8.45am–7.15pm; Mon 9am–1pm) is testament to the family's great wealth, with a huge collection of Renaissance art and frescos. The Palazzo's most important fresco cycle is the *Camera degli Sposi*, in which Andrea Mantegna's frescos depict the court life of Ludovico Gonzaga in intricate detail, right down to his favourite dog and the court dwarf.

The **Palazzo Te** (open Tues–Sun 9am–6.30pm, Mon 1–6.30pm), built by Federigo Gonzaga for his mistress, stands outside the walled part of the city and, with its sweeping gardens, is located opposite the cathedral; this elegant country palace served as an inspiration for Versailles, Nymphenburg and Schönbrunn.

Map on page 204

The Ducal Palace at Mantua once held the nine immense paintings executed by Andrea Mantegna between 1484 and 1492, depicting The Triumphs of Caesar. *The canvases were sold by the Gonzagas to Charles I, and they are now displayed at Hampton Court Palace in London.*

LEFT: Mantua's Piazza Erbe and its clock tower.
BELOW: Virgil, a native of Mantua.

TIP

Don't leave Cremona without trying the city's two culinary specialities: the nougat made of honey and almonds called *torrone*, and the *mostarda di Cremona*, comprised of candied fruits such as apricots, cherries and melons in a sweet mustard sauce.

BELOW: Cremona is the world's violin capital.

● Cremona

Towards Cremona, the banks of the Po are lined with tall poplars and lush, green fields stretching into the distance, many of them used for growing melons. The landscape is punctuated by the occasional cluster of stone farm buildings, reflecting the local tradition of having all farm buildings, including the farmworkers' houses, in a large group. Cremona, capital of the eponymous province, is close to but not directly on the Po. Two-week cruises turn around near the town and head back for Venice, while one-week cruises either start or finish here.

Cremona is indisputably the world's violin capital, its fame dating back to the period between the 16th and 18th centuries, when great names like Nicolò and Hieronymus Amati, Giuseppe Guarneri and, most famous of all, Antonio Stradivari, who was born here in 1644, set out to create the perfect stringed instrument. The streets are lined with the shops of makers of violins and all manner of similar instruments, competing fiercely with Bologna, which has a violin-making industry of its own.

Dedications to Stradivarius are everywhere: the **Museo Stradivariano** (Stradivarian Museum; open Tues–Sat 9am–6pm, Sun 10am–6pm) contains objects from his workshop; there's a statue to him on the Piazza Stradivari; and the Tomb of Stradivari is found in the Piazza Roma. The International Violinmakers School is also located in Cremona, at the Palazzo Raimondi.

The **Cathedral** (open daily 7am–noon, 3–7pm) is an interesting example of Lombard-Roman architecture, started in 1107, seriously damaged by an earthquake of 1117 and consecrated in 1190. The interior contains a vast cycle of 15th-century frescos in the central nave.

The **Piazza del Commune** is the heart of the city, a beautiful square surrounded by palaces and medieval monuments including the **Torrazzo** (open Tues–Sun 10.30am–noon, 3pm–6pm), a mighty bell-tower some 111 metres (364 ft) high, the tallest of its kind in Europe, with sweeping views over the terracotta rooftops. Visit the violin workshop on the first floor and then climb up 487 steps to admire the astrological clock devised by the Diviziolis in 1583.

The finest collection of old stringed instruments can be seen at the **Collezione del Palazzo Comunale**; the oldest violin, by Andrea Amati, dates back to 1566. These priceless instruments are played regularly by a local maestro to keep them in good physical condition, and most visits here or to the nearby **Museo Stradivariano** include a short performance (both open Tues–Sat 9am–6pm, Sun 9am–7pm).

● Parma

Set in wooded, gently hilly countryside south of the Po on the Torrente Parma tributary, Parma is famed for its much-imitated hams and cheeses. The landscape around the town is studded with impressive-looking castles to the south.

Parma itself deserves recognition for more than gastronomy; Verdi and Toscanini composed many great works here, and the **Cathedral** (open daily 9am–12.30pm, 3–7pm) is famous for Correggio's *Assumption of the Virgin* in the cupola, which took

Map on page 204

six years to paint. Charles Dickens famously described Correggio's work in the cathedral as "a fricassee of frogs", although Ruskin claimed that there were only two reasons for getting out of bed in the morning: Mozart's music and Correggio's use of light.

The other important sight is the **Galleria Nazionale** (open Tues–Sun 8.30am–2pm) in the Palazzo della Pilotta, the 17th-century home of the wealthy Farnese family. The gallery contains work by Correggio, Francesco Parmigianino, Fra Angelico, Leonardo, Canaletto and Van Dyck.

The cobbled lanes around the old centre are lined with delicatessens selling the famous Parma ham and Parmesan cheese. There's also a colourful produce market (open daily) in Piazza Ghiaia, south of Palazzo della Pilotta. Genuine parmesan cheese comes from two towns, Parma and Reggio Emilia, which between them have an official logo that should be embossed on the side of the cheese. The unique qualities of both the cheese and Parma ham are attributed to the humid microclimate of the immediate area around Parma. The salty chunks of meat are actually taken to cure in Zibello, on the banks of the River Po.

Stylish handbags and other leather goods don't usually come cheap in Italy, but quality is high.

● Roncole Verdi and Busseto

Northwest of Parma lies the flat river plain known locally as the *bassa* (low), and Verdi country, centred around two small, sleepy villages, Roncole Verdi and Busseto. Both burst into life during the annual Verdi Festival (also held partly in Parma) in the first two weeks of June, when pilgrims flock to the area to hear great romantic operas like *La Traviata* and *Il Trovatore*.

Verdi was born in 1813 in the little town of Roncole, which has since changed its name in his honour to Roncole Verdi; his birthplace, **Casa Natale di Giuseppe Verdi**, is the main attraction (open Mar–Oct Tues–Sun 9.30am–12.30pm, 2.30–6.30pm; Nov–Feb Sat & Sun with reservation 9.30am–12.30pm, 2–4.30pm; buy a pass for all the Verdi sights, including the birthplace and the Verdi Theatre).

BELOW: the region is well known for its cheeses.

His professional career began when Antonio Barezzi, a wealthy merchant, asked him to move to Busseto, a couple of kilometres away, and become a music teacher for his daughter, Margherita. Barezzi became not only Verdi's patron, but also his father-in-law when Verdi married Margherita in 1836.

A monument to Verdi overlooks Busseto's main square, which is also the epicentre of the festival. There's a small museum to the famous son and a theatre seating 300, recently restored, in the Rocca, a fortress that was once the castle of the Pallavicino family. The municipality bought the Rocca in 1856, and the theatre, designed by the architect Pier Luigi Montecchini, was built between 1856 and 1868.

You'll see monuments to Verdi everywhere. A large staircase in the theatre is adorned with a bust by Giovanni Duprè, while the ceiling medallions, representing Comedy, Tragedy, Melodrama and Romantic Drama were painted by Isacco Gioacchino Levi in 1865. Two of Verdi's works, *Ballo in Maschera* and *Rigoletto*, had their premieres here (guided tours every half hour Mar–Oct 9.30am–12pm and 3–6pm. From Nov–Feb 9.30am–12pm and 2.30–4.30pm). ❑

PORTUGAL: DOURO & GUADIANA

Map on page 222

The beautiful scenery of the Douro Valley makes it a favourite river cruise destination. In the south, Guadiana cruises journey from the bright lights of the Algarve to the quiet rural hinterland

The north of Portugal is a wonderfully picturesque corner of Europe, and a cruise on the Douro is a perfect way to explore it. A far lesser-known Portuguese river for cruise holidays is the Guadiana in the south, flowing from central Spain to the Algarve coast, cutting its way through the hills of the arid, little-explored region which lies behind the verdant golf courses and white-washed villas of the coastal strip. Either cruise can be combined with a few days in the enjoyable city of Lisbon.

THE DOURO

The Douro literally translates as "river of gold", from the times of the Phoenicians and the Romans, who mined gold in the Baixo Douro region and used the river to transport the ore to the coast. Some poetically say that the name also derives from the golden sheen of the river as it reflects the sunlight and the arid, sand-coloured hills through which it flows.

The Iberian Peninsula's third-longest river (after the Tagus and Ebro) cuts its way through some of the harshest and most beautiful scenery anywhere on the continent, from the sun-baked badlands of the northern Spanish *meseta* to the terraced hillsides of Portugal's port-wine-growing district. These shale uplands were once arid and inhospitable, but 3,000 years of cultivation have tamed the slopes, now covered by over 40,000 hectares (98,800 acres) of vineyards, and given rise to hundreds of prosperous *quintas*, or wine-growing estates.

The course of the river

The Douro rises in the high hills of Spain's Soria Province to the northeast of Madrid (the river is called the Duero by the Spanish). It then flows west across the heart of Old Castile before curving southwest and marking the border between Spain and Portugal for approximately 98 km (60 miles). At Barca d'Alva it turns westwards towards the Atlantic coast at Porto, meandering through some enchanting countryside en route – sleepy villages, castles and vineyards that have remained largely unchanged for hundreds of years. The total length is 897 km (561 miles), most of which is in Spain. Much of the upper Douro or Duero, however, is unnavigable because of rapids, large amounts of silt and deep gorges. Nine dams have been built along its length, and the river has been harnessed by both countries for its hydroelectric power.

The evolution of river cruising

Evidence of grape pips and vines dating back to the Bronze Age have been found in the Douro region of Portugal. Prosperity first came in Roman times, when

PRECEDING PAGES: the banks of the Douro in Porto. **LEFT:** the splendid Nossa Senhora dos Remédios near Lamego. **BELOW:** *rabelo* wine boats on the Douro *c.*1877.

The Douro is regarded as the world's most difficult major wine-growing region, with harsh, schist soil that contains practically no nutrients, and slopes with an incline of up to 70 percent. The rocky surface has to be smashed down to a depth of 1 metre (3 feet) in order to plant the vines, which send roots down 20 metres (65 ft) through the schist in search of water. The best grapes are grown at the lower elevations; a saying goes that the best port comes from the grapes that can hear the river flowing.

grape cultivation was carried out on a large scale. British merchants settled in the town of Porto in the late 17th century and transformed the region's small wine-export trade, tripling production to 19,000 barrels by 1749. Port wine was actually invented by accident; the rather harsh local wines had to be fortified with spirits to preserve them for long sea voyages, and when the growers tried adding brandy, they discovered that the wine had a completely new and very pleasing taste.

Demand for Douro Valley wines rocketed as a result, and river traffic hit an all-time high in the early 18th century, as flat-bottomed *rabelo* boats, with long rudders and voluminous sails, transported thousands of barrels from the country *quintas* to Vila Nova de Gaia (directly across the river from Porto), where it was aged in cellars. The region was officially demarcated in 1761 by Sebastião José de Carvalho, Prime Minister of Portugal and Marquis of Pombal. This was the world's first *appellation contrôlée*. In the late 19th century, construction of a railway into the hinterland from Porto marked the beginning of the end for the traditional *rabelos* – the last boats went out of service in 1964, and these days most wines are unromantically transported from the growers to the coast by lorry.

World Heritage Site

A few *rabelo* boats remain as tourist attractions – each of the port-wine cellars maintains a couple – and a new kind of craft navigates the swirling waters of the Douro: river cruise vessels. Tourism has grown steadily, and in 2001, the whole of the Douro region was designated a World Heritage Site by UNESCO.

The Douro is navigable for most of its Portuguese course, although there are rapids and occasional flooding in the lower reaches. Five dams and sets of locks have been constructed over the last few decades, allowing some boats to sail much further inland, across the Spanish border. But only vessels with a very shallow draft can enter the river at its mouth, due to sandbars; the river cruisers operating through the wine country do not generally venture into the open sea.

What to expect

Only a handful of river cruisers operate on the Douro, usually offering seven-night itineraries starting and finishing in Porto. Typical stops include Peso da Régua, Pinhão, Vega de Terrón (a jumping-off point for Salamanca in Spain) and Ferradosa (for São João). Apart from the joy of cruising the river as it carves its way through the steep hills, most of the excursions are a coach journey away from the various stops. Each itinerary crosses several dams, including the Crestuma-Lever and the Pachino. Cruises can be combined with a stay in Lisbon and Coimbra, Portugal's former medieval capital, using local trains for transport.

Some river cruise companies will charter specific sailings, while others charter

Douro

Embalse de Ricobayo

Lima

Porto (Oporto)

Vila Nova de Gaia

Crestuma

Crestuma Lever Dam

ATLANTIC OCEAN

Convento de Alpendorada

Carrapetelo Lock

Casa de Mateus

Vila Real

Peso da Régua

Pinhão

Lamego

Douro

São João da Pesqueira

Barca d'Alva

Embalse de Almendra

Vega de Terrón

Huebra

Spain

Tormes

Salamanca

Douro Valley

Corgo

Tâmega

Sousa

Paiva

Tavora

Cão

Tua

Sabor

Duero

Douro

Ria de Aveiro

Portugal

a vessel for the whole season; others still will book you aboard a vessel that is shared by passengers of many other nationalities.

Most of the vessels are modern; the *Vasco da Gama* was built in 2002, the 71-cabin *Fernão de Magalhães* in 2003 and the *Infante D. Henrique* in 2004. These three are owned by French cruise company CroisiEurope, but carry international passengers. There is no official star rating but the company grades these vessels four-star. The *Douro Prince* and the luxurious new *Douro Queen*, which has balcony cabins, hot tubs on deck and a swimming pool, are chartered by American tour operator Uniworld but are also sold in Europe. Local company Douro Azul owns several boats, some of which are used for day trips and two of which, the *Invicta* and *Altodouro*, are used for one-week cruises.

All of these river cruise vessels are comfortable, with twin or double cabins, plenty of deck space and a variety of other facilities from a small gym to a pool on deck. Food on board is typically Portuguese or international, and evening entertainment is low-key, with local entertainers being brought on board on some nights. Some cruises include a couple of evenings ashore.

Destination highlights

● **Porto**

Porto, Portugal's second-largest city and the heart of the port-wine trade, clings to the great gorge of the River Douro, just before the river flows into the Atlantic. The gorge is spanned by several graceful bridges, leading to Vila Nova de Gaia on the opposite bank, where all the great port lodges are located, including Cockburns and Sandeman – their English names reminders of the fact that British merchants controlled the industry from its inception.   ➤ *page 226*

Maps on pages 222, 225

BELOW: traditional *rabelo* boat on the Douro at Porto.

PORTS OF CALL: PORTO

Once a river community, Porto is now a great commercial city, best known for its striking bridges, and the hub of the lucrative port wine trade. The 'granite city' is majestically sited on rocky cliffs overlooking the River Douro, which snakes through its terraced vineyards. The Douro valley is deep and narrow, the banks are high and steep and the old town small, with a confusing maze of streets at its heart. The ancient Ribeira water front district, the historic heart of Porto, was classified a UNESCO World Heritage Site in 1996.

ORIENTATION

Most river cruise vessels moor at the Cais de Gaia on the Vila Nova de Gaia side of the Douro. This is a pleasant and convenient spot, with bars and cafés aplenty, and lies within easy reach of the medieval town.

GETTING AROUND

Porto is well serviced by a network of buses and trams. A new light subway system, Porto Metro, was opened in 2002, and additional lines are under construction. The congested city centre is, however, best navigated on foot – although the hilly location can make it quite tiring.

BUSINESS HOURS

Most shops in the city are open Mon–Fri 9am–1pm, and 3–7pm, Sat 9am–1pm. Almost all stay closed on Sundays, although some supermarkets are open Sunday and all day during the week.

TOP CITY SIGHTS

▲ PONTE DOM LUIS I (THE IRON BRIDGE)
The impressive steel railway bridge looms over the vividly painted houses of the Ribeira district and spans the river to the south bank. Built in 1886, the bridge has two decks, the upper of which will carry the new metro line, and leads directly to port cellars in Vila Nova de Gaia *(see page 225)*.

▶ SÉ (CATHEDRAL)
Crowning the highest point of the granite rock on which much of the old town is constructed is the Cathedral (open 9am–12.30pm, 2.30–6pm). It was built as a defensive fortification in the 12th century, and despite extensive alterations it has retained its fortress-like appearance. The highlight here is a fine baroque Altar of the Sacrament made

from 800kg (1,760lbs) of embossed silver. The small Gothic cloister is decorated with *azulejos* (tiles) depicting the events from the Song of Solomon.

▶ TORRE DOS CLÉRIGOS
The 18th-century Torre dos Clérigos (open daily) is the tallest granite tower in Portugal and has become the emblem of Porto. This was designed, along with its church, by Nicolau Nasoni. Unless you really have no

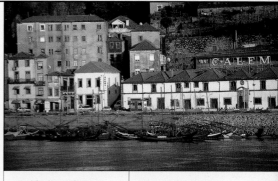

head for heights it is worth climbing the endless spiral staircase with 225 or so steps for the dazzling view over the city, the river Douro and its estuary.

SANTO ILDEFONSO CHURCH

Built in the 18th century, the walls of the church are decorated with *azulejos* by Jorge Colaço depicting scenes from the life of St Ildefonso and allegories from the Eucharist.

▶ STOCK EXCHANGE

On the site of a convent, which burnt down in 1832, is the Stock Exchange (open daily 9am–5.30pm)

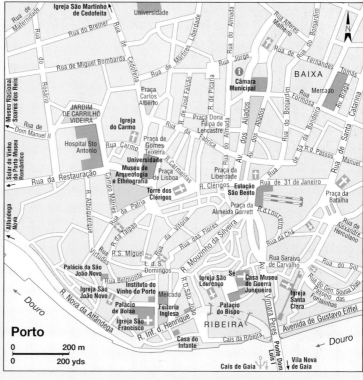

noted for its opulent neo-Moorish reception hall. *(detail pictured below).*

▲ VILA NOVA DE GAIA WINE LODGES

Across the Ponte Dom Luis I, is an industrial zone with ceramic, glass, soap and other factories. But above all, Gaia is the true seat of the port wine industry, where most warehouses or lodges are to be found. There are about 80 port wine lodges: many of the larger ones welcome weekday visitors to tour the installations and taste their wines. Most prominent is **Sandeman** (open Mon–Fri 9am–1pm, 2–5pm), whose distinctive silhouette rises on the skyline.

Porto

0 ———— 200 m
0 ———— 200 yds

*Fado (literally, fate)
is an anguished and
atmospheric
Portuguese style of
singing that always
tells a tragic story.
While its spiritual
heart is Lisbon, the
capital, Porto has its
share of Fado clubs.
Be warned, though,
that the
performances go on
for several hours and
visitors are expected
to listen attentively.*

Inhabited since Roman times, Porto is one of Portugal's loveliest cities, its rows of old gabled houses clustered on the steep hillsides that slope down to the rocky shore. Cruise boats moor up in the heart of the city on the Vila Nova side, within easy reach on foot of the medieval town, the Ribeira district. *For details on what to see in Porto, see pages 224–225.*

● **Peso da Régua**

From Porto the Douro snakes eastwards to Peso da Régua past wooded valleys, fields of almond trees and quiet villages. Shortly after leaving Porto, the boat passes through the floodgates of the Crestuma Lever Dam, one of several built over the last few decades to tame the river, which was previously difficult to navigate. Some cruises stop for the evening at **Bitetos**, with an excursion to the nearby 11th-century **Convento de Alpendorada**, which overlooks the river. The monastery hosts medieval-style banquets and wine-tastings, and provides an atmospheric setting for dinner. The **Carrapetelo Lock**, one of the largest in the world, is also a highlight of this stretch of the river.

The port region proper beings at **Peso da Régua**. At this point, the river suddenly enters a region of steep hills covered with green vineyards, and the occasional lavish manor house set back from the river. Giant lettering on the hillsides denotes each grower's name. Peso da Régua is the home of the Port Wine Institute, and almost all its inhabitants have some connection with the portwine trade; in the past, this was the starting point for the *rabelo* boats, laden with barrels, on their long and treacherous journey to Vila Nova de Gaia on the coast.

For river cruise passengers it's now a departure point for coach tours to Vila Real, 25 km (15 miles) to the north.

BELOW: classic Portuguese fare.

PORTUGUESE CUISINE

Food in Portugal conjures up images of empire, with influences from its erstwhile colonies Brazil, Angola, Mozambique, Goa and Macau much to the fore. The voyages of Vasco da Gama brought back cinnamon and curry powder, and both are still important flavourings in Portuguese cuisine. Common ingredients include fresh fish and seafood, ham, chicken, and fresh vegetables that are typically grown on small, organic farms. It is the quality of the produce that delights many visitors, whether the nutty, earthy potatoes or the juicy tomatoes that taste like an explosion of flavour to those accustomed to bland supermarket varieties. Pork is the dominant meat, and the wonderful charcuterie features in many soups and stews.

Some local specialities in Porto include tripe of veal with beans. The story goes that altruistic locals donated all their meat to the ships departing to conquer the New World, leaving only the tripe for their own consumption. More palatable are the local salt cod *(bacalhau)*, succulent roast lamb and the famous *caldo verde* – a soup of potatoes, cabbage and olive oil. Between spring and early autumn, sardines can be found as street food, cooked on small terracotta braziers. Sweet, egg-based puddings are also popular and go well with a glass of port.

Map on page 222

● Vila Real (Casa de Mateus)

The magnificent 18th-century Baroque house and gardens of **Casa de Mateus** (open daily June–Sept 9am–7.30pm; Mar–May & Oct 9am–1pm, 2–6pm; Nov–Feb 10am–1pm, 2–5pm) lies 3 km (2 miles) outside the busy town of Vila Real. It belonged to the counts of Vila Real, and was the birthplace of the navigator Diego Cão, who discovered the mouth of the Congo River in Central Africa. The estate has beautifully cool, shady formal gardens and a fantastic *allée* of cedar trees. The area is famous for its Mateus Rosé wine, and an image of the house appears on all Mateus Rosé bottles. Vila Real itself has little of interest, although it is the largest town in the region, and is on the edge of a dramatic gorge carved by the River Corgo (a tributary of the Douro).

● Lamego

Lamego, 12 km (7½ miles) south of the river and usually offered as a half-day tour from Peso da Régua on the return journey to Porto, is an important pilgrimage site, overlooked by the the the **Sanctuary Church of Nossa Senhora dos Remédios (Our Lady of the Remedies)**. A superb Baroque-style staircase *(pictured on page 220)* of some 600 steps reaches the church, by which point most visitors are in need of a blessing from the saint. The view from the top, though, is worth it – it is absolutely stunning. In September, thousands of pilgrims flock to the town.

Lamego was once the trading post of the Moors who journeyed across from Spain. They left their legacy in the 12th-century **castle** with an unusual vaulted cistern. The town's **museum** (open Tues–Sun 10am–12.30pm and 2–5pm) houses an impressive collection of furniture, paintings, 16th-century Flemish tapestries, sculpture and jewellery from the Bishop's Palace within which it is situated.

BELOW: terraced hillsides on the Douro near Pinhão.

TIP

The best time to visit the Douro Valley is during the *vindima*, in late September and early October, when the grapes are being collected.

● Pinhão

This small, rustic (and rather run-down) Douro town is best known for its picturesque setting at the confluence of the Corgo and Douro rivers and its proximity to the *quintas*, the country seats of the big names in port production. The railway station has some beautiful *azulejos* (glazed tiles) on the walls, depicting local scenes and culture. Cruise boats stop here to run excursions to the wine-growing estates, where visitors learn about grape crushing, fermentation and blending. Even if you don't drink port, it is worth the visit simply to admire the beauty of the estates, some of them with lavish gardens on the river banks.

● São João da Pesqueira

São João, usually offered as an excursion from Ferradosa or Pinhão, is a sprawling wine-growing village famed for its town hall, which has stunning tiled murals depicting port-wine-making scenes. It is surrounded by port *quintas* on a plateau that overlooks the valleys and vineyards of the Douro in a delightful, picture-postcard setting. As if the scenery could get any more breathtaking, a further excursion follows a twisting mountain road to **São Salvador de Mundo**, a village with nine chapels and sweeping views over the countryside.

● Barca d'Alva

There are two more dams en route to Barca d'Alva, once the upper navigation limit on the Douro. The scenery is softer here, with cherry, almond and olive groves lining the banks, although vines still cling to the steep hillsides in the background. The town itself, usually just a stopping-off place for the night, is only a few hundred yards from the Spanish border.

BELOW: *azulejos* tiles on the Carmo Church in Porto.

● **Vega de Terrón (for Salamanca)**
Across the Spanish border, river boats moor up for the day at Vega de Terrón while their passengers visit Salamanca, a university town since the 13th century. The **Plaza Mayor**, a huge, elegant square surrounded by gracious sandstone buildings, is one of the most impressive and beautiful in Europe. The twin cathedrals, **Catedral Nueva** (16th-century Gothic) and **Catedral Vieja** (12th-century Romanesque), the latter with its spectacular silver Byzantine dome, are also well worth seeing. Paella lunch is usually a feature of the day, although paella is not from this region at all (its origins are in Valencia, hundreds of miles away on the Mediterranean coast).

Maps
on pages
222, 230

THE GUADIANA

Almost within a stone's throw of the verdant golf courses and whitewashed villas of the Algarve, the stretch of coast which extends from Lagos in the far south-western corner of Portugal to Vila Real de Santo António on the Spanish border, lies an arid, little-explored hinterland. Here, life on the stony soil under the punishing sun is tough, the scrub-covered hills used for some cultivation of pines, fruit and olives, and for hunting reserves. Tiny hilltop towns bear many signs of the Moorish occupation, which lasted from AD 711 until the 12th century. The Guadiana cuts its way through these hills, a narrow ribbon of green snaking across a dessicated landscape, with tiny, fortified towns perched on the hilltops and banks.

The Algarve is famous for its beaches; Praia da Rocha, near Portimão, is one of the best.

The course of the river

The 778-km (486-mile) Guadiana rises near Albacete in Spain, flowing west through the sparsely populated Extremadura region to the Portuguese border at

BELOW:
river cruises on the Guadiana began in 2005.

The Guadiana Bridge linking Portugal and Spain opened in 1991. Before this, there was only the ferry service – the nearest road crossing the border was 100 km (60 miles) north.

BELOW: inland from the touristy Algarve, older ways of life quickly resurface.

Badajoz, where it turns southwest. The river forms the border between Portugal and Spain before curving off through the dry hills of the Alentejo region of Portugal, then rejoining the border for the final stretch south to the Atlantic at Vila Real de Santo António. Only a small section of the river, near the Algarve coast, is navigable, and a staggering 1,824 dams have been built upstream.

The evolution of river cruising

The region now known as the Algarve was settled by the Phoenicians, Carthaginians and Romans; the Guadiana played an important role as far back as 1000 BC, when the town of Mertola was founded as an inland port. Waves of Goths and Vandals followed until the region was invaded by Moors from North Africa in AD 711. The Moors stayed for over 500 years before the Christian reconquest, sailing up the Guadiana, building fortresses along its banks and mosques in the hilltop villages. Many place names in the region derive from Arabic, including "Algarve", originally named "Al-Gharb", or "Country of the West".

The Moors were driven out in the 13th century, as Catholic Portuguese rulers began to strengthen their hold on the region. Copper was mined in the Alentejo, and the Guadiana was used to transport the ore to the coast. The great maritime expeditions of the 15th century led to the discovery of the sea route to the riches of the East. Portugal quickly became rich, but it didn't last. By the 17th century maritime supremacy was a distant memory, and declining commodity prices (for pepper and other spices in particular), together with increased competition from the Dutch and British, brought a steady decline. In 1755 a devastating earthquake destroyed much of Lisbon and most of the towns and villages along the Algarve coast. The development of the canned fishing

industry at the end of the 19th century was a boost to this southern region, but it wasn't until the growth of tourism through the 1970s and 1980s, and EU membership in 1986, that the Algarve began to prosper once more.

What to expect

River tourism on the Guadiana is a recent innovation, having started only in 2005 with a single hotel boat. Cruising this relatively unknown river gives a fascinating insight into a region that's so close to the developed coast, yet seems so remote. The company responsible is Douro Azul, which is already well established in the north. A new boat built specially for the Algarve voyage, the 100-passenger *Algarve Cruiser*, is based in Portimão where the cruise begins, visiting Vilamoura and Faro before heading inland along the river.

Destination highlights

Vilamoura is a modern development with a large marina and a wide, sandy beach. At Faro, excursions are run into the old city centre. Continuing east along the Gulf of Cádiz, the boat reaches the frontier town of Vila Real de Santo António where it turns inland along the river.

One of the reasons the Algarve has never really attracted cruising of either the ocean or river variety is the lack of docking facilities, and this is still apparent. In Vilamoura, the boat docks at a makeshift quay by the beach outside the main marina; it cannot even get into Faro because of sandbars at the harbour mouth. Further inland, along the river, conditions are even more primitive, with the large hotel boat often struggling to tie up at tiny Alcoutim. But there is a certain rustic charm about this, and the absence of other large boats is a distinct advantage.

Map on page 230

As well as place names like Algarve and Albufeira, the Arab occupation of the region brought other legacies. Irrigation was introduced by Yemenites, as well as rice cultivation, orange trees, almond, olive, carob and fig trees. Cultivation of all of these remains an important part of the local economy today.

BELOW:
the view across Mertola to Spain.

The architecture of the Algarve region bears marks from its Arabic heritage; one curiosity is the unique design of local chimney pots.

BELOW: the fortress town of Castro Marim, overlooking the Guadiana.

● Vila Real de Santo António

This sprawling town marks the end of the Algarve, where the Guadiana River creates a natural border with Spain. There's a slightly unreal feel about the place, surrounded by salt marshes, out of which rise the occasional ruined castle. Scrubby hills are visible in the distance behind the whitewashed buildings, and the Spanish fishing town of Ayamonte lies across the wide mouth of the river, guarded by sandbars and busy in the mornings with the thud-thud of the engines of fishing boats returning with the night's catch.

Vila Real was completely destroyed in the great earthquake of 1755, and there is little of historic interest today. The town has been in decline somewhat since the opening of a road bridge across the Guadiana in 1991, linking Portugal with Spain and diminishing the role of Vila Real as a border post.

Most visitors head for the resort of **Monte Gordo**, where a wide beach is fringed by pine trees. Alternatively, ferries operate across the river mouth to Ayamonte, a somewhat scruffy place with some lively bars and restaurants. Vila Real is also a base from which to make the one-and-a-half-hour drive to **Seville**, capital of Andalucia, offered as a day trip on this itinerary.

● Alcoutim

The compact 14th-century town of Alcoutim marks the point where the river ceases to be tidal, and was once an important strategic centre. River traffic in the Middle Ages carrying copper from the nearby mines would moor here and wait for the tide to be favourable before continuing up or downstream. A castle was built on the Portuguese side to defend the ships, and an equally stern-looking fortress was soon erected on the Spanish side. The town itself is a tourist centre

today, its streets lined with cafés and restaurants, and there are some fine beaches along the river. The impressive medieval church is one of the best examples of a Renaissance church in southern Portugal.

The Alentejo region proper begins inland from here, beyond the point at which the Guadiana River is currently navigable for bigger boats. It's an expanse of dry, sun-baked hills, almost desert-like in places thanks to the poor soil and underlying slate. Pines, olive and almond trees struggle to survive, and the main income is from hunting the wild boar, quail, hare and partridge that populate the hills. The tiny villages bear signs of the Moorish occupation from the 8th to the 15th centuries; often, a church has been built on the site of a mosque.

● Mertola

Mertola, perched high on a spur of the Guadiana, was founded by the Phoenicians 3,000 years ago as an inland port, and used by the Romans and Moors in subsequent centuries. There are examples of Moorish architecture everywhere, not least in the solid-looking fortifications which encircle the village and the castle which overlooks it. The 12th-century **Church of Santa Maria** is built on a former mosque, with the original doors and some of the pillars intact. The fortress, which is ruined, has wonderful views over the red-tiled rooftops and the confluence of the Guadiana and Oeiras rivers beyond. There's also a small **Islamic Museum**, with one of Portugal's best collections of Moorish ceramics (castle and museum open Wed–Sun July–Sept 10am–1pm, 3–7pm; Oct–June 9am–12.30pm, 2–5.30pm).

Mertola is visited as a coach excursion from Alcoutim. After the visit, the *Algarve Cruiser* returns to the coast, spending a night in Vila Real de Santo Antonio, another night in Vilamoura and ending its voyage back in Portimão. ❏

Map on page 230

Mertola is a good example of a town whose fortunes waned with the silting of the river on which it depended for its prosperity. The export of mineral ores and grain to North Africa had sustained it for many centuries. Without trade, it slipped quietly into decline.

A NATURAL BORDER

The River Guadiana forms the border between Portugal and Spain for much of the cruise, though they part company north of Alcoutim. The area is testimony to the often tense relationship between the two countries: only in 1668 with the Treaty of Lisbon did the Spanish formally recognise that Habsburg rule had come to an end and accept Portuguese independence.

Even today the border region is sparsely populatted, and some roads are of poor quality, although the river cruise passes underneath the strikingly modern road bridge across the Guadiana at Castro Marim. There are remains of fortifications along the border, and, at Alcoutim, the destination of the cruise, a Portuguese (formerly Moorish) castle is matched on the opposite bank by a Spanish counterpart. Signs to the "castle" arouse expectations, but they lead to an empty shell, though the view from it is worth the short walk.

SCOTLAND AND IRELAND

Maps
on pages
241, 242

*Cruising the Celtic fringes of the British Isles offers wild coastal,
loch and mountain scenery in Scotland, gentle bucolic
landscapes on Ireland's Shannon.*

Rather different from the continental European cruises detailed elsewhere in
this guide, the Scottish and Irish itineraries are mostly covered by upmarket
cruise barges. In Scotland, the Caledonian Canal cuts through the majestic
Highland landscapes, while the River Shannon loops its way across the quiet
Irish midlands past small towns and villages and friendly country pubs.

THE CALEDONIAN CANAL

The Caledonian Ship Canal is a partly man-made waterway that runs from southwest to northeast, across the dramatic Great Glen fault of northern Scotland. The
canal – and a string of picturesque lochs – connect the North Sea with the North
Atlantic. The name is misleading, as the entire waterway is not really a canal as
such; in fact only 37 km (23 miles) of the 100-km (62-mile) stretch is man-made.
The rest of this exciting voyage is a journey through lochs Linnhe, Lochy, Oich and
Ness, all running in a slender ribbon, threaded through the Great Glen.

The route is steeped in history, myth and legend, a spectacularly violent and
bloody past unfolding in the setting of the wild and rugged Scottish Highlands.
While simply relaxing on deck and listening to the wonderful tales related by a local
historian is enough for many, there is plenty to see ashore as well, including the
famed Urquhart Castle on Loch Ness, the locks and
aqueducts along the course of the waterway, and, on the
seagoing *Lord of the Glens* cruise, the beautiful Inner
Hebrides around Ullapool.

PRECEDING PAGES: a
mooring in typical
Highland scenery.
LEFT: Irish
entertainment.
BELOW: Neptune's
Staircase.

The course of the Caledonian Canal

The Caledonian Canal stretches from Fort William in
the west to Inverness in the northeast of Scotland,
occupying part of the Great Glen, a geological fault
which slices the Scottish Highlands in two, separating
the Grampian Highlands of the southeast from the
Northern Highlands of the northwest. The fault contains a series of deep lochs (lakes), including Loch
Ness, famed for its mysterious aquatic beast.

As early as 1726, the Great Glen was considered
an ideal site for the construction of a canal which
could link up all the lochs and create one continuous
waterway. The idea was to provide a safe transport
route for naval frigates, one which enabled them to
avoid the stormy waters off the north coast.

The Scottish engineer James Watt surveyed the land
for the British government in 1773, although it was
designed by William Jessop and built jointly by him
and Thomas Telford. Work on the waterway went on
from 1803 to 1822.

The construction of the Caledonian Ship Canal
became, quite unusually for those times, a state-
sponsored scheme – good for the local workforce and

Robert Burns (1759–96) is a cultural icon in Scotland, and considered the nation's poet.

for job creation, as well as being a boon to local shipping. The first vessel to transit the completed waterway was the steam-driven yacht *Gondolier*, on 23 October 1822. The canal was rebuilt and deepened by 1847, but failed to bring commercial success. Today, it is used mainly for pleasure craft and for fishing. Some cruise barges operate the route, and one long-haul river cruise vessel, the luxurious *Lord of the Glens*.

What to expect

A cruise through the Great Glen is a relaxing experience, taking in some of Scotland's most wild and magnificent scenery, with castles, heather-clad hillsides, cosy inns and golf courses galore. The *Lord of the Glens* has all the hallmarks of a small floating manor house. Teak decks and rich wood interiors provide the warmth and feel of a private yacht. The ship has four decks and 27 suites/cabins, and can sail in the open sea as well as on the canal.

Its itinerary takes 10 nights from Ullapool south to the island of Mull and on through the Great Glen. The cruise barge *Scottish Highlander* also travels the Great Glen from Inverness to Fort William on a six-night cruise, through lochs, along rivers and down through the scenic Caledonian Canal.

Destination highlights

● Ullapool

Ullapool is a first taste of northern Scotland's spectacular scenery. The town perches on a spit of land jutting out into Loch Broom on the west coast and is an important fishing port. Crofting, fishing and local customs are all explained in the **Ullapool Museum** (open Apr–Oct Mon–Sat 10am–5pm; winter by prior

arrangement). Near by, **Inverewe Garden** (open March–Oct daily 9.30am–9pm) is a complete contrast, bursting with dazzling flowers and shrubs, including rhododendrons, camelias and giant tree ferns, which grow here thanks to the warming effect of the Gulf Stream.

Map on page 241

● Summer Isles

The *Lord of the Glens* spends some time exploring Scotland's west coast before entering the Great Glen. The Summer Isles lie off Loch Broom, the sea loch that shelters Ullapool. Special local stamps are sold at Tanera Mor's tiny post office, but the main attraction is walking through the beautiful countryside. From the vessel, seals and dolphins can often be spotted.

● Loch Torridon

This sea loch is surrounded by steep, bare mountains, stunning in the sunlight and bleakly menacing on a grey day. Either way, the scenery is awe-inspiring, and sitting on deck is certainly the place to be for this part of the cruise. The village of **Shieldaig**, more of a hamlet in reality, is pretty enough to merit a short wander if the vessel stops. Heading south, the cruise calls in at Kyle of Lochalsh, departure point for the Isle of Skye.

● Eigg, Iona and Mull

These three islands, offered as shore excursions on the *Lord of the Glens* cruise, are varied. **Eigg** is dominated by the pointed An Sgurr, a jagged rock outcrop up which it is possible to walk for breathtaking views of the ship moored below. The island is actually owned by the inhabitants themselves, who bought it from the

BELOW: mooring on the Caledonian Canal near Corpach, with Ben Nevis in the background.

In the Highlands and islands, pubs function as community centres.

previous owner for £1.5 million. In spring, the island is beautiful, the moorlands covered with purple heather and the woods scented with wild garlic.

Iona, lying off the southwest corner of the island of Mull, is the cradle of Scottish Christianity; St Columba and his monks, Celtic evangalists from Ireland, settled here in AD 563. Although Viking raiders pillaged the monastery and killed the monks, Iona became an important place of pilgrimage, and 62 Scottish, Norse and Irish kings, including Macbeth, are buried in the graveyard.

The forbidding **Duart Castle** on the neighbouring island of **Mull** dates from the mid-13th century. Visitors can admire the state rooms and explore the dungeons where Spanish officers from a galleon in the Armada fleet were once held. Climb to the top of the keep and admire the views across the Sound of Mull. Support by the owning Maclean family for the Jacobite cause led to the castle being besieged and bombarded by warships in 1688. Government troops were garrisoned in what was left until 1751, when it became ruinous. In 1911 Sir Fitzroy Maclean bought back the ruin and restored the castle as a family home.

Another highlight on Mull is the village of **Tobermory**, which can come as quite a shock after a couple of days cruising through the Highlands. The façades of the cottages along the waterfront are painted in bright colours, from candy pink to electric blue, and in summer, there will be hordes of tourists. This fishing village is very pretty, nonetheless, its narrow streets and seafront lined with shops.

● Cruising the Caledonian Canal

BELOW: the brightly painted houses of Tobermory.

On the southbound itineraries, the vessel sails from Tobermory, through the lovely Sound of Mull and inland into Loch Linnhe, passing Lismore Island to reach the town of **Fort William**. Although this is technically still the sea, the

mountains rear up steeply on both sides of the loch, which has the appearance of a lake. At Corpach, the ascent of **Neptune's Staircase** begins, a "flight" of eight interconnected locks marking one end of the Caledonian Canal.

The scenery is now becoming really stark, bare mountains scoured of vegetation by ancient glaciers, open moorland grazed by sheep, and tiny crofting villages the only signs of human life. The waterway continues along Loch Lochy, overlooked by **Ben Nevis**, Britain's highest mountain, which may still be snowcapped in late spring. Another man-made stretch, "Laggan Avenue", lined by tall Scots pines, follows before the vessel continues into the **Laggan Locks**. These locks mark the spot of the Battle of the Shirts, a bloody clash between the McDonnel and Fraser clans in 1544, so called because an unusually hot day led the warriors to fight without their shirts on.

The waterway now flows into **Loch Oich**, which is fed from both directions by the sea (a loch is technically a body of water open at one end to the sea) and is the highest point of the canal, 32 metres (106 ft) above sea level. The ruins of Invergarry Castle stand on the loch shore; the castle was burnt down in 1746 following the second Jacobite Rebellion, when it gave shelter to Bonnie Prince Charlie both before and after the terrible battle on Culloden Moor.

The final stretch of this part of the waterway leads to **Fort Augustus**, marking the southwestern end of Loch Ness. The vessel passes through another five locks here, into the deep, mysterious waters of the loch.

● **Loch Ness**

Loch Ness, Britain's deepest body of fresh water, is long, narrow and cold, the waters darkened by peat, and the surrounding mountains plunging into the loch

Map below

BELOW:
fishing is still an important industry in Scotland.

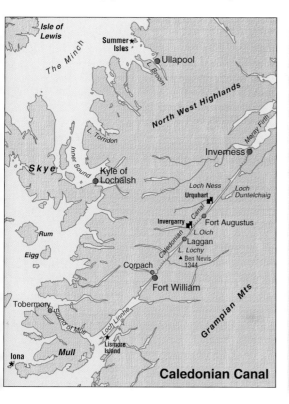

Caledonian Canal

to form sheer underwater cliffs. The legend of the monster has mystified the world since AD 565, when St Columba claimed to have sighted a "water horse" in the River Ness, which feeds the loch. Tourist boards nurture the legend.

One of the main sights on Loch Ness is **Urquhart Castle**, the definitive romantic ruin, built around a strangely shaped rock outcrop on the shore of the loch. The castle dates back to 1230 and has a complex and turbulent past. What is left of it today is by no means Scotland's largest or most impressive castle, but its appearance in many films, and its beautiful setting, certainly make it one of the most photographed.

After Loch Ness, the waterway continues to **Inverness** on the Moray Firth, marking the end of the waterway. For long seen as a dull backwater of Presbyterianism, the city has developed in recent years into a major shopping centre. A number of city-centre pubs have traditional Highland live music, and there are a good number of top-notch restaurants.

IRELAND'S RIVER SHANNON

The River Shannon is the longest river not only of Ireland but all of the British Isles, and rises in the pools at the foot of Tiltinblane Mountain in northwestern County Cavan. It flows for 386 km (240 miles) in a southerly direction before entering the Atlantic Ocean, the long estuary below Limerick accounting for 113 km (70 miles). Virtually dividing Ireland in two and providing an important north–south transport link for centuries, the river has helped to shape the country's social, political and economic history.

BELOW:
typical scenery
along the Shannon.

Today, it's used for pleasure cruising (there is no commercial traffic to inter-rupt the peace), and provides a wonderful way to drift through Ireland's soft,

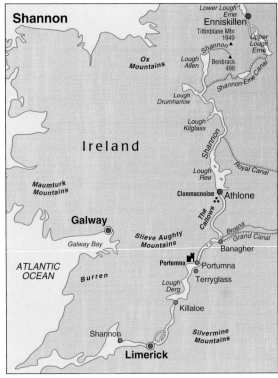

green countryside, stopping at country pubs and going ashore to explore tiny villages and the region's complex Celtic heritage.

There are no river cruise vessels as such on the Shannon, but several smart hotel barges operate on the lower part of the river, from Athlone down to Killaloe. Elsewhere on the water, there are hundreds of self-drive pleasure cruisers and barges in the summer months, bringing Europeans and Americans as well as British visitors in their droves to sample the famous Irish "craic".

The course of the river

The Shannon flows through more than a dozen lakes and weaves its way round more than 100 islands on its complex path from north to south, through the west of Ireland. For much of its course, the river is surrounded by bogs and marshes as it drains the central lowlands of the country, fed by hundreds of tributaries and criss-crossed by Ireland's vast network of inland waterways. The river's shape and form are constantly changing, wide one minute, narrow the next, leaving backwaters, pools, bays and cut-off bends in its meandering wake. The fishing in these quiet spots is superb, with salmon, trout, bream, tench, eel, pike and perch to be had.

The evolution of river cruising

The Greek cartographer Ptolemy mapped the Shannon in 150 BC, and during the first millennium AD looters on Viking longboats sailed upriver as far as Lough Ree, where they founded a settlement. During the Middle Ages, the Shannon was Ireland's great highway – a natural artery that divided the country's central plain. With the advent of road and rail transportation, however, the river was considered less useful, and now earns its keep as one if Ireland's main tourist attractions.

What to expect

A Shannon barge cruise will be peaceful and relaxing, with plenty of opportunity to meet local people, visit pubs, enjoy traditional Irish hospitality and soak up the sights of the green, gently rolling countryside. There are usually opportunities to play golf, walk or cycle for stretches of the journey, as the barges move very, very slowly. Ireland has a fickle climate, and at least a couple of grey, rainy days are almost inevitable.

There are a few luxury hotel barges on the river, including the *Shannon Princess*, which takes 12 guests and drifts slowly downstream from Athlone to Killaloe.

Destination highlights

● **Athlone**

The riverside town of Athlone has been a strategic crossing point of the river for centuries. The town is dominated by its hulking **castle** on the west bank, built by the Normans in 1210 and remodelled several times during its violent past. The vessel continues from Athlone to moor at the ancient monastic site of **Clonmacnoise**, where a monastery has stood since AD 545. Many of the kings of Connaught and Tara are buried here, and, although the monastery is a ruin, you can still see some beautiful stonework and form

Maps on pages 241, 242

When Shannon Airport opened in 1945, it attracted foreign companies to the area, reviving a declining region. Since the 1960s, many high-tech multinationals have been setting up operations here.

BELOW: Irish country pubs are the spiritual home of Guinness.

*The Cross of the
Scriptures and
O'Rourke's Tower
at Clonmacnoise,
spiritual centre of
the Celtic church
from the 7th to the
12th centuries.*

BELOW:
the quayside
at Athlone.

an impression of its original wealth and importance, before it was destroyed for the last time by the English in 1552.

● Banagher

Banagher, on one of the prettiest stretches of the river, is famed for its literary connections; Anthony Trollope lived and worked here in the mid-19th century. Like Athlone, this was an important crossing point of the river for centuries, and for several hundred years was guarded by solid-looking Martello towers and walls, which can still be seen today. But Banagher has a new lease of life now, as one of the biggest boating centres on the Shannon, with a large marina and plentiful shops and pubs catering to the hundreds of visitors on boating holidays.

The scenery surrounding the town is particularly fascinating. Known as **the Callows**, it's a vast tract of water meadows, consisting of reed banks along the river, green pasture and hayfields beyond and peatland in the hazy distance. In summer, the meadows are carpeted with wild flowers, while thousands of ducks and wading birds congregate in the wetlands in winter.

● Terryglass

The picturesque village of Terryglass is another popular boating centre, buzzing with holidaymakers all through the summer. Cruises which stop here allow free time to browse the craft shops and sample the Guinness in the quaint riverside and village pubs. Terryglass is also a base from which to explore the magnificent, semi-fortified **Portumna Castle** (open daily 10am–5pm) in nearby Galway, built in 1618 by Richard Burke, the 4th Earl of Clanricarde, and home to his family for 200 years. The ground floor and

gardens are open to the public, including the 17th-century kitchen garden, filled with organically grown fruit trees, herbs and vegetables.

Map on page 242

● Galway

Medieval Galway City, set on its scenic bay and an easy day trip from the Shannon, has a great atmosphere and *joie de vivre*. One of Ireland's big university cities, it is packed with Irish literary heritage and has been home over time to W.B. Yeats, Patrick O'Connor and Nora Barnacle – walking tours are arranged to take in some of the literary history. The city is a whirlwind of social events, from the famous horse-racing meetings to the annual Horse Fair, Arts Festival and Oyster Festival. The shopping for arts and crafts is superb, and most excursions here include a visit to an Irish crystal factory. Galway also has some good museums, particularly those documenting the region's long equestrian history.

● Killaloe

The southern stretch of the Shannon passes through the impressive expanse of **Lough Derg**, the largest of the Shannon lakes, stretching for 40 km (25 miles) and covering 12,950 hectares (32,000 acres), bordered by rolling hills and countless tiny villages, each one with several pubs offering a warm welcome and a pint of Guinness. Killaloe, at the southern end of the lough and dating back to the 6th century, is famed for the 13th-century **St Flannan's Cathedral**, setting for a celebrated annual classical music festival. Killaloe was the birthplace of Brian Ború, the king who ruled Ireland from 1002 to 1014 and routed the Vikings to free his country of them. A festival in mid-July, Feile Brian Ború, commemorates the event. ❏

The lively Claren-bridge Oyster Festi-val (at Clarenbridge, just south of Galway) marks the start of the Galway Bay oyster season in early September.

BELOW: ruins at Clonmacnoise.

RUSSIA AND UKRAINE

Maps on p256, 278, 286

The vast network of rivers and canals across European Russia and Ukraine are full of interest. Moscow to St Petersburg is the best-known, but other voyages explore the Caspian and Black seas

There's a certain thrill about cruising the complex network of rivers, lakes and canals of Russia and Ukraine; it's a perfect way of exploring a world that was closed to the outside for so long, and one that remains fairly inaccessible away from the main cities for all but the most intrepid traveller.

Ancient babushkas greet the boat as it moors up in a village, proffering bunches of lily of the valley, gaudy Russian dolls, lacquered boxes and bright shawls. Between towns, the rivers meander through fields of potatoes, beets and free-ranging pigs tended by old women with headscarves and pitchforks, or past deep, cool forests or hamlets of colourfully painted wooden houses. Ports of call are rich with history, ornate onion-domed churches displaying exquisite icons. What's more, there are several marvels of engineering along the way, as the rivers and canals pass though huge locks into the vast expanses of lakes and reservoirs, dotted with little wooded islands.

A river cruise also presents the opportunity for what is effectively a short break in both Moscow and St Petersburg, taking in the magnificent gold-domed Kremlin, Red Square and St Basil's, the Winter and Summer palaces and the unparalleled Hermitage – worth several days in its own right.

But a Russian river cruise is more than a sightseeing tour. It's an opportunity to learn about the country's many paradoxes – its fabulously rich cultural heritage and the harsh existence endured by many Russians today; its highly educated population and terrible job shortages; the Russian love affair with vodka, with metaphor, profound statements and impassioned debate. You will get to know your guides and hosts, and learn about Chekhov, Dostoyevsky, Pasternak, Pushkin and Tolstoy; about Russian music and art; and its golden past and uncertain future.

PRECEDING PAGES: choral performance at Uglich Cathedral. **LEFT:** locks on the Moscow–St Petersburg Canal. **BELOW:** at each Russian port of call it is customary to be welcomed by local musicians.

The course of the rivers

The Waterway of the Tsars, as the main Russian water system is often known, is confusing and it's hard at first to picture Moscow, hundreds of miles inland, being linked by rivers, canals and other waterways to the distant Baltic, Black and Caspian seas. In fact, ocean-going ships can sail all the way from the Mediterranean to the Arctic, thanks to this amazing network.

The water route from Moscow to St Petersburg is called the Volga–Baltic Waterway. It is 1,100 km (685 miles) long, and links the Volga, which flows west to east to the north of Moscow, with the St Petersburg industrial area on the Baltic Sea. The route is mainly through forested plains with some farmland and, towards St Petersburg, glaciated lakelands, along wide meandering waterways with small towns and villages

along the banks. There's always something to look at: people fishing, tending their fields, heavily laden river barges, birdlife and, in the towns and cities, a different angle on urban Russia.

Travelling north from Moscow to St Petersburg, the system consists first of the Moscow–Volga Canal, then the Volga River itself, which leads to the Rybinsk Reservoir, a massive flood basin covering the natural beds of many different rivers. Next, three more rivers and two canals form what's known as the Mariinsk System. After travelling the length of these waterways, you'll be at Lake Onega. This huge expanse is linked to the even bigger and very beautiful Lake Ladoga via the Svir River. Finally, the short but commercially important Neva River links Lake Ladoga to St Petersburg and the Gulf of Finland.

The entire system is called the Volga–Baltic Waterway, and is a vital part of Russia's transport infrastructure.

The entire waterway was begun in 1709 to connect St Petersburg with the interior. The major canals were built in the 1930s. The waterway was reconstructed and modernised in the early 1960s, the principal addition being a dam across the Sheksna near Cherepovets, which deepened the waterway as far as the Kovzha River, making it accessible to larger vessels. Although considerably more extensive, this waterway follows the historic Baltic–Volga trade route, in use since the 9th century.

● Moscow–Volga Canal

The canal was dug shovel by shovel by Gulag prisoners in the period between 1931 and 1937, some of the most brutal years of Stalin's dictatorship. The convicts' health and welfare were completely disregarded, but despite its

The Moscow–Volga Canal is 128 km (80 miles) long, although reservoirs take up 20 km (12 miles) of its length. There are nine locks to pass through.

BELOW: plaques at Moscow's Northern River Terminal commemorate the completion of the Moscow–Volga Canal.
RIGHT: champagne on board.

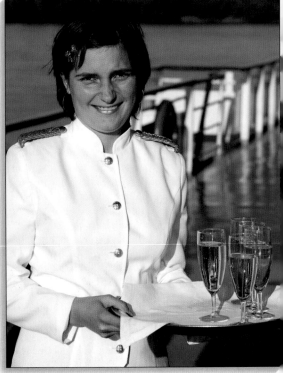

appalling history, the canal is a unique masterpiece of civil engineering; it is said that the amount of soil excavated during its construction exceeds by far that of the Panama and Suez canals.

Maps on p256, 278, 286

● **River Volga**

The Volga has played an important part in the life of the Russian people, and it is characteristically known in Russian folklore as "Mother Volga". For centuries, it has served as the chief thoroughfare of Russia and the lifeline of Russian colonisation to the east. It carries one half of the total river freight of the country and irrigates the vast steppes of the lower Volga region. Grain, building materials, salt, fish and caviar (from the Volga Delta and the Caspian Sea) are shipped upstream; lumber is the main commodity shipped downstream.

At 3,690 km (2,293 miles), the Volga is Europe's longest river. Its source is located 228 metres (748 ft) above sea level, in a small lake set in the Valdai Hills, northwest of Moscow in the Central Russian Uplands. Snow accounts for about 60 percent of its annual discharge, and the river floods in spring and early summer, when it is swollen by meltwater.

From its source, the river flows east to a point above Moscow, continues generally eastwards to Kazan, before turning south and meandering erratically to Volgograd, and finally southeast to Astrakhan and the large delta on the Caspian Sea, located some 28 metres (92 ft) below sea level.

Typically, the section of the Volga featured in river cruise itineraries is from the point where the Moscow–Volga Canal joins the river to the Rybinsk Reservoir. Here, the cruises carry on northwards across the lake, leaving the body of water at the Sheksna Lock, from where the Sheksna River connects the

Icons are sacred in the Russian Orthodox Church. The gold is representative of the Kingdom of Heaven.

BELOW:
autumn cruising along the Moscow–Volga Canal.

reservoir to Beloye Lake. The Volga, however, turns abruptly southeast at the southern end of the reservoir towards Yaroslavl. Some cruises incorporate this section, too, turning round after Yaroslavl and going north again, or carrying on in a southeasterly direction along the Volga to Kostroma, Kazan, Samara and Volgograd.

● **Sheksna River**

The wide Sheksna River, known for its clear waters rich in fish such as pike, perch and bream, flows north through flat, wooded countryside from the Rybinsk Reservoir to the Beloye Lake, with numerous towns and villages along its banks.

● **Kovzha River**

The River Kovzha leaves Beloye Lake and flows north to Lake Onega through a series of six locks; this is the Vytegra Canal, which carries vessels over the watershed to the River Vytegra, just before that river flows into the lake. Along with 220 other villages, the village of Kovzha was flooded as part of the upriver canal construction.

● **Svir River**

The next part of the journey involves crossing Lake Onega, which measures 9,900 sq. km (3,820 sq. miles). The 215-km (134-mile) Svir River is formed from water from Lake Onega, and connects it to the incredibly pure waters of Lake Ladoga to the west, which contains over 1,300 islands in its 17,872-sq.-km (6,900-sq.-mile) area – roughly 1½ times the size of Wales.

BELOW: socialist realist art.

● River Neva

The short River Neva flows out of the vast, freshwater Lake Ladoga, just 74 km (46 miles) to the Finnish Bay of the Baltic Sea. St Petersburg is built on 42 islands in the Neva, and is divided by a system of canals, hence its sobriquet "Venice of the North". Russian lakes are vast; the crossing of Lake Ladoga takes around eight hours and can get excitingly choppy at times!

Maps on p256, 278, 286

● Volga–Don Canal

The Volga–Don Canal (built in 1952) starts at Volgograd and connects the Black Sea/Sea of Azov (into which the Don River flows) with the rest of European Russia. The total length of the canal is 101 km (63 miles), running from Krasnoarmeysk on the Volga, immediately south of Volgograd to Kalach-na-Donu on the eastern shore of the Tsimlyansk Reservoir. There are 13 giant locks along its route, during which the level of the water drops 88 metres (289 ft) to the Volga and 44 metres (144 ft) to the Don. Three reservoirs – Karpovka, Bereslavka and Varvarovka – occupy 45 km (28 miles) of its length.

● River Don

Cruises which head southeast along the Volga beyond Yaroslavl often go all the way to Rostov, on the River Don, which is joined to the Volga at Volgograd by the Volga–Don Canal. A short stretch of the journey is southwest along the Don, a river 1,970 km (1,224 miles) long with its mouth in the Sea of Azov.

● River Dnieper (Ukraine)

The Dnieper (Dnepr) River, at 2,200 km (1,370 miles) is the fourth-longest river in Europe, and has been the commercial artery of Ukraine for centuries. Its source, located 220 metres (722 ft) above sea level, is on the southern slope of the Valdai Hills to the west of Moscow, not far from the source of the Volga. The river flows south, through western Russia, Belarus and Ukraine, passing Ukraine's capital city of Kiev, turning southeast to the cities of Dnipropetrovsk and Zaporozhye, then southwest to the Black Sea.

BELOW: the starred domes of St Dmitri's at Uglich. The stars and blue background symbolise heaven. Other colours have symbolic meaning too – gold for Jesus, green for the Holy Trinity. Green also signifies submission.

The northern section flows through gently rolling hills, some wooded, some farmed, with huge open vistas and brilliant sunsets. The middle Dnieper is characterised by high, sometimes rocky, banks in a forest steppe area. The lower stretches course powerfully across the Ukraine's vast plains, intensively farmed, with gigantic wheatfields prevalent (this is the former breadbasket of the Soviet Union), although the grassy steppe vegetation has been preserved in the nature reserves and in old ravines and gullies. Below Kherson, the Dnieper forms a delta, the many streams of which drain into the Dnieper Estuary. Although the Dnieper has diverse aquatic flora and fauna, damming and diverting its waters for power and water usage have radically altered its natural state, and there are some problems with pollution, particularly in the estuary.

The Dnieper is navigable throughout most of its course and is ice-free for ten months of the year; this

The Caspian Sea is the largest lake in the world and covers parts of Azerbaijan, Russia, Kazakhstan, Turkmenistan and Iran; it measures approximately 1,200 km (750 miles) from north to south and is typically around 320 km (200 miles) from east to west.

makes it a vital transportation artery for Belarus, Russia and Ukraine. The river has the same symbolism to Ukrainians as the Volga does for the Russians.

The evolution of river cruising

Russia and Ukraine rely heavily on their systems of rivers and waterways. Besides the 120 million tons of cargo a year carried through the Russian river and waterways system, both rivers are used extensively as a means of transport and for various leisure pursuits.

After World War II, the then Soviet Union's great European rivers – the Dnieper, Don and Volga – were linked to form an extensive network, and river traffic increased dramatically, with thousands of freight and passenger vessels. After the Soviet Union collapsed in 1991, many former state-run river-transport companies were privatised. Shipping, long a state-run monopoly, was one major industry that started to crumble, along with any form of infrastructure maintenance. Many vessels were laid up, until enterprising Russians and Westerners formed joint partnerships to revive the flagging fortunes of the industry.

The recovery has continued, although today there are merely hundreds of river cruise vessels instead of the thousands that were operating in the Soviet era. The effects of lack of direction and funding, and other considerations, have led to a situation whereby many of the Russian river cruise vessels are now regularly chartered to non-Russian tour operators.

What to expect

BELOW:
docking at Uglich.

There are essentially two types of vessel: those managed and sold by tour operators outside Russia, and those aimed mainly at the Russian market.

Needless to say, the latter are older ships and of low comfort levels by western standards – food may be bland and stodgy, cabins basic and bathrooms often shared, for example. One company, the Orthodox Cruise Company, founded in 1988, operates several river cruise vessels, not only under its own name, but also under charter for non-Russian companies. These companies include such big river cruise specialists as Uniworld (US), Noble Caledonia (UK), Phoenix Reisen (Germany), Viking River Cruises (Germany) and Politours (Spain).

Most river cruise vessels in Russia are large, with capacity for over 250 passengers. Some are air-conditioned and most are clean and tidy, although conditions vary according to the operator: most Western-run vessels have air-conditioning, saunas, bars, libraries and smart sun decks (important as you'll spend a lot of time on deck watching the scenery drift by). Some larger ships have a small indoor swimming pool and sauna, but most have at least a bar and library.

Food and drink

Cuisine on vessels catering to Westerners should be a mixture of Western tastes (salads, vegetarian dishes, plentiful buffets) and Russian specialities like *blinis* or fresh fish from the Volga. There's always a full bar, but wine, even Russian wine, is expensive, and some passengers bring their own on board.

Russian river cruises are usually highly imaginative. As well as the bonus that a lot of excursions are usually included in the price, a typical cruise will have plenty of introductions to Russian culture, from tea ceremonies to vodka-tasting, poetry reading, Russian language lessons, *balalaika* recitals and folk dances on board. Some cruises have a special theme – music, for example.

Several itineraries include concerts ashore, visits to the Bolshoi Ballet in

Maps on p256, 278, 286

Lenin was born at Ulyanovsk on the Volga (see page 275).

LEFT: outside Kirilo-Belorevsky Monastery at Goritsy.

EUROPEAN WATERWAYS

In 2002 the navigable rivers, waterways and canals of the Russian Federation officially became an integral part of the European inland waterways network, as established in the UNECE (United Nations Economic Commission for Europe) European Agreement on Inland Waterways of International Importance. This agreement identifies the main international inland waterways in Europe and establishes uniform infrastructure and operational parameters to which they should conform.

At present, 18 countries are contractors to the agreement: Austria, Bulgaria, Croatia, the Czech Republic, Finland, France, Germany, Greece, Hungary, Italy, Lithuania, Luxembourg, The Netherlands, the Republic of Moldova, Romania, the Russian Federation, Slovakia and Switzerland. One of the goals is to increase commercial river traffic in Europe and reduce the pressure on the congested overland transport routes.

In 1937 the two-headed eagles – the tsarist symbol – were removed from the Kremlin walls and replaced by Communist red stars. Kremlin guards report that two of the stars are made not of glass, but of rubies, and can be identified by their slightly darker hue.

Moscow, or the Moscow State Circus, and performances at the Mariinsky Theatre in St Petersburg, all things that could not be organised independently without considerable hassle.

Guides are usually highly qualified. It's not unusual to find academics earning a crust as tour guides – even university professors and doctors; they simply can't get work elsewhere. Fellow passengers will typically be aged fifty-plus, with an interest in the arts and Russian history. Many Americans visiting Russia are second- or third-generation immigrants, here to see the country of their ancestors.

Cruises tend to be informal, so there's no need to bring a black tie. Sturdy shoes and all-weather clothing are essential, as there's likely to be a considerable amount of walking. Wheelchair passengers, unfortunately, have a hard time and will need assistance all the way, including getting on and off buses, as there are no hydraulic lifts.

Overall, there is much to be said for seeing Russia and Ukraine from the water. River cruise vessels offer a comfortable room with a view, good food and attentive service – something that is still quite difficult to find in most hotels in Russia. You don't even have to carry your own bath plug, as you might do if you stayed in some traditional hotels.

Typical itineraries

The most popular Russian river cruise itinerary is Moscow to St Petersburg or vice versa, with several permutations of itinerary. This popular cruise involves ten different principal bodies of water, although the actual land distance between these two great cities is only 650 km (400 miles). Ten to twelve days is the normal duration for a Moscow–St Petersburg cruise.

The longer tours go east on the Volga as far as Yaroslavl, part of the Golden Ring (Zolotoye Koltso), a loop of seven old towns and cities north of Moscow which formed the cultural and political heart of Russia from the 12th century. All of the cruises allow two or three days in both Moscow and St Petersburg.

An increasingly popular two-week itinerary follows the Volga all the way from Astrakhan, close to the Caspian Sea, to Moscow, taking in Kazan, Samara and Volgograd on the way *(see page 274)*. Dnieper cruises *(see page 280)* in Ukraine are usually from Kiev to the Crimean Peninsula in the Black Sea and back again.

DESTINATION HIGHLIGHTS MOSCOW–ST PETERSBURG

● **Moscow**

The Russian capital is a vast (population 9 million), fascinating and unique city, the start or finish point of your trip. Most cruises begin from the Northern River Cruise Terminal (Rechnoy Vokzal), which is actually 12 km (8½ miles) northwest of the centre, on the

Map: Moscow to St Petersburg

Finland

Lososinka

Kizhi ★

Onezhskoye Ozero (Lake Onega)

Petrozavodsk

Ivinskoye Reservoir

★Valaam

Vytegra

Mandroga

Kovzha Locks

Kovzha

Ladozhskoye Ozero (Lake Ladoga)

Svir

Ozero Beloye (BeloyeLake/ White Lake)

Gulf of Finland

Neva

Goritsy

Sankt-Peterburg (St Petersburg)

Sheksninskoye Vodokhranilishche (Sisminskoye Reservoir)

Sheksna

Sheksna Lock ★

Russia

Rybinskoye Vodokhranilishche (Rybinsk Reservoir)

Kostroma

Yaroslavl

Volga

Uglich Lock ★ Uglich

Kashinka Kalyazin

Kimry

Volga

Dubna

Volga

Dmitrov

Moscow- Volga Canal

Moskva Moskva (Moscow)

Moscow–Volga Canal. River cruise operators usually run shuttles into the city while the boat is docked here. Cruise passengers will normally have two or three days to explore. For first-time visitors, it's probably best to take a guided tour of the big sites like the Kremlin and spend some time wandering the broad boulevards, parks and river banks. A trip on the metro is something everybody should try, through elegant, high-ceilinged stations like ballrooms, with gilded pillars, dazzling frescos and acres of marble. *For details on what to see in Moscow, see pages 260–263.*

Map on page 256

● **Uglich**

From Moscow to the Golden Ring city of Uglich, a small, rather shabby but essentially pretty place, takes almost 24 hours, most boats arriving mid-after-noon for a half-day tour. Leaving Moscow, the boat heads north along the **Moscow–Volga Canal**. As the suburbs melt into the flat countryside, you'll see hundreds of people out on the water, boating, fishing, paddling or simply watching the world go by from their wooden *dachas* (holiday homes) on the river banks.

The river widens as it approaches the mouth of the Kashinka River and passes under the Kashinskiy railway bridge. The Volga was flooded here when the Uglich Hydroplant and reservoir were created in 1940, and the town of Kalyazin was completely submerged. The **belfry** of the town's cathedral, once considered among the finest structures along the Volga, has since been planted on an earthen foundation in memorial and looks bizarre and eerie, protruding from the river. Near by, visible from the river, is a large radio telescope with a 64-metre (210-ft) dish which has been used in international research into quasars.

BELOW: the terminal building at Moscow's Northern River Terminal commemorates the completion of the Moscow–Volga Canal, and is designed to resemble a ship.

The belfry of Kalyazin, memorial of the flooded town in which it once stood.

Just south of Uglich is the Uglich Lock, with its triumphal arch commemorating the Soviet victory in World War II. After passing through, look to the right (east) and you will see the fabulous domes of the Uglich Kremlin. The ship ties up beneath the high embankment near the centre of town and is usually met by swarms of salespeople touting souvenirs.

Uglich was first mentioned in chronicles in 937, but was actually founded as a city in 1148. Boats dock close to the town's magnificent palace, built on the site of the ancient wooden kremlin. The walls were destroyed in the 19th century, but several beautiful buildings remain on the site and can be seen from the river approach.

The red-brick **Palace of the Uglich Princes**, or Prince Dmitri's Palace, is accessed via the former bridge over the former moat, now lined with souvenir vendors. Directly in front is the green-domed **Cathedral**, with the usual collection of icons. To the right as you face the river are the red walls and starred blue domes of the **Church of St Dmitri on the Spilled Blood** (a traditional Russian way of describing churches built on the site of a death), built under Peter the Great in 1692, which has unusual frescos depicting the death of the Tsarevich Dmitri, Ivan the Terrible's only son, in 1591. The church houses the alarm bell that was rung to signal his death. Boris Godunov, the suspected murderer, stripped the bell that sounded the alarm of its tongue when he himself became tsar, and "exiled" it to Siberia. Only hundreds of years later, in 1892, did local townspeople petition for the bell to be "pardoned" and returned to the city. The opera *Boris Godunov* tells the tale of the murder. The church mainly functions as a museum, although there are three services each year. Next door, the red-brick **Palace** itself, where Tsarevich Dmitri lived for seven

years, is one of a very few 15th-century noble dwelling houses extant in Russia; it was begun in 1480 by Andrei Bolshoi, Ivan III's brother.

In addition to three monasteries and a great number of churches from various centuries in assorted states of restoration or dereliction, Uglich has various museums – there is a cluster of them (a doll museum, a museum of prison art and a vodka museum) near the river vessel dock a short distance downriver from the palace.

Map on page 256

● **Kostroma**

Kostroma is beyond Yaroslavl on the banks of the Volga; usually, cruises turn around here and head back towards Rybinsk on the voyage to St Petersburg, calling first at Yaroslavl before saying goodbye to the Volga.

This lovely city has a classical street layout, built after a fire in 1773 destroyed all the wooden buildings that were typical of the times. Today, the streets fan out like the spokes of a wheel from the city centre. The main attraction is an excursion to the **Ipatyevsky Monastery** (open daily 9am–5pm), ten minutes' drive west of the city centre in pretty countryside dotted with little wooden houses, gardens full of flowers and small village churches. The monastery was built in 1332 by Chet, a Tatar prince and an ancestor of Tsar Boris Godunov *(see previous page)*, and its crypt is the burial vault of the Godunov family. The cathedral has glittering gold cupolas and there's a musical bell-tower, modelled after the Ivan the Great Bell Tower in Moscow, which chimes tunes on the hour.

A visit to the monastery can be combined with the **Museum of Wooden Architecture** (open daily 9am–5pm) next door, an outdoor exhibit of the work of local craftsmen – traditional wooden houses, churches and dachas. One of the churches is built without using a single nail.

The main street of Kostroma, Ploshchad Revolyutsii, resembles a film set with its elegant 18th- and 19th-century buildings, which include a UNESCO-listed fire-tower.

BELOW: the alarm bell at the Church of St Dmitri in Uglich.

● **Yaroslavl**

Yaroslavl is one of Russia's oldest, dustiest, but most well-known and fascinating Golden Ring cities. It is also one of the country's most important intellectual centres, with a famous 200-year-old university, as well as being a commercial and industrial centre with a population of 650,000 – the urban area stretches along the banks of the Volga for some 29 km (18 miles). Despite this, the skyline of the city centre – at least when viewed from the river – is one of onion domes and spires; Yaroslavl was a major port from the 17th century, when wealthy merchants attempted to outdo Moscow, putting up one grand ecclesiastical structure after another, complete with lavish decoration and colourful frescos.

The city is located at the confluence of the Kotorosl and Volga rivers, and was founded by the Russian ruler Yaroslav the Wise in the early 11th century. In its beautiful, expansive 19th-century main square (a pleasant 10-minute walk along the merchants' mansion-lined Volga Embankment from the river cruise terminal) you'll find the **Church of St Elijah (Ilya) the Prophet** (open daily 10am–1pm and 2–6pm), with green cupolas and ornate exterior tiles, built by 17th-century fur dealers; you may be treated to a brief choral recital by the monks, an experience that brings ➤ *page 264*

PORTS OF CALL: MOSCOW

Moscow seethes with the stark contrasts of modern-day Russia: lavish hotels, nightclubs, designer shops and restaurants sitting uncomfortably alongside gigantic, brutal communist-era structures, crime, corruption and beggars; elegant women in fur coats walking past destitute old people whose meagre pensions were wiped out with the almost overnight change to a free-market economy.

First-time visitors may prefer to take a guided tour of the big sites like the Kremlin, and spend some free time wandering the broad boulevards, parks and river banks of this vast city.

ORIENTATION

Most river cruise vessels dock inconveniently in the far northwest of the city at the Northern River Terminal (Rechnoy Vokzal). There is another terminal in the south of the city, similarly remote from the centre. This means that most passengers will have to rely on the cruise company tours if they wish to see the sights. If you want to go it alone, it's a 15-minute walk to the nearest metro (Rechnoy Vokzal). The nearest metro station to the southern terminal is Kolomenskaya.

GETTING AROUND

Moscow is vast, but is blessed with a very good (and picturesque) metro system. Taxis are readily available, but make sure you agree a fare before you get in (even if the taxi has a meter) and only use official cabs.

BUSINESS HOURS

Many shops are open Monday–Saturday from 9 or 10am until 6 or 7pm. Some convenience stores are open 24 hours. Shopping malls are usually open until 9pm, and several are open similar hours on Sundays.

TOP CITY SIGHTS

▲ **RED SQUARE, LENIN MAUSOLEUM, GUM AND ST BASIL'S** Standing for the first time in Red Square, Moscow's heart and the backdrop for so many television broadcasts, movies, protests, marches and military displays, is a heady feeling. The red, crenellated walls of the Kremlin run along one side, with the marble monolith of Lenin's Tomb (open Wed, Thurs, Sat & Sun 10am–1pm) in front of them. The amazing cluster of multicoloured, Disneyesque domes of St Basil's Cathedral dominate one end of the square and GUM, the infamous state department store (now a swanky mall) runs the length of the northeastern side.

◄ **KREMLIN** At the heart of Moscow is the Kremlin (Kreml; open Fri–Wed 10am–5pm). Among the sights here are the fabulous Cathedral of the Assumption, and the Cathedral of the Annunciation, a gem of Russian sacred architecture. A visit to the Armoury is the highlight for many visitors – this museum is packed with priceless treasures from the Tsarist past, including exquisite Fabergé eggs, all manner of sumptuous gifts from the royal courts of

café culture, with buskers, pavement artists and a good supply of interesting small shops.

▼ **THE METRO** (main picture on following page). Many of the central stations on Moscow's metro have to be seen to be believed. Deep underground, they present a surreal subterranean world of marble and coloured stone lit by chandeliers and decorated with sculpture and mosaics.

Designed to be the showcase of the Soviet Union's first Five-Year Plan to modernise industry, the metro combined technical innovation with artistic celebration of the working class. It was a symbolic project, intended to show that socialism could achieve anything capitalism could. **Kropotkinskaya** is one of the most beautiful and restrained stations, lined with marble taken from the facade of the demolished Cathedral of Christ the Saviour (now reconstructed nearby). Other notable stations include **Komsomolskaya**, dedicated to the Communist Youth movement, and **Kievskaya** with its stucco frames. Ploschad Revolutsii, Arbatskaya, Mayakovskaya and Belorusskaya are all worth seeing, too.

▶ **THEATRE SQUARE (BOLSHOY CURRENTLY CLOSED)** With the closure of the Bolshoy (Great Theatre) for major renovation work until 2008, the adjacent New Stage (to the west of the theatre) and Maly Theatre (Small Theatre; to the east) are the city's premier stages.

▲ **TVERSKAYA** Traditionally the city's main thoroughfare, Tverskaya runs northwest from Red Square. In Tsarist times this was the road to St Petersburg, and was lined with palaces and mansions. Today, the broad street is lined with a wide variety of shops including the Yesileev Emporium (pictured). Pushkin Square, which leads off Tverskaya, is one of Moscow's liveliest hubs.

Europe, and a collection of magnificent horse-drawn coaches.

This impregnable fortress of the Tsarist, then Soviet, élites is surrounded by imposing red-brick walls 20 metres (65 ft) high and up to 6 metres (20 ft) thick.

◀ **TRETYAKOV GALLERY** Housed in an old mansion, the Tretyakov Gallery (open Tues–Sun 10am–7.30pm; ticket office closes 4.30pm) documents the history of Russian art from the 12th century to the present. Its collection of icons is regarded as the best in the world, and Soviet Realism is also well-represented. Look out for works by Repin (1844–1930), considered Russia's greatest realist painter, and Korovi, master of Russian impressionism.

The New Tretyakov (same hours as main gallery) to the southwest houses the museum's collection of 20th century works.

◀ **THE ARBAT** This pedestrianised street west of the centre has long been the hub of Moscow's

▼ SPARROW HILLS

Anton Chekhov once said of the Sparrow Hills, "If you want to understand Russia, you must come here and look out over Moscow". Today the view is different but still breathtaking. You can easily get here from the Vorobyovye Gory metro stop (exit from the front of the train and follow the path to the right up the hill). Towering over all is the main building of Moscow State University, the greatest of the Stalinist skyscrapers; the campus is located in a beautiful park.

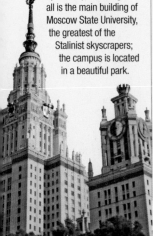

▼ NOVODIVECHY CONVENT AND CEMETERY

Overlooked by the Sparrow Hills, the peaceful and beautifully preserved Novodivechy Convent (open Wed–Mon 10am–5.15pm; closed first Mon of the month) dates back to 1524. The complex includes the Smolensk Cathedral with its five domes and a magnificent interior. Behind the Smolensk Cathedral is the Refectory and Church of the Dormition, built in 1685 and considered an architectural wonder for the lack of supporting pillars in the vast hall.

The Novodevichy Cemetery (open 9am– 6pm in winter, 9am–7pm in summer) is something of a Who's Who of Russia. As well as the grave of Nikita Khrushchev, you can see Chekhov's modest *style moderne* gravestone; the monument to Vladimir Mayakovsky; the clown Yuri Nikulin and the ballet dancer Ulanova; and the monuments to the aircraft designers Tupolev and Ilyushin. The Anarchist Prince Kropotkin is also buried here, as is the famous film director Eisenstein. By the south wall is the grave of Raisa Gorbachev: a simple gravestone with a delicate and graceful muse standing watch.

▼ PUSHKIN FINE ARTS MUSEUM

The Pushkin Fine Arts Museum (open Tues–Sun 10am–7pm) features a compilation of the magnificent art collected by Russian noblemen in the 18th and 19th centuries. The museum was conceived to present the finest examples of Western art to the public. There is a great deal to see. Highlights include Botticelli's *Annunciation*, a

superb Rembrandt collection, and works by Brueghel, El Greco, Tintoretto and Rubens. The holy grail for most visitiors, though, is the marvellous collection of Impressionist and post-Impressionist art, with works by Monet, Cézanne, Gauguin and Van Gogh, amongst others.

▲ IZMAILOVO MARKET

Out in the eastern suburbs, this huge market – also known as Vernisazh – is a treasure trove for souvenir hunters. Matroshka dolls and other wooden toys, icons, and Soviet memorabilia in all its kitsch excesses can be found here. It is also a good place to look for carpets and rugs from Central Asia. Outside the main market, traders from various far-flung parts of the old Soviet Union sell clothes and bric à brac,

while numerous food stalls present an opportunity to sample the cuisine of Armenia, Georgia and the Central Asian republics.

▶ ALL-RUSSIA EXHIBITION CENTRE (VVTs)

Some of the most spectacular Soviet-era monuments can be seen in and around the All-Russia Exhibition Centre in the north of the city. Exit the VDNKh metro station to see the Gagarin Memorial *(pictured)*, commemorating the first manned space-flight in 1961. Close by are The Worker and Collective Farm Girl, gigantic steel sculptures of Stakhanovite resolve. The pavilions inside the exhibition centre are part trade fair, part shopping centre.

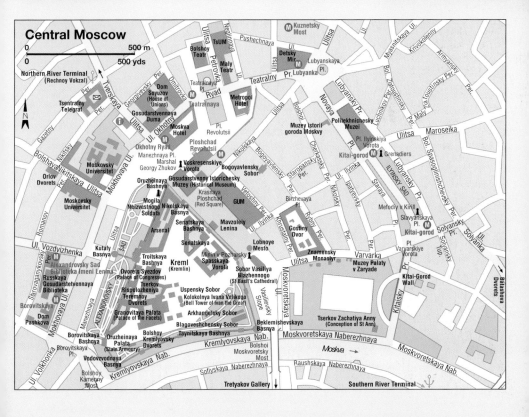

Decorative tilework at Yaroslavl's Church of St Elijah.

the building to life. Overlooking the Kotorosl River a few minutes' walk further south is the 12th-century **Saviour Transfiguration Monastery** (open Tues–Sun 10am–5pm), with shining gold domes. It's easy to get church fatigue, as there really is a house of worship on every corner, in which case, visit the **Music and Time Museum** (open Tues–Sun 10am–7pm), on the Volga Embankment, an impressive collection of antique clocks and musical instruments.

● Goritsy

The crossing of the Rybinsk Reservoir usually takes place at night, so you won't see much of this huge, shallow expanse. The boat then continues through the smaller Beloye Lake (White Lake). Cruises are timed to leave Yaroslavl at about midday, arriving at the colourful village of Goritsy, on the Sheksna River, which flows out of the northern end of the Rybinsk Reservoir, around 10am the following morning, for a short tour either of the village or the nearby Kirilo-Belozersky Monastery.

The boat docks near the centre of the village. The scenery around here is tranquil and pastoral, with unpaved roads, brightly painted wooden houses along the river and farmers toiling in the fields. Most houses have a small plot of land, on which potatoes, carrots and cabbages are grown, and some house-holders invite guests into their homes, to see how a typical rural Russian lives. Needless to say, an element of commercialism has crept into this, and some visitors are also disappointed to find the middle of the village overrun with souvenir vendors. None the less, it's worth learning a few greetings in Russian if you're planning to visit a home, or to offer a small gift. Despite the river traffic, people here live in poverty.

BELOW: the Church of St Elijah in Yaroslavl.

Kirilo-Belorevsky Monastery, usually offered as a guided tour, was founded in 1397 by Kiril Belozersky on the shore of Lake Siverskoye, and prospered from the 15th to the 17th centuries by trading salt and fish. It is surrounded by walls, which contain three churches with typical onion-dome towers.

Map on page 256

● Lake Onega

As the river nears the vast expanse of Lake Onega, an extension of the heavily glaciated landscape of eastern Finland, it becomes the Volga–Baltic Canal again and passes through a series of six locks. At one point where the canal is particularly straight, you can see all six, lined up ahead of the boat. It's worth being on deck to witness the passage through the locks, which are an impressive feat of engineering.

Lake Onega is Europe's second-largest freshwater lake (9,720 sq. km/3,750 sq. miles – the largest is Lake Ladoga, *see page 268)* and lies 15 km (9 miles) from the town of Vytegra, which is on the canal. The lake is 248 km (154 miles) long and its greatest width is about 80 km (50 miles); it's also surprisingly deep for a glacier lake, at 150 metres (350 ft). There are, in all, some 1,650 islands in this vast lake, and more than 50 rivers flow into it.

Onega is part of the republic of Karelia, which extends from St Petersburg to the Arctic Circle. It's a sparsely populated but very beautiful region, mostly forest and water, with some 60,000 lakes scattered across the gently undulating landscape, gouged and scoured over the millennia by huge glaciers.

Much of the population is scattered along the shores of the lake, mainly occupied in the timber trade, fisheries and mining industries. Stalin deported prisoners here between 1931 and 1933 to dig the White Sea Canal, a network

BELOW: the Russian Orthodox religion is thriving after years of persecution under communist rule.

TIP

It's useful to take a
pair of binoculars on
any river cruise, but
especially in Russia,
with its vast
landscapes. At any
time of the year
except midsummer,
you may be glad of a
woolly hat!

of waterways leading to the Arctic, and their descendants remain here today.

Salmon, *palya* (a kind of trout), burbot, pike, perchpike and perch are among the fish caught in the lake, and over 1,000 species of bird have been recorded around its perimeter. The shores are low-lying and sandy in the south and rocky in the north, with smooth boulders instead of beaches. In winter the lake freezes over, but the ice melts in May and summers are usually warm, with long, light evenings. You'll see other lake traffic as you make the crossing to Kizhi, towards the northern end; in fact, steamboats have plied the waters of Lake Onega since 1832.

Pack some seasickness tablets, as the waters can be whipped up into quite a swell, particularly later in the season. River cruisers have to have a special classification to cross these large lakes, so they are not completely flat-bottomed – this helps stability, but seasickness can still be a problem.

● Kizhi Island

Kizhi, a long, skinny island at the northern end of Lake Onega, is best known for the amazing **Open-Air Museum of Architecture** (open late May–mid-Oct daily 9am–8pm), a fascinating display of everything from wooden 19th-century peasants' houses to old watermills, windmills and threshing mills. The entire island serves as the museum and is protected as a UNESCO World Heritage Site. The boat docks at a landing stage surrounded by kiosks, and it's a short walk to the entrance of the main museum area.

Kizhi's most famous building is the three-tiered, fairy-tale-like **Transfiguration Church**. It is the world's largest wooden church, was built in 1714 entirely without nails and has 22 onion domes (cupolas), although the shape is meant to look like the flame of a candle, not an onion. Some 32,000 aspen wood shingles

BELOW: bankside
entertainer.
RIGHT: Kizhi's
spectacular
Transfiguration
Church.

cover the cupolas, which gleam in the sunlight with a silver sheen. Adjacent is the **Church of Intercession**, which was also constructed nail-free.

The actual village of Kizhi is a 30-minute walk from the river cruise vessel berthing place. In the summer months, ensure you have some mosquito repellent with you. There are also poisonous snakes in the undergrowth, so be careful in long grass.

Map
on page
256

● Petrozavodsk

Petrozavodsk is a four-hour cruise across the lake from Kizhi. It was founded in 1703 by Peter the Great and is the capital of the Republic of Karelia, and its largest city. Two languages (Karelian and Russian) are spoken here and, throughout the town you can see Latin inscriptions everywhere. The city, much favoured by the tsars and Bolsheviks as a place of exile for their opponents from St Petersburg, was home to a shipbuilding industry. It was also the site of Russia's first cannon-casting foundry. Today it's a laid-back, peaceful place, with wide, tree-lined boulevards and parklands along the Lososinka River, which flows through the city into the lake. Petrozavodsk is also a starting point for expeditions into the Karelian wilderness, and you'll see campers and backpackers, as well as tourists from neighbouring Finland, around town.

Most buildings in rural Russia are still made out of wood, and painted in cheerful colours.

There's not a huge amount to see; boats normally call here for a performance by Kantele, a colourful and impressive Karelian folk ensemble, followed by free time to stroll along the lake shore, which is dotted with sculptures.

Leaving Petrozavodsk, the boat heads south through the lake to the River Svir, which is partly canal and flows for 224 km (140 miles) into Lake Ladoga, Europe's largest freshwater lake.

BELOW: Kizhi Island.

In 1941–3, the 'Life Road' (linking besieged St Petersburg, or Leningrad, as it was then, with the rest of the country) operated across Lake Ladoga, with vehicles travelling in convoy across the ice in the winter months to bring supplies.

● **Mandroga**

Some cruises make a lunch stop at the village of Mandroga. This is a new creation; the original village was destroyed during World War II and rebuilt as recently as 1996 on the initiative of private entrepreneur Sergei Gutsait, with several pretty re-creations of traditional wooden houses. The permanent population of the village numbers less than 50, and it really serves as a tourist resort, offering picnics of barbecued *shashlik* (shish kebabs) and Russian red wine. There's a small vodka museum, arts-and-crafts workshops, a bakery where fresh *blinis* are sold and the inevitable hordes of "entrepreneurs" trying to sell Russian dolls and lacquered boxes. If the pressure gets too much, you can take a stroll through the birch and alder woods.

● **Lake Ladoga**

The vast Lake Ladoga is the largest in Europe, and the second-largest in the Russian Federation after the Caspian Sea. It covers an area of 17,700 sq. km (6,840 sq. miles) and is fed by the Volkhov, Svir and Vuoksa rivers; its outlet is by way of the Neva River which flows into the Gulf of Finland. The average depth is 51 metres (167 ft). Some 660 islands are scattered across the lake, mainly in the north.

Lake Ladoga freezes at the edges from November/December, and in the centre between January and March. As the lake is subject to violent storms (it's actually classed as a sea, and river boats have to be specially certified to be allowed to sail on it), a chain of navigable canals has been constructed around its southern shores. Beaches indent the lake, and its banks are overgrown with willows, alders, birches and pines. Much of the forest around the lake is pristine wilderness, and, along the banks, there's a wide variety of wildlife, including a unique

BELOW: Russian winter pursuits are strictly for the hardy.

subspecies of the ringed seal. The main industry for the inhabitants of the area is commercial fishing.

Map on page 256

● Valaam

The Valaam Archipelago in the north of Lake Ladoga is famous for the 14th-century Transfiguration Monastery, once a fortress built to defend the lake from Swedish invaders, and later a prison. The **Valaam Monastery** became one of the leading Orthodox centres in the region in the 14th century, although it is clear that time and decay have both taken their toll. The journey adds 200 km (120 miles) to the cruise and is not part of all itineraries.

The voyage along the Neva from Lake Ladoga to St Petersburg is brief. As the river enters the suburbs, passengers have a chance to reacclimatise to the feel of a big city after the peace of the wilderness.

● St Petersburg

St Petersburg, one of the most northerly cities in the world, is Russia's largest port, and its second-largest city, built on 42 islands in the broad delta of the River Neva, and criss-crossed by canals, spanned by over 400 bridges. Founded by Peter the Great in 1703, the city, which is European in its design, celebrated its 300th anniversary in 2003. The amazing art treasures of the Hermitage alone could fill five days, but in addition, there are breathtakingly opulent palaces, stunning churches, monuments and museums to explore. St Petersburg is the home of Russian ballet and the inspiration of great Russian poetry, music and literature.

From around 11 June to 2 July, when the sun doesn't sink below the horizon and the dusk meets the dawn, the city comes alive for what are ➤ *page 274*

The red lighthouse at the southern end of Lake Ladoga marks a settlement where, legend has it, a band of pirates were so thankful to be saved from a storm on the lake that they "went straight" and founded a monastery. Tchaikovsky visited the island and dedicated a movement of his 1st Symphony to it, entitled "Gloomy Land, Misty Land".

LEFT:
Peter the Great.

KARELIA

A vast region of forests and lakes, Karelia straddles the Finland–Russia border, and is perhaps best-known by the orchestral overture and suite composed by Sibelius following his honeymoon there. Much of Karelia was ceded to Russia (from Sweden) in the Treaty of Nystad in 1721, when Peter the Great was tsar. Travellers arriving by boat at the region's capital of Petrozavodsk ("Peter's Factory") are further reminded of this link by a huge bronze statue of the Tsar on the shoreline; he is depicted in full-dress uniform with his sword and right hand pointing towards the River Lososinka's mouth, where a gun foundry was set up in 1703. The monument was cast in St Petersburg. Sibelius continued to draw inspiration from the region, notably the great Karelian/Finnish epic of the *Kalevala*, which inspired such hauntingly beautiful pieces as *The Swan of Tuonela* and *Lemminkäinen*. Traditional folk music can still be heard in the city.

PORTS OF CALL: ST PETERSBURG

St Petersburg, the second largest city in Russia and one of the world's major cities, has been at the very centre of Russian history and culture since Peter the Great founded it at the beginning of the 18th century. The city remains an intensely stimulating and cultured place, home to one of the world's top art museums and full of wonderfully elegant and harmonious architecture. It is a city reinventing itself after decades of neglect, and has remained the most European of Russia's cities, drawing its inspiration from the West.

ORIENTATION

River cruisers dock on the Neva several miles upstream towards Lake Ladoga, long before the river flows through the heart of the city. There's no terminal building as such, and boats are tied to a pier, three or four abreast, so if yours is the furthest out, you'll have to clamber over the others to disembark, which is awkward for those with mobility difficulties. The area around the terminal is residential and industrial, with no major attractions and a slightly grim feel.

GETTING AROUND

The metro is the quickest way to get around. Tokens are bought at station ticket offices and include changes between the four lines. Trains run from 6am to 1am. Buses, trolleys and trams are less straightforward to use than the metro, but very cheap. Buy tickets either from the driver or at kiosks all around the city. Stops with "A" signs are for buses, and "T" signs for trams.

BUSINESS HOURS

Most shops are open Monday–Saturday 10am–6, 7 or 8pm, though in the city centre there are 24-hour convenience food stores. More and more businesses are working the entire day, forgoing closure at lunchtime, although most banks still close for one hour, either 1–2pm or 2–3pm. Shopping malls are usually open until 9pm, and several are open similar hours on Sundays.

TOP CITY SIGHTS

▲ ► HERMITAGE/WINTER PALACE

St Petersburg's famous art gallery, the Hermitage (Ermitazh) houses one of the world's great collections, so vast that only one-twentieth can be put on display at any one time. It is renowned for its collection of Western European art, including early 13th-century Italian works, French Impressionists and modern art. Of equal interest is the architecture of the interior such as the ornate Jordan staircase *(pictured opposite)*. The Hermitage complex is made up of four buildings. At its heart is the Winter Palace (Zimniy Dvorets), former winter residence of the tsars and tsarinas. Open Tues–Sat 10.30am–6pm, Sun until 5pm.

◄ THE RUSSIAN MUSEUM

Housed in

Mikhailovsky Palace, one of the city's finest examples of neoclassical architecture, the Russian Museum (Russkiy Muzey) showcases the world's largest collection of Russian art. There are some 400,000 works in total, ranging from medieval icons to the latest in conceptual art. Open Wed–Sun 10am–6pm, Mon 10am–5pm.

EXCURSIONS

PETERHOF, west of St Petersburg, was built by Peter the Great and was the primary country residence of the tsars, especially during the 18th and early 20th centuries. It comprises several dozen buildings, nine of which are now museums. The palace is situated on the south coast of the Gulf of Finland, and can be reached by hydrofoil from the Dvortsovaya naberezhnaya in front of the Hermitage.

▼ PETER AND PAUL FORTRESS

On the tiny island of Zayachy stands the star-shaped Peter and Paul Fortress (Petropavlovskaya krepost), built by Peter the Great to protect the city from the threat of Swedish attacks. It also served as a high-security jail for political prisoners. Today, it has become a favourite area for relaxation, and in the summer many city-dwellers flock to the beach in front of the fortress to sunbathe. Open Thur–Mon 11am–6pm.

◄ PALACE SQUARE AND ALEXANDER COLUMN

Behind the Hermitage is the impressive Palace Square (Dvortsovaya Ploschad), a key landmark in the city's turbulent history. In 1905 it was the scene of the so-called "Bloody Sunday" massacre, when tsarist troops opened fire on unarmed strikers sparking the 1905 Revolution. The square also took centre stage in the build up to the events of 1917, when a small army of Bolsheviks stormed the Winter Palace from here, seizing power.

In the centre of the square stands the Alexander Column (Aleksandrovskaya kolonna), a triumphal monument erected to commemorate the victory of the Russian army over the French during the Napoleonic Wars. The base of the towering column is decorated with bas-reliefs of figures representing the great rivers Russian troops had to cross in pursuit of Napoleon.

▶ NEVSKY PROSPEKT

The 4.5-km (3-mile) Nevsky prospekt, which begins in Dvortsovaya Square in the heart of town, is the most famous street in St Petersburg. It is the city's most fashionable address and is popular for shopping, eating out and people-watching. Apart from the splendid architecture and impressive historic buildings along this stretch, there is plenty of activity at street level, and it remains the city's business and entertainment hub.

Not to have walked Nevsky, as the locals refer to it, is not to have visited St Petersburg.

▲ ST ISAAC'S CATHEDRAL

The gleaming golden dome of St Isaac's Cathedral (Isaakiyevskiy Sobor), plated with 100 kg (220 lb) of pure gold, soars majestically over its square, and is visible for miles around. The cathedral's façades are adorned with massive red-granite columns, while the lavish interior is inlaid with lapis lazuli. Open Thur–Tues 11am–6pm.

▼ AURORA CRUISER

The legendary Aurora Cruiser played a pivotal role in 20th-century Russian history. A shot from its guns signalled the start of the storming of the Winter Palace (the seat of the provisional government) by the Bolsheviks in October 1917. Today, the cruiser is moored on Petrogradskaya Embankment, and now houses a naval museum. Open Wed–Sun 10.30am–4pm.

▶ KAZAN CATHEDRAL

Kazan Cathedral (Kazanskiy Sobor; open daily until 8pm; large groups prohibited during mass) is an architectural masterpiece. Designed by Andrei Voronikhin and modelled on St Peter's in Rome, the cathedral was built between 1801 and 1811. The most distinguished feature is the magnificent semi-circular colonnade made up of 96 Corinthian columns. Enormous 15-metre (49-ft) long bas-reliefs adorn both ends of the building and depict biblical themes.

▶ PETER THE GREAT'S CABIN

In 1703, local carpenters built Peter the Great a small cabin from which he could supervise the construction of the Peter and Paul Fortress. The cabin, which took just three days to complete, is now a museum (Domik Petra Pervogo; open Wed–Mon 11am–5pm, closed last Mon of the month) and was the first residential building in St Petersburg. It is filled with Peter the Great's original belongings. The cabin

Mariinsky's stage, including Anna Pavlova and Vatslav Nijinsky.

retains its historic atmosphere, providing one of the best impressions of life in the city during its first decade. It is lined with stone on the outside, but is still rough pine in the inside.

▶ **MARIINSKY THEATRE**
The imposing Mariinsky Theatre (Mariinsky teatr), formerly known as the Kirov, (open for performances only) was named in honour of Alexander II's wife, Maria.

Ballet, opera and classical concerts can be seen here in the plush 18th-century surroundings. During its golden age around the turn of the 20th century, Russia's top ballet stars graced the

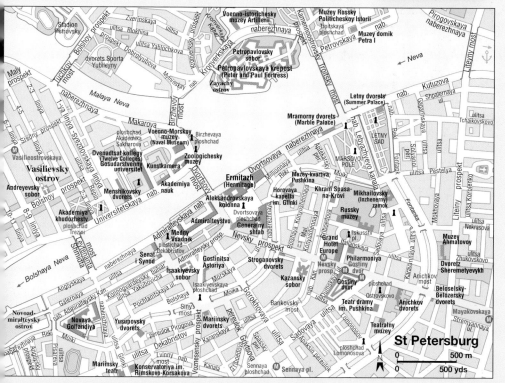

St Petersburg

poetically known as "white nights", with street entertainment all night and lovers walking hand-in-hand along the banks of the Neva and Nevsky Prospekt, the city's main thoroughfare. But if you're taken by the romance of the city, also consider coming back in mid-winter, when the river freezes over for ice-skating and the air is cold and clear. *For details on what to see in St Petersburg, see pages 270–273.*

THE VOLGA: MOSCOW TO ASTRAKHAN

This is a more unusual itinerary than Moscow–St Petersburg, travelling virtually the whole length of the River Volga between Moscow and Astrakhan close to the Caspian Sea, or Rostov-on-the-Don near the shores of the Sea of Azov. It is perhaps suited to those who have already done the more traditional route and want to explore the heartland of Russia in more depth.

Some cruises run south to north to finish in Moscow, others start in the capital and head south. From Moscow, the cruse first navigates the Moscow–Volga Canal *(see pages 250, 257)* to join the Volga, and then calls at Uglich, Kostroma and Yaroslavl *(for details on these cities see pages 257–259).*

● Nizhni Novgorod

Nizhni Novgorod is the third-largest city in Russia, and its former name (from 1932 to 1991) was Gorky, in honour of the writer Maxim Gorky, who was born here. It is, however, perhaps better-known to non-Russians as the city to which Andrei Sakharov was exiled in the 1980s after the outspoken Nobel Laureate criticised the Soviet Union for invading Afghanistan. His house can now be visited, although because it's a little off the beaten track, it is not always part of the shore excursion.

Nizhni Novgorod has been an important trading centre since the 13th century, and became famous for its huge trade fair of floating barges, Yarmarka, a tradition that continues today. The city is also a major manufacturing centre for river cruise vessels, naval vessels, submarines, trains, cars (the largest car factory in Russia is located here) and military trucks, as well as electrical equipment. The presence of the military factories meant the city was closed to outsiders for decades.

The river station is just below the walls of the 16th-century Kremlin. Most of the buildings inside the Kremlin are government offices, but you can visit the 17th-century **Cathedral of the Archangel Michael** (open daily 9am–2pm), and see the eternal flame, a monument to the heroes of World War II. As well as the **Sakharov Museum** (open Sat–Thurs 10am–5pm), you can see a variety of wooden houses where Gorky lived, including the **Gorky Museum** (open Tues, Wed, Fri–Sun 9am–5pm).

● Kazan

The Volga at Kazan is wide and slow-moving, winding through hilly country bisected by ravines. Kazan is the capital of the Tatar Republic – "Tatarstan", which declared its autonomy from the rest of Russia in 1990, although this has not yet been granted.

Almost half of the one million inhabitants are, in any case, Russian. The Tatars themselves were once a warlike and nomadic Turkish tribe. The city was founded in the 13th century by Mongols who had occupied Russia, and became the seat of the mighty Golden Horde (Tatar) Empire until it was conquered by Tsar Ivan the Terrible in 1552. The old Tatar fortress was rebuilt as a striking Russian kremlin, the white walls and towers of which date back to the 16th and 17th centuries.

Much of the city was burnt to the ground during a revolt in the 18th century. Catherine the Great rebuilt it on a gridiron pattern, including the **Cathedral of SS Peter and Paul**. Today, Kazan is a busy Volga port, half-Russian and half-Tatar, its exotic-sounding name matched by its blend of Muslim and Christian cultures – there are elements of Asia, including several mosques, sitting alongside the onion-domed churches. Kazan State University, founded in 1804, is where two famous Russian figures studied, Vladimir Lenin and Leo Tolstoy.

Most stops here include a city tour, but if you want to explore independently, see the **Museum of the Republic of Tatarstan** (open Tues–Sun 10am–5pm) and the colourful central market, piled high with tropical fruits, vegetables, flowers and some distinctly unappetising cuts of meat, including pigs' and horses' heads.

● **Ulyanovsk**

Around 74 km (46 miles) downstream from Kazan, the Volga is joined by the Kama, its largest tributary, flowing in from the Ural Mountains to the east. Just south of here is the town of Ulyanovsk (formerly Simbirsk), occupying both banks. It was founded in 1648 to protect the southeastern outskirts of the Russian

Maps on pages 256, 278

A samovar, traditional Russian implement for brewing tea.

BELOW: hand-crafted souvenirs.

state from incursions. It is most famous for being Lenin's birthplace, hence its name: Lenin's original surname was Ulyanov – "Lenin" was one of the many revolutionary *noms de guerre*.

Samara was once a trading centre of bread, wool and leather, but is famed in Russia today for the products of its chocolate factory, Rossia.

● Samara

Located on a sharp bend on the River Volga at its confluence with the Samar River, Samara was founded in 1586 as a fortress to protect the Volga trade route. Formerly called Kuybyshev (it reverted to Samara in 1991), it is the administrative centre of Samara Province, and is now a major industrial centre, although it has the feel of a holiday resort as you cruise along the sluggish Volga on a hot day, with people sunbathing on the beaches and strolling along the parks and gardens that line the river banks.

The most fascinating thing to see here is **Stalin's Bunker** (open Mon–Fri 11am–1pm, 2–3pm; guided tours only), buried nine storeys below the Academy of Culture and Art. Even though Stalin never used it, you'll have the feeling of looking at a piece of political history.

● Saratov

The sprawling industrial city of Saratov is the administrative centre of Saratov Province. Like many other Volga ports, it was founded (in 1590) as a fortress to protect the trade route along the river from nomadic raiders. In the 19th century, Saratov became a major commercial centre, especially after the railway to Moscow was built in the 1870s.

BELOW: richly painted ceilings are a feature of Russian Orthodox churches.

The river here is at least 3 km (2 miles) wide, even wider in places, with parks and promenades along its embankment, Naberezhnaya Kosmonavtov. This

stretch of the bank was named in honour of Yuri Gagarin, the first man in space, who lived and studied in Saratov; there's a statue of him on the promenade.

The city's largest pre-revolutionary industry, flour milling, is still important, and glass, brick and other building materials, footwear, clothing and foodstuffs are also produced. Timber rafted down the Volga is processed at Saratov's sawmills and made into furniture. Petroleum and natural gas occur in the locality and help contribute to Saratov's important chemical industries. In the 1960s a large dam and hydroelectric station were completed at Volsk on the Volga immediately above the city. While the suburbs are heavily industrial and not especially pleasant, there are a few museums, including the **Gagarin Museum** (open Mon–Fri 9am–4pm), which gives an insight into the life of the cosmonaut. The city also has a curiously German feel; a lot of German settlers lived here before it was occupied by the Nazis in World War II, and many visit today.

● Volgograd (formerly Stalingrad)

Famous for its role in World War II, Volgograd has a long history. During the 13th century the area around the lower Volga was occupied by the Golden Horde. When the Kazan and Astrakhan khanates eventually collapsed in the second half of the 16th century, a new town called Tsaritsyn was built on the island where the Tsaritsyn River flows into the Volga.

It was designed to protect Russia's southeastern borders. Peter the Great attached great importance to Tsaritsyn and built a barrage more than 60 km (38 miles) long and a rampart about 12 metres (40 ft) high. In the late 18th century, the area was settled by a sizeable colony of Germans, and over the following decades became established as an important river port and commercial centre.

Map on page 278

Tea and coffee are popular in Russia. Locals typically drink tea without milk, while the quality of coffee is variable.

BELOW: vessels on the Volga.

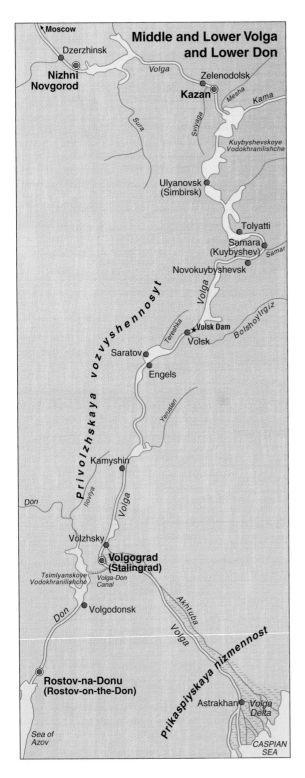

Middle and Lower Volga and Lower Don

Moscow
Dzerzhinsk
Nizhni Novgorod
Volga
Zelenodolsk
Kazan
Mesha
Kama
Sviyaga
Sura
Kuybyshevskoye Vodokhranilishche
Ulyanovsk (Simbirsk)
Tolyatti
Samara (Kuybyshev)
Samar
Novokuybyshevsk
Volga
Privolzhskaya vozvyshennosyt
Tereshka
Volsk Dam
Volsk
Bolshoy Irgiz
Saratov
Engels
Yeruslan
Kamyshin
Don
Ilovlya
Volga
Volzhsky
Volgograd (Stalingrad)
Tsimlyanskoye Vodokhranilishche
Volga-Don Canal
Volgodonsk
Don
Akhtuba
Volga
Rostov-na-Donu (Rostov-on-the-Don)
Prikaspiyskaya nizmennost
Astrakhan
Volga Delta
Sea of Azov
CASPIAN SEA

Renamed Stalingrad in Soviet times, the city was totally destroyed in one of the most famous battles of World War II. The true number of casualties may never be known, but at least a million Russians and 200,000 Germans died in what proved to be the turning point in the Russian resistance to Hitler.

Today the city hosts many memorials and several museums dedicated to the fallen heroes. Tours include a visit to the very moving **Mamai Hill**, overlooked by a huge statue of Mother Russia. The Memorial depicts a group of grieving citizens carrying wreaths to put on the heroes' graves. Behind the sculpture is a ramp flanked by granite blocks engraved with the dates of all the major battles that took place near the town. The ramp ends with an 11-metre (36-ft) high sculpture of a warrior with a submachine-gun and a grenade in his hand. Behind him rises a wide staircase with high walls on both sides showing the town's ruins. The staircase leads to a gigantic sculpture of a female figure symbolising the **Mother Russia**, a sword high in her hand.

● **Volga–Don Canal**

For cruises going to Rostov, the next part of the journey south is along the Volga–Don Canal, built in 1952, and leading from Volgograd to the River Don, connecting all five seas of the European part of Russia into one water-transport system. The total length of the canal is 101 km (63 miles). There are 13 giant locks along its route, from which the level of the water drops 88 metres (289 ft) to the Volga and 44 metres (144 ft) to the Don. Three reservoirs – Karpovka, Bereslavka and Varvarovka – occupy 45 km (28 miles) of its length, and a lot of the time you'll be cruising through what feel like vast lakes, with woodlands and dachas along the banks.

● **Rostov-on-the-Don**

A regional capital and large industrial city, Rostov-on-the-Don is both a river port and a seaport on the small Sea of Azov (part of the Black Sea), and is

Map on page 278

known as the Gateway to the Caucasus. It's also linked by pipeline to the petroleum fields of Caucasia. The city, founded in 1749 as the customs post of Temernika, when the river mouth was still in Turkish hands, lies on the fringes of Russia's vast steppes and was once a Cossack outpost and trading centre. Today, the river is busy with hydrofoils, tug boats, barges, cruise vessels and yachts, as well as large ocean-going ships making their way right across Russia from the Black Sea.

There are several busy beaches along the left bank of the river, lined with cafés, restaurants, outdoor kebab grills, karaoke bars and casinos. On summer nights, there's dancing under the stars and the area is buzzing until late. There are not many sights, although a visit to the **Nativity of the Virgin Cathedral** can be combined with browsing in the **Open-Air Market**. The **Botanical Garden** features a number of species from Eastern and Central Asia, as well as 500 types of tropical plant in its glasshouses.

The battle for Stalingrad lasted from July 1942 to February 1943, and was perhaps the greatest German defeat of World War II. Over 330,000 German soldiers surrendered when they were encircled by the Soviet army.

● Astrakhan

As an alternative to ending a cruise at Rostov-on-the-Don, some vessels continue down the Volga from Volgograd through the huge expanse of the Volga Delta to Astrakhan, an important fishing port situated on the delta about 100 km (60 miles) from the Caspian Sea, at a point where the river breaks into hundreds of smaller arms and flows through mile upon mile of marshlands.

Astrakhan itself came into being after Ivan the Terrible established a kremlin here in 1558, and is a city of bridges and canals. You will notice the presence of fishing vessels – fishing, fish-processing and caviar-preserving centres provide the city's major year-round industries, although caviar production is under serious threat due to catastrophic overfishing.

BELOW: part of the war memorial at Volgograd, formerly Stalingrad.

Orthodox Easter is taken extremely seriously, and is an interesting time to visit Russia and Ukraine.

BELOW: Russian sturgeon can reach an extraordinary 7 metres (24 ft) in length, and weigh up to 900 kg (1,200 lbs).

Sights worth visiting in Astrakhan include the hilltop kremlin, the solid walls of which encircle two beautiful cathedrals and a chapel, as well as a number of minor cultural exhibits. From the Red Gate, there are sweeping views of the city below, along the banks of the vast river.

One of the most popular activities is a cruise of the **Volga Delta**, an incredibly diverse area inhabited by hundreds of species of waterfowl, fish and mammals such as muskrats and otters. Only tour agencies and fishermen with special permission have access to the delta, so you need to book ahead. Fishing is permitted, but the fish must be thrown back. May and June are best avoided because of the black clouds of mosquitoes which will descend on any boat, while August is the time when giant lotus flowers are in bloom – a spectacular sight.

If you're simply wandering around, the wide walkway which extends along the river is lined with outdoor restaurants, street vendors selling their produce and fish, lovers and families taking a stroll, and friends enjoying the fresh air. Street vendors sell the ubiquitous *shashlik* (grilled meat kebabs), as well as small piles of green plum tomatoes, dried peppers and herbs, and dried fish.

UKRAINE CRUISES (DNIEPER AND CRIMEA)

Cruising the Dnieper from Kiev to the river's mouth at the Black Sea provides an opportunity to explore the lesser-known river ports of Ukraine and to venture out into the Black Sea to visit the Crimean towns of Sevastopol and Yalta. Relatively few Western tour operators sell this route, which takes about 15 days' round trip from Kiev. The river scenery is attractive particularly as it nears the delta on the Black Sea, with rolling hills and fertile countryside. Winters further north are harsh, though, and the Dnieper is navigable for only ten months of the year.

● Kiev

One of the oldest cities in Eastern Europe – it belonged to Lithuania and Poland until it was united with Russia in 1654 – Kiev still retains, in parts, elements of its former grandeur, mainly in and around the central network of broad avenues lined with chestnut trees. The city was severely damaged during World War II, but by the mid-1950s it had been largely rebuilt. By the 1970s it had become a modern river port with a well-developed economic and cultural life. Kiev's status as a major European capital was established during the emergence of an independent Ukraine in the early 1990s (the issue of Ukraine's true independence from Russia hit the headlines in 2004 with the emergence of Viktor Yushchenko as President – *see margin*). Today, a vast statue of "Mother Ukraine" stands high on a hill outside the city overlooking the river as she keeps watch over her "children". River cruise vessels moor at the river station, set in woodlands on the bank, a short drive from the city centre.

Kiev's major sight is the magnificent **St Sophia's Cathedral** (open Fri–Wed 10am–5pm), with 13 shining domes and rich in frescos and mosaics, was completed in 1031 in honour of the defeat of the nomadic Pechenegs by Yaroslavl the Wise. The Byzantine layout and design, as well as the name taken from the Hagia Sophia in Constantinople, reflect all the authority and prestige that Kievan Rus enjoyed at the time. It was the spiritual heart of the early Rus state and remains a treasure of Eastern Slav civilisation. The cathedral was restored and enlarged at the end of the 17th century, when many of the external intricacies were added in Ukrainian baroque style.

Vulitsya Kreshchatik is the main hub of modern Kiev, a sophisticated avenue of restaurants, cafés and shops, pedestrianised at weekends and holidays, and

Maps below & p278, 286

Ukraine's President Viktor Yushchenko was swept into power in January 2005 following mass protests against the defeat of his what was seen as a rigged election. The "Orange Revolution" has been seen as a hugely significant move for the country as it turns away from Russia and looks towards Europe.

BELOW:
Kreshchatik, Kiev's main thoroughfare.

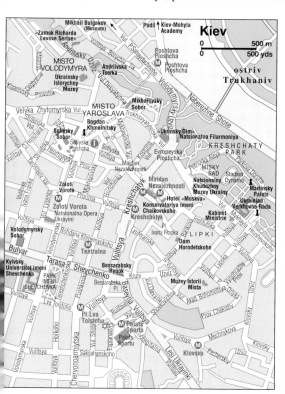

The River Dnieper was the scene of the first baptisms when Christianity was introduced to Russia by Prince Vladimir in 988. The importance of the river for trade is reflected in an old Russian proverb akin to "All roads lead to Rome": "Your tongue will lead you to Kiev."

famous for the rows of chestnut trees that soften the lines of its post-war architecture. The city authorities have tinkered extensively with Kreshchatik since the mid-1990s. **Maidan Nezalezhnosti (Independence Square)** lies off Kreshchatik and was remodelled to mark the 10th anniversary of independence in 2001; it attracts crowds of Ukrainians, street entertainers and vendors throughout the year. The square was the focus of the so-called Orange Revolution *(see margin, page 281)* in late 2004.

Andriivska Tserka (St Andrew's Church) was designed with exquisite grace by Rastrelli, the Italian architect who shaped 18th-century St Petersburg. It marks the entrance to one of Kiev's most likeable streets, **Andriivsky Uzviz** (Andrew's Descent), which winds its way down to the **Podil** region by the river. This is Kiev's Montmartre, full of artists and cafés, and the best place to shop for souvenirs.

About 3 km (2 miles) southeast of the town centre is the resplendent **Kievo-Pecherskaya Lavra** (Kiev Pechersk Monastery; open Wed–Mon 9.30am–6pm), a complex of churches, caves and museums founded in 1051 where you can easily spend a whole day. The monastery spreads down to the river, and the crowd of domes and cupolas poking above the woodland slopes is one of Kiev's most memorable sights. The name "Pechersk" comes from the subterranean passages, chapels and caves *(pechera)* that have been dug into the rock. The monastery barely survived the onslaught of the Tatars in the 13th century, but remained an important site of pilgrimage for Orthodox Christians throughout the Middle Ages. In the 18th century it acquired its present Ukrainian baroque appearance, and under the Soviets it was turned into a museum. Since 1988 most of the monastery has been returned to the Orthodox Church.

Kiev also has a **Museum of Folk Architecture** (open Thurs–Tues 10am–5pm) on its outskirts, housing over 200 structures moved here from various regions of Ukraine or constructed on the spot, mainly out of wood. You'll also see folk costumes, fabrics, embroidery, carpets, ceramics, musical instruments, paintings, tools and household articles.

Leaving Kiev, cruises spend a day sailing southeast along the Dnieper through gently rolling hills dotted with forest groves, villages, wide lakes and reservoirs, past villages and wooden dachas.

BELOW: view of the spires of Kiev's Pechersk Monastery.

● **Dnipropetrovsk**

Dnipropetrovsk lies close to where the Dnieper merges with the Samara in a pleasant setting of undulating, forested hills on a bend in the wide, slow-flowing river with vast, open landscapes. In autumn, the turning leaves on the trees are brilliant shades of yellow, red and fiery orange.

Founded in 1783 as a fortress settlement called Yekaterinoslav, it was known as Novorossiysk from 1796 to 1802, when its old name was restored and it became a provincial centre. Despite the bridging of the Dnieper in 1796 and the growth of trade in the early 19th century, Yekaterinoslav remained small until industrialisation began in the 1880s. Nowadays, it's a huge industrial centre with a thriving iron-and-steel industry. It was renamed Dnipropetrovsk in 1926.

The city is surprisingly green along the wide Dnieper River and has attractive embankments, long boulevards and spacious parks. There are several theatres and a philharmonic hall in the city, and visits usually include the **History Museum** on Zhovtneva Square in the heart of the city, giving an insight into Ukraine's past (open daily 10am–5pm).

● Zaporizhzhya

Zaporizhzhya sprawls below the point where the river once cascaded over a series of rapids, long-since drowned. The urban centre really only developed after 1927, when the hydroelectric station was built. Disaster struck during World War II, when the dam was destroyed, but it was subsequently rebuilt.

Zaporizhzhya's history began in 1770, when the fortress of Aleksandrovsk was built to ensure government control over the Zaporizhzhya Cossacks, whose headquarters were on nearby Khortitsa Island from the 16th to 18th centuries. For nearly 300 years the Zaporizhzhya Cossacks served as the rallying point for Ukrainian struggles against social, national and religious oppression. Tours of Zaporizhzhya include a Cossack show, with stunning acrobatic horsemanship performed on beautiful white horses.

● Novaya Kakhovka

The small town of Novaya Kakhovka lies along the shores of the Kakhovka Reservoir, on what was once semi-arid steppe country. In 1950, the construction of the Kakhovka Hydroelectric Power Station changed everything, and the town of New Kakhovka was born, with special emphasis on parks, gardens and green surroundings. There is not much to see as an independent visitor; walking along the river banks is pleasant enough but most tours use the stop here to hold a folklore performance in the Palace of Culture.

Maps on pages 281, 286

Dnipropetrovsk was founded by Catherince the Great's lover and administrator, Potemkin, as a summer residence for her as well as a fortress.

BELOW: tranquil scenery along the Dnieper.

● Kherson

South of Zaporizhzhya the lower Dnieper flows through rich, fertile land, with vines, watermelons and corn grown in the fields along its banks. Kherson, sometimes spelled Herson, is a hilltop city and the administrative centre of the eponymous province in southern Ukraine. The city sits high on the west bank of the lower Dnieper River about 25 km (16 miles) from the mouth, on the edge of its huge delta. The city has wide, sandy beaches, packed with sunbathers on hot summer days.

Founded in 1778 by the military leader and statesman Grigory Potemkin as a fortress to protect the newly acquired Black Sea frontage of Russia, Kherson became the first Russian naval base and shipyard on the Black Sea. Potemkin is buried in St Catherine's Cathedral in the centre. The main activity offered here, though, is to board a small boat and cruise the waterways of the Dnieper Delta, drifting through narrow canals watching bird and animal life en route to Fishermen's Island.

● Odessa

Situated on the northwest shore of the Black Sea, Odessa's architecture has a strong French influence. The Odessa Opera House, with its Italian Baroque façade, is prized throughout the former Soviet Union. Some cruises spend an evening in port so guests can attend a performance here.

River vessels dock at the cruise terminal (at this point, your river cruise becomes an ocean-going one), a short walk from the famous **Potemkin Steps**. The steps have 10 landings, and these become wider when going from top to bottom; thus, an interesting optical illusion is created. If you stand at the top of

BELOW: Odessa's Deribasovskaya street is full of bars, cafés – and odd photo opportunities.

the stairway and look down, you see only steps. If you stand at the bottom of the stairway and look up, you see only landings.

Visit the fabulous **Opera House** (open Tues–Sun 10am–6pm; performances from 6.30pm), its ceiling decorated with images from Shakespeare's plays. Unfortunately, the building is badly in need of renovation, with large cracks appearing on exterior walls. It was destroyed by fire in 1873 and rebuilt ten years later; its design is similar to that of the State Opera in Vienna (indeed it was designed by two Viennese architects, Fellner and Helmer). The hall itself is renowned for its wonderful acoustics, and was greatly admired by such composers and artists as Schalyapin, Rimsky-Korsakov and Tchaikovsky; Glazunov, Rimsky-Korsakov and Tchaikovsky all conducted here.

Another worthy site is the **Uspensky Cathedral** (also known as the Dormition or Assumption), with its five blue-and-white domes. Also worth visiting are the **Statue of the Duke of Richelieu**, the **Vorontsov Palace** on the waterfront and the **Archaeological Museum** (open Tues–Sun 10am–5pm), with exhibits from the Black Sea area and Egypt.

Half an hour's drive away, at Nerubayskye, is the entrance to the **Catacombs**, an amazing network of over 1,000 km (620 miles) of tunnels extending under the city and its surroundings, which were used by smugglers, revolutionaries and, most notably, World War II partisans. A visit to the small **Resistance Museum** is usually included.

Tour companies also operate visits to the **Uspensky Monastery**, 40 minutes away, for anyone interested in the Russian Orthodox Church. There is an icon museum near by, as well as the summer residence of the Patriarch of Moscow and All Russia.

Map on page 286

The Black Sea coastal areas of Ukraine and Russia bask in a favourable climate, enabling the cultivation of water-melons and other warm-weather crops.

BELOW: the Crimean coastline at Yalta.

Sevastopol was almost entirely destroyed by the Crimean War siege, only 14 buildings remaining intact. Almost a century later, a 250-day siege during World War II laid waste to the city again.

● Sevastopol

From Odessa, the boat sets sail into the Black Sea for the Crimean Peninsula, where Sevastopol is positioned just above the southwestern tip in a natural harbour. In town, visit the **Panorama** (open May–Sept daily 9.30am–6pm, Oct–Apr Tues–Sun 9.30am–6pm), a huge circular tableau depicting the defence of the city during the Crimean War, and the **Maritime Museum** (open Wed–Sun 10am–6pm), which traces the history of the Black Sea Fleet. There's good shopping, with plenty of street stalls and open-air galleries (you can pay in US dollars), and a wide choice of places to eat (reasonable if you drink the excellent local wine; expensive otherwise). The indoor **Flower Market** near the Hotel Ukraine is worth seeing; a lot of people buy flowers here to place at the war memorials.

Balaclava, scene of the Charge of the Light Brigade during the Crimean War in the mid-19th century, is only half an hour's drive away. There will be plenty of taxi drivers offering tours. There's a viewpoint on Sapoune Heights that overlooks the battlefield. You can also see the North Valley, where Russian guns were positioned, and the port, which was the main British supply base.

The ancient Greek city of **Chersonesos**, situated on a headland by the sea, is worth a visit as a well-preserved example of an ancient countryside settlement, with many of the stone houses and allotments still in existence, their foundations dating back to the 5th century BC.

● Yalta

Vaguely subtropical Yalta is a fashionable harbour and resort town, where the former Russian nobility built summer palaces. This, and the beautiful setting against the Crimean mountains, lends it the raffish air of an eastern Riviera.

BELOW:
The Swallow's Nest near Yalta dates from 1912.

Map on page 286

On the approach to the port, which is surrounded by wooded hills and vineyards, look out for the dramatic **Swallow's Nest**, a turreted tower perched high on a hill. Yalta is said to have more health resorts and spas than any other city in the world (there are reportedly more than 100 spas), including one established in 1900 at the instigation of the writer-physician Anton Chekhov.

The centre is five to ten minutes' walk from the dock. The hub of everyday town life is around the mouth of the little Bystraya River, although visitors flock to the shops and restaurants on the seafront promenade stretching west. The main sight in Yalta itself is the **Chekhov Residence** – known as the "white dacha" it was built by the famous writer in 1898 and is now a museum (open June–Sept Tues–Sun 10am–5.15pm, Oct–May Wed–Sun 10am–4pm). The delightful **Nikitski Botanical Gardens** (open daily June–Aug 8am–8pm, Sept–May 9am–4pm) are on a hill just outside of town. Further out (24 km/15 miles from town), the **Levadia Palace** (open May–Nov Thurs–Tues 10am–5pm, also closed Mon Dec–Apr) was the summer residence of Tsar Nicholas II and the scene of the famous conference between Churchill, Stalin and Roosevelt in 1945, when the post-war map of Europe was drawn up. A typical shore excursion to see the Palace takes around three hours.

Some cruise lines offer excursions to the **Massandra Palace**, the summer residence of Alexander III (open May–Oct Tues–Sun 9am–6pm; Nov–Apr Wed–Sun 9am–4pm), which later became a favourite of Stalin, and is located two and a half hours from Yalta. There's usually an opportunity to taste the famous Massandra wine in the tasting hall of the dacha. There's also a nature reserve at **Alushta** in the spectacular Crimean Mountains, a short drive from the port, home to some 2,600 species of wild plants as well as an abundance of birdlife. ❑

A hydrofoil service connects Yalta with other resorts along the scenic Crimean coast.

BELOW: souvenir stall in downtown Yalta.

THE NILE

A cruise down the Nile is the perfect way to see Egypt and the awe-inspiring grandeur of its ancient sites. Most itineraries operate from Aswan to Luxor, with a couple of days in Cairo

Maps on pages 292, 296

A Nile cruise is a journey back through the millennia to a time when the Pharaohs believed they were immortal and people worshipped the gods of the five elements: earth, water, sky, air and the sun. Vast temples, elaborate necropolises, huge obelisks and incredible statues were erected along the banks of the Nile as each king tried to create his own legacy, celebrate victories and pay homage to the gods. The antiquities today are breathtaking, set against the exotic and beautiful backdrop of the Nile Valley as the river carves its way through Upper Egypt.

Without the lush green ribbon created by the Nile, Egypt would be barren desert. Almost all of the country's population of 66 million is crammed into just five percent of the land, most people living within a mile or so of the river. Either side of the narrow, cultivated strip, the Eastern Desert and Western Desert are quick to encroach, forming a harsh landscape of huge sand dunes, mountains shaped by wind, erosion and sandstorms, and empty plains of slate and rock. Life along the river itself is a curious mix of ancient and modern: skinny donkeys pulling carts laden high with sheaves of maize, and old men smoking hookah pipes of apple tobacco outside ramshackle internet cafés overlooked by mobile-phone masts.

PRECEDING PAGES: cruising past the Old Cataract Hotel at Aswan. **LEFT:** the amazing entrance to Abu Simbel. **BELOW:** a felucca.

Days begin fresh and cool, as busloads of visitors are ferried from the ranks of river cruisers to the temples, to admire the antiquities in the soft morning light. By midday, the sun is white-hot. The boats have left, the market stalls are quiet again and the towns along the banks revert to their normal sleepy pace. As the sun sinks lower in the sky in the late afternoon, the whole river appears to be bathed in gold, before a rapid, fiery sunset gives way to black, unlit night. Now, the towns come alive, with families out walking, bars blaring Arabic television, and tempting aromas wafting from food stalls, where *pida* breads are piled high and kebabs are fried on makeshift stoves.

A Nile cruise is a quick and convenient way to absorb this fascinating place. Whether you choose the most popular itinerary, between Luxor and Aswan, or take three soporific days drifting through the vast expanse of Lake Nasser, you'll take a crash course in Egyptology, visiting temples and tombs, learning the rudiments of the intricate hieroglyphic script and the complex funeral rituals of the Pharaohs, as well as exploring the riverside towns.

The course of the river

The River Nile (called Iteru by the ancient Egyptians) is 6,695 km (4,160 miles) long from source to mouth, making it the longest river in the world. It is formed jointly from the waters of the Blue Nile and the White

Cairo's markets, such as Khan al-Khalili and Maydan al-Atabah, are fascinating places to visit.

Nile, which rise separately far to the south in Ethiopia and Uganda, on the western flanks of the great East African Rift Valley. Their waters, fed mainly by the annual rains on the Ethiopian Highlands, merge at Khartoum, capital of Sudan, before coursing northwards through increasingly arid Saharan landscape towards Egypt. Between Khartoum and Aswan the river tumbles over a series of six cataracts, or rapids (the First Cataract, at Aswan, used to represent the southern border of Egypt, and the ancient Egyptians believed it to be the source of the Nile, from where the river went south into the Sudan and north into Egypt). Before entering Lake Nasser, the river reverses its roughly south–north course and flows back to the southwest, forming a feature called the Great Bend of the Nile. The river then heads north through Upper Egypt, threading its way past hundreds of small islands and several locks towards Cairo before reaching its huge marshy delta on the Mediterranean coast at Alexandria.

In order for boats to get over the cataracts, canals were constructed to run alongside the river. The topography of the area between the Second Cataract and the

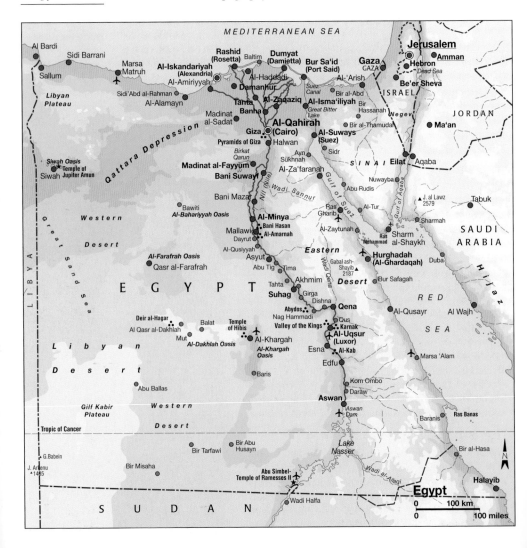

First (at Aswan) was changed for ever in 1889 with the construction of the Aswan Dam, in an attempt to control the annual floods, which were destroying farmland along the Nile Valley in Egypt. The dam was extended and strengthened in 1912 and 1933. In 1946, the surging waters of the reservoir which had been created behind the dam almost broke over the top, and the Egyptian government decided in 1952 that a new, stronger dam was needed upstream.

Maps on pages 292, 296

The Aswan High Dam

The $1 billion Aswan High Dam, funded partly by Russia after the US withdrew its offer of loans, took 18 years to build and was opened in 1970, 6 km (4 miles) upstream of the old dam. The huge reservoir created behind it, Lake Nasser, was named after the former president, Gamal Abdel Nasser, who died in 1970. Some 17 percent of the lake is in Sudan, and the two countries have an agreement for the distribution of water.

The benefits of the dam are better navigation of the river, flood control and a renewable source of energy that meets 50 percent of Egypt's needs. There are several disadvantages, though. The dam is filling with silt, which is no longer carried downstream and deposited on the banks as rich sediment. No sediment means erosion, and salination of the soil has become a serious problem, both of the levees, which are intensively farmed, and of the Nile Delta, which is shrinking and eroding.

Lake Nasser is 500 km (312 miles) long, 50 km (31 miles) wide and 70 metres (230 ft) deep at its deepest point. A new channel, the Sadat Canal, was constructed in Wadi Toshka (a dried-up river bed) in 1978 to drain off water from the lake every time the level reached 178 metres (584 ft) above sea level, and in the late 1990s astronauts in space began to notice the clear formation of four lakes in Egypt's Western Desert. The Toshka Lakes are being developed into new agricultural and residential areas, which by 2020 are expected to be home to 3 million Egyptians and to increase the country's arable land by 10 percent.

The river swells in summer, when tropical downpours in Ethiopia force a throughput that appears at its maximum flood strength in August and September. Its level then falls in November and December. The lowest water level is from March to May.

The Nile Valley from Aswan to Cairo is fertile, the heavily farmed levees lush with sugar cane, grasses, banana palms, cotton and various other agricultural crops. South of Cairo, from the air, it's a bottle-green ribbon across the yellow desert, but beyond Aswan in the ancient region of Nubia, the temperature can easily be 10°C (18°F) higher, and the river takes on a silvery sheen in the heat haze, the rocks and dunes of the Eastern and Western deserts alongside its banks.

The evolution of river cruising

The Nile has been used to transport goods and people ever since humans first settled in the region. A gradual drying of the North African climate from around 8000 BC encouraged local tribes to gravitate towards the river, which in turn encouraged the development of a sedentary, agricultural economy.

BELOW: bulrushes by the Nile.

The first known navigation of the entire Nile took place as recently as April 2004, when geologist Pasquale Scaturro sailed from Lake Tana in Ethiopia to Alexandria on the delta, making an IMAX film, Mystery of the Nile, *as he travelled.*

The first great kingdom of Egypt was formed by King Menes in around 3000 BC, and was followed by a series of powerful dynasties ruling for the ensuing three millennia. During this time, the ancient Egyptians built incredible tombs and monuments along the Nile, with elaborate barges being used to transport stone from the quarries at Aswan. When the river was high, the voyage from Thebes (now Luxor) to Memphis (near Cairo) took around two weeks, but in the dry season, the same journey could take up to two months. The felucca sailing boats, which still ply the waters today, were able to sail upstream in winter, thanks to the prevailing winds which blow from north to south.

Fabulous discoveries

It was only in the 18th and 19th centuries that archaeologists began to uncover the ancient tombs and temples, buried in a couple of thousand years' worth of sand and silt (inside some of the monuments, some of these pioneers' graffiti can still be seen carved into the soft sandstone). Their fabulous discoveries made Egypt into one of the world's first tourist destinations, and the setting for what must have been the first organised river cruises. Murray's original *Handbook to Egypt* was published way back in 1835, and the first steamers appeared on the Nile shortly after. Some of the early tourists took a trip up the Nile, but one needed to be resourceful and self-reliant to cope with the difficulties and such occasional hazards as sandstorms and robbery by Bedouin. The first organised river cruises specifically for tourists were set up by Thomas Cook in 1869 *(see panel opposite)*.

The world's attention was focused on Egypt in 1922, when Howard Carter discovered the tomb of Tutankhamun in the Valley of the Kings, near Luxor, prompting a new rush to see the treasures he had uncovered. In 1937, Agatha

BELOW:
enjoying the balmy breezes on deck.

Christie stayed at the Old Cataract Hotel in Aswan and wrote *Death on the Nile*, the famous murder-mystery set on a Nile steamer.

Package tourism as we know it today began to boom on the Nile in the 1970s and continued to grow through the 1980s, since when fortunes have been mixed: the first Gulf War in 1991 had a serious impact on tourism, and has been followed by a prolonged period of instability in the Middle East that has had a sporadic effect on tourism. In 1997, a group of German tourists were shot dead at the Temple of Queen Hatshepsut near Luxor, causing a huge drop in visitor numbers. The terrorist attack on the Red Sea resort of Sharm el-Sheikh (Sharm al-Shaykh) in 2005 did little to help the fortunes of tourism on the Nile.

Egypt is, however, an enduring and romantic destination. Today, there are some 230 passenger cruise boats in operation and a further six on Lake Nasser. The river is used much less nowadays for commercial transport, barges having been usurped by road and rail, but you will still see some laden with stone from the quarries, as well as hundreds of feluccas transporting tourists and locals.

What to expect

The typical Nile cruise is a three- or four-day voyage between Luxor and Aswan or vice versa. This takes in the temples of Kom Ombo, Esna and Edfu between the two towns and spends some time in Luxor, gateway to the Valley of the Kings and the Valley of the Queens. Alternatively, some boats cruise from Aswan to Dendera, 60 km (37 miles) north of Luxor, taking about a week. Abu Simbel, some 280 km (175 miles) south of Aswan, is offered as a day trip by air from Luxor or Aswan, or on a four-day cruise across Lake Nasser.

In recent years the Nile has become severely silted, which has prevented river

Maps on pages 292, 296

Osiris and Isis, legendary King and Queen of Egypt, were torn apart when Osiris was nailed into a gold coffin by his evil brother, Seth, and cast into the river. The annual floods of the Nile were once considered to be the tears of Isis.

BELOW: passengers on a Nile steamer, 1901.

THOMAS COOK AND THE NILE

The first travel company to operate Nile cruises was Thomas Cook, when, in 1869, he took 30 travellers up the Nile by steamer. Cook hired two English-built steamers, the *Benha* and the *Beniswaif*; neither was very clean, and his party "encountered fleas, though not bedbugs". By chance, they found themselves following the party of Edward, Prince of Wales, in six steamers, amply supplied with 3,000 bottles of champagne and 4,000 bottles of claret.

Soon, Thomas Cook was operating pleasure cruises by steamer all the way from Alexandria in the north to Wadi Halfa in the far south of Egypt, and sometimes beyond to Khartoum in Sudan. In 1872, the company opened an office in Cairo and prepared to serve the thousands of military personnel who were to pour through the Suez Canal on their way to the East. In 1884 John Mason Cook (son of Thomas Cook) was asked by the British Government to set up a relief expedition up the Nile to rescue Major General Charles Gordon from Khartoum. Together with his Egyptian managers, he oversaw a huge operation to move 18,000 troops, almost 40,000 tons of supplies, 40,000 tons of coal and 800 whaleboats. In order to transport the coal from Tyneside (England) to Boulac and Assiout via Alexandria, 28 large steamers and 6,000 railway trucks were required.

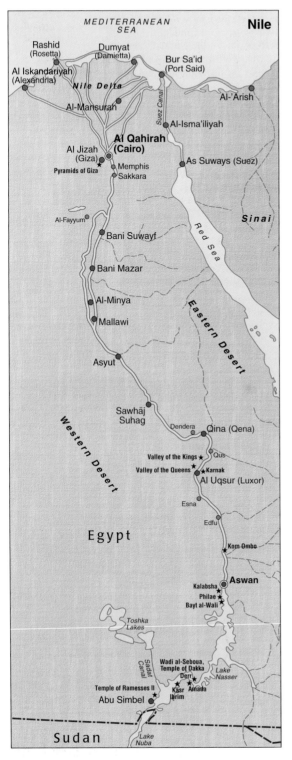

cruise vessels from sailing north to Cairo. Most people fly into the city at the start of their holiday, or out of it at the end, and spend a few days there exploring the Pyramids and other sights. In the past, longer cruises of 11 to 14 days from Cairo down to Aswan were always popular. These are likely to resume in the not-too-distant future (probably 2007), as a government-funded project is now under way to dredge the river bed, making it navigable for boats with a shallow draft.

The cruise boats on the Nile and on Lake Nasser are naturally of varying standards, and the staffing system is different from that on a European river cruise. Each ship has a manager, whose role is essentially that of a hotel manager. There's no captain; the vessel is controlled by three pilots, two of whom must always be on duty. Pilots have to have 15 years' experience on the Nile before they can sail a river cruiser, and they know the river intimately. If you're invited for a bridge visit, don't be alarmed by the lack of controls. There are no depth sounders or radar – everything is done by sight and experience. Boats sailing downstream have priority over those sailing upstream, as they take longer to stop in an emergency. The boats communicate with one another by horn or flashing lights, with a radio for emergencies only. Every cruise will include a few tense moments as wayward feluccas cut across the bows of an advancing river cruiser.

Value for money

There is no official star rating of boats, and you certainly get what you pay for. One way of guaranteeing a degree of luxury is to book a cruise on a boat operated by a hotel group such as Oberoi or Sonesta, or through an upmarket tour operator like Thomas Cook Signature or Abercrombie & Kent. One of the single biggest concerns of visitors to Egypt is hygiene, and the manager of a good Nile cruiser will allow guests to inspect the kitchens and be happy to explain about the water-filtration system. All boats take water from the Nile, and there are minimum standards of filtration allowed, but if you are going to eat salad or have ice in your drinks, it is absolutely essential to make sure the water has been passed through an extra filter.

Cabins on the better boats are spacious, with either big picture windows or French balconies; you can't actually stand on these but you can open the doors. But do ask yourself if it's worth paying extra for a balcony; you'll probably spend one night moored at Aswan and two at Luxor, with a strong chance that the boats will be stacked three deep, giving you an unenticing view of somebody else's cabin. There is talk of erecting pontoons at Luxor so the boats can dock perpendicular to the river and get around this problem. Another reason not to bother with a balcony is that mosquitoes will get in if you sleep with the windows open.

Food and facilities

Food on Nile cruisers is either buffet-style or table d'hôte, and will normally be a mixture of international and Egyptian dishes – lots of dips, falafel, fragrant rice and pasta, chicken and beef kebabs and stews. Well prepared, these are delicious. Most boats nowadays will happily cater for vegetarians. Alcohol is heavily taxed and is expensive. Egyptian wines take some getting used to (it helps if you like a resiny flavour), but are perfectly adequate.

Fellow passengers will be of all ages, although there are not usually any facilities for small children, and this is essentially a cultural voyage, not a holiday for people wanting nightclubs and sports facilities. Many boats carry an Egyptologist, or a guide who will remain with you for the whole cruise.

People with mobility difficulties will have real trouble on a Nile cruise, getting across three or four boats, in and out of buses and feluccas and, in particular, getting inside the tombs in the Valley of the Kings.

Map on page 296

When the explorer Robert Curzon first encountered the Nile in the 1830s, the water did not taste as good as he had been led to believe. He found that no one drank it until it had stood for a day in a large earthen jar, the interior of which had been rubbed with a paste of bitter almonds.

BELOW: traditional wheelwrights.

The best time to take a Nile cruise is between December and February, when the heat is less intense. August is almost unbearably hot, although September to November is good value and popular with visitors from France, Spain and Italy, who are less sensitive to heat than northern Europeans. There are fewer crowds at the antiquities during these months, too. Do note, however, that the water level on the river can be low between October and May; this is to conserve water in Lake Nasser. The result of this is that transits of the locks at Esna (between Aswan and Luxor) can take a long time, due to the build-up of traffic, not only of river cruise vessels but also cargo vessels and feluccas. In June and December the locks at Esna may be closed for maintenance, and passengers will be ferried to Luxor by coach. It's best to avoid booking at this time, as Luxor is a marvellous place to experience in the evenings and early mornings, and, when the locks are closed, you'll probably see it only on day trips by coach.

Destination highlights

● Cairo

Starting or finishing a holiday with two or three days in Cairo is a good idea, as it fills in some of the gaps that will be revealed during a visit to Upper Egypt (the city is not currently on cruise itineraries, although this should be changing soon – *see page 296)*. Visit the Valley of the Kings at Luxor, for example, and then see the mummies and the amazing treasures from the tombs in the Egyptian Museum, especially the solid gold coffin of Tutankhamun. Visit the Pyramids of Giza and begin to appreciate the astonishing accuracy of the architects of ancient Egypt, before moving on to the great temples of the south. After Cairo's round-the-clock noise – the roar of traffic, the calls to prayer from the great mosques and the general din of an intensely packed city – Luxor and Aswan, although relatively significant towns, seem like sleepy villages. *For details on what to see in Cairo, see pages 300–301.*

● Cruising Lake Nasser

A cruise across Lake Nasser, the biggest reservoir in the world, is a completely different experience from a Nile cruise, with its constant river traffic and busy excursion programme. A few temples aside, the lake voyage from Aswan to Abu Simbel, 200 km (125 miles) to the south, is simply three days of silence and emptiness, with just the desert and the brilliant night sky to contemplate; it is a wonderfully tranquil voyage.

The lake is an amazing sight – glassy and calm, surrounded by curious, pyramid-shaped mountains with flat tops. There's no greenery at all, just endless desert, the deep blue of the sky and the shimmering heat haze. Guides tell stories of spectacular creatures that inhabit the lake's waters – 10,000 ferocious crocodiles, up to 8 metres (26 ft) in length, and Nile perch weighing up to 100 kg (220 lb). Although the shores of the lake are sparsely populated, a handful of companies run fishing expeditions for perch, as well as tiger fish and giant catfish.

The creation of Lake Nasser following the completion of the Aswan High Dam in 1960 has flooded the area once known as Nubia, a region of great impor-

BELOW: looking across the island-strewn Nile at Aswan to the tomb of the Aga Khan.

tance to the ancient Egyptians and the location of some 22 impressive temples – at least, that is the number that had been discovered when the urgent salvage operation began to move as many antiquities as possible out of the way of the advancing water. It is estimated that about 800,000 Nubians were displaced and resettled when the reservoir was built, and you'll see a lot of them living and working in Aswan today – tall, elegant and very dark-skinned.

Some 17 of the Pharaonic monuments of Nubia that would otherwise have been drowned by the rising waters along the Nile were rescued from oblivion and moved either to the river banks or downriver. The Temple of Abu Simbel is the best-known and most spectacular. Five monuments were lost, partly because the UNESCO funding had run out and partly because they were not in a good enough state of repair to move, thanks to various earthquakes and years of being buried in the desert sand.

The first cruise vessel on Lake Nasser started operations only in 1993; the vessel, the *Eugenie*, had to be dismantled, then taken in pieces from Cairo and reassembled close to the First Cataract.

Map on page 296

All of Upper Egypt's towns were originally built on the east bank of the Nile, with tombs situated on the west bank. This is because the west is where the sun sets, representing death.

● The Temple of Abu Simbel

Located in the deep south of Egypt close to the Sudanese border, Abu Simbel has only been accessible by road since 1985, prior to which access was exclusively by boat. The magnificent site is a highlight for many visitors to Upper Egypt, now accessible by air (the most popular option), boat or a long, hot road journey from Aswan. The vast structure was built by Ramesses II between 1275 and 1225 BC, ostensibly as a dedication to Amun-Ra, Ra-Horakhty and Ptah, but in all probability as a vast ego boost to the Pharoah himself. ➤ *page 302*

BELOW:
on Lake Nasser.

PORTS OF CALL: CAIRO

Cairo is a vast, chaotic urban sprawl of around 20 million people, the largest city in Africa. It is a multicultural melting pot, a modern-day metropolis and a magnificent Oriental bazaar all rolled into one. Its reputation for dust, filth and noise, though valid, is only part of the picture in this city. The heat is fierce between April and October. Visitors eager to encounter the real Cairo, and not just the city of temples and mosques, should head for the narrow alleys in the old part of the city where Cairenes treat the streets as their living room. The centre of Cairo is bisected by the Nile, with the corniche (as the river banks are known) lined with five-star hotels and prestigious office blocks.

ORIENTATION

River cruises at the time of writing operate only to Luxor but the intention is to open more locks at Esna and to dredge the Nile, which is silting up, to allow boats to continue to Cairo. This is expected to happen at some point in 2007. River trips from Cairo are mainly felucca rides and they go from jetties all over the city centre.

GETTING AROUND

The excellent Cairo metro is inexpensive, quick and clean and the best way to get around. Buses are overcrowded, taxis are cheap.

BUSINESS HOURS

Shops are open 9am–7 or 8pm in winter and 9am–8 or 9pm in summer, often closing for lunch between 1.30pm and 4pm. Many shops are closed on Fridays and Saturdays. Major museums and sites are mostly open daily from 8am until 5 or 6pm.

TOP CITY SIGHTS

▲ PYRAMIDS (GIZA AND SPHINX)

These monumental wonders are southwest of the city. The Pyramids of Giza are truly awe-inspiring and are the only surviving structures of the Seven Wonders of the ancient world. The mythical creature of the Sphinx was carved from natural limestone and is suffering badly from erosion.

▶ EGYPTIAN MUSEUM

The enormous Egyptian Museum (open daily 9am–7pm) holds the world's greatest collection of Egyptian artefacts, with 155,000 exhibits documenting 4,500 years of history. Among the highlights are the treasures found in the tomb of Pharaoh

Tutankhamun by Howard Carter in 1922.

▼ MUSEUM OF ISLAMIC ART

This dusty, but wonderful, museum has a huge treasury of miniatures, carpets and textiles, weapons and assorted

block the view of the architecture hereabouts: the inner courtyards are especially magnificent.

▶ SULTAN HASAN MOSQUE

This mosque (open daily winter 8am–5pm, summer 8am–6pm) is one of the finest examples of Islamic architecture in the world. The walls are 117 ft (36 metres) high and so solidly built that the mosque was twice used as a fortress – first in 1381 during a Mamluk revolt and then again in 1517 during the Ottoman invasion. The intricately carved stucco friezes and marble ornamentation are the main features.

▶ IBN TULUN MOSQUE

The Ibn Tulun Mosque (open daily 7am–5pm) was built in AD 879 on the site where, according to legend,

Abraham was sent to sacrifice his son. It is constructed of red brick and stucco. The unusual minaret is a famous Cairo landscape and has a spiralling external staircase. The mosque is impressive both for its simplicity and grand scale – its courtyard alone covers 2.5 hectares (6½ acres) and

the sycamore wood frieze of Qur'anic verses is more than 2 km (1¼ miles) long.

artefacts, providing a complete overview of artistic development since Islamicisation. (Open Sat–Thur 9am–4pm, Fri 9am–11.30am, 1–4pm.)

▼ KHAN AL-KHALILI BAZAAR

Cairo's colourfully exotic Khan al-Khalili bazaar (open 10am–7 or 8pm) is the place to buy leather goods, hookahs, jewellery and antiques. Don't let the merchandise on display

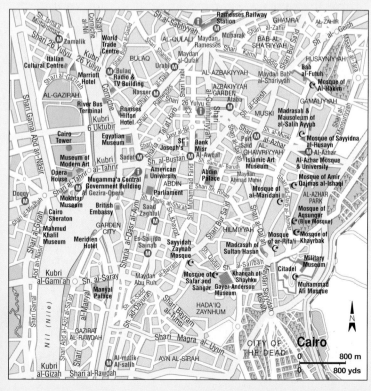

Four giant statues of Ramesses in various poses, each one 20 metres (66 ft) high, were hewn out of a single piece of sandstone and guard the entrance to an inner sanctuary, 65 metres (213 ft) inside the mountain. Statues of the three gods and the Pharoah sat in a carefully calculated spot within this inner space, penetrated by a beam of sunlight on 21 February and 21 October each year for just a few minutes, illuminating Ramesses II, Amun-Ra and Ra-Horakhty but allowing Ptah, the god of darkness, to remain unlit. A smaller, but almost as impressive, temple sits next to what's now known as the Large Temple, dedicated to Nefertari, Ramesses II's favourite wife, and Hathor of Abshek, a goddess with exceptionally varied associations and in three forms: a cow; a woman with the ears of a cow; and a woman with horns, a solar disc over her head and two plumes.

The temples were rediscovered, buried deep in the sand, in 1813 when Johann Ludwig Burckhardt stumbled across the upper parts of the huge statues. Giovanni Battista Belzoni found the entrance to the main structure in 1817. The temple was moved in 1965, being painstakingly sliced into blocks, piece by piece, and reassembled 210 metres (about 690 feet) from the original site, and 61 metres (200 feet) higher. The alignment was almost, but not quite, accurate, so the beam of light enters the sanctuary a day later now than Ramesses intended.

There are daily sound-and-light shows in several languages; the day trips leave long before these, but the lake cruisers spend the night here with an opportunity to see the show.

● Wadi al-Seboua

Around seven hours south of Aswan on Lake Nasser, Wadi al-Seboua consists of a couple of minor temples scattered across the barren, sun-baked hills. Wadi

al-Seboua itself is the last temple built by Ramesses II in Nubia, guarded by an avenue of sphinxes with the heads of falcons. A mile or so away (reached on foot or by tractor) is the **Temple of Dakka**, dedicated to Thoth, the god of wisdom.

● **Derr**

The Temple of Derr, also commissioned by Ramesses II, is another rescued monument with well-preserved reliefs depicting scenes of the Pharaoh. Unlike the Luxor temples further north, Derr is not lit and is viewed by torchlight, which adds an element of mystery and excitement.

● **The Temple of Amada**

Amada Temple is the oldest of the Nubian relics, a boxy structure built in the 15th century BC. It was moved in one solid block to preserve the paintings in the sanctuary and had to be hoisted on to a flat, extra-wide railway car and pushed at a painfully slow pace along a short distance of track. When the track ran out (there is no railway this far south in Egypt), the crew repeatedly pulled up the track behind the car and relaid it in front. The process of moving the temple 2.5 km (1½ miles) took six months.

The final stretch of the Lake Nasser cruise passes **Kasr Ibrim**, a more recent structure and currently the site of an archeological dig. Boats don't stop here but from the water you can see the remains of a Roman garrison and the arches of a 14th-century mosque built on the site of an earlier Orthodox cathedral. The rest of Kasr Ibrim is under water; it is the only vestige of Nubia's past left alone by the lake and not moved by UNESCO.

Map on page 296

TIP

The banks of the Nile are good places for spotting birds, among them the brilliantly coloured bee-eater, the pied kingfisher, and the Nile Valley sunbird. Black kites and the occasional Egyptian vulture can be seen overhead. Bring binoculars.

BELOW: some Nile cruisers have a small plunge pool on deck.

● Aswan

Egypt's southernmost city sprawls dustily on high ground on the east bank of the river, 130 metres (400 ft) above sea level, its centre a lush, green oasis of palm trees. The Nile braids itself around several small islands here, and the corniche is lined with hotels, their tropical gardens facing the sand dunes of the opposite bank. Feluccas zigzag backwards and forwards across the river, particularly during late afternoon when the wind picks up and the heat lessens, and *calèches* (decorated carriages drawn by malnourished horses) clatter up and down the riverfront. River cruisers are moored three deep along the Nile, a reminder that tourism is Aswan's most important industry nowadays.

Aswan is much quieter than Luxor, and small enough to walk around comfortably, at least, along the river bank and to the market. In summertime, however, the temperatures can be extremely high, often reaching 48°C (118°F). Winter is a more manageable 22–25°C (72–77°F); it even gets chilly at night.

The town is located in front of the older of the two dams, the old dam and the Aswan High Dam, on what was once the First Cataract of the Nile. Historic accounts tell of boats having to be rescued from the foaming waters, but the scene is considerably more tranquil today. The dam is not Aswan's *raison d'être*, though; it originally developed around stone quarries which were exploited by the Egyptians some 1,500 years before Christ, and there are tombs near by predating that era by another 1,500 years. Before the era of road and rail, this was also the northern terminus of the camel-caravan routes from Sudan, a journey across the desert of 40 days. Nowadays, however, tourism and the dam are the main businesses. Aswan was also made famous when Agatha Christie wrote part of her best-selling novel *Death on the Nile* in the impressive **Old Cataract**

BELOW: small village on the Nile near Aswan.

Hotel, located on **Elephantine Island**. The hotel today is a romantic colonial structure with beautiful gardens and a lovely terrace where guests take afternoon tea and watch the feluccas on the river below.

Map on page 296

Also on Elephantine Island is the small **Aswan Museum** (open daily 7am–4pm, until 5pm in summer), with exhibits from the Temple of Satet; the garden offers a welcome shady refuge. The ticket also permits entrance to the ruins of **Yebu** and to the **Nilometer**, constructed during Roman times to measure the river's rise, on the site of an earlier one. From the Old Kingdom onwards a strict watch was kept on the rise and fall of the Nile. Up until the 19th century, when Western technology began to revolutionise the management of water, frequent and regular readings were taken from here. Those responsible for the cultivation of crops and the maintenance of embankments and canals could thus know in advance what to expect; and other administrators could calculate tax assessments (a bumper crop year would mean more opportunity to boost tax).

According to a text at Edfu, if the Nile rose 24 cubits at Elephantine, it would provide sufficient water to irrigate the land satisfactorily. If it did not, disaster would surely ensue. Just such a failure, which lasted for seven years, is recorded on a block of granite a short way upstream: "By a very great misfortune the Nile has not come forth for a period of seven years. Grain has been scarce and there have been no vegetables or anything else for the people to eat." There are several other Nilometers along the river – for example at Rawdah Island in Cairo, dating from AD 861, and at Kom Ombo *(see page 308)*.

The Nile at Philae, between the two Aswan dams.

A popular trip in the late afternoon is a felucca ride across to **Kitchener's Island** (also called Plantation Island) to see the botanical gardens and stroll through long, shaded *allées* of palm trees. Across the water, you can see the **Aga Khan**

BELOW: Lady Duff Gordon, Victorian adventurer.

LADY DUFF GORDON AT ASWAN

One of the best-known Britons in Egypt during the 19th century was the remarkable Lady Duff Gordon. When she showed signs of tuberculosis during the 1850s, her doctors advised travel, and in 1862 she began a seven-year residence in Egypt. Most of it was spent in Luxor, where she was visited by many travellers from Britain. In 1863 she visited Aswan and was invited to join some slave merchants for dinner: "Oh! how delicious it felt to sit on a mat among the camels and strange bales of goods and eat the hot tough bread, sour milk and dates, offered with such stately courtesy. We got quite intimate over our leather cup of sherbet (brown sugar and water), and the handsome jet-black men, with features as beautiful as those of the young Bacchus, described the distant lands in a way that would have charmed Herodotus." The damage being done to ruins by thoughtless people appalled her: "The scribbling of names is quite infamous, beautiful paintings are defaced by Tomkins and Hobson, but worst of all Prince Pückler Muskau has engraved his and his *Ordenskreuz* (religious cross) in huge letters on the naked breast of that august and pathetic giant at Abu Simbel. I wish someone would kick him for his profanity." Lady Duff Gordon's vivid letters to her family were published and received considerable acclaim.

Timeless scenery on a backwater of the Nile.

BELOW:
the venerable
Old Cataract
Hotel at Aswan.

Mausoleum on the west bank. This is not open to the public, but it is the burial place of the late leader of the Ismaili sect, one of the richest men in the world.

Aswan has a bustling market street, **Sharia al-Souq**, where spices and scents are sold, together with an incredible supply of Egyptian souvenirs from "no hassle" stalls,where overenthusiastic vendors try to lure passers-by inside "just to look, not buy". If you do buy, haggling is essential and expected; it's part of the culture. Expect to reduce most items by about 75 percent.

Tours of Aswan also include a visit to the **stone quarries**, where you scramble up a steep path to see the amazing unfinished obelisk, 41 metres (135 ft) long, partly hewn out of the white rock. The work that went into cutting a single chunk of marble out of the quarry, engraving it and moving it down to the river, some 3,000 years ago, is quite astonishing.

● **The Temple of Philae**

Visits to Aswan typically include a drive across the dam, which measures 2,440 metres (2,660 yds) across, and a short boat ride to the island of Agilqiyya to explore the beautiful **Temple of Philae**, located on the reservoir between the two dams, and dedicated to Isis, goddess of magic. The temple is decorated with the image of her alter ego, the cow-eared Hathor, goddess of revelry and fertility. Philae is one of the prettiest of all the Egyptian temples, and it's hard to imagine that it was dismantled and moved from a lower location 150 metres (490 ft) away as the Nile waters began to rise. The structure, began by Ptolemy II around 260 BC and continued by a further five Pharaohs of the Ptolemy dynasty, has several components, including two huge pylons (as the towers of Egyptian temples are called) covered with reliefs and hieroglyphic writing, with an under-

lying theme of the love story between Isis and Osiris. All around the lower walls of the pylons there are smooth indentations where worshippers have gouged out dust from the sandstone as a symbol of good luck.

● Kalabsha

Kalabsha Temple is a short drive south from Aswan and is visited while the boat is still docked in the town. This is a Nubian temple, dedicated to the local god Mandulis, and is much more recent than the other temples along the Nile, having been built in the reign of the Roman Emperor Augustus (Octavian; 30 BC–AD 14). The temple has some stunning reliefs with intricate details of the crowns of the Nubian gods. The whole structure was moved from its original site, 55 km (34 miles) south of Aswan, in the 1960s.

● Bayt al-Wali

A short walk along the shore from Kalabsha is Beit el-Wali, another construction of Ramesses II, and another temple rescued from Lake Nasser. Beit el-Wali commemorates Ramesses II's military victories in Libya, Syria and Nubia. It's a small temple, but you can pick out the military scenes on the walls, and inside, some of the colours have lasted surprisingly well. A large statue of Ramesses II lies collapsed on the sand outside the temple; a poignant end for a Pharoah so keen to be remembered.

● Kom Ombo

The stretch of the river between Aswan and Luxor is particularly beautiful. Spend the voyage on deck, just looking at life drift by: water buffalo standing

Map on page 296

TIP

Aswan offers some of the loveliest views of the Nile. For those who wish to experience a felucca, it's a wonderful place to hire one of these elegant vessels for a short voyage around the islands.

BELOW: if it's too hot to walk, take a camel.

*Hieroglyphs at Kom
Ombo.*

motionless in emerald-green fields; herds of goats kicking up dust; small children playing football; people fishing from old wooden boats; the occasional train snaking its way across the desert landscape. The levees on the inside of the river bends are crammed with crops and small villages, while the outsides of the bends have been cut deep into the rock, forming steep ochre cliffs which change colour as the afternoon shadows lengthen.

Just 32 km (20 miles) to the north of Aswan lies the Ptolemaic temple of Kom Ombo, built on a sweeping bend of the river. The temple is dedicated to two gods: Sobek, the crocodile-headed god, who was worshipped before the time of the pharaohs; and Haroeris, the falcon-headed god of war, more popularly known as Horus the Great, son of Isis. Kom Ombo is a double temple surrounded by a thick outer wall, with two entrances, two halls and two sanctuaries. Guides point out the amazing reliefs towards the rear of the temple, clearly depicting surgical tools, including bone saws, scalpels and dental tools. Ancient prescriptions are engraved in cartouches, the formulae known only to the surgeons who invented them.

In the Chapel of Hathor to one side, there are three mummified crocodiles in a remarkable state of preservation. Look out, too, for the Nilometer, one of several along the river *(see page 305)*. As well as measuring the level of the water, this Nilometer was used to house crocodiles, which were common in the Nile prior to the construction of the Aswan Dam.

● Edfu

Further along the river, 105 km (65 miles) south of Luxor and surrounded by fields of sugar cane, is the temple of Edfu, one of the best-preserved in the

BELOW:
a statue of Horus,
god of war, at Edfu.

whole of Upper Egypt. This is the Temple of Horus, the god of war, started by Ptolemy III in 237 BC and completed in 59 BC. Two beautiful black-granite statues of Horus depicted as a falcon guard the entrance, and the sanctuary inside is in an amazing state of preservation. In the New Year Chapel, there's a superb relief of Nut, the goddess of the night, who was believed to swallow the sun every night and give birth to it again at dawn.

Map on page 296

● Esna

Only the longer cruises take time to call at the Temple of Khnum at Esna, much of which is still buried. The town has grown up all around the temple, which lies a full 9 metres (30 ft) below the modern buildings.

Khnum was the god of creation, depicted with a ram's head; he was believed to have fashioned mankind from Nile mud, using his potter's wheel. The temple is a Greco-Roman structure, constructed in the reign of Ptolemy VI and finished by Roman emperors; some of the decorations are believed to be as recent as the 3rd century AD.

An idea of the time taken to construct Egypt's temples is given by the record detailing the Temple of Edfu, which took 180 years, 3 months and 14 days.

The other notable feature of Esna is the locks, where river cruisers form long queues to pass through to the next, lower level of the Nile. New locks are under construction to ease the traffic, but for now, this can create a long delay. It's interesting, though, to observe the river traffic. There isn't much commercial shipping on the Nile nowadays, but at Esna barges laden with stone line up with the floating hotels.

● Luxor

The city of Luxor grew out of what was Thebes, the 4,000-year-old ruined capital of ancient Egypt's New Kingdom (1550–1069 BC), built on the eastern banks of the River Nile. Ancient Thebes was a busy and prosperous place, surrounded by monuments and tombs of unimaginable splendour, with lavish temples built for the gods Amun, Mut and Khons. The city was, however, sacked in 672 BC and left to decay. By Roman times, Thebes was already a ruin.

BELOW: life in rural Egypt remains largely untouched by the modern world.

Luxor has often been called (particularly by Egyptians) the world's greatest outdoor museum; it is believed that only around 30 percent of the fabulous antiquities have been unearthed. The excavations go on, and new discoveries are being made all the time, adding a real element of excitement to the place. *For details on what to see in Luxor, see pages 310–313.*

● Dendera

The vast majority of northbound cruises end in Luxor, but a few continue 60 km (37 miles) north along the Nile to Qena city and the granite Temple of Dendera, a Greco-Roman offering to the goddess Hathor. The temple was started by Ptolemy II and completed by the Roman emperors. It has a beautiful hypostyle hall, supported by 24 columns, each with a capital bearing a carved face of the goddess. The ceiling is decorated with vultures, winged discs and images of the moon, sun, stars and planets, as well as the usual depictions of the goddess Nut, swallowing the sun every night and giving birth to it again in the morning. ❏

PORTS OF CALL: LUXOR

Luxor is a manageable, pleasant city, thoroughly geared to tourism. The east bank of the Nile is solid with river cruisers; too many, almost, as only those on the outside of the ranks enjoy the magnificent view across the river to the sandy hills of the west bank and the thrilling secrets they conceal.

Although towns were always built on the east bank and tombs on the west, Luxor's west bank is becoming developed, with alabaster workshops and farming villages dotted around the fertile fields. A drive across here at dawn is still magical, the rising sun reflecting off the glassy water of the irrigation canals and turning the mountains a soft shade of golden yellow. Every morning, a cluster of hot-air balloons takes off and drifts silently over the Nile and the valleys of the Kings and Queens.

ORIENTATION

Nile cruise vessels dock along the east bank in a long string, so some can be quite a distance from the centre. This isn't necessarily a problem, as there are *calèches* (horse-drawn carriages) everywhere. The main areas of interest in the town are the Corniche, along which *calèches* form a constant stream, bearing travellers on a well-trodden route between the Luxor Museum, the market, the Luxor Temple, which is in the middle of the town, and the riverboats.

GETTING AROUND

Taxis are the easiest way to get around Luxor. The *calèches* is a more leisurely mode of transport, but agree a price before you start your journey. *Arabayas* (microbuses) also operate around the town and are quite inexpensive.

BUSINESS HOURS

The opening hours of shops are not regulated, and are mostly related to the visiting times of monuments nearby. Some shops in Luxor are open 8am–5pm, others stay open until 10 or 11pm – each trader opens and closes to demand. Friday is the official day off.

TOP SIGHTS

▲ **LUXOR TEMPLE** Luxor Temple, like Karnak *(see page 312)* is dedicated to Amun and Mut. The impressive entrance is guarded by two enormous statues of Ramesses II, who ordered the construction of the great pylon. A lone, graceful obelisk towers 25 metres (82 ft) over the statues; its partner was given to the city of Paris in 1833 and now adorns the Place de la Concorde.

Interestingly, a mosque was constructed on top of the temple in the 14th century and is still in use today. It's a strange sight, one form of architecture so obviously built on top of something

are open until you arrive at the site. Each one is unromantically named "KV" and then a number, according to the order in which the tombs were officially mapped in the 19th century. The entrance fee covers any three tombs except KV62, the tomb of Tutankhamun, for which an extra charge is made.

Most tombs don't actually contain any human remains, but the hieroglyphs and paintings on the walls are stunning, with incredible colour that has remained unchanged over the millennia. The usual style is three corridors, an antechamber and a sunken sarcophagus chamber, where the

mummy would be installed. Texts from the Book of the Dead, the Book of the Gates and the Book of the Underworld adorn the walls, telling the story of the Pharaoh's life and preparing him for the experiences he will have in the next life. KV2, the tomb of

Ramesses IV, is particularly impressive, with dazzling colour adorning the walls. Seti I's burial place (KV17) is also wonderfully colourful, with 11 chambers and side rooms and stunning reliefs.

Tutankhamun's tomb is small and unimpressive; what caused all the excitement in 1922 when it was discovered by Howard Carter was the incredible richness of its contents – gold statues, shrines and jewels, untouched by grave robbers. The mummy was encased in three coffins, two of gilded wood and one of solid gold, encrusted with lapis lazuli and turquoises. The gold mask is now in the Egyptian Museum in Cairo. The tombs are open daily 6am–6pm summer, 9am–5pm winter.

completely different, but what was once the mosque's door is now a window, several metres above the ground. When the mosque was built, the temple itself was several metres under the surface, buried in silt. Open daily 6am–9pm, until 10pm in summer.

▲ VALLEY OF THE KINGS/ TOMB OF TUTANKHAMUN

Across the river from Luxor, the pharaohs were buried in a honeycomb of tombs set in what is now known as the Valley of the Kings. For many, this is the real highlight of a Nile cruise. Above ground, there's little to see apart from hordes of visitors blinking as they emerge into the sunlight, the real treasures lying deep inside the mountains in an unassuming blind valley. There are 66 known tombs, built for the pharaohs of the 18th, 19th and 20th dynasties, which are opened to the public in rotation. You won't know which tombs

KARNAK (TEMPLE COMPLEX OF AMUN-RA)

(picture on page 311, top right)
Karnak is absolutely breathtaking because of its sheer size. The complex covers an amazing 40 hectares (100 acres) and took 1,300 years to build; the great Temple of Amun,

the king of the gods, is the largest in the world supported by columns, and could easily accommodate Notre Dame in Paris.

Construction began in the reign of King Sety I (1294–1279 BC). The entrance to the site is via an avenue of sphinxes *(picture on page 311)* with rams' heads, remarkably intact, which leads to two enormous pylons. Statues of the king stand between the forelegs of each sphinx. The Great Hypostyle Hall is incredible, supported by 134 columns, each 23 metres (75 ft) high with an open, papyrus-shaped capital so vast that 50 people could stand on it. Several smaller temples occupy the site, too.

Beside the complex is a sacred lake in which the priests would perform nocturnal rituals, and now the setting for most of Karnak's famous sound-and-light show, performed every night.

Visitors are guided slowly through the site after dark, mysterious voices echoing out as evocative lighting illuminates different aspects of the ancient site. For atmosphere, it's unbeatable. The temple complex is open daily, 6am–6.30pm in summer, 6.30am–5.30pm in winter.

◀ RAMASSEUM

What remains of Ramesses II's mortuary temple, the Ramasseum, is a majestic monument to this prolific Pharaoh (he reigned for over 60 years and had over 80 children).

A short distance south of the Ramasseum, the road from Luxor passes the Colossi of Memnon – two huge seated figures, each 20 metres (66 ft) tall, of Amenhotep III. The statues are all that remain of that Pharaoh's temple and are cut out of single blocks of sandstone.

▼ VALLEY OF THE QUEENS / TOMB OF NEFERTARI

About a mile away from the Valley of the Kings is the Valley of the Queens, where so far, 80 tombs dating from 1300 BC to

1100 BC have been discovered. The tomb of Nefertari, the principal wife of Ramesses II, is one of the most beautiful in Egypt, with the walls completely covered in dazzling paintings. In the past there have been many restrictions on entry to the tomb. At present it is closed to the public.

on an ambitious expedition, bringing back images of giraffes, monkeys and leopards, which are carved on the walls. The structure and the hieroglyphs remain intact.

◄ LUXOR MUSEUM

The Luxor Museum is within a short walk of Luxor Temple, and completes the picture, with a display of Pharaonic relics from both temples. Luxor also has a small Mummification Museum, housing mummies, coffins and the tools used by physicians in ancient Egypt. Open daily 9am–1pm and 5–10pm (4–9pm in winter).

► WINTER PALACE HOTEL, LUXOR

The venerable Old Winter Palace Hotel, on the bank of

the Nile is an elegant, colonial-style building which attracts a lot of visitors. This is one of the places where Howard Carter stayed in the 1920s when he was searching for the tomb of Tutankhamun.

◄ TEMPLE OF HATSHEPSUT

The unusual temple of Queen Hatshepsut was built in the 15th century BC for the only queen to rule Egypt during the time of the Pharaohs. The temple is quite unlike any other, with three tiers of elegant columns connected by a series of ramps. The vertical

columns reflect the natural columns in the dramatic rock wall that forms a backdrop to the structure. The temple itself is dedicated to Amun and Hathor, with a smaller chapel built in honour of Anubis, the god of embalming. Outside are the stumps of two trees, from Punt (now Somalia), where the queen travelled

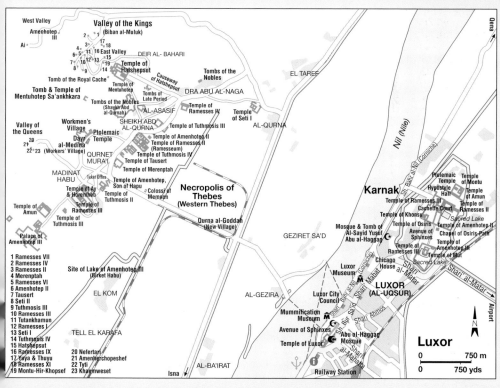

Luxor

0   750 m
0   750 yds

TRAVEL TIPS

P LANNING A TRIP

EVERYTHING YOU NEED TO KNOW BEFORE YOU DEPART

For a descriptive analysis of river cruising and river cruise companies, see pages 25–37.

Choosing a Cruise

River Cruise Vessels

In a brochure, distinguishing one river cruise vessel from another isn't easy. They're similar in appearance, and, at first glance, all seem to have the same facilities. The reality, though, is that vessels and river cruise products are not the same, nor do they deliver the same cruise or dining experience.

On pages 355–60 of this guide is a comprehensive listing of river cruise vessels in service across Europe, European Russia and the Nile, with independent ratings by the Maritime Evaluations Group.

To illustrate some points of difference, a summary of five vessels follows.

A'Rosa Bella (Arkona Reisen)

This river cruise vessel debuted in 2002, having been built in Warnemunde, especially for the River Danube. The *A'Rosa Bella* and its sister vessels, which serve the German-speaking market, each have a bright pair of pursed red lips holding a rose adorning the bows, epitomising their younger, funkier style.

The *A'Rosa Bella* measures 124.5 metres (408 ft) long, with a beam of 14.4 metres (47 ft). It has three decks plus an upper, open sun deck. There are two full-length accommo-dation decks, plus a few cabins on a third deck. All 48 cabins on Deck 2 feature a French balcony (the doors open, but there's only just room for your feet – you can't sit outside), while the 46 cabins on the lower Deck 1 and six cabins on Deck 3 (located

adjacent to the main foyer, the Centrum), feature a picture window.

Cabin décor is bright, breezy and contemporary. Passenger capacity is 242 in 100 cabins. All cabins feature two lower beds (these can be placed together to make a queen-sized bed), a writing desk, television and private bathroom with shower enclosure, washbasin and toilet.

The public rooms consist of the forward Aida Lounge, with large panoramic windows and a novel arrangement of its bar, so that passengers face each other instead of the barman.

The Markt Restaurant is open 24 hours a day. With its show galley, open grill and open seating, the dining room brings people together and is an excellent focal point. In other words, there's no sit-down dining, no set menu, no tablecloths (placemats only) and no assigned seating – a fresh approach for a river cruise vessel. The restaurant has panoramic windows and doors that lead on to the open aft deck for alfresco dining.

A notable feature of the *A'Rosa Bella* is its Fitness/Wellness Centre. This is located forward of the main staircase in the centre of the ship, and consists of a doughnut-shaped gymnasium connected to Finnish saunas, massage/treatment rooms, steam baths and changing areas. In addition, the vessel carries 50 trekking bicycles for the active types the company wants to attract. A tipping box is provided (tips are shared by all the crew).

Mozart (Peter Deilmann River Cruises)

The *Mozart* is a large, extremely spacious vessel, originally built in 1987 and acquired by Peter Deilmann

River Cruises in 1993. It is the forerunner of the rush to design and build larger and ever better vessels within the size constraints of Europe's rivers and locks. When it was introduced it was hailed, quite rightly, as Europe's most luxurious vessel – and despite stiff competition, this is a position it still just about holds.

The vessel is 120.6 metres (395 ft) long, with a beam of 22.8 metres (75 ft). It has three decks plus an upper, open sun deck. From uppermost to lowermost deck, the names are Papageno Sun Deck, Don Giovanni Deck, Tamino Deck and Dorabella Deck, named after characters from Mozart's operas.

The front of the vessel appears to be split into two sections, thus giving it the look of a catamaran hull, although this is not exactly true. The hull itself is actually a (single) monohull, although the vessel is wide, as it was built to operate on

Brochures

Remember that brochures are designed by company marketing departments to attract and tempt you to take a cruise. Within their glossy pages, every vessel appears to be the "Best in Europe" or "Best on the Nile".

Brochures are best used to determine which itinerary and cruise attracts you most. Use any vessel rating stars only as a basic guideline – each operator grades its own, usually with four or five stars, but that this is only really of value for comparing vessels within one operator's fleet. The listings section on pages 355–60 uses the fully independent rating system of the Maritime Evaluations Group.

the River Danube. The maximum passenger capacity is 212. Note, however, that there is no elevator.

There are two accommodation decks, 99 cabins in seven different price categories. Unusually for a river cruise vessel, there are also three interior cabins, each of which has a third berth available.

The size of the cabins is a very generous 18.8 sq. metres (203 sq. ft); the suites measure a superb 37.7 sq. metres (406 sq. ft). All cabins feature dark-wood cabinetry, closet space, sofa, drinks table, dressing table with mirror, telephone, television, VCR and radio.

The beds feature fine-quality European duvets with feather pillows and eiderdowns (pillows made of synthetic material are available on request). 100 percent cotton towels are provided, as are 100 percent cotton bathrobes (on request).

There are three principal public rooms, the lounge and the dining room. Due to the design of the vessel, the lounge has large, panoramic windows at the front, giving passengers a splendid bird's-eye view of the river ahead. The bar has sensibly been placed at the aft section of the lounge, and extends along the starboard side (a baby grand piano is located on the port side) so that passengers have maximum viewing space forward. A wrap-around promenade deck allows passengers to walk around the forward lounge and past the dining room.

On the deck below, a small, heated swimming pool occupies the forward space, and swimmers can also look forward to the river ahead. On the port side is a massage room. There is also an infirmary and a qualified doctor on board, and the vessel flies the German flag.

The interior décor is dark, and, although it is quite pleasing to some, it does represent a rather heavy northern German influence – but then, the vessel's main market is German-speaking. The artwork is from Peter Deilmann's own collection.

The dining room has both smoking and non-smoking sections. There is one seating for all meals, at assigned tables, which means you could be seated with strangers. The dining room has window-side tables, and there is a central self-serve buffet display counter. Wine is not included with meals, but there is a wine list featuring mainly German and Austrian varieties. The crew of 80 includes personnel of several different nationalities. The euro is the currency on board.

Viking Primadonna (Viking River Cruises)

The *Primadonna* is a very spacious vessel which was launched in July 1998 as the *Delphin Queen*, and renamed *Primadonna* in 2001. The vessel is 113.3 metres (372 ft) long, and has a beam of 17.3 metres (57 ft). It features a wide interior promenade that is two decks high, and can be used as a sidewalk café, for exhibition space or customised for special theme cruises. The maximum passenger capacity is 196.

There are three accommodation decks and three sizes of cabin: 8.1 sq. metres (87 sq. ft), 12 sq. metres (129 sq. ft) and 16 sq. metres (172 sq. ft). Although not large, all cabins have outside views through large picture windows. There are two whole decks of cabins with private balconies (40 in all) that are neatly, creatively angled in such a way that each has its own two-person bench seat and floor-to-ceiling glass windows. In addition, four cabins are provided for the mobility-limited, with wider doors, and a large bed and sofa bed; all are adjacent to a glass-walled elevator.

All cabins have wood-panelled walls and are very well equipped, with twin beds (electrically operated so that foot and head sections can be raised and lowered independently), bedside reading lights, television/VCR, cordless, satellite-linked direct-dial telephone, personal safe, individual climate control, illuminated closets and minibar. A switch lets you turn announcements off or on, as required. The fully tiled bathrooms feature 100 percent cotton towels, hairdryer, large shower enclosure, toilet, shelves for personal toiletries, and 100 percent cotton bathrobe.

A glass-walled elevator travels between three of the four decks, as well as a sit-on stairlift on two aft stairways that go to the open-air sun deck. Unusually, this vessel also has a laundry service. Breakfast and snacks can be provided in your cabin.

Public rooms include an observation lounge, entertainment/lecture salon, and a dining room that seats all passengers in one seating at tables for four or six. The open sun deck is used for afternoon tea, buffets or for lounging in the sun.

Breakfast and lunch are provided in a self-serve buffet style, while dinner is a served meal. In addition, mid-morning bouillon, afternoon tea and a light midnight snack are provided.

River Cloud (Sea Cloud Cruises)

The *River Cloud*, introduced in 1999, is 110 metres (360 ft) long, has a beam of 11.4 metres (37.4 ft) and

carries a maximum of 90 passengers. It is a top-of-the-range river cruise vessel and product.

There are 45 cabins, of quite generous proportions, measuring 12–19 sq. metres (129.1–204.5 sq. ft). There are three price categories, according to cabin size and location. The cabins are very well equipped, and features include a large panoramic window, cherry-wood cabinetry, half-height wood panelling along the walls, two beds with European duvets and cotton pillows of 100 percent cotton, combination television/VCR, radio, telephone and individual climate control. The bathrooms feature 100 percent cotton towels, hairdryer, large shower enclosure and a fully tiled bathroom with anodised gold and brass fittings. Shampoo, conditioner, soap, body lotion, sewing kit and shoehorn are supplied. Soft drinks and bottled water are supplied free in a minibar (the cabins do not have refrigerators, though).

The dining room features arched windows, dark-wood-accented ceilings and wall decorations. Breakfast and lunch are self-serve buffet-style, while candlelit dinners are a sit-down affair with assigned seating. Table wines are included for lunch and dinner (although this will depend on which company has the vessel under charter), and a small premium wine list is also available. The food is extremely creative, and very attractively presented.

Other facilities include a 24-hour reception desk, shop, main salon with dark-wood ceiling accents and dance floor with baby grand piano and bar, library, hair salon and small fitness room with sauna. The *River Cloud* also has hardwood steamer chairs on its teakwood uppermost outdoors deck, as well as a wrap-around promenade deck outdoors.

River Navigator (Vantage Deluxe World Tours)

The *River Navigator*, launched in 2000, is 110 metres (360 ft) long, with a beam of 11.4 metres (37 ft). The maximum passenger capacity is 140, and the vessel is aimed at the US market.

There are three accommodation decks. The cabins are of reasonably decent proportions, at 45.7 sq. metres (150 sq. ft) or 68.5 sq. metres (225 sq. ft) for a junior suite. Suites and cabins are priced in four bands, according to size and location.

All cabins are smoke-free (as is the rest of the vessel, with the exception of the main lounge, which has both smoking and non-smoking sections), and are equipped with a television, in-room movies and CNN, telephone and private bathroom with shower and hairdryer. The beds are convertible and turn into a sofa for daytime use. Junior suites also feature a DVD player, minibar, coffee/tea maker, better linens, better artwork and a lounge area. The bathroom features a shower and built-in hairdryer.

There are two principal public rooms: the lounge, with piano music each evening, and the dining room. There is also a library with travel books, games and a small gift shop/boutique. The dining room, with its large, river-view picture windows, features one-seating dining and an open seating plan, so you can sit with whomever you wish.

Saxonia (Scylla Tours)

The *Saxonia*, which was launched in June 2001, is 82 metres (269 ft) long, has a beam of 9.5 metres (31 ft) and a draft of just 1.05 metres (3½ ft). There is room for just 88 passengers. There are only two decks (plus an open, uppermost sun deck), so it is ideal for travel along Europe's shallow rivers such as the Elbe, Moselle, Neckar or Saar. The navigation bridge is retractable, allowing the vessel to sail under the low bridges along various river routes.

There are two decks of passenger cabins. Highly practical twin "Murphy" beds can be pulled down from the wall for night-time use, while in the daytime these are completely hidden from view, giving the cabin more space and more of a private lounge feeling. European goose-down duvets are provided. The cabin décor features maple-wood panelling; fittings and furnishings include a walk-in closet with full-length dressing mirror, hairdryer and safe. Other features include a combination television/VCR, radio with alarm clock, telephone, refrigerator, individual climate control and a single 220-volt electrical socket.

The bathroom has a separate shower enclosure, white washbasin with blue/black marble surround and 100 percent cotton towels.

There are only two public rooms, the restaurant and the observation lounge, the latter featuring a ship's bow-shaped bar located at the front of the lounge. The carpeting throughout the vessel is in the same blue with gold motif that Scylla Tours (the owner of the vessel) places aboard all its vessels, and is both appealing and practical.

Because the vessel has a shallow draft and only two decks, there is no elevator. Instead, a wrought-iron stairway with brass handrail, located in the centre of the vessel, goes from the upper to the lower deck.

The dining room is attractive, and features wrought-iron and etched-glass room dividers, and a central buffet station. Breakfast consists of a self-serve buffet (although hot items can be ordered from the galley), while lunch and dinner are full-service meals. Dining is at tables that are assigned for the duration of the cruise. The catering is extremely good; plenty of choice is provided, the self-serve buffets have ample selections and there is always an excellent array of cheeses. Table wines are included with lunch and dinner.

Cabins

Almost all river cruise vessels offer outside-view cabins, and you often pay a premium for a bigger window or a balcony. A balcony is undeniably a luxury and is great for sitting quietly and watching the world go by. It is unlikely, however, to offer total privacy, and you'll still smell your neighbours' cigarette smoke and hear their chatter. If you are sensitive to noise, ask for a cabin well away from the bar and restaurant.

There are usually two or three decks of cabins to choose between, the uppermost being the most expensive. If you have mobility difficulties, check that the vessel has a lift or ask for a cabin near the gangway.

With a bit of cunning, you can secure a better view on a Nile cruise. As vessels head north from Aswan to Luxor, they almost always tie up on the left bank of the Nile (except in Aswan, where they're on the right bank). Unfortunately, they also tend to moor two or three deep. But if you ask for a starboard cabin and your vessel gets the outside position, your view across the Nile while in port, particularly in Luxor, where you will spend a couple of nights, will be uninterrupted. In a port cabin, you will only ever be looking at the river bank or the vessel next to you while tied up. Reverse this logic for southbound cruises.

River Cruise and Barge Cruise Contact Details

Booking from North America

Abercrombie & Kent, Inc.
1520 Kensington Road,
Suite 212, Oak Brook, Illinois,
IL 60523-2156, USA
Tel: 630-954-2944
Fax: 630-954-3324
www.abercrombiekent.com

Avalon Waterways
5301 South Federal Circle,
Littleton, Colorado,
CO 80123, USA
Tel (toll-free): 1-866-755-8581
www.avalonwaterways.com

European Waterways
Go Barging–European Waterways Ltd
35 Wharf Road, Wraysbury,
Middlesex TW19 5JQ, UK
Tel (toll-free): 1-800-394-8630
Fax: +44 (0)1784 483072
www.gobarging.com

Grand Circle Travel
347 Congress Street, Boston,
Massachussetts, MA 02210, USA
Tel: 800-959-0405
(toll free: 1-800-321-2835)
www.gct.com

Orient-Express Trains & Cruises
10 Weybosset St, Suite 500,
Providence, Rhode Island,
RI 02903, USA
Tel: 401-351-7518
(toll-free: 800-524-2420 (ORIENTX))
Fax: 401-351-7220
www.orient-express.com

Peter Deilmann River Cruises
1800 Diagonal Road, Suite 170,
Alexandria, Virginia, VA 22314, USA
Tel: (toll-free): 1-800-348-8287
E-mail: pdcmail@deilmann-cruises.com
www.deilmann-cruises.com

Sea Cloud Cruises, Inc.
32–40 North Dean Street, Englewood,
New Jersey, NJ 07631, USA
Tel: 201-227-9404
(toll-free: 1-888-732-2568)
Fax: 201-227-9424
E-mail: info@seacloud.com
www.seacloud.com

Uniworld River Cruises, Inc.
Uniworld Plaza, 17323 Ventura
Boulevard, Los Angeles, California,
CA 91316, USA
Tel: 800-733-7820
(international callers: 818-382-2700)
Fax: 818-382-7829
www.uniworld.com

Value World Tours
17220 Newhope Street, #203
Fountain Valley, California,
CA 92708, USA
Tel: 714-556-8258 (reservations, toll-free: 800-795-1633)
Fax: 714-556-6125
E-mail: travel@vwtours.com
www.vwtours.com

Vantage Deluxe World Tours
90 Canal Street, Boston,
Massachussetts,
MA 02114-2031, USA

Tel (toll-free): 1-800-322-6677
Fax: 1-617-878-6154
www.vantagetravel.com

Viking River Cruises, Inc.
5700 Canoga Avenue, Suite 200,
Woodland Hills, California,
CA 91367, USA
Tel: 1-818-227-1234
www.vikingrivers.com

Booking from Europe

Abercrombie & Kent
St George's House, Ambrose Street,
Cheltenham, Glos. GL50 3LG, UK
Tel: +44 1242-547-700
(UK only: 0845 0700 610)
Fax: (UK only) 0845 0700 607
www.abercrombiekent.co.uk

Arkona Reisen GmbH
Steinstr. 9, 18055 Rostock, Germany
Tel: +49 (0)381-4 58 50 00
Fax: +49 (0)381-4 58 51 09
E-mail: info@arkona.de
www.arkona.de or www.arosa.de

Blue Water Holidays
The Old Mill, Firth Street, Skipton,
North Yorkshire BD23 2PT, UK
Tel: +44 1756 639609
(UK only: 0845 226 2475)
E-mail: info@bluewaterholidays.com
www.bluewaterholidays.com

European Waterways
Go Barging–European Waterways Ltd
35 Wharf Road, Wraysbury,
Middlesex TW19 5JQ, UK
Tel: + 44 (0)1784 482439
Fax: +44 (0)1784 483072
www.gobarging.com

Noble Caledonia Ltd
2 Chester Close, Belgravia,
London SW1X 7BE, UK
Tel: +44 (0)20 7752 0000
Fax: +44 (0)20 7245 0388
www.noble-caledonia.co.uk

Peter Deilmann River Cruises
Suite 101, Albany House,
324/326 Regent Street,
London W1B 3BL, UK
Tel: +44 (0)20 7436 2931
Fax: +44 (0)20 7436 2607
E-mail: info@peterdeilmanncruises.co.uk
www.peterdeilmanncruises.co.uk

Phoenix Reisen GmbH
Pfälzer Strasse 14, 53111 Bonn,
Germany
Tel: +49 (0)228-7 26 28-0
Fax: +49 (0)228-7 26 28-999
www.phoenixreisen.com

Scylla Tours AG
Uferstrasse 90, CH-4019 Basel,
Switzerland
Tel: +41 61-638 81 81

Fax: +41 61-638 81 80
E-mail: info@scylla-tours.com
www.scylla-tours.com

Sea Cloud Cruises GmbH
Ballindamm 17, D-20095 Hamburg,
Germany
Tel: +49 (0)40-30 95 92-0
Fax: +49 (0)40-30 95 92-22
E-mail: info@seacloud.com
www.seacloud.com

Titan Travel Ltd
HiTours House, Crossoak Lane
Salfords, Redhill, Surrey RH1 5EX, UK
Tel: +44 1293 422433
Fax: +44 1293 440034
www.titanhitours.co.uk

Transocean Tours Touristik GmbH
Stavendamm 22,
D-28195 Bremen, Germany
Tel: +49 (0)421-3336-0
Fax: +49 (0)421-3336-100
E-mail: mail@transocean.de
www.kreuzfahrt-transocean.de

Travel Renaissance Holidays Ltd
28 South Street, Epsom,
Surrey KT18 7PF, UK
Tel: +44 (0)1372 744 455
(UK only: 0870 850 1690)
Fax: +44 (0)1372 724871
E-mail: info@travelrenaissance.co.uk
www.travelrenaissance.co.uk

Venice Simplon–Orient-Express
(Afloat in France)
Sea Containers House, 20 Upper
Ground, London SE1 9PF, UK
Tel: +44 (0)20 7805 5060
(UK only: 0845 077 2222)
Fax: +44 (0)20 7805 5908
www.orient-express.com

Venice Simplon–Orient-Express
Deutschland GmbH (Afloat in France)
Sachsensring 85, 50677 Köln
Tel: +49 (0)221-33 80 300
Fax: +49 (0)221-33 80 333

www.orient-express.com
Voyages Jules Verne
21 Dorset Square, London
NW1 6QG, UK
Tel: +44 (0)20 7616 1000
www.vjv.co.uk

Cruising with Children

River cruises can certainly be
educational for children, but families
will have to make their own
entertainment on board. River cruise
vessels will not have things like a
children's playroom, babysitting or
kids' movie channels on the TV, and
there is unlikely to be a children's
menu. Breakfast and lunch are usually
buffet service, which is no problem,
but you may have to ask special
favours of the chef in the evening –
and feel under pressure to have your
children behave at the dinner table
when they are in a minority on board.

Having said this, there is no
reason why young children would not
enjoy certain river cruises – the
Rhine Valley, for example, or the Po.
Vienna to Budapest is worth
considering, as both cities are very
child-friendly. The Nile has many
distractions that children would enjoy
(camels, felucca rides, markets,
tombs), but you would probably have
to keep temple visits to a minimum.

Another option is a luxury barge
holiday, which, if you book the whole
barge, is ideal for families, with
plenty of opportunity for children to
stretch their legs on the towpath and
on bicycles, and frequent stops.

The Elbe, the long Danube cruises
and the Russian waterways would
probably be less suitable for small
children and by nature attract a much
older market in any case.

If you do take small children on a
river cruise, consider packing a lot of
books, board games and a portable
DVD player.

Travellers with Disabilities

Sadly, river cruise vessels are not well adapted to catering for travellers with disabilities. Cabins modified for wheelchairs are like gold dust, and the vast majority of vessels don't have any at all.

The good news, though, is that with careful planning, even the fairly frail can take a river cruise. Most vessels have lifts. The vessel won't move around like an ocean-going ship, so the danger of falling is minimal. Getting on and off can be difficult but not impossible, and, in any case, you will be in the company of many others of a certain age who do not move fast. Long walking tours can be a problem – but there are always shore excursions that involve less walking and more sitting on a coach.

When to Go

There are advantages to every season in Europe. Early spring and late summer will be less crowded and can have beautiful weather. In July and August the weather is often at its best and most reliable, although it can be too hot for some, and there will be more crowds. You may want to time your cruise to coincide with certain events, such as the Rhine in Flames festival in high summer, or the paprika harvest in Hungary, or the beautiful autumn colours along the Danube's Wachau Valley. Special winter cruises operate on the Rhine and Danube to take in the Christmas markets – if you're lucky, you will get crisp, cool weather and snow on the ground, but rain and slush are just as likely.

Russia tends to be hot and humid in summer, so spring and autumn are better times to travel. Take insect repellent for travel in August and September, when midges can be a problem, and something warm for the evenings in spring and autumn.

In Egypt, the seasons are different. Nile cruises operate year round, the peak months being January to March, when it's cooler. August is really too hot for anybody except the most dedicated sun-worshipper. September is tolerable if you take things slowly, with the added advantage that there will be hardly any crowds at the temples.

What to Take

River cruise vessels may carry some basic supplies, but it's better to take what you need.

There is generally no limit to the amount of personal baggage you can take on your river cruise, if you can fit it in your cabin. Towels, soap, shampoo and shower caps are provided aboard most vessels but toiletries will probably be basic brands or unbranded, so take your own favourites. Storage space really is at a premium, so be prepared to share coat-hangers with your partner!

Do tag your luggage with your name, the name of the vessel, cabin number, sailing date and embarkation point (tags are provided by the cruise operator with your tickets, but it is surprising just how many people forget to carry out this simple but essential pre-cruise task). Baggage transfers from airport to ship are generally smooth and problem-free when handled by the cruise operator. Your luggage will be taken from the transfer bus direct to your cabin, which is why it's important to tag it.

Liability for loss or damage to baggage is contained in the passenger contract, which is part of your ticket. Do take out insurance for lost or stolen belongings. The policy should extend from the date of departure until two or three days after your return home.

Clothing

If you think you might not wear it, don't take it; closet space aboard all river cruise vessels is at a premium. So, unless you are on an extended holiday that includes a river cruise, keep your luggage to a minimum.

In the summer, where the weather is warm to hot, casual wear should include plenty of lightweight cottons and other natural fibres, or high-tech "wicking" fibres. Synthetic materials do not "breathe" as well and often retain heat. Clothes should, however, be as opaque as possible to counteract the ultraviolet rays of the sun. It's easy to underestimate this when you're on deck in a pleasantly cooling breeze.

Take a lightweight cotton sweater or windbreaker for the evenings, when the vessel's air-conditioning will seem even more powerful after a day in the sun. Pack sunglasses and a hat that stays on – gusts of wind on rivers are common.

Certain areas (such as Egypt, for Nile cruises) may be dusty as well as dry. In these latitudes, the weather can be changeable and cool in the evenings from October to March, so remember to take a couple of sweaters and a windbreaker. In the summer months, Egypt is breathtakingly hot, and you will need lots of changes of clothes, as well as something respectable for entering tombs or mosques. Capri pants and a cotton wrap are ideal for women; wandering round Egyptian towns in shorts and a tank top shows a lack of respect, and you're likely to be hassled.

For spring or autumn river cruises in Eastern Europe or Russia, take some warm comfortable clothing in layers, plus a raincoat or parka for the northernmost port calls. Unless you are travelling to northern ports such as St Petersburg during winter, you will not need thermal underwear.

Aboard the vessel, dress rules are relaxed during the day, but in the evening what you wear should be tasteful. Men should take a blazer or sports jacket and a tie or two for the dining room and for any formal occasions. For women, a cocktail dress is as smart as you need to be on the formal nights.

No matter where in the world you are travelling, comfortable low- or flat-heeled shoes are a must for women, except for formal nights. Light, airy walking shoes are best for walking – Europe's medieval streets are cobbled and uneven, so comfort is more important than style. Rubber soles are best for walking on the deck of a river cruise vessel.

Cruising Dress Code

While river cruise vessels don't have strict dress codes like those of ocean-going ships, on some you may see the suggested dress for the evening mentioned on the daily programme. Broadly speaking, you should interpret it like this:

Informal: Jacket and tie for men; cocktail dress, dressy pantsuit or the like for women.

Casual/smart: Long trousers (no shorts or jeans), proper collared and sleeved shirt for men; skirt or slacks and smart top for women.

Casual/relaxed: Slacks over sweater or open shirt (no tie) for men (no beach wear or muscle shirts); blouse with skirt, trousers/slacks, or similar comfortable attire for women. Shoes are always required in the dining room and bar of a vessel.

Documents

A passport is the most practical proof of your citizenship and identification. Visas are required for some countries (allow time to obtain these). Most visitors to Egypt have to obtain a visa in advance. Russia, too, requires a visa for almost every nationality.

On most river cruises, you will hand in your passport to the purser upon embarkation. This helps the vessel to clear customs and immigration inspection on arrival in ports of call. Your passport will be returned prior to the vessel's arrival in the port in which you will finally disembark.

Flying... and Jet Lag

Modern air travel is fast and efficient. Even experienced travellers, however, may occasionally find that the stress of international travel persists long after the flight is over.

Eastbound flights cause more pronounced jet lag than westbound flights. Jet aircraft are generally pressurised to some 2,400 metres (7,850 ft) in altitude, causing discomfort in the ears and the stomach and swollen feet. A few precautions should reduce the less pleasant effects of flying around the world. Plan as far in advance of your cruise as you possibly can. Take a daytime flight, so that you can arrive at, or close to, your normal bedtime. Try to be as quiet as possible prior to flying, and allow for another five hours of rest after any flight that crosses more than five time zones. If you need to stay awake on arrival in your destination until local bedtime, try to be outside in sunlight, which represses the creation of melatonin, the hormone which promotes sleep. If you need to go to sleep, even if you feel wide awake, stay in a darkened room.

Note that babies and small children are less affected by changes in time because of their shorter sleeping and waking cycles. But adults generally need more time to adjust.

Medication

Take any medicine and other medical supplies that you need, plus spare eyeglasses or contact lenses. If you are taking a long cruise, ask your doctor for names of alternatives, in case the medicine you are taking is not available.

Remember to take along a doctor's prescription for any medication (make sure you can read it easily), especially when you are flying into foreign countries to join a ship, as customs may be difficult without documentation.

Do not pack medication in any luggage to be checked in when flying, but take it in your carry-on, and divide it between your bag and that of your travelling companion.

Money Matters

Most river cruise vessels in Europe now operate primarily in euros, but a few operate in other currencies.

Major credit cards and travellers' cheques are accepted on board (few river cruise operators take personal cheques). You sign for drinks and other assorted services as part of the "cashless cruising" policy.

In most ports of call you'll find an ATM for getting cash, but don't rely on this. Sometimes, the vessel may be moored out of town, and in more obscure ports in Russia or Eastern Europe, there may not be ATMs. Egypt, however, is not a problem; vessels always moor up in towns and there are several banks.

Remember to take lots of small-denomination notes when shopping in local markets, and familiarise yourself with the value of the local currency before setting out to haggle. In Russia, for example, prices are almost always quoted in US dollars, euros or, occasionally, sterling – you don't even need to change money into roubles. Just watch the exchange rate that market vendors use, as it will inevitably be in their favour. In Egypt, the situation is the same, although you'll usually get the best value if you pay in Egyptian pounds. Don't expect to use credit cards in local markets, although shops take them.

Pets

Pets are not allowed aboard river cruise vessels.

Photography

It is hard to find any situation more ideal for photography than a cruise. Your photographs enable you to share your memories with others at home. If you purchase film anywhere, remember to check the expiry date. Don't buy film or instant cameras in Egypt – they have almost always been left in the sun and will probably be damaged.

If you use digital, take enough memory cards with you, as it's unlikely on most cruises that you will come across a shop that will download everything onto CD during your trip. Buy a storage device for your pictures, or take along a small laptop. In Egypt, keep digital cameras covered when not in use, as the dust blowing around will get to them. Do not be alarmed at the many X-ray machines and scanners in Egypt – they will not harm the camera or its contents. Bear in mind that at some antiquities, you need to pay for a photo permit if you want to take your camera inside. Otherwise, you will have to check it in.

When you take photographs in ports of call, it is important to respect the wishes of local inhabitants. Ask permission to photograph someone close-up. Most will smile and tell you to go ahead. But some people are superstitious or afraid of having their picture taken and will shy away from you. Some will expect a tip. Do not press the point. Also, in some countries, taking photographs of military installations, aircraft, ships or vehicles may be prohibited. It is wise to ask advice and/or permission first.

Travel Insurance

River cruise operators, tour packagers and travel agents routinely sell travel-cover policies that, upon close inspection, appear to wriggle out of payment due to a litany of exclusion clauses, most of which are never explained to you, the policyholder. Read the policy carefully and take note of clauses about pre-existing medical conditions and security concerning valuables.

Give yourself enough time to shop around and don't accept the first travel-insurance policy you are offered. Do read the contract carefully and make sure you know exactly what you are covered for. Medical emergency repatriation is absolutely critical, wherever you are travelling in the world.

Check out the procedure you need to follow if you are the victim of a crime (such as your wallet or camera being stolen while on a shore excursion). Incidentally, if anything does happen, always obtain a police report as soon as possible. Ask your guide or somebody from the vessel to help you with this. You will not be able to make a claim without it. Note that many insurance policies will only reimburse you for the second-hand value of an item that has been lost or stolen, rather than the full cost of replacement. You will also probably be required to produce the original receipt for any such items claimed.

Watch out for exclusions for "hazardous sports". These could include things typically offered as shore excursions aboard your river cruise vessel, for example, horse riding (there goes that horse riding on a puzta in Budapest, for example) or cycling (renting a bicycle is popular on many European cruises).

If you purchase travel cover over the internet, do check the credentials of the company that is underwriting the scheme. It is best to deal with well-established names, and not to take what appears to be the cheapest deal offered.

L IFE ON BOARD

A FULL A–Z RUNDOWN OF WHAT TO EXPECT ON BOARD

For a descriptive account of life on board and the facilities you can expect, see pages 39–51. For more information on cabins see page 317.

Comment Cards

On the last day of the cruise you may be asked to fill out a company "comment card". Be truthful when completing this form, as it serves as a means of communication between you and the cruise line. If there have been problems with the service or any other aspect of your cruise, do say so.

Disembarkation

Disembarkation is a simple matter aboard river cruise vessels. During the final part of your cruise, the cruise director will give a quick, informal talk about disembarkation.

The night before, place your main baggage outside your cabin on retiring. It will be collected and off-loaded on arrival. Leave out fragile items, liquor and the clothes you intend to wear for disembarkation and onward travel. Anything left in your cabin will be considered hand luggage, to be hand-carried off when you leave.

Before leaving the vessel, remember to claim any items you have placed in the safety deposit boxes, and leave your cabin key in the cabin.

On barge cruises, the process is much less formal. The crew will help with baggage on the day of disembarkation and passengers will usually be taken to the train station or airport as part of the service.

Etiquette

An international outlook is required when joining a river cruise. Try to embrace cultural differences with the other passengers. Any other culture en masse can be intimidating, but most people want to be friendly.

If you do not like your assigned table in the dining room, ask the maître d' if you can be moved. This often happens, and the people you've left behind will soon forget about it.

On a shared table, it's acceptable to order your own wine. If you all get along particularly well, it's equally OK to take turns to buy the wine.

Be considerate to fellow passengers and keep the noise down in your cabin. Walls are thin, and nobody appreciates a television blaring all night. On barge cruises, you are living in very close proximity to other people and tolerance is essential, however luxurious the surroundings. Drinks are included on most hotel barges so splitting the bill is not an issue.

Events on Board

Entertainment

Entertainment on river cruises is certainly low-key. It may consist of a local dance troupe who come on board for an evening, or a pianist and/or singer in the bar. There may be an evening of games or quizzes, too. Most vessels have a music system in the bar and, if the atmosphere is right, may have dancing. Often, though, you will be in port in the evening, and guests will scatter far and wide to investigate the nightlife.

During the day, entertainment may vary from wine or vodka (in Russia) tasting to language lessons, poetry readings or cookery demonstrations.

On barge cruises, you make your own entertainment and, usually, conversation over digestifs or an impromptu recital on the piano (if there is one) from a fellow passenger is as lively as it gets. On some nights, depending on where the barge is moored, you can go ashore to check out the local nightlife.

Lectures

River cruise operators often bring experts and guest speakers on board, which can be fascinating. Subjects covered will always relate to the region through which you are passing.

Facilities on Board

Air-Conditioning

Aboard most river cruise vessels, the temperature in your cabin can be regulated by an individually controlled thermostat, so you can adjust it to suit yourself. The temperature in public rooms may be kept cooler than you are used to. On Russian river cruises (particularly in the spring and autumn) heating, rather than air-conditioning, will be provided. If you have the luxury of a balcony, you can have the doors open, although not at the same time as the air-conditioning is on, and you will need to close them when you go out, for security reasons.

Bed Linen

On European river cruises and cruise barges, European duvets are usually provided, rather than sheets and blankets. Anti-allergenic pillows may be available, although it is wise to make your request known at the time of booking.

Communications

Most river cruise vessels (but not cruise barges) have a direct-dial satellite-telephone system. You can call from your cabin to anywhere in the world, but this is expensive. It is much cheaper to use your mobile (cellphone) if it is set up for international roaming – check with your service provider before departure. Remember that if somebody calls you while you are abroad, you pay for the international part of the call. Some of the newer vessels have internet/email access (see page 50).

Exercise Room/Sauna

If a river cruise vessel does have an exercise room, it will be very small. Keep fit by walking as much as possible when you're ashore. Some ships have a sauna or steam room.

Gift Shops

The gift shop/boutique/drugstore will offer a small selection of souvenirs, gifts and toiletries, as well as a basic stock of essential items. Opening hours are posted at the store and in the daily programme. Don't rely on it though; planning ahead and packing sensibly is a better option.

Laundry and Dry Cleaning

Some river cruise vessels offer a laundry and pressing service (but no dry cleaning).

Library

Most river cruise vessels have a library, offering a small selection of books (in several languages), reference material and periodicals, as well as board games such as Scrabble, backgammon and chess.

Money Changing

There's no need to carry cash, except when you go ashore. It is now the norm to cruise cash-free, and to settle your account with one payment (by cash or credit card) prior to disembarking on the last day. Often this is arranged by making an imprint of a credit card when you embark, permitting you to sign for everything. Before the end of the cruise, a detailed statement is delivered to your cabin. Some cruise lines may discontinue their "cashless" system for the last day, which can be irritating – this means you must carry and pay with cash for all purchases; euros or US dollars are normally accepted on European cruises.

Sometimes, particularly in Egypt, money-changers are brought on board the vessel on the penultimate day of the cruise. A cynic might observe that this would ensure all the passengers had cash when it came to settling the final bill – and tipping the crew. While using this service is hassle-free, you are likely to get a better rate from a bank ashore.

Movies and Television

Aboard most river cruise vessels, video/DVD movies are shown on the in-cabin television system, or may be obtained from the library. Pretty well all vessels have television in the rooms, but the satellite signal can never be guaranteed, especially when the vessel is on the move.

Spa/Beauty Salon

Make appointments as soon after boarding as possible (particularly on short cruises). Charges are comparable to those ashore. Typical services: haircut for men and women, styling, permanent waving, colouring, manicure, pedicure, and leg waxing. Aboard some river cruise vessels, the beauty salon may also provide massage treatments.

Swimming Pool

Many river cruise vessels have a small plunge pool on the top deck, and possibly a hot tub or two. A pool is particularly important on the Nile, when it can be incredibly hot. Sitting in the hot tub watching the scenery go by is especially pleasant.

Visiting the Bridge and Engine Room

It is possible to visit to the engine room, if you so wish (ask at the reception desk). Note, however, that this is an extremely compact space, and will inevitably be very noisy and quite dirty, due to the fact that engines are of the diesel type. You may be allowed to visit the bridge, too, which is fascinating, although you will be asked to leave as the captain manoeuvres the vessel into ports. The navigation bridges on Nile cruise vessels are amazingly primitive, with no radar, depth sounder or charts. The vessels are driven instead by experienced pilots, who know every inch of the river.

Barge Cruises

Most luxury barges have a hot tub on deck, and some even have a plunge pool. You can expect beautifully maintained interiors, luxurious cabins, as well as a stereo and sometimes a piano. There is not usually a TV or video and if you want to make calls, you should expect to use a cellphone or a public payphone along the way. The idea of a barge holidays is, after all, to escape.

Food and Drink

Dining

Food on a river cruise is not the huge event it may be on an ocean cruise, where you can eat round the clock and there is a wide choice of restaurants and menus. Fortunately, this means that you don't need to anticipate large weight gain during your cruise! Mealtimes are social, convivial and a good time to make new friends and taste some new dishes.

Meals are all taken in the dining room, unless the vessel has the facility for dining on deck. Breakfast and lunch are usually open-seating, while dinner on most vessels is at assigned tables at a fixed time. You can, of course, dine ashore if the vessel is in port.

Food will usually reflect the cuisine of the area in which the vessel is cruising, so expect German, Hungarian, Russian or Egyptian influences, depending on where you are. North Americans may find some of the Eastern European cuisine a little stodgy. Expect a fair amount of meat with sauces, and very sweet desserts. If you are vegetarian, let the cruise line know in advance, but do not set your sights on anything wildly creative or exciting. Stock up on the salad buffet at lunchtime instead. Other special diets may be hard to cater for, such as low sodium, vegan, etc. Anyone following a kosher diet should probably resign themselves to travelling as a vegetarian.

If you get a chance, take a tour of the galley. You will be amazed at how many elaborate dishes, breads and pastries can be prepared in such a tiny place. Many people are particularly impressed on a Nile cruise when they are invited to see the galley. It shows that the hotel manager is confident that the hygiene – a common bugbear in Egypt – is first-rate on his or her vessel.

Wine and Liquor

The cost of drinks on board is typically the same as on land, since river cruise vessels seldom have access to duty-free liquor. Drinks may be ordered in the dining room or at any of the vessel's bars.

In the dining room, you can order wine with your meals from a small, reasonably priced wine list. Some river cruise operators (particularly French and German companies) may include basic table wines for lunch and dinner.

If you don't finish a bottle of wine with a meal, ask the waiter to write your table number on it and save it for

you. Ordering like this is cheaper than buying wine by the glass.

Room Service

Breakfast, beverages and snacks may be available aboard a small number of river cruise vessels, although there is not usually any room service for dinner.

Barge Cruises

Food and drink are highlights of a luxury barge holiday. Expect candlelit, five course dinners using the finest local ingredients, with a different wine for each course. Breakfast is usually continental, with fresh local bread if the chef has had a chance to buy any that morning, or bread baked on board. Lunch may be served on deck, weather permitting. Special requests can usually be catered for and the chef will discuss the following day's menus with guests every evening. On most barges, all alcoholic drinks are included in the price.

Health and Safety

On-board Injury

Slipping, tripping and falling are the typical sources of on-board injury. This does not mean that river cruise vessels are unsafe, but there are some things that you can do to minimise the chance of injury. If you suffer from injury aboard your river cruise vessel, feel it is the company's fault and want to take some kind of legal action against the company, you would be required to file suit in the state (or country) designated in the ticket. Thus, if your river cruise vessel is registered in Switzerland, then any lawsuit must be filed in Switzerland. This is known as the Forum Clause.

Cabin Hazards

Aboard many river cruise vessels (particularly older vessels – those built before 1990) raised "lips" (typically between 15.2 cm/6 inches and 30 cm/12 inches) separate the bathroom from the sleeping area.

Aboard the older vessels, it is wise to note how the door lock works. Some require a key on the inside in order to unlock the door. Leave the key in the lock, so that in the event of a real emergency, you do not have to hunt for the key.

On Deck

Aboard most river cruise vessels (particularly older ones), watch out for raised lips in doorways leading to open deck areas. On the uppermost (outside) deck, some raised lips may be encountered (particularly on European river cruise vessels, where bridges are of low height) as part of the equipment that is raised and lowered hydraulically.

Wear sensible shoes with rubber soles (not crêpe) when walking on the open decks. Do not wear high heels. Walk with caution when the outer decks are wet after being washed, or if they are wet after rain. This warning applies especially to metal decks and stairways. There is nothing more painful than falling onto a solid steel deck.

Do not throw a lighted cigarette or cigar butt over the side of the vessel (even if you see crew members do it). The water might seem like a safe place to throw such items, but they can easily be sucked into an opening in the vessel's side or onto an aft open-deck area, only to cause a fire (and of course, it is also environmentally unfriendly).

How to Survive a Fire

Vessel fires generate heat, smoke and often panic. In the unlikely event that you are in one, try to remain calm and think logically and clearly.

When you board your river cruise vessel and get to your cabin, check and remember the way from there to the nearest emergency exits (typically aft and in the middle of the vessel). Count the number of cabin doorways and other distinguishing features to the exits in case you have to escape without the benefit of lighting, or in case the passageway is filled with smoke and you cannot see clearly. Some river cruise vessels use "low location" lighting systems, which are either the electro-luminescent or photo-luminescent type.

Exit signs are located just above floor level, but aboard older vessels the signs may be above your head, a position that is virtually useless, as smoke and flames always rise. Note the nearest fire-alarm location and know how to use it in case of dense smoke and/or no lighting.

In the event of fire in your cabin, report it immediately. Then get out of your cabin if you can and close the door behind you to prevent any smoke or flames from entering the passageway. Finally, sound the alarm and alert your neighbours. If you are in your cabin and there is fire in the passageway outside, feel for the cabin door. If the door handle is hot, soak a towel in water and use it to turn the handle of the door. If there is a raging fire in the passageway, cover yourself in wet towels and go through the flames. It may be your only means of escape, unless you have a cabin with a balcony, and large floor-to-ceiling sliding patio doors. If there are no flames, and if everything looks clear, go to the nearest emergency exit or stairway. If there is smoke in the passageway, crawl to the nearest exit. If the exit is blocked, then go to an alternate one.

It may take considerable effort to open a fire door to the exit, as they are heavy. Don't use the elevators, as they may stop at a deck that is on fire or full of smoke.

Sun Protection

Be sensible in the sun, particularly on the top deck, where the breeze is deceptively cooling and the sunlight is reflecting off the water all around you. Always wear a strong sunscreen, on deck and when walking around in port. Also bring a wide-brimmed hat (that won't blow away) and cover up with garments in a thick weave. If you must sunbathe, restrict yourself to early morning and late afternoon – avoid the midday sun, especially in places like the south of France and Egypt.

Drinking Water

Water on board is drinkable, although it may be heavily chlorinated. In Egypt and Russia, it's best to drink bottled water. If in any doubt at all about the hygiene on board in these countries, avoid ice in drinks and don't eat salad items that will have been washed in the vessel's water.

Incidentally, there is no reason to expect to be ill on a Nile cruise. If you choose a good, trustworthy operator, your vessel should be spotlessly clean. If you are cruising on a tight budget, be very careful indeed.

Insects

Mosquitoes are often a problem on deck in the evenings, so take repellent and wear long sleeves and long trousers.

Egypt is not a malarial zone, so only the usual precautions against irritating bites are necessary. Other vaccinations, however, are required for Egypt and possibly Russia/Ukraine; check with your doctor before travelling.

Barge Cruises

The same rules apply to barges. In addition, while a barge holiday is ideal for families, parents will have to be very careful about young children falling overboard as they clamber around the deck.

Smoking on barges is usually restricted to the deck area.

Information

Some river cruise companies, notably Viking, supply very useful booklets detailing every sight along the route. You can sit on deck with these, spotting villages, locks, castles and other notable attractions. Others simply offer a printed daily programme, with times of excursions and meals.

Barges are more informal. The following day's activities will be discussed with the skipper over dinner. Most barges carry plenty of local information and a guest comment book with tips on what to see.

Security

All cabins aboard river cruise vessels can be locked, and it is recommended that you keep your cabin locked at all times when you are not there. Old-style keys are made of metal and operate a mechanical lock; most will be plastic key cards that operate electronically coded locks. Cruise lines do not accept responsibility for any money or valuables left in cabins, and suggest that you store them in a safety deposit box at the purser's office, or in your in-cabin personal safe (if one is supplied).

You will be issued a personal boarding pass when you embark (the latest high-tech passes may include your photo, and other pertinent information). This serves as identification, and must be shown at the gangway each time you board. The system of boarding passes is one of many ways in which cruise lines ensure passenger safety.

In Egypt, expect to walk through scanners at every place you visit, in hotels, restaurants, when walking across other vessels and when boarding your own.

Barges do not have key cards, generally speaking. Most have locking cabin doors but the house party atmosphere is supposed to engender an element of trust between passengers. The barge will always be locked if all passengers and crew are ashore.

Shore Excursions

River cruise operators plan and oversee optional excursions, assuming that you have not seen a place, and aim to show you its highlights in a comfortable manner and at a reasonable price.

Coaches or minibuses are usually the principal choice of transportation. This cuts costs and allows the tour operator to narrow the selection of guides to only those most competent, knowledgeable, and fluent in whatever language the majority of passengers speak, while providing some degree of security and control. You may find yourself on a multilingual coach if your vessel has passengers from all over

the world, and it can be tiresome to have commentary in three languages.

Most excursions give little in-depth history, and guides are often not acquainted with details beyond a superficial general knowledge. The exceptions are Russia, where you are likely to be guided by a local academic, and Egypt, where most guides are highly qualified Egyptologists with an encyclopaedic knowledge of history and architecture. River cruise operators run shore excursions in three ways. They are either all included in the price (a huge bonus when budgeting for a holiday), can be pre-booked as a package, or can be booked on board as the cruise progresses. Shore-excursion information may be forwarded with your cruise tickets and documents.

Only take along what is necessary on a shore excursion; leave any valuables aboard the vessel, together with any money and credit cards you do not plan to use. Groups of people are often targets for pickpockets in popular sightseeing destinations and major cities. Also, the coloured disk you may be asked to wear for "identification" instantly marks you out as a "rich" tourist for shopkeepers.

If you are hearing-impaired, make arrangements with the shore-excursion staff to assist you in departing for your excursions at the correct times.

Barge Cruises

Shore excursions are included in the price of the more upmarket barge holidays and will be activities tailored to a small group, like an exclusive wine tasting in a chateau, or a stroll around the local market with the barge's resident guide. At the beginning of the week, the guide will discuss any special interests with the guests. Most barges carry bicycles, so you can cycle along the towpath.

Going it Alone

To see a city at your own pace, go alone or with a small group. Travel by taxi or bus, or walk directly to the places that are of most interest to you.

If you hire a taxi for sightseeing, negotiate the price in advance, and do not pay until you get back to the vessel or to your final destination. If you are with friends, hiring a taxi for a full- or half-day sightseeing trip can often work out far cheaper than renting a car, and you also avoid the hazards of driving. Naturally, prices vary according to destination, but if you can select a driver who speaks your language, and the taxi is comfortable, even air-conditioned, you are ahead.

Remember to bring a driving licence

and photo ID for hiring any vehicle; note also that driving is on the right in mainland Europe, Russia and Egypt.

Research the destination thoroughly before you arrive, and take a good map. Always check that train, bus and ferry times coincide with the vessel's arrival and departure. Make reservations for particularly special lunch venues and check in this guide to see if important museums and galleries are open; many close for one day a week, or for a couple of hours at lunchtime. Plan shopping trips to avoid early-afternoon shop closures.

Remember that it is your responsibility to get back to the vessel on time and, if you miss it, to catch up with it at the next port.

Smoking/Non-Smoking Areas

River cruise operators want all passengers to have a good holiday, but there are some rules to be observed. In public rooms, smoking and non-smoking sections are available. In the dining room, however, cigar and pipe smoking are not permitted at all, although cigarette smoking may be allowed in a special section. On some vessels, the smoke smell can permeate the whole ship, for example, if people smoke on deck near the air-conditioning intake. Some river cruise operators have dining rooms that are totally non-smoking. Examples include Global River Cruises and Vantage Deluxe World Tours. In Italy, smoking is now banned inside in public places, as it is in Ireland.

Smoking on barges is usually restricted to the open deck.

Tipping (Gratuities)

Many travellers feel that the river cruise vessel should host its passengers, and that the passengers should not host the crew by means of tips, so the question of tipping can be awkward and embarrassing.

However, the accepted river cruise industry standard for gratuities is around $5–6 (€5–6) per person, per day. Tips are given as a lump sum at the end of your cruise, and divided equally between all on-board personnel. You can add them to your onboard account, or put cash in an envelope. A few cruise lines include gratuities in the overall fare, so do check first.

On a barge holiday, the suggested tip is 5 percent of the vacation cost (excluding the flight). This may seem high, but the level of service is usually of the highest standard.

PRACTICAL INFORMATION BY COUNTRY

AUSTRIA

Fact File

Area: 83,838 sq. km (32,370 sq. miles).
Capital: Vienna.
Population: 8 million, of which around 1.6 million live in Vienna.
Language: German.
Religion: Roman Catholic; smaller numbers of Protestants and Muslims (5 percent each).
Currency: euro (€).
Time zone: see page 327.
International dialling code: 43.
Websites: www.austria-tourism.at; www.wien.gv.at

Entry Requirements, Customs and Health

As for all countries in the European Union, refer to box on page 326.

Money Matters

The main credit cards and travellers' cheques are widely accepted by the bigger hotels and most shops in cities. Otherwise, ATMs are by far your best option for obtaining local currency; cash dispensers at most banks accept the major European debit cards. Banks and exchange offices will change foreign currency at the current rate of the Viennese stock exchange.

There is no limit to how much local money visitors may bring into or take out of Austria.

VAT Reimbursement

For purchases over a specified amount, non-EU citizens are entitled to reclaim the VAT (Mehrwertsteuer) if they are taking the goods out of the EU. The salesperson must complete form "U 34", which you will need to present on departure to airport or border customs officials for stamping. Then you can post the form to the shop for reimbursement by cheque or bank order.

Tipping

It is customary to leave a 10–15 percent tip for good service. Bills at hotels and restaurants include a service charge, but porters and maids should be tipped a couple of euros or so. Taxi drivers, tour guides, cloakroom attendants and hairdressers also expect a 10 percent tip. In general, rounding up the bill seems to be good form.

Public Transport Vienna

Maps and Tickets

Maps for buses, trams and U-Bahn (underground) are available at main stops, as well as at the central public-transport information offices at Karlsplatz and Stephansplatz. Tickets can be bought from a conductor or a machine on trams and buses, from the booking office or a machine for mainline or city trains. A single ticket for a journey by tram, bus and underground, which covers changes made without interruption, costs €1.50. Discount tickets can be bought in advance from a tobacconist's (Tabaktrafik) or transport offices (Verkehrs-betriebe). Travel passes are available for 24 hours (€5) and 72 hours (€12).

Also worth considering is the Vienna Card, a 72-hour ticket currently costing €16.90, which is valid on all public transport and entitles the holder to discounts at museums and other attractions.

U-Bahn (Underground)

Five lines cover all the main parts of the city. Tickets can be purchased from machines or ticket offices.

PLANNING A TRIP

LIFE ON BOARD

RIVER VESSEL LISTINGS

A – Z

The lines are:
• U1
Kagran–Stephansplatz–Karlsplatz–
Reumannplatz.
• U2
Schottenring–Volkstheater–Karlsplatz.
• U3
Ottakring–Stephansplatz–Landstrasse–
Simmering.
• U4
Hütteldorf–Karlsplatz–Schwedenplatz–
Heiligenstadt.
• U6
Florisdorf–Spittelau–Westbahnhof–
Meidling–Philadelphiabrücke–
Siebenherten.

Schnellbahn (S-Bahn)

Rapid-transit suburban trains depart
from the Südbahnhof for outlying
districts. The unit fare applies in the
central zone, standard fares outside.
Other points of departure are Wien
Nord and Wien Mitte. The S-Bahn
also connects to the airport, as does
the City Airport Train.

Trams (Strassenbahn)

With some 35 tram routes, this is
Vienna's most important form of
public transport. On most trams (and
buses) the driver serves as the
conductor. These vehicles carry a blue
sign front and rear with the word
Schaffnerlos (without conductor). If you
have a ticket, enter by the door
marked *Entwerter* and have it
stamped; otherwise get in at the front
and buy your ticket from the vending
machine. For trams with conductors,
enter at the rear to buy a ticket or have
it stamped. The most useful lines are:
• 1 and 2 around the Ringstrasse.
• 38 from Schottentor to Grinzing.
• 52 and 58 from the Westbahnhof
to the city centre.

Buses

The airport bus service runs between
the City Air Terminal at Landstrasse
Hauptstrasse (Hilton Hotel) and the
airport every 20 or 30 minutes. Allow
half an hour for the journey. The main
city-centre routes are:
• 1a from Schottentor to
Stephansplatz.
• 2a from Burgring to Graben.
• 3a from Schottenring to
Schwarzenbergplatz.

Opening Times

In general, shops are open
Monday–Saturday 9am–6pm, with
some smaller shops closing for lunch
and on Saturday afternoons. Banks
are open Monday–Friday
8am–12.30pm and again from
1.30–3pm, often to 5.30pm on
Thursday.

Public Holidays

1 January: New Year's Day.
6 January: Epiphany.
March/April/May (variable):
Good Friday/Easter Monday.
1 May: Labour Day.
May (variable): Ascension;
Whit Monday; Corpus Christi.
August (variable): Assumption.
26 October: National Day.
1 November: All Saints' Day.
8 December: Immaculate Conception.

EU Entry, Customs, Health and Currency

The European Union states covered
in this guide are Austria, Czech
Republic, France, Germany,
Hungary, Ireland, Italy, Netherlands,
Poland, Portugal, Slovakia and the
UK. For all other countries, see
individual listings.

Entry Requirements

To enter a country in the EU you need
a passport (or any form of official
identification if you are an EU
citizen). Visas are not needed if you
are an American, Commonwealth
citizen or EU national (or come from
most other European or South
American countries). Health
certificates are not required unless
you have arrived from Asia, Africa or
South America.

Customs Regulations

In theory, there are no customs
barriers for alcoholic drinks and
tobacco when travelling between EU
countries. However, there are still
recommended allowances.
  The following quantities can be
exceeded, provided proof is shown
that the goods bought are for
personal consumption (for example,
a family wedding) and not for resale.
  Customs allowances for each
person over 18 years of age are:
• 10 litres of spirits or liqueurs
over 22 percent volume
• 20 litres of fortified wine
• 90 litres of wine (of which no
more than 60 litres may be
sparkling wine)
• 200 cigars or 400 cigarillos or
3,200 cigarettes or 3 kg tobacco
• 110 litres of beer
  Non EU-visitors can bring in
€7,600 in currency. Vistors over 17
years of age from a non-EU country
(this applies to Andorra, which is
outside the EU) are entitled to
import the following articles duty-
free: 200 cigarettes or 100 small
cigars or 250g of tobacco, 1 litre of
spirits and 2 litres of wine and
beer, and 50g of perfume.

25–6 December: Christmas.

Shopping

To shop in Austria generally means to
go to Vienna, where the best choices
are within the Ring. The shopping
district in most other towns and
cities will be compact and often close
to the train station.
  The winding streets of Vienna's
Inner City – especially between the
Hofburg, Graben and Kärntner

US citizens should check duty-
free allowances with the US
Customs Department before
departure and on return must
complete the CBP Declaration Form
6059B.
  Canadian travellers returning
home must declare all goods
acquired abroad. It is important to
keep original receipts for possible
inspection. Personal exemptions
available to Canadian residents
returning from a trip abroad are
$750-worth of duty-free goods,
including alcohol and tobacco.
  Upon returning to Australia,
citizens can bring in 250 cigarettes
or 250g of loose tobacco, and
1.125 litres of alcohol.

EU Health Coverage

From January 2006 the E111,
entitling Europeans to free medical
treatment within the EU, will be
replaced by the European Health
Insurance Card (EHIC). The card is
valid for three to five years and
covers any medical treatment that
becomes necessary during your
trip, because of either illness or
accident. You may have to make a
contribution to the cost of your
care. The easiest way to obtain
a card is to apply online at:
www.dh.gov.uk/PolicyandGuidance/
HealthAdviceforTravellers.
  It is, however, always advisable
to take out private health
insurance, regardless of whether
you are covered by an EHIC.
  The number to call for emergency
services throughout Europe is 112.

The Eurozone

Most EU countries have used the
euro (€) as their national currency
since January 2002 (the exceptions
are the UK, Sweden, Denmark and
countries that joined in 2004).
  Notes are unvarying throughout
"euroland", but each of the member
countries mints its own coins –
which are valid throughout the EU.

Strasse – are the best places for shopping. Some of the world's finest cakes and pastries abound at confectioners such as Demel and Oberlaa; and Adolf Loos-inspired furnishings and fixtures are well in evidence throughout the Inner City.

Elsewhere, Mariahilferstrasse is the other main shopping area: a long series of shops (including the famous Amadeus bookstore) which only peter out at the Westbahnhof. Smaller shopping zones can be found in the university district (near the Votivkirche) and Siebenstern-gasse, where a hip crowd takes over. Flea markets take place on Saturday in the Naschmarkt and elsewhere.

Typical souvenirs include Tyrolean costumes and walking sticks in the Innsbruck area, local wine in Lower Austria, bottles of pumpkin-seed oil and hand-blown glassware in Styria and Mozart balls in Salzburg. Salzburg's north-of-the-river streets and the pedestrianised Maria-Theresien-Strasse in Innsbruck are also good for browsing.

Tourist Offices

Austria (National Office)
4, Margaretenstrasse 1, Vienna, tel: (01) 587 2000 or 588 660; fax: (01) 588 6620; www.austria.info.
Vienna
1, Albertinaplatz/Ecke Maysedergasse, tel: (01) 24 555; e-mail: info@info.wien.at; www.wien.info
Open daily 9am–7pm.

Telecommunications

Making an international call from your hotel is more expensive than calling from post offices or from one of the many telephone booths. Note that, when dialling Vienna numbers from outside the city, you must include the area code 01 (within Austria) or 1 (outside Austria). The international code for Austria is 43.

Security and Crime

Austria's crime and theft rate is quite low compared to other parts of Europe. Nevertheless, in Vienna it is advisable to take the same precautions you would in any city, keeping valuables out of sight and watching out for pickpockets. If your passport is stolen, the police will give you a certificate to take to your consulate.

Time Zones

Below are listed the different time zones for the countries covered in this guide. Note that one hour should be added for daylight-saving time from late March to late October, unless stated otherwise.

GMT (Greenwich Mean Time)
Ireland
Portugal
UK

GMT + 1 hour (also known as Central European Time or CET)
Austria
Croatia
Czech Republic
France
Germany
Hungary
Italy
Netherlands
Poland
Serbia and Montenegro
Slovakia

GMT + 2 hours
Bulgaria
Egypt (daylight-saving time late April to late September)
Romania
Ukraine

GMT + 3 hours
Russia – all areas covered in this guide (daylight-saving time late March to late September)

Emergency Telephone Numbers

Police: 133
Ambulance: 144
Fire: 122

BULGARIA

Fact File

Area: 110,933 sq. km (43,000 sq. miles).
Capital: Sofia.
Population: 7.9 million.
Language: Bulgarian.
Religion: Bulgarian Orthodox with a substantial Muslim minority.
Currency: lev.
Time zone: see box on this page.
International dialing code: 359.
Website: www.bulgariatravel.org

Entry Requirements

EU and most other Western nationals do not require visas for short stays; only passports are required.

Customs Regulations

Duty-free allowances for visitors are: 1 litre of spirits, 2 litres of wine, 200 cigarettes or 50 cigars. To avoid complications upon departure, declare anything of value, including jewellery and cameras, when entering the country.

Health and Insurance

There are no specific health risks particular to Bulgaria, though you should take out adequate health-insurance cover before departing as a matter of course. In an emergency telephone 150 for an ambulance. Emergency medical treatment is free, but you may have to pay for some medicines, and you should tip the doctor and nurses. If it is private medical care you are after, head for IMC Medical in Sofia, at 28 ul Gogol, tel: 02-944 93 26.

Tap water is safe to drink, though the low cost of the bottled variety means that very few visitors actually do. Mosquitoes are a problem in the summer, so insect repellent is a must. Stray dogs can be a problem in Sofia and Varna. Though outbreaks of rabies are rare, should you be bitten, go to a hospital immediately for a rabies injection.

Money Matters

The Bulgarian lev is pegged to the euro. It's best to bring cash (euros or dollars) to exchange into lev, although some services, especially taxis, can unofficially be paid for in euros – notes only (don't expect change). Private exchange offices offer better rates than banks. Credit cards are becoming more widely accepted, universally in the best hotels and resorts. Cash machines (ATMs) are widespread, particularly in the capital and the coastal resorts. Travellers' cheques are rarely accepted and a high commission is payable.

Tipping
A tip of 10 percent is sufficient in restaurants and for taxi drivers. Barbers and hairdressers expect to receive the same.

Opening Times

Shops mostly open Mon–Fri 9am–7pm, with speciality stores open 10am–6pm; most shops also open 9am–1pm on Saturday.

Banks are open Mon–Fri 8–11.30am and 2–6pm. Some open Sat 8.30–11.30am.

However, opening times for shops and banks can be unpredictable; your cruise line should be able to give guidance on specific places.

Public Holidays

1 January: New Year's Day.
3 March: National Day (Day of Liberation).
March/April/May (variable): Orthodox Easter Sunday and Monday.
1 May: Labour Day.
6 May: St George's Day (Day of Bulgarian Army).
24 May: St Cyril and Methodius Day (Day of Culture and Literacy).
6 September: Unification of Bulgaria Day.
22 September: Independence Day.
1 November: Day of the Spiritual Leaders of Bulgaria.
25–6 December: Christmas.

Shopping

While it would be an exaggeration to say that Bulgaria is a shopper's paradise, it does offer some of the best shopping in the Balkans. Economic reform may not have been as fast as that of other former Communist countries, but when it comes to consumer commerce, the Bulgarians now lead the way.

In the days of the "wild East" – immediately following the collapse of the Communist regime – almost anything could be bought in Bulgaria for any price. Although those days have gone, you will still find a few forbidden fruits in the country's flea markets, most notably counterfeit CDs and DVDs.

Markets and Malls

Prices in general can be divided into two categories: cheap (if the product is made in Bulgaria) and expensive (if the product is imported). While haggling has long been a Balkan necessity, it is now frowned upon in all but the most provincial markets. Try it in a chic boutique in Sofia and the police may be called.

Most of Bulgaria's groceries are still purchased early in the morning at markets, and produce is strictly seasonal. Imported goods can be found out of season only in expensive supermarkets. Almost everything else is sold in standard high-street shops or malls. The biggest mall is TZUM, in central Sofia.

There are also a number of flea markets for those who know where to look. The biggest and best is the one in front of the Alexander Nevski Cathedral in Sofia. If you are looking for a genuine Third Reich fountain pen, then this is the place to come, while busts of Lenin and Stalin and posters of Todor Zhivkov and other Communist heroes are also popular. Russian army hats are two a penny, while medals, watches and other Soviet memorabilia – all of which may or may not be original – can be bought for peanuts. Directly next to the flea market is another one, selling Orthodox iconography and naive art which, while not cheap, is good quality and a very good place to hunt for souvenirs.

The Black Sea coast's numerous street hawkers sell little else but sunglasses, beachwear and accessories, most of which are terribly poor in terms of quality.

What to Buy

Traditional Bulgarian handicrafts offer a wide choice of wares. These include lace, pottery, woodcarvings and iconography. Bulgarian souvenir shops are ubiquitous, though the souvenirs themselves can be of variable quality. Reproductions of Orthodox iconography and wood-carvings can be bought all over the country, with the best quality being found in Sofia in the art market outside the Alexander Nevski Cathedral. As a general rule, the stuff sold by hawkers and stallholders outside the more famous Bulgarian monasteries should be bought only in a souvenir emergency, as quality is patchy at best.

Iconography

If you are after genuine antique icons, as opposed to reproductions, you should contact a professional art dealer and have a reasonable idea of what you are looking for. Exporting antiques is a difficult process, requiring a long paper chase that a dealer will be able to handle with ease. Only the brave should attempt to do it on their own. There are a number of galleries in Sofia clustered together on the streets around the Radisson Hotel. Any of them will be delighted to help.

Pottery

The manufacture of fine pottery in this part of the world dates back as far as the Thracians, and the work of Bulgarian potters is traditionally sacred, with know-how a closely guarded secret kept within families of potters. Over the last hundred years or so the craft has somewhat died out, and today only a few potteries remain, mostly as working museums. The Etura complex near Gabrovo is a fine example of this kind of living

museum and an excellent place to purchase exquisite handmade Bulgarian pottery, as is the market in pl Samodivska in Veliko Tarnovo.

Embroidery and lace

Etura is also a good location to find these crafts, though the best place is probably along the coast, especially in Varna, as there is so much choice and competition between the old ladies who throng the market that surrounds the Cathedral of the Virgin Mary. Quality here is high and prices are reasonable, though not cheap. You can try haggling, but few stall-holders speak English.

Tourist Offices

Bulgaria
1, Sveta Nedelia Square, 1000 Sofia; tel: 02-987 97 78; fax: 02-989 69 39; www.travel-bulgaria.com
UK
Embassy of the Republic of Bulgaria 186–188 Queen's Gate, London SW7 5HL; tel: 0870 060 2350; fax: 020 7584 4948; www.bulgarianembassy.org.uk

Telecommunications

The country code for Bulgaria is 359. The city code for Sofia is 02. You can dial internationally from most hotel rooms (at an extravagant cost), and most public phones also permit direct dialling. All public phones require a phonecard, available from news-stands and kiosks.

If you need to send or receive a fax, do so from a post office, as hotels charge well over the odds for the privilege. Internet cafés are fairly common, and an increasing number of hotels also offer internet access via laptop plug-ins in rooms.

Security and Crime

Crime against foreigners has increased in recent years. Don't carry all your cash in one place, and avoid displaying large sums of money. Behave sensibly and be aware that street crime in the cities of Eastern Europe is generally as rife as it is in any big city in the world.

It's a good idea to deposit any valuables in the safe if you are staying in a hotel, or to take as little as possible with you when you go ashore. Keep valuables out of sight and hang on to your bags.

Emergency Telephone Numbers

Police: 166
Ambulance: 150
Directory enquiries: 144

CROATIA

Fact File

Area: the mainland is approximately 56,500 sq. km (21,800 sq. miles). The islands total 3,300 sq. km (1,274 sq. miles).
Capital: Zagreb.
Population: 4,800,000.
Language: Croatian.
Religion: largely Roman Catholic.
Currency: kuna (kn/HRK).
1 kuna = 100 lipa.
Time zone: *see page 327.*
International dialling code: 385.
Website: www.croatia.hr

Entry Requirements

Every visitor needs a valid passport, but for stays of less than 90 days many Europeans (including all EU citizens) and those from the US, Canada, Australia and New Zealand do not need a visa to enter Croatia. South Africans require a 90-day visa and should seek advice from any Croatian Embassy.

Customs Regulations

Visitors may bring personal possessions and the following items into Croatia duty-free: 2 litres of wine, 1 litre of spirits, 60 ml of perfume, 250 cl of toilet water, and either 200 cigarettes, 100 cigarillos, 50 cigars or 250 g of tobacco. Foreign currency can also be taken freely into the country. The transportation of kuna is restricted to 2,000 kn per person.

Expensive goods such as cameras and laptop computers should be reported to customs officials upon arrival to prevent difficulties when leaving the country.

Health and Insurance

It is safe to drink the tap water throughout Croatia, and visitors do not require any inoculations to travel here. The most common health problems experienced by visitors are the result of sunstroke, sunburn and dehydration, exacerbated by too much alcohol.

During summer, insect repellent is recommended, as is the wearing of jelly shoes when swimming in rocky areas, due to spiny sea urchins. Contact with these is painful and requires medical attention.

The UK, Ireland and many European countries have an agreement with Croatia that offers their citizens free medical care. However, all visitors should take out private travel insurance to cover any unforeseen medical expenses.

Money Matters

The national currency is the kuna (kn), divided into 100 lipa (lp). Although the euro is not an official currency in Croatia, prices are frequently quoted in both kuna and euros.

ATMs are readily available, and debit or credit cards carrying the Maestro, MasterCard, Visa, Cirrus and Plus symbols can be used to obtain cash. You will rarely find ATMs in villages. Currency can also be obtained in exchange offices, hotels and at any post-office counter.

Credit cards are not accepted everywhere, even among the most expensive shops, hotels and restaurants, so check in advance.

Euro or US-dollar travellers' cheques can be exchanged at any bank and many exchange offices for a commission of up to 2 percent. You must take your passport.

Tipping

Hotel and restaurant bills usually include tax and service, but it is customary to round up your bill to the nearest 10 kn and to leave an extra tip for exceptional service. Taxi drivers often round up the fare or overcharge tourists, so an additional tip is not needed.

Opening Times

Shops and **department stores** open Mon–Fri 8am–7pm and Sat 8am–2pm. In the resorts shops often open Mon–Fri 8am–1pm, close for the afternoon and open 5–11pm. **Banks** are open Mon–Fri 7am–3pm and Sat 8am–2pm. **Café-bars** open daily 7am–midnight and most restaurants open from midday to midnight. **Museum** opening times vary, but are generally Mon–Sat 9am–1pm or later. Some are open until 8pm in the summer.

Many Croatian towns and resorts have a fresh-food **market** and a general market. These are open Mon–Sat 8am–2pm. Markets selling souvenirs often have extended opening hours.

Offices are generally open Mon–Fri 8am–4.30 or 5pm.

Public Holidays

1 January: New Year's Day.
6 January: Epiphany.
March/April (variable): Easter.
1 May: Labour Day.
22 June: Anti-Fascist Resistance Day.
25 June: Croatian National Day.
5 August: Victory Day and National Thanksgiving Day.
15 August: Feast of the Assumption.
8 October: Independence Day.
1 November: All Saints' Day.
25–6 December: Christmas.

Shopping

Croatia is not normally considered a great shopping destination, but visitors will be pleasantly surprised. The cities, especially Zagreb, have a good range of designer stores and interesting shops. Nearly everything is available here that you would find in any other major European city. The towns and villages have smaller outlets selling local produce and handicrafts, and in the coastal resorts the work of local artists is on sale.

Food and drink

Often the best places to buy the freshest fruit and vegetables are the bountiful local markets, still very much alive today despite the increasing number of shopping malls and supermarkets. Markets in the holiday resorts also sell souvenirs; as a result, they tend to have extended opening hours.

Food items to look out for are the excellent salty sheep cheese from the North Dalmatian island of Pag, as well as the delicious Pršut smoked ham, which is served in thin slices all along the coastline, but particularly in Dalmatia. Croatian olive oil is also highly rated, as are its truffles, which are found in the Istrian interior. Kulen sausage from Slavonia is a spicy and tasty treat that travels well.

Croatia is also gaining a reputation for its wines, with a multitude of varieties available. Istria and Dalmatia produce the best-known and most highly regarded wines, but family-run and larger vineyards can be found all over the country. Wine is disproportionately expensive in the country due to high production costs and the relatively small domestic market, but the quality is high. There is an increasing number of specialist wine shops, especially in the resorts.

Jewellery and clothes

Items of jewellery, especially silver pieces and necklaces made from Adriatic coral, can be found in all of the coastal resorts in summer, sold from small shops or temporary stalls. The jewellery is often made in the outlying villages. Handmade silk neckties *(kravata)* are also popular, as is lace from the island of Pag, where the local women have made it by hand for centuries. From Rijeka comes the distinctive traditional *morãiç* jewellery.

Arts and crafts

Over the last few years the arts-and-crafts scene in Croatia has developed tremendously. Most tourists encounter it in the coastal resorts in the form of skyline depictions of the historic sights. More interesting are the individual paintings and artworks that surface in small shops.

Tourist Offices

Croatia

For information from the Croatia National Tourist Office (Hrvatska Turistiãka Zajednica), visit their website at www.croatia.hr

UK

2 The Lanchesters, 162–164 Fulham Palace Road, London W6 9ER; tel: 020 8563 7979; e-mail: info@cnto.freeserve.co.uk

US

Suite 4003, 350 Fifth Avenue, New York, NY 10118; tel: 212-279-8672; e-mail: cntoNY@earthlink.net

Telecommunications

Most public telephones only accept phonecards *(telekarta)*, which can be bought from tobacco kiosks or post offices. Direct-dial international and domestic calls can also be made from larger post offices, where you pay at the end of the call. Local, national and international calls can be made from most hotel telephones, but at a very high call rate.

Security and Crime

Crime rates in Croatia are lower than in most European countries and crime against tourists is rare. Simple precautions such as not leaving valuables in vehicles, carrying personal belongings securely and avoiding walking alone in dark areas at night minimise the risk. It is advisable to photocopy the identification pages of your passport, so that if it is lost or stolen the consulate will be able to issue a replacement quickly.

Emergency Telephone Numbers

Police: 92
Fire: 93
Ambulance: 94

CZECH REPUBLIC

Fact File

Area: 78,886 sq. km (30,500 sq. miles).
Capital: Prague.
Population: 10.2 million.
Language: Czech.
Religion: Unaffiliated 59 percent, Roman Catholic 27 percent, Protestant 2 percent, other 3 percent.
Currency: crown (koruna ãeská or Kã in the Czech Republic).
Time zone: *see page 327.*
International dialling code: 420.
Website: www.czechtourism.com

Entry Requirements, Customs and Health

The Czech Republic is in the European Union; *see box on page 326.*

Money Matters

Credit cards are widely accepted, especially in the larger cities. Cash is still used for most transactions, however. The easiest way to obtain cash is from an ATM. In Prague alone there are more than 100 cash machines connected to the worldwide Cirrus (Mastercard) and PLUS (Visa) networks. All of them dispense crowns (local currency) and have instructions in English. Travellers' cheques are accepted by some souvenir shops, hotels and restaurants as well as by banks, but often what looks like an exceptionally good rate may be accompanied by an inordinately high commission.

Exchange

In most shops and kiosks, payment is made in crowns, though an increasing number of places will accept and exchange euros, particularly in Prague. Shops and hotels accepting credit cards will normally have the requisite signs on the door. International exchange rates are published in newspapers and displayed at banks and exchange bureaux. There is no shortage of places to change your money in the city centre. Banks are usually open normal working hours.

Tipping

The customary tip for waiters and waitresses is 10 percent (up to 15 percent in the more expensive restaurants). For taxi tips, round up to the nearest 10 crowns. Give hotel porters, bellboys and washroom attendants 20–40 crowns.

Public Transport Prague

The various means of public transport are cheap and well synchronised. The network includes trams and buses, the metro and the funicular up Petfiín Hill. Tickets can be purchased in shops, at the kiosks, automatic ticket machines and newsagents. Remember that bus and tram drivers do not sell tickets. One-, three-, seven- and 15-day passes are available. For single-use tickets on the bus and tram (15 minutes travel time) or the metro (four stops), buy an 8-crown ticket. For one hour's worth of travel on all forms of public transport buy a 12-crown ticket. Be sure to have the right ticket: plain-clothes inspectors abound, and they will fine you if you do not have a valid ticket.

For ticket sales and further information contact the information office of the Public Transport Executive: Travel Information Centre, TIC Muzeum station (subway lines A and C), tel: 222 623 777, or the Mûstek metro station exit area beneath Jungmannovo Square, tel: 222 646 350 (open Mon–Fri 7am–6pm), or visit www.dp-praha.cz

Metro

The modern underground system links the centre with the suburbs and provides for convenient changes inside the city. It is a remarkably clean and fast means of public transport. The three lines have been developed with an eye towards expediency, and by transferring it is possible to reach just about all the important tourist attractions in the city. Because of the frequency of the trains (3–12 minutes), you don't need to allow more than about 30 minutes even for journeys into the suburbs. The metro operates 5am–midnight.

Metro signs outside the stations are small and square and decidedly inconspicuous, with a white M on a green, yellow or red background, depending which line the station is on.

Taxis

After midnight, with the exception of night buses, taxis constitute the sole form of public transport available in Prague. But be warned: Prague's taxi drivers have a reputation for ripping off tourists. Always insist that the meter is running before starting out, and try to use only official taxis, which can be recognised by their sign and by the licence number posted inside the vehicle. You'll find a number of taxi stops in the centre of Prague, as well as in front of larger hotels. You can order an official taxi by calling, tel: 266 776 677.

Opening Times

Shops in Prague open 9am–7pm on weekdays and 10am–1pm on Saturday, though many are now extending their hours. Those in the centre, catering largely to the tourist trade, often remain open late almost year round.

Late-night grocery shops are scattered around the city centre (one of the most central being the Bílá labut store at Wenceslas Square). **Banks** open 8am–5pm or 6pm from Monday to Friday, with some minor variations. Exchange offices remain open until 7pm, some until 10pm.

Public Holidays

1 January: New Year's Day.
March/April/May (variable): Easter.
1 May: May Day.
8 May: Liberation Day.
5 July: Feast Day of SS Cyril and Methodius.
6 July: Anniversary of the death of Jan Hus.
28 September: Czech Statehood Day.
28 October: Independence Day.
17 November: Struggle for Liberty Independence Day.
24–6 December: Christmas.

Shopping in Prague

If you are looking for souvenirs in Prague, the vendors on Charles Bridge or the market on Old Town Square are good bets. Sketches or paintings of the main sights may make for good and inexpensive options. Marionettes and costume jewellery are also on sale in the boutiques leading to the Old Town Square as well as elsewhere. If you prefer to take home antiques, you should be aware that the export of antique items of domestic historical significance is subject to strict controls. Most antiques dealers should be able to advise you on how to get a permit.

Classical music buffs can also take advantage of decent-quality and low-price CDs. Bohemian glass is a big favourite, and there are dozens of outlets in the city centre. Shop around as there are bargains to be found.

Relatively cheap and good-quality shoes are on offer at Bat'a at the bottom of Wenceslas Square.

A Prague ham or salami may be a nice idea. In terms of drinks, a bottle of Czech Becherovka or Moravian Slivovice represent distinctively local and cheap options.

Tourist Offices

Prague
PIS, the Prague Information Service, provides tourists with all necessary information. Their main office is at Na Příkopů 20, Praha 1, tel: 12444 (infoline); other offices are at Staroměstské radnice 1, Praha 1, and the Main Railway Station (Hlavní Nádrali). See also www.pis.cz. Offices are usually open in the summer Mon–Fri 9am–7pm, Sat–Sun 9am–5pm, with shorter hours Mon–Sat in the winter. A telephone information service is available on 420 1244, Mon–Fri 8am–7pm.

UK
Czech Tourism, 13 Harley Street, London W1G 9QG; tel: 010 7631 0427.
Čedok Travel Limited, Suite 22–3, 5th Floor, Morley House, 314/322 Regent Street, London W1B 3BG; tel: 020 7580 3778, fax: 020 7580 3779; e-mail: travel@cedok.demon.co.uk.

US
Protravel, 515 Madison Avenue, 10th Floor, NY 10022; tel: 212-755-4550; e-mail: nathalie@protravel.com; www.protravelinc.com

Telecommunications
Telephone
Even if you are dialling a number within the same area code, or between area codes within the Czech Republic, you dial the entire nine-digit number. The telephone systems have improved beyond all recognition in the past few years. You can use coins or phonecards (which are available in most newsagents). There are rows of telephones at most metro stations as well as on the streets. As ever, bear in mind that hotels will charge considerably more than public telephones.

Fax and Internet
In most of the larger hotels you can both send and receive a fax or take advantage of internet facilities to send e-mail. There are also centrally located internet cafés springing up all over Prague.

Security and Crime

The Czech Republic is a relatively safe country to visit, but the incidence of offences like robbery

and fraud has increased, particularly in Prague. It's therefore a good idea to deposit any valuables in the hotel safe or leave them at home. Also beware of pickpockets. There are professional gangs roaming busy shopping and tourist areas as well as the metro, trams and buses. In an emergency either consult with your hotel reception or contact the police directly by dialling 158. If you either lose or have your personal documents stolen, contact your embassy representative immediately.

Emergency Telephone Numbers

Emergency: 112
Ambulance: 155
Police: 158
Fire: 150

EGYPT

Fact File

Area: 1,002,000 sq. km (626,000 sq. miles).
Capital: Cairo.
Population: over 66 million.
Language: Arabic (official). English and French are widely understood by educated people.
Religion: Muslim (mostly Sunni), Coptic Christian minority (around 10 percent).
Currency: Egyptian pound (LE) = 100 piastres.
Time zone: *see page 327.*
International dialling code: 20.
Website: www.egyptnow.com

Entry Requirements

All travellers entering Egypt must have a passport valid for at least six months and a valid visa. For most visitors, including EU and US nationals, it is easiest and cheapest to get a tourist visa at the point of arrival. They can be obtained from Cairo International Airport, Sharm al-Shaykh and Alexandria Port among other points of entry.

Customs Regulations

Visitors are permitted to enter Egypt with 250g of tobacco, or 50 cigars, 1 litre of alcohol, and personal effects. Duty-free purchases of liquor (three bottles per person) may be made at ports of entry or at the tax-free shops in Cairo. If you have any expensive electronic equipment you may be required to declare it on arrival so that authorities can check that it is with you when you leave (and has not been sold).

Health and Insurance

No inoculations are needed at present, but it's best to check with your doctor before travelling, to ensure you take all necessary precautions. Rabies is present in Egypt, so be wary of animals. Make sure you have adequate medical insurance cover before travelling.

The most common ailments experienced by tourists are dehydration and upset stomach. Take the following precautions to minimise the risks:

• Drink plenty of bottled water (this is widely available) and always carry a supply with you. Do not drink tap water.

• Do not drink the Nile water, swim in it, or walk barefoot along its banks: the water contains bilharzia, a parasitic flatworm.

• Wash your hands before eating.

• Eat well-cooked meat and peel fruit before eating it.

• Avoid ice in drinks except in luxury hotels.

• If you eat at buffets, ensure that cold dishes have been well chilled.

• Be aware that milk and dairy products may be unpasteurised in non-tourist establishments.

Pharmacies

These have a green crescent sign decorated with a red cross or serpent. Local medicines may not have the same names as at home. Check with the hotel doctor before buying anything of which you are not sure.

Doctors and Hospitals

The large hotels have English-speaking doctors on call. The Anglo-American Hospital in Cairo is west of the Cairo Tower on Zamalek Island, tel: 02-735 6162/6315.

Money Matters

Banks are available at the airport for currency exchange. Egyptian currency is the Egyptian pound (LE), divided into 100 piastres (PT). Credit cards are used in most major hotels, but not always in shops. It is advisable to bring some US-dollar travellers' cheques or use the ATM machines, which are widespread in the cities, to withdraw cash.

Tipping

In Egypt, the practice of tipping, or baksheesh, is widespread. Children and beggars may approach you in the street asking for baksheesh.

Although you don't need to give them money, it is a good idea to carry plenty of small banknotes to give to those who provide a service.The following people will expect tips for their services:

Porter	2LE per bag
Waiter	10 percent if service not included
Toilet attendant	1LE
Maid	50LE per week
Taxi driver	1–5LE
Tour guide	10 percent
Cruise guide	50LE per client
Felucca boatman	2LE per passenger

Public Transport Cairo and Luxor

From Cairo Airport

Options from Cairo airport include limousine, taxi and bus. A kerbside limousine service at fixed fares is offered by Misr Limousine (tel: 02-259 9381) and others. Official Cairo taxis are mostly black and white. Fees are often the same as the limousine service.

The best bus to take to and from the airport from Downtown Cairo is No. 356, which runs 6am–11pm every 20 minutes from Terminal 1 via Terminal 2, Heliopolis and Abbaseya, to the Abdel Mouneem Riyad bus station just behind the Egyptian Museum. The bus leaves from the bus stop outside the airport car park.

From Luxor Airport

Luxor International Airport, with a new, fully air-conditioned terminal building completed in 2005, is 6 km (4 miles) east of the city, just off the 02 highway which runs along the east bank of the Nile River. A regular bus service is available between the airport and the city, but it is generally very crowded. The best way into Luxor is by taxi; the trip operates on a flat-fee basis and takes about 15 minutes, depending on the traffic.

By Bus around Cairo

The large red-and-white and blue-and-white buses are usually extremely overcrowded. As well as being claustrophobic, they provide ample opportunity for petty theft and unwelcome sexual encounters. New blue-and-white air-conditioned buses are much more comfortable, as are the less crowded but slightly more expensive minibuses. Most buses start or pass by the Abdel Mouneem Riyad terminal, behind the Egyptian Museum on Maydan at-Tahrir. Here are a few interesting routes for the adventurous tourist:

• No. 337 to Muhandesseen
• No. 13 to Zamalik
• No. 400 airport to Downtown
• No. 66 Nile Hilton in Midan Tahrir to Khan al-Khalili
• No. 72 from the Nile Hilton in Midan Tahrir to the Citadel
• Nos. 800/900 from Midan Tahrir to the Pyramids.

More comfortable are the smaller orange-and-white minibuses which do not permit standing. Here are a few major routes (from Maydan at-Tahrir):

• Nos. 24, 27, 35 to Ramesses statue, Abbassiyah and Roxi
• No. 27 to Ramesses statue, Abbassiyah and the airport
• No. 82 to the Pyramids.

By Metro around Cairo

In Cairo the metro system is identified by circular signs with a big red M. The metro is clean and efficient and an easy way to get around. Note that every train has a special carriage for women. The system runs 5.30am–12.30am north–south from Heliopolis to Helwan through the heart of the city. Another line was opened from the northern suburb of Shubra al-Kheima to Bulaq al-Dakrour, and other lines are under construction.

Opening Times

Shops The Egyptian weekend is Friday and Saturday, so most open Sun–Thurs 9am–6pm, usually closing for lunch 1.30pm–4pm, reopening until 8pm in winter and 9pm in summer. The Khan al-Khalili bazaar in Cairo is open daily 10am–7 or 8pm (later in summer and during Ramadan). **Banks** are open Sun–Thurs 8.30am–1.30pm.

Public Holidays

1 January: New Year's Day.
25 April: Liberation of Sinai Day.
1 May: Labour Day.
23 July: Anniversary of the 1952 Revolution.
6 October: Armed Forces Day.
In addition, there are Islamic and Coptic holidays throughout the year.

Shopping

Bazaars

Khan al-Khalili and the surrounding area, in Cairo, is one of the oldest bazaars in the Muslim world. A veritable treasure trove of shopping opportunities, the labyrinth of narrow alleys is divided into "quarters", each with its own speciality. The tent-making quarter, where large ceremonial tents are fashioned by hand from brightly dyed Egyptian cotton, is particularly interesting. The Khan, as it is known locally, is not just a tourist bazaar. The Egyptians shop here, too, and it offers a chance to mingle with them to find artefacts from around the country. There is a smaller but no less atmospheric bazaar at Luxor.

Bear in mind that you'll need a strong will and a sense of humour to shrug off the sales pitch of Egyptian shopkeepers. If you take a guide or interpreter with you, it is customary for them to receive a percentage on every purchase you make.

Archaeological Sites

Mini tourist markets have sprung up around most of the major archaeological sites. They all sell much the same items as the larger bazaars and souks, but prices are likely to be higher. The quality of goods varies from one stall to another, and a common ploy is to sell inferior stone painted to look like marble or alabaster, so be wary of bargains. Always study any item carefully before purchase. Prices drop at the end of the day, after the tour groups leave, especially out of season.

What to Buy

Alabaster and marble
Carving skills have been passed down through the centuries, notably in villages near the Valley of the Kings and around the marble quarries at Aswan. From beautiful copies of ancient pieces to inexpensive souvenirs, you will be spoilt for choice. Small items, such as scarab beetles – considered lucky in Egypt – are sold in shops, but also by young children and street hawkers around the archaeological sites.

Antiques
Pharaonic and Islamic antiquities can only be exported through a few shops. Each sale should be accompanied by a letter of authenticity and permission to export the item. Street vendors selling antiquities are selling fakes, worth purchasing for their own merit, but not as authentic articles.

Appliqué
This craft, probably traceable to ancient Egypt, when appliqué banners billowed from the tops of temple gates, comes in Pharaonic and Islamic designs in the form of pillowcases, tablecloths and wall hangings. You'll find examples of the craft in bazaars throughout Egypt.

Copper and brass
These metals have long been used for practical items such as water carriers, samovars or cooking pots, and they make excellent souvenirs. Older pieces have the patina of age, whereas new pieces – usually made on-site – are

bright and shiny. Trays can be found in all sizes, and those with a wooden stand make good portable tables.

Cotton
Egyptian cotton, with its long fibres, is arguably the finest in the world. The thousands of hectares under cultivation in the Nile Delta are one of the country's most lucrative export earners. Almost everywhere you go you'll find practical items such as the *gellabiya* – the long shirt-like garment, a variation on the *gellaba* – and T-shirts, normally featuring images of camels and pyramids.

Jewellery
Given the amount of gold found in Egyptian tombs, it's not surprising that gold is a good buy. Precious metals are sold by weight, with very little added to the price for workmanship. Precious stones and semi-precious stones, including topaz, lapis lazuli and aquamarine, can be bought loose or set in rings, necklaces, bracelets or brooches. Copies of ancient hieroglyphic cartouches also make popular souvenirs – a jeweller can have your name made up into a cartouche of Egyptian script in a couple of days.

Perfume
Egypt grows and exports jasmine, geranium, rose, violet, camomile and orange for perfumiers in France, from whom essence is then reimported. Nefertari products, available from the better craft shops, are locally made, 100 percent natural beauty products, made with olive oil and natural essential oils.

Tourist Offices

Egypt
Cairo: 5 Adly Street; tel: 02-391 3454. You'll also find smaller offices at the Pyramids and at Cairo International Airport.
Luxor: Corniche an-Nil; tel: 095-238 2215.
Canada
1253 McGill College Avenue #250, Montreal, Quebec H3B 2Y5; tel: 514-861-4420.
UK
170 Piccadilly, London W1V 7DD; tel: 020-7493 5283;
www.egypttreasures.gov.eg; www.egyptnow.com
US
630 Fifth Avenue, Suite 2305, New York, NY 10111; tel: 212-332-2570; www.egypttourism.org

Telecommunications

Most five-star hotels offer a direct-dial service, although it is cheaper to call from a telephone office; calls must be paid for in advance, with a

three-minute minimum. You can also call from one of the many Menatel cardphones; cards can be bought from telephone offices. Between 8pm and 8am the cost of phone calls is greatly reduced.

The Central Telephone and Telegraph offices (8 Shari' Adli, 13 Maydan at-Tahrir, 26 Shari' Ramesses) are open 24 hours a day. Others are open daily 7am–10pm.

There is an increasing number of cyber cafés in all the main cities.

Security and Crime

There is a large presence of tourist police in the tourist areas since the terrorist attacks of recent years. Common caution is advised at all times. Social restrictions on women in Egypt can make foreign women seem particularly enticing to young Egyptian men. The number of petty thefts has increased, although you are still more likely to have a lost wallet returned intact in Egypt than in most Western countries. If you do experience problems, you should report immediately to the nearest tourist police post or police station.

Lost or stolen passports must be reported to the police immediately. New passports can be issued in a matter of hours at the consular office of your embassy in Egypt, but you'll require a copy of the police report verifying the loss.

Emergency Telephone Numbers

Police: 122
Ambulance: 123
Fire: 180

FRANCE

Fact File

Area: 543,965 sq. km (210,026 sq. miles).
Capital: Paris.
Population: around 60 million.
Language: French, but regional languages still exist.
Religion: Roman Catholic, Muslim and other minorities.
Currency: euro (€).
Time zone: *see page 327.*
International dialling code: 33.
Website: www.franceguide.com

Entry Requirements, Customs and Health

As for other European Union countries, *see the box on page 326.*

PLANNING A TRIP

LIFE ON BOARD

A–Z

RIVER VESSEL LISTINGS

Money Matters

The French currency is the euro (€). Credit cards are widely accepted, though sometimes American Express is not. French bank cards use a PIN but you should also be able to sign the receipt. Credit and bank cards can be used at ATMS to withdraw money, and instructions will be available in English.

Tipping

You do not usually need to add service to a restaurant bill in France. A charge of 10 percent is added automatically as part of the bill. To be sure, check that it says *Service compris* on the menu, or ask *"Est-ce que le service est compris?"* Taxi fares also include service, but drivers don't mind a bit extra.

Public Transport Paris

Métro and RER

Despite being one of the world's oldest subways, the Paris Métro is quick and efficient. It operates 5.30am–12.30am, and its comprehensive map and signage make it difficult to get lost; the lines are identified by number and the names of their terminals. It operates in conjunction with the RER, suburban regional express trains, which operate on five lines, A–E.

Flat-fare tickets are valid for both the subway and the bus, but a book *(carnet)* of 10 gives a considerable saving. Buy them at bus or Métro stations and some *tabacs*.

Another option is the Paris-Visite card, which is valid for one to five consecutive days on the Métro, bus and railway in the Paris/Ile de France region. It also gives discounted entry to various tourist sites; it is available from main Métro and SNCF stations and the airports. For shorter stays, buy the Mobilis card, which allows an unlimited number of trips in any one day on the Métro, bus and suburban trains and the night buses (zones 1–5). Buy it from Métro offices or the Central Tourist Office in the Champs-Elysées.

A combined Louvre/RATP ticket offers two journeys on public transport and priority access to the Louvre. Information on all passes is available from RATP, tel: 08 92 68 77 14, www.ratp.fr, or Allo France in the UK.

By Bus

Details of bus routes and timetables are generally available free from bus stations *(gares routières)*, which are often situated close to railway stations, or tourist offices.

Taxis

Taxis are most readily available at airports and railway stations. In Paris there are almost 500 taxi ranks, but be careful in the capital to hail only a genuine taxi (with a light on the roof); other operators may charge exorbitant fares. Taxi drivers in Paris operate on three tariffs:

- Tariff A 7am–7pm
- Tariff B 7pm–7am
- Tariff C at night in the suburbs and during the day in the outlying districts of Hauts-de-Seine, Seine Saint-Denis and Val-de-Marne, when the taxi has no client for the return journey.

A 10 percent tip to the driver is usual. Any complaints about Paris taxis should be addressed in writing to the Service des Taxis, Préfecture de Police, 36 Rue des Morillons, 75015 Paris.

Opening Times

Shops normally open Mon–Sat 8am–noon and 2–7pm. Department stores in cities open 9am or 10am–7pm or 8pm. *Boulangeries* (bakeries) open at 7am even on Sunday. Supermarkets and hypermarkets open 9am–9pm, except Monday when they often start at noon or 1pm. Shops (and banks) in country areas open for shorter periods than town branches and nearly always close for the midday meal between noon and 2pm or even 3pm. During the summer season, however, shops stay open until fairly late.

Banks open Mon–Fri 8.30am–noon and 2–4.30pm, but 9am–5.30pm in large cities; they are closed Sat–Sun and sometimes Monday.

Chemists open 8am–12.30pm and 3–7pm. A sign in the chemist's window will indicate the nearest *pharmacie de nuit* (late-night chemist).

Museums: national museums close on Tuesday, while municipal museums are closed on Monday. There are no fixed opening times for smaller museums. Ask at the local tourist office *(Syndicat d'Initiative or Office du Tourisme)*.

Post offices (PTT – Postes et Télécommunications, Télédiffusion) open Mon–Fri 9am–7pm (in rural areas Mon–Fri 8am–noon and 2–5pm) and on Saturday until noon.

Shopping

Paris

Paris, naturally, has an exceptional range of shops from the fashion houses in the 8th arrondissement,

Public Holidays

1 January: New Year's Day.
March/April/May (variable): Easter Monday.
40 days after Easter: Ascension Day.
1 May: May Day/Labour Day.
8 May: Victory in Europe Day 1945.
Seventh Monday after Easter: Pentecost.
14 July: Bastille Day.
15 August: Assumption of the Virgin Mary.
1 November: All Saints' Day.
11 November: Armistice Day.
25 December: Christmas Day.

particularly around the Faubourg St-Honoré, to the more affordable, but still chic department stores *(grands magasins)*, such as Galeries Lafayette and Printemps, both of which are on boulevard Haussmann. The Marais is a focus for youthful fashion boutiques and quirky gift shops. The biggest flea market in the world is Les Puces de St-Ouen at Porte de Clignancourt in Paris, open Sat–Mon 6am–7.30pm. Insight Guides' *Shopping in Paris* is full of detailed information for dedicated shoppers.

Markets

Markets are a riot of colour and bustle; the best have all kinds of stalls, from flowers to domestic animals. Local cheeses, honey, wine, pâté and other specialities are often offered for tasting to encourage browsers to buy. They usually start early in the morning and close at midday, although some bigger ones are open in the afternoon too.

Flea markets *(marchés aux puces)* are fun to look around – you may even find a genuine bargain antique amongst all the old junk.

Shopping by Area

Burgundy/Champagne: superb food and wine are the highlights here. As well as burgundies, this is the home of the genuine article: champagne. It's also where cassis comes from, the blackcurrant liqueur which when added to white wine makes kir. Dijon mustard is another product of the area. In Dijon itself the market square (off rue Quentin and rue Bannelier) has superb stands of foods and specialities amongst pretty cafés and restaurants.

In Beaune there is a covered market selling a whole range of local produce and specialities; it includes one of the last remaining mustard makers, Edmond Fallot.

Dordogne: Another gastronomic heaven, with specialities including foie gras, *confit* and *magret de canard*, truffles and *huile de noix* (walnut oil). Bordeaux is not far from here, with its world-class clarets. Other souvenirs include soap, baskets and porcelain.

Loire: The Loire Valley is famous for its white wines, including Muscadet, Saumur, Pouilly Fumé and Sancerre; the region also produces fine leather goods, and Gien and Tours are well known for their chinaware.

Midi: Toulouse and the surrounding area are home to many delicious foods: cassoulet, for example, a rich concoction of goose or duck, mutton, sausages and haricot beans; Toulouse *saucisses*; *confit de canard* (conserved duck); and foie gras, the goose liver pâté you either love or hate. Armagnac, a fiery brandy from the Gers, also makes an excellent souvenir.

Provence: Specialities from Provence include lavender sachets, fine fabrics, perfumes from Grasse and hand-painted tiles. *Santons* are also typical of the region; they are clay figurines, traditionally representing characters from the nativity. Or there's *savon de Marseille* (soap), and cicada-inspired creations – *la cigale* is the symbol of the region.

Provençal food specialities include olive oil, *anchoïade* (mashed salted anchovies, olive oil and garlic on bread), *tapenade* (purée made from capers, black olives, anchovies and olive oil, used as a dip or spread), *calissons d'Aix* (sweets made from ground almonds blended with candied fruit), home-made jams and honeys, truffles and *herbes de Provence*.

Rhône Valley: Lyon in the Rhône-Alpes is often considered the gastronomic heart of France. In this region you will find fresh fish from the lakes and mountain streams, fine-flavoured beef, tasty hams, superb sausages and excellent cheeses, such as Tôme de Savoie, Vacherin, Bleu de Bresse and Reblochon. Beaujolais wines to look out for include Juliénas, Morgon and Brouilly, and fuller-bodied wines include Crozes-Hermitage.

Tourist Offices

France

Lyon: Lyon Convention and Visitors' Bureau, Place Bellecour, BP 2254, 69214, Lyon CEDEX 02; tel: 04 72 77 69 69; fax: 04 78 42 04 32; e-mail: info@lyon-france.com; www.en.lyon-france.com

Paris: Office de Tourisme de Paris,

25 rue des Pyramides, 75001; tel: 08 92 68 30 00; www.parisinfo.com Branches at: Opéra-Grands Boulevards, Gare de Lyon, Eiffel Tower, Gare du Nord, Montmartre, Carrousel du Louvre. For information on the area around Paris (Ile de France), tel: 01 44 50 19 98.

Canada

1981 McGill College Avenue, Esso Tower, Suite 490, Montreal, Quebec, H3A 2W9; tel: 514-288-4264.
30 St Patrick Street, Suite 700, Toronto, Ontario M5T 3A3; tel: 416-593-4723.

UK

178 Piccadilly, London W1V 0AL; tel: 09068 244 123; e-mail: info.uk@franceguide.com; www.franceguide.com

US

444 Madison Avenue, NY 10022, New York; tel: 514-288-1904.
676 N. Michigan Avenue, Suite 3360, Chicago, IL 60611-2836; tel: 312-751-7800.
9454 Wilshire Boulevard, Suite 715,Beverly Hills, CA 90212-2967; tel: 310-271-2693.

Telecommunications

Card-operated telephones are now common throughout France, and the old coin-operated machines are a threatened species. Post offices or *bar-tabacs* sell *télécartes* for either 50 or 120 units. The cheap tariff for long-distance calls applies Mon–Fri 7.30pm–8am, Sat 1.30pm–Mon 8am, and on public holidays. You'll find internet cafés in major cities.

Security and Crime

Take sensible precautions in the cities, as you would anywhere. Be especially aware of pickpockets, who can be quite devious. Keep your money and valuables safely tucked away out of sight.

Emergency Telephone Numbers

Ambulance: 15
Police: 17
Fire *(sapeurs-pompiers)*: 18

GERMANY

Fact File

Area: 357,000 sq. km (138,000 sq. miles).
Capital: Berlin.
Population: 83 million.
Language: German, plus small

minorities speaking Frisian and Sorbian.
Religion: About one third Protestant, one third Roman Catholic, one third other religions or agnostic/atheist.
Currency: euro (€).
Time zone: *see page 327*.
International dialling code: 49.
Website: www.germany-tourism.de

Entry Requirements, Customs and Health

Germany is in the European Union; *see page 326 for details.*

Money Matters

Credit and Debit Cards

Major credit cards are accepted in department stores and most other shops in Germany, plus hotels, airlines, petrol stations and the majority of restaurants. However, there are still many occasions, especially in smaller shops and pubs, when credit cards are not accepted, so it is advisable to carry some euros, just in case. Note that you cannot use travellers' cheques as payment, as they have to be cashed at a bank beforehand.

Credit and debit cards also give you access to money from cash machines in Germany. Remember that most banks charge a commission and fee every time you use your credit card abroad; check exact details with your own bank before travelling.

Tipping

Restaurant bills always include a 15 percent service charge. However, it is common to reward good service with a gratuity of around 5–10 percent. In taxis it is also usual to add a little extra as a tip.

Tax/VAT

VAT *(Mehrwertsteuer)* in Germany is charged at two rates: 16 percent and 7 percent. The reduced rate is applied to food, newspapers, books, theatre tickets and so on. All other goods and services, such as car rental or restaurant meals, are taxed at 16 percent. This is normally included in the final price, but shown as an extra on most bills.

Non-EU residents may get the tax reimbursed provided they fill in a sales form when buying the article from specially designated "tax-free" shops. This then has to be stamped and the article shown at customs before you leave the country for you to receive your refund.

Public Transport
Germany

A widespread network of public transport systems exists, and in large cities such as Berlin, Cologne and Frankfurt the bus routes are integrated with the underground (U-Bahn), the tram and the above-ground suburban railway (S-Bahn). The same ticket may be used on all four means of transport.

In many towns, reduced-rate tickets are sold for unlimited daily, weekly or monthly travel. There are also special tourist offers like the Welcome Card in Berlin, which includes three days of free travelling on public transport, plus many discount coupons for sightseeing or cultural events (similar offers exist in other cities).

The Berlin Transport Company (BVG) operates a number of services specifically for tourists (Nos. 100 and 200 cover most of the major sites), as well as an express bus shuttle service between the airport and the city centre. Tel: 030-19449 for details (lines open 24 hours); e-mail: info@bvg.de; www.bvg.de. Tickets can be bought from ticket machines. Inspections are frequent, and passengers travelling without valid tickets will be fined on the spot.

Opening Times

Shops: Typical opening hours for department stores and shopping malls in the big cities is Monday–Friday 10am–8pm, with other shops open 9am–6pm, but often until 8pm on Thursdays. In smaller towns and villages shops usually close at 6 or 6.30pm, but may have longer opening hours on Thursday and Friday. Some shops open at 7 or 8am. Bakeries, of course, start selling fresh bread and rolls early on, and at pavement kiosks daily papers go on sale at around 6 or 7am.

On Saturdays small shops normally open 8am–1 or 2pm, and department stores close at 4 or 5pm. Sundays are still considered sacrosanct in Germany and there is normally no trading, with the exception of bakeries, newsagents, souvenir shops and a few others.

Banks usually open weekdays 9am–4pm (possibly closed at lunch-time), but they are expanding their services, at least in big cities. Exchange bureaux (Wechselstuben) are open until 6pm, sometimes longer, and also on Saturday.

Post offices retain their traditional opening hours: 8am–6pm, and until noon on Saturday. At railway stations and airports you will find post offices open until later.

Restaurants and pubs normally close at midnight or 1am. Nightclubs and some bars have licences for extended hours. In Berlin there are no late-night restrictions.

Public Holidays

1 January: New Year's Day.
March/April/May (variable): Easter.
1 May: Labour Day.
May (variable): Ascension Day.
May/June (variable): Whitsun.
3 October: Day of German Unity.
25–6 December: Christmas.
The following are religious holidays in some areas:
6 January: Epiphany.
May/June (variable): Corpus Christi.
15 August: Ascension.
31 October: Reformation Day.
1 November: All Saints' Day.

Shopping

Germany has a well-earned reputation for high-quality manufactured goods, and a stroll around any large department store will reveal any number of consumer desirables. There are also plenty of more or less tacky souvenirs.

As elsewhere in Europe, chain stores and department stores occupy the prime sites, while humbler establishments like antique shops and second-hand bookdealers can be found in side streets, or in particular parts of town. The Antik und Flohmarkt beneath the railway arches near Berlin's Friedrichstrasse is a treasure trove of antiques. Modern shopping arcades – Passagen – are often very inviting, especially in the biggest cities; Berlin has state-of-the-art examples opening off redeveloped Friedrichstrasse.

Flea markets like the weekend one in Berlin's Charlottenburg are a great attraction, while Christmas markets are full of atmosphere as well as good ideas for presents. Museum shops are a good source of original souvenirs.

Antiques
The more prosperous periods in German history produced quantities of fine things, notably during the Jugendstil (the local version of art nouveau) and art deco eras. Ceramics, lamps and similar objects are often of very high quality and are available at reasonable prices. Early 19th-century Biedermeier furniture is also very desirable.

Fashion
Everything is available, from designer fashions to second-hand chic.

Traditional Bavarian wear can look very smart in Bavaria, but how often would you sport lederhosen or a dirndl at home? A Loden coat could be a better buy. Leatherwear is usually of a high quality.

Porcelain
This long-established industry is still turning out fine products. Among the leading factories are Nymphenburg and Rosenthal, Meissen (both in Munich), KPM in Berlin, and Villeroy & Boch at Mettlach in the Saarland.

Souvenirs
As well as cuckoo clocks, timepieces of all kinds are made in the Black Forest. Toys make good souvenirs too, with centres of excellence in Nuremberg (mechanical toys, including the world's best model railways) and the Erzgebirge mountains in Saxony (carved items).

Tourist Offices

Germany
Berlin: Berlin Tourismus Marketing, Am Karlsbad 11, 10785 Berlin; tel: 030-250025; fax: 030-25002424; www.berlin-tourism.de
Cologne: Köln Tourismus, Unter Fettenhennen 19, 50667 Köln; tel: 0221-23345; fax: 0221-23320; www.koeln.de
Frankfurt: Tourismus & Congress Frankfurt/Main, Kaiserstrasse 56, 60329 Frankfurt/Main; tel: 069-21238800; fax: 069-21237880; www.frankfurt.de
Munich: Information Centres at Main Train Station and Marienplatz. Tel: 089-233 96 500; e-mail: tourismus@muenchen.de; www.muenchen-tourist.de
Nuremburg: Tel: 0911-2336-131/2; e-mail: tourismus@nuernberg.de; www.tourismus.nuernberg.de
Ulm: Stadthaus, Münsterplatz 50, D-89075 Ulm; tel: 0731-161 2830; fax: 0731-161 1641; e-mail: info@tourismus.ulm.de; www.tourismus.ulm.de

Canada
German National Tourist Office, 480 University Avenue, Suite 1410, Toronto, Ontario M5G 1V2; tel: 416-968-1685; fax: 416-968-0562; e-mail: info@gnto.ca; www.gnto.ca

UK
German National Tourist Office, no walk-in office; tel: 020 7317 0908; fax: 020 7317 0917; e-mail: gntolon@d-z-t.com; www.germany-tourism.co.uk

US
122 East 42nd Street, New York, NY 10168-0072; tel: 212-661-7200; fax: 212-661-7174; email: gntonyc@d-z-t.com; www.cometogermany.com

Telecommunications

The country code for Germany is 49. For domestic enquiries, tel: 11 8 33; for international, tel: 11 8 34.

Calls can be made from hotel rooms, but more cheaply from phone booths. Most of these accept phone-cards in various denominations, and some accept credit cards. You can buy phonecards from post offices, newspaper kiosks and petrol stations.

Most British mobile phones will work in Germany, but check charges before leaving.

Security and Crime

Take the same precautions you woud in any large city; beware of pick-pockets in crowds, do not leave your luggage unaccompanied at any time and put valuables in the hotel safe.

Emergency Telephone Numbers

Police: 110
Fire brigade: 112
Ambulance: 112

HUNGARY

Fact File

Area: 93,033 sq. km (35,920 sq. miles).
Capital: Budapest.
Population: 10 million.
Language: Hungarian (Magyar).
Religion: Roman Catholic, with Protestant, Orthodox and Jewish minorities.
Currency: forint (Ft or HUF).
Time zone: *see page 327.*
International dialling code: 36. The city code for Budapest is 01.
Websites: www.gotohungary.co.uk; www.hungary.com; www.budapestinfo.hu

Entry Requirements, Customs and Health

Hungary is in the European Union; *see box on page 326.*

Money Matters

The unit of currency in Hungary is the forint (Ft), with 1, 2, 5, 10, 20, 50, 100 and 200 forint coins. Notes are issued to the value of 200, 500, 1,000, 2,000, 5,000, 10,000 and 20,000 forints.

There are no limits on the amount of currency which may be imported and exported, but large sums of money should be declared to the authorities in order to guarantee re-export without hitches.

Most banks will change money, especially branches of the OTP, the Hungarian savings bank. ATMs accepting most major debit/credit cards are to be found throughout Budapest. Hotels, travel agencies, tourist offices and campsites will also change money, and exchange rates are similar to those at a bank.

VAT Refunds

Hungary has 25 percent VAT (ÁFA) imposed on many goods. A traveller can claim it back if no more than 90 days have elapsed between purchase and export and the value exceeds 50,000 forints. Customs officials must confirm that goods are in original condition. No more than 183 days may elapse between purchase date and refund. Travellers must bring the refund to the attention of the customs official or subsequent requests will be invalid. No refund will be made for goods used within Hungary.

For more information, ask your local Hungarian tourist office or contact Global Refund Magyarország Rt. in Budapest, tel/fax: 212 4906, www.globalrefund.com, or the Tourinform Head Office, 1052 Deák tér (Sütő utca 2.); www.tourinform.hu

Tipping

In restaurants and bars a tip of 10–15 percent is expected, depending on the service. The same applies to services rendered by taxi drivers, hairdressers and porters.

Public Transport Budapest

Public transport in Budapest is good, rapid and cheap. An integrated net-work of trams and buses, the underground railway (metro) and the suburban railway (HÉV) provide access to all parts of the city in any direction. Tickets (best bought in bulk in advance) can be obtained from vending machines, at stations, at tobacconists, at metro ticket offices and in travel agencies. Each ticket is only valid for one journey. They are not valid for transfers. If you are caught fare-dodging, you will have to pay a 2,000 Ft fine.

Operating Hours

Metro, buses: 4.30am–11pm.
Trams: 4am–midnight.
24-hour and night-time routes:
Information about the public trans-port system can be obtained from Fővinform (day and night), tel: 317 1173, or visit www.bkv.hu

Discount Cards

You may find the **Budapest Card** useful. This card is valid for two or three days, and included in the price is unlimited public transport within the city, discounts on various museums, tours, spas, restaurants and shops. It is available from metro stations, travel agencies, tourist informa-tion offices, hotels and at the airport. See www.budapestinfo.hu

Buses/Trams

In Budapest there are about 30 tram and over 200 bus routes. Express buses have red numbers and only stop at certain points. The 14 trolley-bus routes mainly link up with the metro routes; route 73 is a direct link between the Western and Eastern Railway Stations. To reach the airport from the city, the Volánbus departs every half-hour from the central bus station at Erzsebet tér.

Metro

The metro system is by far the quickest way of getting around. There are three routes. The "little metro" (1) links the city centre with Mexikói út. Route M2 runs west–east, from the Southern Railway Station (Déli pályaudvar) under the Danube to the other bank, passing the Eastern Rail-way Station (Keleti pályaudvar) and on as far as Örs vezér tere. The M3 runs north–south on the Pest bank from Újpest központ to Kőbánya-Kispest. The M1 is signed in yellow, the M2 in red, the M3 in blue. The three routes intersect at the busy downtown hub of Deák tér.

Taxis

Taxis are fairly reasonably priced, providing you make sure to take one bearing a phone number and a company name, not just a sign saying "Taxi". Within Budapest there are around 150 taxi ranks, and it is also acceptable to hail a cab. However, it's slightly less expensive to order a taxi to your pick-up address, and there's nearly always an English-speaking operator to take your call. When ordering a cab from the street, look for one of the following:
6x6 Taxi, tel: 266 6666
Buda Taxi, tel: 233 3333
City Taxi, tel: 211 1111
FŒ Taxi, tel: 222 2222
Radió Taxi, tel: 377 7777

Other Forms of Transport

Cable railway: This nice little ride runs from Clark Adam tér opposite the Chain Bridge up Castle Hill. Every 3 minutes, 8.30am–8pm.

Rack railway: From Városmajor up Széchenyi Hill. Every 15 minutes, 4am–12.25am.

Children's railway: From Széchenyi Hill to Hüvösvölgy (Cool Valley) covering 12 km (8 miles). Apart from the driver, the train is manned by children and young people. Fares vary according to length of journey. Tickets available at stations.

Chair lifts: From Zugligetu út up János Hill. Terminus near the viewing tower. Operates 8am–4pm (winter), until 5pm (summer).

Microbus: Runs on Margaret Island. Tour guide (in Hungarian).

Horsedrawn omnibus/carriage: A horsedrawn omnibus from the turn of the 20th century runs through Óbuda.

Opening Times

Most shops and department stores in town centres open Mon–Fri 10am–6pm and Sat 9am–1pm. Some shops also stay open until 8pm on Thursday, and there are convenience stores that stay open around the clock. Some of the new hypermarkets on the outskirts of Budapest, most notably Tesco, are open 24 hours.

The following shopping centres in Budapest are open Mon–Sat 9am–9pm and Sun 10am–4pm:
• Duna Plaza, XIII, Váci út 178;
Mamut Center, II, Lövoház utca 2–6;
• WestEnd City Center, VI, Váci út 1–3 (next to Nyugati Train Station).

There are many 24-hour stores offering basic consumer goods. They advertise either "non-stop", or "éjjel-nappal". After 10pm there is sometimes a small surcharge.

Food shops: Mon–Fri 7am–7/8pm; Sat 7am–4pm; closed Sun, with the exception of some supermarkets (8am–1pm or 24 hours).

Banks: Mon–Fri 8am–5pm, with some banks now adopting Saturday morning opening hours.

Pharmacies: Mon–Fri 8am–6pm, Sat 8am–1pm, with a weekend emergency cover service.

Museums: Major ones: Tues–Sun 10am–6pm; smaller museums may have reduced hours.

Public Holidays

1 January: New Year's Day.
15 March: National Day.
March/April (variable): Easter Monday.
1 May: Labour Day.
20 August: St Stephen's/Constitution Day.
23 October: 1956 Republic Day.

25–6 December: Christmas.
If the holiday falls on a Thursday or Tuesday, the Friday or Monday will be taken off and added to the weekend.

Shopping

Buda's Castle Hill and Pest's Váci utca are lined with crystal and gift shops where you can buy hand-crafted items like leather purses, colourful pottery and porcelain, which make excellent presents or souvenirs.

Note that the prices for embroidery and lace (from Kiskunhalas, for example) can be quite steep. Bear in mind that lacemaking and embroidered place mats or tablecloths represent a great deal of work that can only be done by hand. In hotels, there is a commission business that also pushes up prices.

Food is another excellent gift: salamis (from Pick or Herz, for example) make nice presents, though they may well contain donkey or horse meat. Hungary also has several excellent wine regions, notably Tokaj, Villány, Balaton, Kecskemét, Szekszárd and Sopron, where you might pick up some special wines. Finally, there is paprika. Note the words *csípös* (meaning hot, as in peppery) and *csemege* (which means sweet).

Tourist Offices

Hungary
Tourism Office of Budapest, V, Marcius 15 ter 7; tel: 1-322 4098/1-488 0475 or 438 8080; www.tourinform.hu
Other tourist offices in Budapest: VI, Oktogon, Liszt Ferenc tér 11, tel: 322 4098; Nyugati Western Railway Station, VI; tel/fax: 302 8580; Buda Castle, I, Szentháromság tér; tel: 488 0475; V, Városház utca 7, tel/fax: 428 0377.

UK
Hungarian National Tourist Office, 46 Eaton Place, London SW1X 8AL; tel: 020 7823 1032; fax: 020 7823 1459; www.gotohungary.co.uk
Malév, Hungarian Airlines, 6th Floor, Devonshire House, 1 Devonshire Street, London W1W 5DS; tel: 0870 9090 577; e-mail: london@malev.hu

US
Hungarian Tourist Board, Embassy of the Republic of Hungary, 150 East 58th Street, 33rd floor, New York, NY 10155; tel: 212-355-0240; www.gotohungary.com.
Malév USA, 90 John Street, Suite 312, New York, NY 10038, tel: 212-566-9944; www.hungarianairlines.com

Telecommunications

Most public phone boxes use phone-cards, issued by Matav (the Hungarian telecommunications company) and available from tobacconists, post offices, supermarkets, petrol stations, stationery stores, etc.

National phone calls are cheaper between 8pm and 7am, but there is no off-peak reduction for inter-national calls.

Security and Crime

Crime increased sharply in Budapest in the 1990s, and certain precautions should be taken. Avoid certain neighbour-hoods at night: the Eastern Train Station, the narrow streets around Rákóczi tér and Blaha Lujza tér. Your judgement is called for as in any other major metropolis. Do not carry purses and cameras too obviously; do not count wads of money in public – take only what you need. Pickpockets are very skilled in Hungary. They tend to operate in crowded places (such as shops, subway stations, Váci utca). Should you fall victim to a crime, contact the police at once.

Money-changers are no longer a common sight, but if you meet one, just say no thanks.

Much of the criminal activity that takes place is mafia-style and only really affects either other criminals or victims such as drug addicts, prosti-tutes and shop owners subjected to extortion. Prostitution has flourished since the Communist embargo was lifted, and is also a by-product of hard economic times.

Emergency Telephone Numbers

Ambulance, Emergency Rescue Service: 104 (or 311 1666 for an English-speaking operator)
Fire: 105
Police: 107

IRELAND

Fact File

Area: 70,300 sq. km (27,135 sq. miles).
Capital: Dublin.
Population: 3.9 million.
Language: English and Irish (Irish Gaelic).
Religion: predominantly Roman Catholic.
Currency: euro (€).

Time zone: *see page 327.*
International dialling code: 353.
Website: www.ireland.ie

Entry Requirements, Customs and Health

Ireland is in the European Union; *see box on page 326.*

Money Matters

Exchange Facilities

Banks are accustomed to exchanging euros and pounds. Major post offices, including the GPO in Dublin, have a bureau de change. Some international travel agencies also change money and travellers' cheques. Be sure to take along your passport as proof of identity when cashing travellers' cheques.

The O'Connell Street Tourist Information Office in Dublin operates money-exchange services from 9am–5.15pm Monday to Friday.

Credit Cards and Travellers' Cheques

These are widely accepted in Irish shops, hotels, restaurants and car-rental firms. Cashpoints at banks throughout the island offer cash advances on major cards.

Tipping

Most hotels and restaurants include a service charge, so tipping is unnecessary. If not, 10 percent of the bill in a restaurant or a couple of euros a day for cleaners is expected in the Republic. Taxis are usually tipped by rounding up the fare.

Public Transport Dublin

Dublin Bus *(Bus Atha Cliath)* runs services in the Dublin area. For bus information, tel: 01-873 4222 or check the website, www.dublin bus.ie. Timetables for bus and train services, including details of various money-saving tourist tickets, are sold in newsagents. Dublin Area Rapid Transit (DART) provides a swift and frequent rail link through the city, from Howth in the north to Greystones in the south. For information on fares and schedules, see www.irishrail.ie. The new LUAS tram system also provides a light-rail service to outlying suburbs, tel: 1800 300 604, www.luas.ie.

Opening Times

Shops are generally open Monday to Saturday 9am–6pm, with late-night shopping until 8 or 9pm on Thursday (and Fridays for some stores).

On Sundays some supermarkets and bigger stores open from midday until 5 or 6pm.
Banks open 10am–4pm, except one day a week (usually Thursdays) when they stay open until 5pm. Banks outside the city centre may close for lunch from 12.30pm–1.30pm.

Public Holidays

1 January: New Year's Day.
17 March: St Patrick's Day.
March/April (variable): Good Friday, Easter Monday.
May: May Day (first Monday).
June: Bank Holiday (first Monday).
August: Bank Holiday (last Monday).
October: Bank Holiday (last Monday).
25–6 December: Christmas.

Shopping

Traditional crafts still flourish, partly as a source of merchandise but partly out of a very Irish sense that the excellence cultivated by past generations is worth nurturing. Cut crystal, a craft which had just about died out, was resurrected in the 1960s and today flourishes in Waterford and elsewhere.

Ireland's internationally renowned wool-textile industry has moved its emphasis from the old homespun, handwoven tweed to very finely woven scarves, stoles and dress fabrics. Linen and lace remain remarkably delicate.

Pottery has developed fast as a craft industry, and new studios are opening all the time. Basket-weaving remains widespread and provides such souvenirs as table mats and St Brigid crosses.

Tourist Offices

For information in Ireland, tel: 1850 230 230; from the UK, tel: 0800 039 7000; from anywhere else, tel: 00-353-669-792 083.
Ireland
Dublin: Fáilte Ireland, Baggot Street Bridge, Dublin 2; tel: 01-602 4000; www.ireland.ie
Amiens Street, Dublin 1; tel: 01-855 6555; www.visitdublin.com
Also at Dublin Airport (Arrivals Hall) and Dun Laoghaire Ferry Terminal (St Michael's Wharf).
Ireland West Tourism (Galway, Mayo, Roscommon): Aras Fáilte, Forster Street, Galway; tel: 091-537700; fax: 091-537733; e-mail: info@ irelandwest.ie; www.irelandwest.ie
UK
Nations House, 103 Wigmore St, London W1U 1QS; tel: 0800 039 7000.

US
345 Park Avenue, New York, NY 10154; tel: 212-418-0800, fax: 212-371-9052.

Telecommunications

About 50 percent of public phones are cardphones. Phone cards are widely available from post offices, newsagents and supermarkets and are sold in denominations of 10, 20 and 50 units. A local call from a public telephone costs 30 cents in the Republic.

International calls can be dialled direct from private phones, or dial 114 for the international operator. To contact the local operator, dial 10. The long-distance services of AT&T, Sprint and MCI are also available.

Security and Crime

In Dublin, take the same precautions you would in any city. Do not carry round large sums of cash, beware of pickpockets and keep valuables out of sight.

Emergency Telephone Numbers

For emergency services, such as police, ambulance, fire service, lifeboat and coastal rescue, tel: 999 or 112 and ask for the service you need.

ITALY

Fact File

Area: 301,164 sq. km (116,280 sq. miles).
Capital: Rome.
Population: around 57 million.
Language: Italian.
Religion: predominantly Roman Catholic.
Currency: euro (€).
Time zone: *see page 327.*
International dialling code: 39.
Websites: www.enit.it; www.turismovenezia.it

Entry Requirements, Customs and Health

As for other European Union countries – *see box on page 326.*

Money Matters

Italy is a society that prefers cash to credit cards, except for large purchases, or, for instance, hotel bills. In the case of petrol stations, more modest restaurants and smaller shops, it is usual to pay in cash. Check beforehand if there is any doubt. Most shopkeepers and restaurateurs will not change money, so it is best to change a limited amount at the airport when you arrive, or you can use an ATM to get money out.

Travellers' cheques are still recommended in Italy, as they can be replaced if stolen or lost. Note, however, that commission will be charged for changing them.

Banks generally open Mon–Fri 8.30am–1.30pm and for one hour in the afternoon (usually between 3pm and 4pm). Commission tends to be higher in hotels than in banks.

Tipping

A service charge of approximately 15 percent is added to hotel and restaurant bills. If hotel prices are quoted as all-inclusive (tutto compreso), the service charge is included, but not necessarily the IVA (VAT/sales tax); ask if you're not sure. In addition to the restaurant bill's service charge, it is customary to give the waiter something extra. Bellboys, doormen, bartenders and service-station attendants all expect a tip of a euro or two, depending on the situation.

Public Transport Venice

To/from Venice Airport

Venice's **Marco Polo Airport** is at Tessera on the mainland, 9 km (5½ miles) north of Venice. To reach Venice there is a public bus to Piazzale Roma (30 minutes), taxis (20–5 minutes), or the hourly Alilaguna water bus, which crosses the lagoon to Piazza San Marco via the Lido and takes about 75 minutes, depending on your stop. Between 11.30am and 3.30pm the waterbus is quicker and costs about €12 (2005 rates). The luxury option is to take a private water taxi; these cost about €80 and are identifiable by their black-on-yellow numbers.

If you are taking a taxi, make sure it's an official one with a meter, and ask what the fare is likely to be before you set off. Taxis have the right to negotiate prices with passengers. Extra charges for luggage and for trips at night, on public holidays and to and from the airport are posted inside every cab. For a tip, it is normal practice to round up the fare.

Treviso Airport is an alternative for travellers to Venice or the Lakes. A reliable coach service runs to Venice.

Venice Card

This innovation, aimed at tourists, comes in two colours: blue, offering unlimited access to local public transport services and toilets, and orange, which also offers access to municipal museums, including the Palazzo Ducale. To obtain the card you should book it 48 hours in advance, either by accessing www.venicecard.it or by calling: 899 909090 when in Italy or 003 041-271 4747 from abroad. The price structure is quite complex and depends on age and length of stay.

Water Buses

Venice's water buses (vaporetti, and the smaller and faster motoscafi) ply the Grand Canal and shuttle between islands. Tickets can be bought from bars, kiosks and at most stops. Apart from ordinary single tickets (buy one and get it validated when boarding or you'll have to pay a surcharge), there are passes valid for 24 hours. Venice has several water-taxi stations. Although theoretically the rates are fixed, they tend to vary according to distance; state your destination when purchasing your ticket. This also applies to trips by gondola.

Opening Times

Shops are usually open 9am–12.30pm and 3.30 or 4pm–7.30 or 8pm. In Venice and other areas serving tourists, many shops remain open on Sunday, while elsewhere almost everything is closed on that day. Shops often also close on Monday (sometimes in the morning only) and some shut on Saturday – again not in tourist areas.

Public Holidays

1 January: New Year's Day.
March/April/May (variable): Good Friday, Easter Monday.
25 April: Liberation Day.
1 May: Labour Day.
15 August: Assumption of the Virgin Mary.
1 November: All Saints' Day.
8 December: Immaculate Conception.
25–6 December: Christmas.

Shopping in Venice

One of the great adventures of shopping in Venice is separating the treasure house from the tourist trap, distinguishing priceless gems from

pricey junk. By and large, the better, more expensive shops are around Piazza San Marco. The shopping street of Mercerie has quality boutiques growing progressively moderate in price as they approach the Rialto from Piazza San Marco; so does the area west of Piazza San Marco. For cheaper purchases, head for the Strada Nuova leading behind the Ca' d'Oro towards the railway station.

The bargains or at least more authentic and tasteful products are to be found far from these main tourist centres, in artisans' workshops on the Giudecca, in the Dorsoduro behind the Zattere – to be hunted down or stumbled upon by chance.

For a cross-section of Venetian craftsmanship in more moderately priced jewellery, as well as ceramics and glass mosaics, take a look at Veneziartigiana, just off San Marco in Calle Larga, or in the artisanal shops on the Frezzeria.

Glassware

You'll see the famous Venetian glassware all over the city; prices in the Murano island factories are rarely better than elsewhere, but you do get a free demonstration and transportation thrown in. Necklaces of crystal or coloured beads are popular for children, the antique glass beads collectables for adults. When choosing gifts to be shipped, remember to bypass the extremely fragile items and always ask for handling and insurance rates before you buy, as they can frequently double the price.

Laceware

Visit Burano to see intricate laceware being made in the time-honoured manner in the island's small museum. The real thing is exquisite but exorbitantly priced, with many lesser-quality, machine-made pieces from the Orient being passed off as locally handmade. Modern reproductions and interpretations of traditional patterns can be bought around Piazza San Marco.

Paper and masks

The venerable craft of handmade paper goods, stationery and bookbinding is easy to find. You can give your fancy-dress outfits a touch of Venetian class with the finely crafted papier-mâché masks made by workshops for Venice's Carnival.

Fashion

The range of fashion boutiques around San Marco is small but select, with an emphasis on top-class shoes and other leather goods made in the Brenta area outside Venice.

Tourist Offices

The main office is on the western corner of Piazza San Marco and offers both general information and booking for some tours and events: apt Venezia, San Marco 71/f, Calle dell'Ascensione/Procuratie Nuove, tel: 041-529 8711; fax: 041-523 0399; Mon–Sat 9am–3.30pm.

The equally convenient but less busy office is on the St Mark's waterfront, in a pavilion beside the public gardens. It also has a good Venice-themed bookshop: apt Venezia, Ex-Giardini-Reali (tel: as above; Mon–Sat 10am–6pm).

The tourist office at the railway station is also handy: apt Venezia, Ferrovia Santa Lucia (8am–6.30pm), as is the one at the airport: apt Marco Polo (9.30am–7.30pm).

Canada
17 Bloor Street East Suite 907, South Tower, M4W 3R8 Toronto, Ontario; tel: 416-925-4882/ 925-3725; fax: 416-925-4799; e-mail: enit.canada@on.aibn.com
UK
1 Princes Street, London W1B 2AY; tel: 020 7408 1254; fax: 020 7399 3567; e-mail: enitlond@globalnet@.uk; www.enit.it
US
Chicago: 500 North Michigan Avenue, Suite 401, Chicago, IL 60611; tel: 312-644-0996, fax: 312-644-3019, e-mail: enitch@ italiantourism.com
New York: 630 5th Avenue, Suite 1565, New York City, NY 10111; tel: 212-245-4822, e-mail: enitny@italiantourism.com; www.italiantourism.com

Telecommunications

In Italy you have to include the area code when dialling a number, even if you are calling from within that area. Another oddity is that you must always include the initial 0 in the area code when calling Italy from abroad.

Public phones are found in bars and shops displaying a yellow dialling symbol. In addition to coins and phone tokens (gettoni), most accept prepaid phonecards (schede telefoniche), available from tobacconists and many bars. Beware of exorbitant hotel charges for direct calls and service charges for toll-free calls on their phone lines.

Security and Crime

The main problem for tourists is petty crime – pickpocketing, bag-snatching and theft from cars; it is wise to have insurance cover against this and to take basic, sensible precautions against theft. If walking, especially at night, in the tiny alleys of Venice, try to blend in and avoid wearing flashy jewellery that may attract attention.

If you are the victim of a crime (or suffer a loss) and wish to claim against your insurance, it is essential to make a report at the nearest police station and get documentation to support your claim. If you need a policeman, dial 113 (112 for the Carabinieri, a national police force).

Emergency Telephone Numbers

Police (also ambulance and fire): 113
Carabinieri: 112
Fire: 115
Medical Emergencies: 118

NETHERLANDS

Fact File

Area: 33,950 sq. km (13,000 sq. miles).
Population: 16.3 million.
Capital: Amsterdam.
Seat of Government: The Hague.
Currency: euro (€).
Language: Dutch.
Religion: Roman Catholic (40 percent), Protestant (30 percent).
Time zone: see page 327.
International dialling code: 31 + 20 (Amsterdam), 70 (The Hague), 10 (Rotterdam).
Website: wwww.holland.com

Entry Requirements, Customs and Health

As for other European Union countries, see box on page 326.

Money Matters

Changing Money

The best rates of exchange are at national banks; beware high commission rates at hotels. Major credit cards are accepted in all main hotels, restaurants and shops.

The GWK (Grenswisselkantoren NV) is a national financial institution where you can exchange any currency and also use credit cards or travellers' cheques. The GWK exchange office inside Centraal Station, Amsterdam, is open Mon–Sat 7am–10.30pm, Sun 9am–10.30pm. Change is also available at post offices (at good rates) and banks.

There are automatic cash dispensers all over the city. Most can be accessed by foreign credit cards and charge cards, or cash cards with the Cirrus or Plus symbol. GWK and other currency exchange outlets also accept major credit cards.

Tipping

Tips are included in taxi fares and prices in restaurants and bars, so all that is required is to leave some small change if you think the service warrants it – but service personnel won't object to receiving a tip and have become used to the fact that many visitors (in contrast to their fellow citizens) do tip. In most restaurants, a tip of 10 percent will be considered generous, or at least adequate.

Public Transport Amsterdam

Its compact size and layout means that the centre of Amsterdam can be largely covered on foot. However, the public transport network can be useful for tourists. It consists of tram and bus routes and four metro lines. All operate from 6am until midnight, after which there are night buses.

One-day or multiple-day tickets are valid on all public transport lines within the city and can save you time and money. Otherwise, use a strippenkaart – strip ticket; the more strips you buy, the cheaper they come. These are valid for one hour's travel, and the amount you use depends on the number of public transport zones you cover. The city is divided into zones, and you cancel one strip more than the number of zones you will be travelling within – two strips for one zone, three strips for two zones, and so on. It sounds complicated, but in practice it works well.

Tickets are available from the GVB Tickets & Info office next to Centraal Station, as well as at railway stations, tourist offices, post offices, some tobacconists and at major hotels. Tickets purchased on trams and buses cost more than those bought in advance.

From the Airport

There is a 24-hour rail service from Schiphol, the Netherland's principal airport, to Amsterdam Centraal Station, with up to six trains an hour at peak times, and in late evenings around one an hour. Trains also depart frequently to Amsterdam RAI Station and Amsterdam Zuid/WTC (South/World Trade Centre) Station. The journey time to Centraal Station is about 20 minutes. Taxis to the city centre leave from in front of Schiphol Plaza and cost around €45.

Trams

Within the city centre, trams are the best means of getting around. Tickets must be stamped by the conductor at, or towards, the rear, or in the machines that are usually located next to the doors. If you have no ticket, enter at the front and buy a ticket from the driver. If the tram has a conductor, enter at the rear, where there is a small counter.

On busy tram routes such as nos. 2 and 5 to the Museum Quarter, teams of *zakenrollers* (pickpockets) are active, especially in summer and holiday periods. Be aware of your personal property at all times.

Tram line 26, inaugurated in May 2005, travels east from Centraal Station to connect the many new developments in the old harbour zone along the south shore of the IJ waterway.

Buses and Metro

You are unlikely to use buses or the metro system unless you are travelling outside the city centre. Both are clean and efficient. On the metro you must stamp your ticket in the machines provided – these are usually found close to the steps leading to the platforms.

Canal Buses

The canal buses are modern, glass-topped launches which pick up passengers at 11 major points along three different routes. They take you through some of the loveliest parts of Amsterdam en route to various museums and tourist attractions. Day passes, which enable you to hop on and off at your whim, are available.

The museum boat service stops at nine major museums at 75-minute intervals – well worth considering if you intend doing a lot of sightseeing. You can buy a day ticket from the office opposite Centraal Station, where the boat service starts. The canal bus 52-seat cruiser provides a regular service between Centraal Station and the Rijksmuseum, with three stops on the way. For further information, tel: 623 9886.

Using the canal bus or museum boat gives reduced entrance fees to many museums.

Taxis

Cabs cannot be flagged down (though sometimes they do stop), but should be found at key locations throughout the city (in front of Centraal Station, and at Rembrandtplein, Leidseplein, Museumplein, the Dam, Waterloo-plein and many other locations, for example outside public buildings such as Concertgebouw), or by dialling 0900 677 7777 (50 cents per minute); www.taxi.nl. Meters are used, and the cost is calculated according to the zone and the time of day. On longer journeys it is always wise to establish the cost before you set off. You can also make use of the water taxi in front of Centraal Station (tel: 622 2181).

Opening Times

Most shops are open from 8.30am or 9am until 6pm Monday–Friday. Late-night shopping is Thursday until 9pm. Most shops close at 5pm on Saturday. All shops close for one half-day a week, usually Monday, when they open at 1pm. Many grocery stores, such as the Albert Heijn chain, are open most evenings until either 7pm or 9pm. Some shops have Sunday hours of 1–7pm. Many department stores and speciality shops in the city centre are also open on Sunday from noon to 5pm. Banks and government offices are normally open 9am–5pm Monday to Friday.

Public Holidays

1 January: New Year's Day.
March/April (variable): Easter.
30 April: Queen's Birthday.
1 May: Labour Day.
4 May: Remembrance Day.
5 May: Liberation Day.
May (variable): Ascension.
June (variable): Pentecost.
15 December: Kingdom Day.
25–6 December: Christmas.

Shopping in Amsterdam

For general shopping the main streets are Kalverstraat and Nieuwendijk; for exclusive boutiques try P. C. Hooftstraat, and for the more offbeat shops head to the Jordaan, northwest of centre, where many of the local artists live. Two shopping malls are worth a visit: Magna Plaza opposite the Royal Palace and Kalvertoren on Kalverstraat.

Most museums have good gift shops, especially the Jewish Historical Museum, Amsterdam Historical Museum, Maritime Museum, NEMO and the Nieuwe Kerk. The Rijksmuseum and Van Gogh Museum have a shared gift shop on Museumplein.

Antiques

The VVV Tourist Office produces brochures on shopping for antiques and diamonds. These give maps, route descriptions, places of interest and a list of addresses and shop specialities.

Or you can start at Nieuwe Spiegelstraat (opposite the Rijksmuseum), which is lined with small and immaculate antique shops. Look out for old Dutch tiles, copper and brass, glass, pewter, snuff boxes, clocks and dolls. In markets, beware of imitation antique copper and brass, made in Tunisia.

Art and prints

The major museums and art galleries, particularly the Stedelijk and Rijksmuseum, have excellent reproductions of paintings in their collections. There are numerous commercial galleries selling original oil paintings, watercolours, drawings, engravings and sculpture. For old prints and engravings, try Antiek-Markt de Looier, 109 Elandsgracht.

Clothes

The major department stores are around Kalverstraat and Nieuwendijk, but the biggest and most prestigious is De Bijenkorf, 1 Dam. For designer labels, try P.C. Hooftstraat, Rokin, Van Baerlestraat and Leidsestraat. For quirky boutiques, the Jordaan or the side streets between the canals are the places to go. Also try Magna Plaza shopping mall opposite the Royal Palace or the Kalvertoren mall on Kalverstraat.

Jewellery

Jewellery shops all over town have eye-catching displays of modern and traditional pieces, some original and designed on the spot. Note: the fact that Amsterdam is a major diamond-cutting centre doesn't mean you'll get diamonds cheap. For modern jewellery designs, visit Hans Appenzeller at 1 Grimburgwal or Anneke Schat at 20 Spiegelgracht.

Porcelain

Cheap imitations of the familiar blue Delftware are sold all over town. The genuine article, always with a capital "D", is sold at Royal Delft's official retail branch, De Porceleyne Fles, 12 Muntplein. You can watch painting demonstrations in their showrooms. Focke & Meltzer, with branches at 149 Gelderlandplein and the Okura Hotel, have a good choice of porcelain and glass, and some attractive reproduction Delft tiles. For a huge range of antique tiles, try Eduard Kramer, 64 Nieuwe Spiegelstraat.

Other gifts

Tulips and bulbs are always popular. If you fail to get them at the flower market *(see below)* you can buy them at higher prices at Schiphol Airport. Other things typically Dutch are cigars (the best-known shop is Hajenius, 92 Rokin) and chocolates made by Van Houten,

Verkade or Droste (Pompadour at 12 Huidensstraat has a superb selection, as does Jordino, who also makes exquisite Italian ice cream at 25 Harlemmerdijk). There's always Edam and Gouda cheeses and, of course, clogs.

Markets

Amsterdam's street markets are a source of amusement and interest.
Flower market: Singel. Mon–Fri 9am–6pm, Sat 9am–5pm. Probably Amsterdam's most famous market, housed in boats and bright with colours and perfumes even in the depths of winter. Prices are reasonable and quality is excellent.
Flea market: Waterlooplein. Mon–Sat 10am–5pm. Lively and fun.
Farm produce: Noordermarkt or Oudemanhuispoort. Sat 10am–4pm.
Book market: Oudemanhuispoort. Mon–Sat 10am–4pm. Unusual books and prints. More interesting is the extensive antiquarian book market, held every Friday 10am–6pm at Spui and during the summer one Sunday each month at Dam Square or next to the Muzeiktheater.
Stamp market: Nieuwezijds Voorburgwal. Wed & Sat 1–4pm. Stamps and coins.
Open-air antique market: Nieuwmarkt. Daily 9am–5pm May–September.
Antiques, curiosities and junk: "De Looier", 109 Elandsgracht. Sat–Thurs 11am–5pm. Indoor market.
Flea and textile market: Noordermarkt/Westerstraat. Mon 9am–1pm. An interesting mix of people and junk. Have a cup of coffee and a piece of *apelgebaak* at the corner Winkel Café – some say it is the best in the city.
Bird market: Noordermarkt. Sat 8am–1pm.
Art market: Thorbeckeplein. Apr–Oct Sun 10.30am–6pm. Artists sell their own drawings and paintings – some of the work is very good.
General markets: Albert Cuypstraat: Mon–Sat 9.30am–5pm; Westerstraat: Mon 9am–1pm.

Tourist Offices

The main tourist office (VVV) is opposite Centraal Station at 10 Stationsplein, tel: 201 8800; fax: 201 8850; open daily 9am–4.30pm; e-mail: info@atcb.nl; www.holland.com or www.vvvamsterdam.nl. There is another office inside the station at platform 2, open daily 9am–4.30pm, and a VVV bureau at 1 Leidseplein, open daily 9am–5pm (Apr–Aug Thurs–Sat until 7pm). The telephone and fax

numbers and e-mail and internet addresses are the same for all offices.
The GVB Tickets & Information office, also at Stationsplein, alongside the dock to your left as you exit, tel: 0900 9292 (50 cents per minute), provides information and ticket sales for local and city public transport. Open Monday–Friday 7am–9pm, Saturday and Sunday 8am–9pm.
Canada
Netherlands Board of Tourism, 14 Glenmount Court, Whitby, Ontario, L1N 5M8; tel: 905-666-5960; fax: 905-666-5391.
UK
Netherlands Board of Tourism, PO Box 30783, London WC2B 6DH; tel: 020 7539 7950; fax: 020 7539 7953; www.holland.com/uk
US
Netherlands Board of Tourism, 355 Lexington Avenue, 19th Floor, New York, NY 10017; tel: 212-370-7360.

Telecommunications

When dialling an Amsterdam number from outside the city, the area code to use is 020 (or 20 from outside the Netherlands). Most telephone boxes take phonecards (€5, €12.50, €25 and €50), which you can buy in post offices, large stores and cafés.
If you bring your mobile phone with you, remember that to call a local number you have to dial the international access code (eg 00 from the UK), followed by the code for the Netherlands (31) and Amsterdam (20). Calls are expensive because you are still operating through your service provider at home.

Security and Crime

Amsterdam is a centre of the drugs trade, and much crime here is drug-related. As a visitor, you are unlikely to be affected by big-time drugs-related crime, but you should take sensible precautions against becoming a victim of petty crime like pickpocketing and bag-snatching. Keep a careful watch on wallets, bags and other valuables, especially on public transport, at busy transport centres like Centraal Station and Schiphol Airport. And exercise some caution in certain areas after dark: the red-light district – mostly safe but some of its narrow alleys may not be; deserted canalsides; and Vondelpark.
In an emergency, call the police *(politie)* on 112. For non-emergencies, there are police stations around the city. Police headquarters is at 117 Elandsgracht, tel: 559 9111.

Emergency Telephone Numbers

Ambulance, Police and Fire services: 112
National non-emergency police: 0900 8844

POLAND

Fact File

Area: Poland is 690 km (430 miles) east–west and 650 km (400 miles) north–south. The total land area encompasses 312,685 sq. km (120,728 sq. miles).
Population: 38.5 million.
Language: Polish.
Capital: Warsaw.
Religion: 95 percent Catholic (Roman and Greek).
Currency: Polish złoty (zł or PLN), divided into 100 groszy (gr).
Time zone: *see page 327.*
International dialling code: 48.
Websites: www.polandtour.org; www.poland-tourism.pl; www.poland.net

Entry Requirements, Customs and Health

Poland is in the European Union; *see box on page 326.*

Money Matters

Currency and Exchange

Foreign currency can be exchanged at the airports and banks, as well as most hotels. *Kantors* are ubiquitous private exchange houses, often very informal-looking, that exchange cash only. They offer the best rates (no commission). Your passport is only necessary when changing money at banks. It's wise to keep all your exchange receipts until you leave the country. Any offers to exchange currency from people on the street are likely to involve counterfeit currency.

Credit Cards and Travellers' Cheques

Major international credit cards (Visa, MasterCard and American Express) are increasingly accepted in most hotels, restaurants and shops, but are not usually accepted at supermarkets, museums and even railway stations. Travellers' cheques can only be cashed at the foreign exchange desk of banks.

ATMs

Cash machines, known as "Bankomats", are widespread in

Polish cities and offer competitive international exchange rates.

Tipping

It is usual to leave about 10 percent of the total bill as a tip in a restaurant, hairdressers and for taxi drivers.

Opening Times

Offices are generally open Monday to Friday 9am–6pm. Shops open 10am–6pm Monday to Friday and 9am–2pm on Saturdays. In general shops are closed on Sundays, but more and more larger stores are staying open all week. There are plenty of small neighbourhood shops open 24 hours a day.

Banks open Monday to Friday 8am–6pm without lunch break. Post offices open Monday to Saturday, 8am–8pm.

Public Holidays

1 January: New Year's Day.
March/April/May (variable): Easter.
May: Labour Day (first Monday).
3 May: Constitution Day.
15 June: Corpus Christi.
15 August: Assumption.
26 August: Our Lady of Czestochowa.
1 November: All Saints' Day.
11 November: Independence Day.
25–6 December: Christmas.

Shopping

The demise of Communism in 1989 and the move to a free-market economy have had a dramatic impact on Poland as a shopping destination. Drab state-owned stores are a thing of the past. The pound, dollar, euro and other currencies don't go as far today as they once did, but foreign visitors and their Polish counterparts can only be pleased with the opening of trade and vastly improved selection of goods on the market. In major cities like Warsaw and Kraków, Poland doesn't lag far behind Western Europe and North America for commercial opportunities. Even with the end of Communism and inflation, Poland remains considerably cheaper than Western European destinations.

Crafts and antiques

For folk art and other handicrafts, start at branches of Cepelia stores, a chain of folk-art and souvenir shops in large cities. Rustic Poland excels at folk art and handicrafts, including hand-carved wooden (usually religious) figures; leather goods from the Tatra Mountains; embroidery and lace; hand-painted eggs (especially at

Easter); and colourful naive art and glass paintings, especially that of Zakopane.

For antiques, the dominant player is the Desa chain (though there are many smaller, independent dealers as well). In Kraków and Warsaw, there are numerous branches, all with different stock.

Speciality shopping markets and unique venues exist in several cities. These include the famous, long-established Cloth Hall stalls, loaded with crafts and amber jewellery, in Kraków; Warsaw's swank, boutique-lined ul. Nowy Świat; and ul. Mariacka in Gdańsk's Main Town for amber jewellery. Open-air markets and bazaars include: in Warsaw, Dziesięciolecia Stadium in Praga, across the river, and Koło Bazaar, in Wola; in Kraków, the traders' market between the railway station and the Barbican; and in Gdańsk, Kupcy Dominikańscy (on Pl. Dominikański 1).

Bargaining is generally only acceptable at the large open-air markets, though if you ask for a discount at an antiques store or art gallery, you may well be granted one.

Ceramics and pottery

Distinctive Kashubian pottery and that known as Ceramika Artystyczna Bolesławiec are sold the world over, but are considerably cheaper in Poland.

Poster art

Poster-making for the arts is a thriving and valued art form in Poland, and some of the finest poster artists in the world are Polish. You'll find vintage and contemporary posters for familiar Western films and the greatest hits of theatre and opera, as well as more obscure titles. Contemporary poster designers include Górowsky, Stasys and Sadowski.

Vodka

If you want to take back an authentic bottle of Polish vodka, or wódka (pronounced "voot-ka"), look for Wyborowa, Extra Żytnia or any of the flavoured vodkas, such as Żubrówka (with a blade of "bison grass" in the bottle) and Myśliwska (juniper-flavoured).

Tourist Offices

Poland

Warszawskie Centrum Informacji Turystycznej, Zamkowy Square 1/13, 00-26 Warsaw; tel: 22-635 1881; fax: 22-310 464. Local "Info Centrum" are listed at www.poland-tourism.pl

UK

Polish National Tourist Office, Westec House, West Gate, London W5 1YY;

tel: 08700 675010; e-mail: info@visitpoland.org; www.visitpoland.org

US

Polish National Tourist Office, 5 Marine View Plaza, Hoboken, NJ 07030; tel: 201-420-9910; e-mail: pntonyc@polandtour.org

Telecommunications

Public Telephones

Public phones take either tokens *(leton)* or cards *(karta)*, both of which are available at kiosks and post offices. There are plenty of public phone boxes, although many of them don't work, so it is often better to head for a post office if you need to make a call. For a long-distance call it is better to use a credit-card phone, found at airports and in the foyers of almost all hotels. These are considerably cheaper than making calls from your room.

Internet Services

There is a special phone number (0 202122) that provides an internet link from any point in Poland without a subscription fee. The user name and password is PPP.

Security and Crime

Theft is not unusual in places frequented by tourists. It is better to keep any valuables and jewellery in the hotel safe or stowed safely. If you are the victim of a theft, report it immediately to your guide, or to your hotel reception, and also to the police. The emergency police number is 997. If you lose all your money or your passport, seek advice from your nearest consulate or embassy.

Emergency Telephone Numbers

Ambulance: 999
Fire: 998
Police: 997

PORTUGAL

Fact File

Area: 92,072 sq. km (33,549 sq. miles) including Madeira and the Azores.
Capital: Lisbon.
Population: 10.3 million.
Language: Portuguese.
Religion: predominantly Roman Catholic.
Currency: euro (€).
Time zone: see page 327.
International dialling code: 351.

Websites: www.visitportugal.com; www.portugal.org

Entry Requirements, Customs and Health

These are the same as for other European Union countries – see box on page 326.

Money Matters

The easiest way to obtain euros is to use your credit card (or debit card) in one of the numerous ATMS, usually called *Multibanco*. Otherwise, money is best changed at banks, rather than at hotels or travel agencies; this works out cheaper than the commission paid on travellers' cheques.

Major credit cards can be used in most hotels, restaurants and shops, but check in advance to avoid embarrassment. Country restaurants and *pensãos* may only accept cash.

Tipping

Hotel and restaurant bills are generally all-inclusive, but an additional tip of 5–10 percent is common and even expected in restaurants. Hotel porters, per bag, generally receive €0.50. Taxi drivers do not normally expect a tip, though one should be given for any special services or information rendered.

Public Transport Portugal

From Porto Airport

Porto's Francisco Sá Carneiro Airport (tel: 22-948 2552; www.ana-aeroportos.pt) is 20km (13 miles) northwest of the city centre. The Aerobus runs between the airport and the city centre every 30 minutes, stopping at some hotels. A cheaper option is local bus no. 56 or 87.

Buses and Trams

Bus and tram stops in cities usually have a small route map and an indication of which buses stop there. You can buy your ticket on the bus, or you can buy passes or blocks of tickets from kiosks and some shops (if in doubt, ask at the tourist office).

Porto has several bus terminals. Rede Expressos (www.rede-expressos.pt) buses go to most destinations in Portugal, and depart from the Paragem Atlântico terminal on Rua Alexandre Herculano 370. Renex have frequent buses to Lisbon and Braga and some buses to the Algarve, and depart from Rua das Carmelitas 32. STCP (tel: 0808-200 166; www.stcp.pt) operates Porto's bus

network and one tram route. International buses depart from Praça da Galiza 96.

Trains

Porto's main train station is Estação Campanhã, which handles trains to destinations throughout Portugal as well as international trains. The more centrally located Estação São Bento handles suburban and regional trains. Frequent trains run between the two stations.

A new metro system in Porto (www.metro-porto.pt/uk/) makes it much easier to get around the city. Although there are several underground stations in the city centre, most of the trains run along the streets like trams.

Taxis

Most taxis are black with a green roof and a "taxi" sign. City taxis have meters, but are entitled to charge an extra 20 percent at night and an extra sum for each item of luggage. If there is no meter, it is essential to establish a price before your trip starts. Most taxis use taxi stands, but some cruise the streets looking for passengers.

Opening Times

Most **shops** in Portugal open for business Mon–Fri 9am–1pm and 3–7pm, Saturday 9am–1pm, and are closed Sunday and holidays. Some malls and supermarkets are open on Sunday and all day during the week. **Banks** open Mon–Fri 8.30am–3pm and are closed Saturday, Sunday and holidays. **Museums** usually open 10am–12.30pm and 2–5pm, and are generally closed on Mondays.

Public Holidays

1 January: New Year's Day.
End February: Carnival/Mardi Gras.
March/April (variable): Easter.
25 April: Liberation Day.
1 May: Labour Day.
10 June: Camões Day/National Day.
May/June (variable): Corpus Christi.
15 August: Assumption Day.
5 October: Republic Day.
1 November: All Saints' Day.
1 December: Independence Day.
8 December: Immaculate Conception.
25 December: Christmas Day.

Shopping

Traditional crafts are still practised throughout Portugal. Intricate works of gold and silver, hand-painted ceramics, basket work and classic

wool rugs are sold in small shops and outdoor markets across the country. The Thursday market in Barcelos, north of Porto, has lots of handicrafts for sale.

Brass, bronze and copper
Candlesticks, pots and pans, old-fashioned scales, bowls and trays can be found across Portugal. *Cataplanas*, a broad-domed copper dish which looks like two woks on top of each other, make a delightful decorative or functional souvenir. The Moorish tradition of producing cooking utensils from beaten metal is maintained in the town of Loulé, in the Algarve.

Carpets and rugs
Attractive and excellently crafted handmade rugs, mostly from the Alentejo region, have been produced for centuries. Arraiolos wool rugs are colourful and rustic-looking; the small town of the same name has a few dozen small dealers.

Ceramics, pottery and azulejos
Portugal is renowned for its colourful, hand-painted glazed pottery and tiles. You can buy a single blue-and-white tile, an address plaque for your house, or an entire set of plates. Some shops will paint tiles to order or copy a photograph. Ceramics can be heavy and fragile to carry, but some outlets can have them shipped to your home. Each region has its own distinctive style, ranging from the intricately painted faience animals of Coimbra to the ubiquitous roosters of Barcelos and the black clay pottery of Chaves. The shops along the N125 in the Algarve sell more ceramics and pottery than anywhere else in Portugal.

Embroidery
A great many embroidered items, including tablecloths and napkins, are sold all over Portugal – especially at street markets. Look for the delicate hand needlework that comes from the island of Madeira – items that are exceedingly well crafted but still comparatively inexpensive.

Other gifts
Of course, port also makes a great souvenir. If you want something lighter to take home, cork is a good option; Portugal is the world's leading producer of cork. You'll find place mats, intricate sculptures and other designs.

Tourist Offices

Portugal
Most towns have tourist offices, providing maps and information, though smaller ones close at weekends off season.
Faro: Rua da Misericórdia 8–12,

8000 Faro; tel: 289-803 604.
Airport: There is an information service desk at the meeting point in the terminal building (tel: 289-800 617) for details of flights, disabled facilities, opening hours and public-transport timetables. Cultural and tourist information is also available on arrival from the ICEP desk at the airport, tel: 289-818 582.
Porto: Tourist Welcome Centre Casa da Câmara (old City Hall), Terreiro da Sé, 4050-573 Porto; tel: 223-325 174; e-mail: turismo.casadacamara@ cm-porto.pt; www.portoturismo.pt. Also at Praça D. João 1; tel: 222-057 514.
ICEP Information Centres: Francisco Sá Carneiro Airport, EN 107 Pedras Rubras, 4470 Maia; tel: 229-412 534; fax: 229-412 543; e-mail: icep_pta@hotmail.com
Canada
Portuguese Trade and Tourism Commission, 60 Bloor West, Suite 1005, Toronto, Ontario M4W 3B8; tel: 416-921-7376; fax: 416-921-1353.
UK
Portuguese National Tourist Office, 11 Belgrave Square, London SW1X 8PP; tel: 0845 355 1212 (brochure line); 020 7201 6666, fax: 020 7201 6633, e-mail: tourism.london@iapmei.icep.pt; www.visitportugal.com
US
Portuguese National Tourist Office, 590 5th Avenue, 4th floor, New York, NY 10036. Tel: 800-767-8842 or 212-354-4403; www.portugal.org

Telecommunications

All phones are equipped for international calls and accept coins, phonecards or credit cards, the latter being by far the easiest way to make an international call.

A phonecard can be bought at kiosks and many shops. Instructions for using the phone are written in Portuguese and English. You can also make calls (international and local) from post offices. Go to the window for a cabin assignment and pay when the call is finished. The main post office in the bigger cities usually has internet access.

Many village stores and bars in Portugal have metered telephones. Phone first, pay later, but be prepared to pay more than the rate for call-box or post-office calls. As elsewhere, calls made from hotels are higher still.

Mobile Phones

Mobile phones with reciprocal GSM network arrangements will function throughout most of the country. Alternatively, the three national cellular networks (Vodaphone, TMN and Optimus) have short-term rental facilities at the main airports.

Security and Crime

Portugal has a well-deserved reputation for non-violence. It remains one of the few developed countries where you can both feel and be safe when walking almost anywhere at any time of day or night. This is changing in one or two of the larger cities, though, and petty theft is becoming a problem in some of the more run-down areas, and close to some of the larger shopping centres.

Emergency Telephone Numbers

Ambulance, Police: 112
Fire: 117

ROMANIA

Fact File

Area: 237,500 sq. km (91,700 sq. miles).
Capital: Bucharest.
Population: 22.4 million.
Language: Romanian; minorities speak Hungarian and German.
Religion: Romanian Orthodox with substantial Catholic and Muslim minorities.
Currency: leu (RON).
Time zone: *see page 327.*
International dailling code: 40.
Websites: www.romaniatourism.com; www.turism.ro

Entry Requirements

EU and US citizens do not require visas; other nationalities do; visit www.mae.ro to check.

Customs Regulations

Duty-free allowances for visitors are: 1 litre of spirits, 2 litres of wine, 200 cigarettes or 50 cigars.

Health and Insurance

There are no specific health risks particular to Romania, though you should take out adequate health insurance before travelling. General standards of health care, in urban areas at least, are satisfactory, though in the countryside health care is often very ad hoc. In an emergency call 112 for an ambulance. Emergency medical treatment is free, but you may have to pay for some medicines. You will also be expected to "tip" doctors and nurses (who are underpaid) very well. Failure to do so can result in very poor, in some cases non-existent, treatment.

Tap water is safe to drink, though the low cost of the bottled variety means that nobody actually does. Mosquitoes are a problem in most parts of the country during the summer, and insect repellent is a must. Stray dogs are a massive problem in most cities, especially Bucharest. Bites are common, more in summer than winter, and you should be very careful. If you are bitten you will need to have an anti-rabies injection urgently.

Money Matters

The best deals for currency exchange are at bureaux de change, though official tourist offices also exchange currency. Very high rates are charged for cashing travellers' cheques, if they are accepted at all. Cash machines do exist but they are often out of service. Credit cards are becoming more accepted and can be used in larger hotels, restaurants, car-rental companies and stores in main tourist cities.

In July 2005, Romanian currency was subject to redenomination: one new leu (plural lei) (RON) is worth 10,000 old lei (ROL). So, one US$ equals 28,300 old Romanian lei or 2.83 new Romanian lei. The old lei will be legal tender until 31 December 2006.

Tipping

You are expected to tip waiters and waitresses in restaurants (but check your bill to ensure that service is not already included), domestic hotel staff and doormen. In these cases, a 10 percent tip is seen as obligatory, regardless of whether you have been happy with the service. Indeed, the notion of a waiter going out of his way actually to earn a good tip is unheard of.

Unusually, taxi drivers do not expect to be tipped, and you should do so only if you have taken a taxi on a particularly short journey, in order to make the ride worth the driver's time and trouble.

See also under Health for information about tipping doctors and nurses.

Opening Times

Shops mostly open Mon–Fri 9am–7pm, and Sat 9am–1pm, with speciality stores open 10am–6pm.
Banks are open Mon–Fri 9am–4pm.

Public Holidays

1 January: New Year's Day.
March/April/May (variable): Easter Monday (Romanian Orthodox).
1 May: Labour Day.
1 December: Day of National Unity.
25–6 December: Christmas.

Shopping

For bargains you will need to stick to locally produced items, such as leather shoes. Romania has a thriving textile industry, and produces clothes for many big-name brands. Many seconds and copies find their way into Bucharest's fashion markets.

Handicrafts and iconography
Traditional Romanian handicrafts worth looking out for include pottery, woodcarvings and iconography. Romanian souvenir shops are ubiquitous, though the souvenirs themselves can be patchy in quality. Look out for replica painted Easter eggs, which make super gifts.

Reproductions of Orthodox iconography and woodcarvings can be found all over the country, with the best quality being found in Bucharest, in some of the little shops in Hanul cu Tei. As a rule, the goods sold by hawkers and stallholders outside the more famous Romanian sights and monasteries should be purchased only in a souvenir emergency, as quality is mediocre at best. An exception is the excellent craft market at the foot of Bran Castle.

If you are after genuine antique icons as opposed to reproductions, you should contact a professional art dealer and have a reasonable idea of what you are looking for. Exporting antiques is a difficult process requiring a long paperchase that a dealer will be able to handle for you. Only the brave should attempt to do it on their own. There are a number of galleries in Bucharest, clustered together on the streets around the Lipscani area and in the National Theatre.

Embroidery and lace
Intricate embroidery and lace can be found in good souvenir shops; the one at the National Peasant Museum in Bucharest is especially well stocked. The craft markets at Bran Castle and on the road between Sinaia and Predeal are also worth exploring for high-quality work, though don't expect bargains: prices for such painstaking work are high.

Tourist Offices

Bucharest
Tel: 021 314 99 57; fax: 021 314 99 60; e-mail: romovare@ mturism.ro
UK
22 New Cavendish Street, London WIM 7LHI; tel: 020 7224 3692; fax: 020 7935 6435; e-mail: infoUK@RomaniaTourism.com
US
355 Lexington Avenue, 19th Floor, New York, NY 10017; tel: 212-545-8484; fax: 212-251-0429; e-mail: infoUS@RomaniaTourism.com; www.RomaniaTourism.com

Telecommunications

The country code for Romania is 40. The city code for Bucharest is 021, for Brasov 0268. The first 0 is dropped if calling from abroad. To make an international call from Romania, dial 00.

You can dial internationally from most hotel rooms (though at great cost). All public phones allow direct international dialling. Most newsstands sell phone cards (look out for Avem cartele Romtelecom). You can receive or send a fax at a post office. Internet cafés are everywhere, and cheap to use. Most good hotels also now offer in-room internet access.

Security and Crime

Street crime is generally as rife as it is in any big city in the world, and crime against foreigners has increased in recent years. Take the usual precautions: don't carry all your cash in one place and avoid displaying large sums of money.

It's a good idea to deposit any valuables in the safe if you are staying in a hotel, or take as little as possible with you when you go ashore.

Emergency Telephone Numbers

General emergencies: 112
Ambulance: 961
Police: 955
Fire: 981
International Operator: 971
Operator: 991

RUSSIA

Fact File

Area: 17.1 million sq. km (6.6 million sq. miles).
Capital: Moscow.

Population: 146 million (Russian 81.5 percent, Tatar 3.8 percent, Ukrainian 3 percent, others 11.7 percent).
Language: Russian.
Religion: Russian Orthodox, with Muslim and other minorities.
Currency: rouble.
Time zone for area covered: see page 327.
International dialling code: 7.
Websites: www.russiatourism.ru/eng; www.russianembassy.org; www.russia-travel.com; www.moscow-guide.ru (for Moscow)

Entry Requirements

You will need a visa to enter Russia, but this will normally be arranged for you via your tour operator. If this is not the case you should apply to the Russian embassy or consulate; allow ample time, as it may take a month or so. You'll need a valid passport, an official application form, hotel reservation (for business travellers and tourists) and three passport photographs.

You have to have your passport and visa registered within three days of arrival in Russia – failure to do so may result in a heavy fine upon departure. It's a good idea to carry your passport and visa with you at all times, since the police have the right to check your identity at will. Keep a photocopy of important documents on board the ship.

Customs Regulations

When entering Russia you must fill in the customs declaration. It must be returned to the customs office, along with another customs declaration which you fill in on leaving the country.

As customs regulations change frequently, it is best to check with the Russian consulate or embassy in your home country about restrictions and limitations before travelling. Export duties may be imposed on any items which are determined by customs officials at the point of departure to be of commercial use.

Health and Insurance

Make sure you take out adequate medical insurance before leaving for Russia, and that you are covered for an emergency flight home. Medical services are available free to British citizens in state-run hospitals. The following private clinics are also available:
Moscow: American Medical Center, Grokholsky Pereulok 1; tel: 095-933-7700; European Medical

PLANNING A TRIP
LIFE ON BOARD
A–Z
RIVER VESSEL LISTINGS

Centre Group, Spiridonievsky
Pereulok 5; tel: 095-933-6655;
www.emcmos.ru
St Petersburg: American Medical
Center, Serpukhovskaya Ulitsa 10;
tel: 812-326-6272; American
Medical Clinic, Naberezhnaya Reki
Moiki 78; tel: 812-740-2090,
www.amclinic.com
   For minor ailments a doctor can
be called through your hotel service
desk. There may be a small charge
for prescriptions. All sorts of Western
medicines are available in the shops.

Money Matters

There is no limit to the import of hard
currency, but the sum must be
declared on entry. The amount
exported should not exceed the
amount declared when entering the
country. Unspent roubles should be
changed back into hard currency
before you leave the country.
   The black market has largely
disappeared. ATMs can be found in
major cities on main thoroughfares
and at central metro stations.
   All large hotels have an official
exchange counter where you can
buy roubles with cash, travellers'
cheques or credit cards. Do compare
rates before changing currency
though, as they vary considerably. You
will need your customs declaration
form, on which all your money
transactions must be recorded.
Keep this form, as you will need to
show it when leaving the country.
   Most tourist-related businesses
and restaurants accept credit cards.

Tipping

Tipping is an accepted practice.
Waiters and taxi drivers appreciate
around 10–15 percent. Porters will
take what's acceptable anywhere else
in the world. Guides, interpreters and
maids also appreciate tips.

Opening Times

Most stores in Russia are open
Monday–Saturday 9 or 10am to 6, 7
or 8pm. Malls usually stay open until
8pm or later, and often open on
Sundays. There are 24-hour
convenience food stores in cities.
More and more businesses work the
entire day, foregoing closure at lunch
time. But some organisations, such
as banks, do close for one hour,
either 1–2pm or 2–3pm.

Public Holidays

1–5 January: New Year Holidays.
7 January: Orthodox Christmas Day.
23 February: Army Day.

8 March: Women's Day
March/April/May (variable):
Orthodox Easter.
1 May: Labour Day.
9 May: Victory Day.
12 June: Independence Day.
4 November: Unity Day.

Shopping

The best places for interesting
souvenirs are the markets, where you
can haggle over prices. Remember to
take a small pocket calculator with
you – it makes it easier when
bargaining. Anything that is
considered to be of historical or
cultural value (in the opinion of the
customs officer, that is) cannot be
taken out of the country. This
includes art, old manuscripts,
antiques, coins, medals and so on.
Anything bought in a shop or an art
gallery is safe enough (keep the
receipts), but you could possibly have
trouble with objects bought on the
street or in the markets.
   Good buys include amber
jewellery, art and caviar – make sure
you keep the receipt to show
customs on departure as caviar is a
restricted item.

Moscow

Moscow's main shopping areas are
in Tverskaya Street, Petrovsky Street
and Novy Arbat. The best-known
department store is GUM,
conveniently situated right on Red
Square. Its main competitor is TSUM
(WEV), across the street from the
Bolshoi Theatre; it gets very crowded
here, but can be rewarding for
bargain souvenirs such as samovars,
fur hats and jewellery. Up the road
from TSUM, at Petrovska Street 10, is
Petrovsky Passage, a smaller, less
crowded, upmarket version of GUM.
The "must-see" street is the Arbat,
which is crammed with souvenir
stalls, though prices can be quite
high. The weekend market at
Izmailovsky Park, in the city's
northeastern suburb (metro
Izmailovsky Park), is worth a trip.

St Petersburg

Shopping is centred around Nevskiy
Prospekt. The two big stores are
Gostinny Dvor and Passage.
Souvenir hunters should make their
way to the market situated near the
Cathedral of the Resurrection on
the Griboyedov Canal.

Tourist Offices

Moscow
Chistoprudni Blvd 5/10, Suite 214,
Moscow; tel: 095-980-8440;

fax: 095-980-8441.
Canada
1801 McGill Avenue, Suite 930,
Montreal, Quebec H3A 2NA;
tel: 514-849-6394.
UK
Russian National Tourist Office,
70 Piccadilly, London W1J 8HP;
tel: 020 7495 7570; e-mail:
info@visitrussia.org.uk;
www.visitrussia.org.uk
US
224 West 30th Street, Suite 701,
New York, NY 10001; tel: 646-473-
2233, toll-free 877-221-7120;
e-mail: info@rnto.org

Embassies/Consulates

Moscow

Canada
Starokonyushenny Peryulok 23;
tel: 095-105-6000; after-hours
emergency, tel: 095-1056-055.
Open 9.30am–5pm.
UK
Smolenskaya nab. 10; tel: 095-
956-7200; fax: 095-956-7201.
Open 9am–1pm; 2–5pm.
US
Bolshaya Devyatinskiy Per 8;
tel: 095-728-5000.

St Petersburg

Canada
Malodestkoselskiy prospekt 32B;
tel: 812-325-8448.
UK
Proletarskaya Diktatury 5; tel: 812-
320-3200. Open 10am–5.30pm
weekdays.
US
Furshtatskaya ulitsa 15; tel: 812-
331-2600; after-hours emergency,
tel: 812-331-2888. Open
9.30am–5.30pm weekdays.

Telecommunications

The Russian telephone system is
hopelessly overburdened, and
making a domestic call is often a
frustrating process involving busy
lines and wrong numbers. New
public phones which take
phonecards (sold in various
denominations in metro stations,
post offices and banks) can be
used for local, intercity and
international calls.
   Fast, easy, and reliable (but also
very expensive) are the satellite
phone booths that are now to be
found in most tourist hotels. These
operate with a prepaid phonecard
or major credit card, and allow you
to dial direct to anywhere in the
world. Instructions in English are
clearly displayed, as are rates
per minute.

Security and Crime

Don't carry all your cash in one place, and avoid displaying large sums of money. Be especially careful while buying souvenirs from street vendors – thieves may be watching to see where you keep your money. Tuck your bag and camera firmly under your arm while shopping. The rule to observe is to behave sensibly and be aware that street crime here is as rife as it is in any big city in the world.

Corrupt police officers, especially in St Petersburg, are probably the only major worry a visitor to Russia will have. President Putin recently singled out crooked cops as one of the biggest problems in the country and has vowed to rein them in. Still, it's likely that it will be a while before significant progress is made.

Violent crime in Russia is mostly connected to conflicts in the world of Russian business, and if you are in the country for pleasure, there is little reason to worry about your safety.

If you are the victim of abuse or a crime, it is best first to contact your consulate *(konsulat)* and ask them to assist in speaking to the police.

Emergency Telephone Numbers

Fire: 01
Police: 02
Ambulance: 03

SERBIA & MONTENEGRO

Fact File

Area: 102,173 sq. km (39,449 sq. miles). There are two member states – Serbia and Montenegro. The state of Serbia includes two autonomous provinces: Vojvodina, and Kosovo and Metohija, which is administered by the United Nations as a protectorate.
Capital: Belgrade (pop. 1.6 million).
Population: 10 million. In Serbia, (excluding Kosovo and Metohija) Serbs account for 83 percent; in Kosovo and Metohija Albanians account for 88 percent; in Montenegro 62 percent are Montenegrin. Other sizeable national minorities include Hungarians, Romanians, Slovaks and Bulgarians.
Language: Serbian (which uses the Cyrillic alphabet), Albanian and the languages of the many minorities.
Religion: most Serbs adhere to the Eastern Orthodox religion. Kosovan Albanians are Muslim.
Currency: Serbia: dinar (CSD), made up of 100 paras. Montenegro: euro (€).

Time zone: *see page 327.*
International dialling code: 381.
Websites: www.serbia-tourism.org; www.gov.yu/start; www.visit-montenegro.com

Entry Requirements

Most nationalities do not require a visa, just a valid passport. For further information, refer to: www.serbia-tourism.org

Customs Regulations

You may bring into the country 1 litre of wine, 0.75 litres of strong alcohol, 200 cigarettes or 50 cigars or 250 grams of tobacco, 0.25 litres of eau de cologne or a smaller quantity of perfume, as well as medicine provided it is for your personal use.

Health and Insurance

Doctors are well trained but medical facilities are limited, and medicines and basic medical supplies are often unavailable. Hospitals usually require payment in hard currency. Health insurance with emergency repatriation is essential; visitors may be asked to pay first and seek reimbursement later.

Vaccination against typhoid is sometimes advised. Mains water is normally chlorinated and, whilst relatively safe, may cause mild abdominal upsets. Bottled water is available and is advised.

Rabies is present in the country, so avoid contact with animals. For those at high risk, vaccination before arrival should be considered. If you are bitten, seek medical advice without delay.

Money Matters

International credit cards Visa, MasterCard and Diners are accepted in most shops, hotels and restaurants in the bigger towns and cities. The cheapest way to obtain cash is to use an ATM, but you'll also find numerous banks and bureaux de change who will exchange currency.

Tipping

The waiting staff in restaurants and hotels expect around 10 percent, as do taxi drivers.

Opening Times

Shops: open Mon–Fri 9am–8 or 9pm (some shops take a long lunch break); Sat 10am–3pm; Sun closed.
Banks: open Mon–Fri 8am–4pm or 9am–5pm; Sat 8 or 9am–2pm; Sun closed.

Post offices: open Mon–Fri 8am–7pm; Sat 8am–3pm; Sun closed.
Chemists: open Mon–Fri 8am–8pm; Sat 8am–3pm.

Public Holidays

1–2 January: New Year.
6–7 January: Orthodox Christmas.
15 February: Statehood Day of the Republic of Serbia.
March/April/May (variable): Easter.
1–2 May: International Labour Day;
9 May: Victory Day.
29 November: Republic Day.

Shopping

Many traditional crafts are being revived following the chaos of the war. The city of Pec, in the west of Kosovo, was a major religious centre in medieval Serbia and the birthplace of fine Pec filigree work, which you may find throughout the country. Other special purchases include embroidery, lace, leatherwork, metalwork and Turkish coffee sets. You may also want to take home a bottle of the national drink, Slivovitz, a kind of plum brandy. The small glasses traditionally used to drink it also make good souvenirs.

The markets are great to browse round, and contain an interesting array of crafts and an eclectic selection of goods from nearby Albania, Macedonia and Greece.

Belgrade

A good place to go for gifts and souvenirs is Kalenic Market (Kalenich Market); it's a huge fruit and vegetable market near St Sava's Cathedral on Vracar, but it also has an area devoted to selling what looks like anything and everything: antiques, Yugoslavian memorabilia, old coins, stamps, books, records, vintage clothes, jewellery, etc. Be sure to haggle if you want a good price.

Some of the large halls at the Belgrade Fairground (located by the Sava River south of the city centre) have been converted into a shopping centre, with shops selling clothing, cosmetics, food and gadgets. When a fair is being held here there are lots of interesting stalls selling locally made artefacts and souvenirs.

The souvenir shop of the Ethnographic Museum of Serbia (Studentski trg 13) sells traditional Serbian artefacts. Here you will find copies of silver medieval jewellery, textile furnishings, authentic folk costumes, china from the village of Zlakusa, well known for its potteries, and icons painted on wood or glass.

Tourist Offices

Serbia
National Tourism Organisation of Serbia (NTOS), Decanska 8/V, 11000 Belgrade; tel: (11) 334 2521; fax: (11) 322 1068; www.serbia-tourism.org
Montenegro
National Tourism Organisation of Montenegro, Cetinjski put 66, Trg. Vektre, 81000 Podgorica; tel: (81) 235 155-8; fax: (81) 235 159; www.visit-montenegro.com
Canada
Embassy of Serbia and Montenegro, 17 Blackburn Avenue, Ottawa, Ontario K1N 8A2; tel: 161-3233-6289; fax: 161-3233-7850.
UK
7 Dering Street, London W1S 1AE; tel: 020 7629 2007; fax: 020 7629 6500; e-mail: sales@jatlondon.com
US
Embassy of Serbia and Montenegro, 2134 Kalorama Road, NW, Washington DC 20008; tel: 202-332-0333; fax: 202-332-3933.

Security and Crime

Once virtually non-existent, violent crime is now more common in the big cities following the impact of the war. Be extra vigilant for pickpocketing in public places and on public transport. If you do intend to travel round the country, refer to the guidelines laid down by the foreign office at www.fco.gov.uk

Emergency Telephone Numbers

Police: 92
Fire service: 93
Ambulance: 94

SLOVAKIA

Fact File

Area: 49,035 sq. km (18,933 sq. miles).
Capital: Bratislava.
Population: 5.4 million.
Language: Slovak.
Religion: predominantly Roman Catholic.
Currency: crown (Slovenská koruna or Sk in Slovakia).
Time zone: see page 327.
International dialling code: 421.
Websites: www.slovakiatourism.sk; www.sacr.sk

Entry Requirements, Customs and Health

Slovakia is in the European Union; see box on page 326 for details.

Money Matters

The unit of currency is the crown (Slovenská koruna or Sk in Slovakia). There has been talk of both the Czech and Slovak republics joining the Eurozone as early as 2007, but 2008/2009 seems more likely.

Credit cards are widely accepted, especially in the larger cities. Cash is still used for most transactions, however. Probably the easiest way to obtain cash these days is from an ATM. Travellers' cheques are accepted by some souvenir shops, hotels and restaurants, as well as by banks, but often what looks like an exceptionally good rate may be accompanied by an inordinately high commission.

Opening Times

Shops open Mon–Fri 8am–6pm; Sat 9am–12 noon; closed Sun.
Banks open Mon–Fri 8am–5pm; closed Sun.
Post offices open Mon–Fri 7am–7pm; Sat 7.30am–12.30pm; closed Sun.

Public Holidays

1 January: New Year's Day.
6 January: Epiphany.
March/April (variable): Easter.
1 May: May Day.
5 July: Day of the Slav Missionaries.
29 August: National Day.
1 September: Constitution Day.
15 September: Patron Saint's Day.
1 November: All Souls' Day, Day of Freedom and Democracy.
24–6 December: Christmas.
Various Christian holidays, for example the Feast of Corpus Christi and the Assumption of the Virgin Mary, are celebrated in different regions but are not considered national holidays.

Shopping

Bratislava's range of shops is improving fast. You can find most of what you want in the Old Town and on SNP Square. A bottle of Slivovica – Gazdovská is among the best – will make a good present, as will Tokaj wine and porcelain or locally produced fabrics. There are new galleries springing up in the centre of town which also offer good buys.

Souvenirs include pottery, porcelain, woodcarvings from the eastern and central parts of Slovakia (especially from Spisská Belá, Michalovce and Kyjatice), hand-embroidered clothing and food items. There are a number of excellent shops specialising in glass and crystal, while various associations of regional artists and crafts people run their own retail outlets. Two of the most famous brands are Modra and Tatran, which have an international reputation for craftsmanship.

Tourist Offices

Slovakia
SACR, the Slovak Tourist Board, can be contacted at Namestie L. Stura 1, PO Box 35, 97405 Banska Bystrica; tel: (421 48) 413 61 46–48; fax: (421 48) 413 61 49; e-mail: sacr@sacr.sk; www.sacr.sk
See also: www.travelguide.sk; www.tourist-channel.sk; www.slovakia.org; www.slovakiatourism.sk
UK
Embassy of the Slovak Republic, 25 Kensington Palace Gardens, London W8 4QY; tel: 020 7243 0803; e-mail: mail@slovakembassy.co.uk

Embassies

UK: Panská 16, 811 01 Bratislava; tel: (02) 5998 2000/2237.
US: PO Box 309, 814 99 Bratislava; tel: (02) 5443 3338

Telecommunications

Telephone
The telephone system has improved beyond recognition in the past few years. There are rows of telephones at most metro stations, as well as on the streets, which take either coins or cards, available at most newsagents. As ever, bear in mind that hotels will charge considerably more than public telephones.

Fax and Internet
In most of the larger hotels you can both send and receive a fax or take advantage of internet facilities to send e-mail. There are also centrally located internet cafés springing up all over Slovakia.

Security and Crime

Slovakia is a relatively safe country to visit, but the incidence of offences like robbery and fraud has increased measurably. It's therefore a good idea to deposit any valuables in the hotel safe. Also beware of pickpockets. There are professional gangs roaming busy shopping and tourist areas as well as buses and trams. In an emergency either consult with your hotel reception or contact the police directly by dialling 112. If you either lose or have your personal documents stolen, contact your embassy representative immediately.

Emergency Telephone Numbers

Ambulance: 155
Police: 112
Fire Brigade: 112

UKRAINE

Fact File

Area: 603,700 sq. km (233,100 sq. miles).
Capital: Kiev (pop. 2.6 million).
Population: 48.4 million.
Language: Ukrainian is the official language; Russian is widely spoken.
Religion: Orthodox with substantial Roman and Greek Catholic and Protestant minorities.
Currency: hryvna (hrn).
Time zone: see page 327.
International dialling codes: 380.
Website: www.ukraine.com

Entry Requirements

A valid passport and visa are required. If your tour operator is not getting your visa for you, you should contact the Ukrainian embassy or consulate in your country. Travellers from countries where there is a Ukrainian embassy or consulate cannot obtain visas on arrival, so make sure you have one before you get here.

Customs Regulations

You are exempt from customs formalities if you are carrying less than US$1,000 (or equivalent) and up to US$10,000 with customs declaration.

Health and Insurance

Travel insurance is compulsory for all travellers. In theory, free medical treatment is available for all citizens and travellers who become ill. However, as in most parts of the former Soviet Union, health care is a serious problem. For minor difficulties, visitors are advised to ask the management at their hotel or cruise boat for help. For major problems, you should contact your

embassy for advice on where to get medical aid. It is advisable to take a supply of those medicines that are likely to be required (but check first that they may be legally imported), as medicines can prove difficult to obtain.

All water should be regarded as a potential health risk. Water used for drinking, brushing teeth or making ice should have first been boiled or otherwise sterilised. Only eat well-cooked meat and fish, preferably served hot. Pork, salad and mayonnaise may carry increased risk. Vegetables should be cooked and fruit peeled.

Money Matters

Ukraine has a cash economy, and travellers' cheques are rarely used, although they will be accepted in the major Ukrainian banks. Use of credit cards is limited to the more expensive hotels, tourist restaurants, international airlines and select stores. Credit-card fraud is rife, so take extra care when paying by this method. Changing currency is legal only at banks, currency-exchange desks at hotels, and at licensed exchange booths.

Opening Times

Shops are usually open Mon–Fri 9am–6pm, Sat 9am–noon or 2pm. More and more businesses forgo closure at lunchtime, but many small shops do close for an hour between noon and 3pm. Most stores are closed on Sunday, though some open 10am–4pm, and supermarkets and out-of-town hypermarkets are open all day in large towns and cities.
Banks are usually open Mon–Fri 9am–5pm but many close at 3.30pm.

Public Holidays

1 January: New Year's Day.
7 January: Russian Orthodox Christmas Day.
23 February: Defenders of the Motherland Day.
8 March: International Women's Day.
April/May (variable)**:** Easter.
1–2 May: Labour Day/Spring Holiday.
9 May: Victory Day.
12 June: Russian Independence Day.
7 November: Great October Socialist Revolution Anniversary.
12 December: Constitution Day.

Shopping

Folk art is still alive and well in Ukraine; souvenirs to look out for include painted wooden boxes,

plates and spoons, earthenware pottery, embroidered cloths and linen and woollen rugs. At open markets you will also find an interesting range of home-made produce, like honey, and sausages of all varieties.

The best place in Kiev for souvenir shopping is Andrievsky Uzviz, a long, descending cobblestoned street, which is also the setting for outdoor fairs, festivals and concerts. Here, in the art galleries, shops and studios, you will find a great selection of original souvenirs, antiques and paintings. If you do buy antiques, especially icons, be sure to follow the correct procedure for export or they will be confiscated by customs officials. Any reputable art dealer should be able to help you.

Tourist Offices

Ukraine
National Tourist Organisation, 36 Yaroslaviv Val Street, Kiev 1034; tel: (380) 4427 22912; fax: (380) 4448 63351; e-mail: nto@nto.org.ua; www.uatravel.com
UK
Intourist, 7 Princedale Road, Holland Park, London W11 4NW; tel: 0870 112 1232/020 7792 5240; fax: 020 7727 4600; e-mail: info@ intourist.co.uk; www.intouristuk.com.
US
The Consulate General of Ukraine, 240 East 49th Street, New York, NY 10017; tel: 212-371-5690; fax: 212-371-5547; email: gc_usn@mfa.gov.ua; www.ukrconsul.org

Embassies

In UK
60 Holland Park, London W11 3SJ; tel: 0870 005 6983; fax: 020 7792 1708.
Consular/visa section:
Ground Floor, 78 Kensington Park Road, London W11 2PL; tel: 0870 005 6983; fax: 020 7727 3567.

In Ukraine
Canada
31 Yaroslaviv Val Street, Kiev 01901; tel: (44) 464 1144; fax: (44) 464 0598.
UK
9 Desyatinna Street, Kiev 01025; tel: (44) 490 3660.
Consular/visa section:
Artyom Business Centre, 4 Glybochytska Street, Kiev 04050; tel: (44) 494 3400.
US
6 Mykoly Pymonenka Street, Kiev 01901; tel: (44) 490 4422; fax: (44) 484 4256.

Telecommunications

Every city and large town has a telephone centre from where you can make national or international calls. You pay in advance at the counter, and you will get change for any unused time. Alternatively you can buy a Utel phonecard and use designated Utel telephones to make international calls; they are found in main post offices, telephone centres and upmarket hotels. To call overseas from Ukraine, dial 810 followed by the country code, area code and number.

Local and national calls can be made from public phones using a phonecard, which you can buy from kiosks and post offices.

You should have no trouble finding an internet café in the main towns and cities.

Security and Crime

Don't carry all your cash in one place, and avoid displaying large sums of money. Behave sensibly and be aware that street crime is on a similar level to any big city in the world.

It's a good idea to deposit any valuables in the hotel safe, if you are staying in a hotel, or to take as little as possible with you on a shore visit. Beware of pickpockets in crowded places. Keep valuables out of sight and hang on to your bags.

Emergency Telephone Numbers

Fire, Police and Ambulance: 112
Fire: 01

UNITED KINGDOM (SCOTLAND)

Fact File

Area: England: 50,056 sq. miles (129,645 sq. km); Scotland: 30,414 sq. miles (78,772 sq. km); Wales: 7,967 sq. miles (20,635 sq. km); Northern Ireland: 5,242 sq. miles (13,571 sq. km).
Capital: London (England), Edinburgh (Scotland), Cardiff (Wales) and Belfast (Northern Ireland).
Population: England: 50 million; Scotland: 5.1 million; Wales: 2.9 million; Northern Ireland: 1.7 million.
Language: English. In Wales 20 percent of residents also speak Welsh; in Scotland 25 percent speak Scots and a small minority speak Gaelic; in Northern Ireland minorities also speak Irish and Ulster Scots.

Religion: mostly Protestant (Church of England): the monarch is the titular head of the Church; the primate is the Archbishop of Canterbury. There are sizeable Church of Scotland and Roman Catholic populations, and minority Muslim, Sikh, Hindu and Jewish populations.
Currency: pounds divided into 100 pence. Scotland issues its own notes, which are not technically legal tender in England and Wales, though banks and many shops accept them.
Weights and measures: officially metric, although imperial measurements are still widely used, notably for distances (miles) and beer in pubs (pints).
Time zone: see page 327.
International dialling code: 44.
Website: www.visitbritain.com

Entry Requirements, Customs and Health

See box on page 326. In the case of a serious accident or emergency, dial 999. For free health advice call NHS Direct on 0845 4647.

Money Matters

Most banks open between 9.30am and 4.30pm Monday–Friday, with Saturday morning banking common in shopping areas. International credit or cashpoint cards can be used in ATMs, or cash machines, in conjunction with a personal number, to withdraw cash.

The major banks offer similar exchange rates, so it's worth shopping around only if you have large amounts of money to change. Banks charge no commission on travellers' cheques presented in sterling. If a bank is affiliated to your own bank at home, it will make no charge for cheques in other currencies either. But there is a charge for changing cash into British currency. Some high-street travel agents, such as Thomas Cook, operate bureaux de change at comparable rates. There are also many privately run bureaux de change (some of which are open 24 hours a day), where exchange rates can be low but commissions high.

Tipping

Most hotels and restaurants automatically add a 10–15 percent service charge to your meal bill. It's your right to deduct this amount if you are not happy with the service provided. Sometimes when service has been added, the final total on a

credit card slip is still left blank, the implication being that a further tip is expected: you do not have to pay this. You don't tip in pubs, cinemas or theatres, but it is customary to give hairdressers, sightseeing guides, railway porters and cab drivers an extra amount of around 10 percent.

Opening Times

Town-centre shops generally open 9am–5.30pm Monday–Saturday, while supermarkets tend to be open 8 or 8.30am–8 to 10pm from Monday to Saturday and 10 or 11am–4 or 5pm on Sunday. Many small towns and villages have a half-day closing one day in the week, and shopping centres in towns and cities are likely to have at least one evening of late-night shopping.

Offices usually operate 9am–5.30pm Monday–Friday with an hour for lunch.

British pubs are generally open between 11am and 11pm Monday–Saturday (later in Scotland) and noon–10.30pm on Sunday, although some now take advantage of new legislation which allows them to stay open later at night. Some may close for periods during the day, and pubs can apply for an extended opening hours licence for special events such as New Year's Eve.

Public Holidays

1 January: New Year's Day.
March/April (variable): Easter.
May: May Day (first Monday); Spring Bank Holiday (last Monday).
August: Summer Bank Holiday (last Monday).
25–6 December: Christmas.
On public holidays all banks are closed. Roads are usually a nightmare as people head for the coast or to see relatives, while others head for London.

Shopping in Scotland

Glasgow is Scotland's major shopping city, with the smart, upscale Princes Square, the newer Buchanan Galleries and the pedestrianised Buchanan Street. In Edinburgh the main shopping is on Princes Street. For gifts, tartans and other Scottish wares in Edinburgh, try the Royal Mile.

You'll find an array of Scottish goods in many shops all over the country, from tartan scarves, neckties and heraldic clan crests to oatcakes and Scottish mead. You can even buy a set of bagpipes.

Art and antiques

The Scottish art scene is an active one. Look for prints and affordable works by young Scottish artists. Victorian antiques and old prints and maps are also a good buy.

Crafts

Interesting stoneware and salt-glazed pottery comes from the Highlands, while potters, jewellery-makers and other craftspeople live on the isles of Mull and Skye. Unusual "heather-gems" jewellery is made from stems of heather. Look for wood and stag-horn carvings, Celtic designs, handknits and prints and greeting cards by local artists.

Crystal

There are several major Scottish lines of handmade crystal. Edinburgh Glass, Stuart Crystal in Crieff, and Caithness Glass in Oban, Perth and Wick are incised with distinctive thistle or star designs. Scotland also produces some of the finest glass paperweights in the world; leading makes include Selkirk, Caithness and Perthshire.

Kilts and tartans

A number of more serious shops in Edinburgh, Glasgow, Stirling and Aberdeen specialise in made-to-measure kilts, or full Highland dress. These shops will be glad to help you find your family tartan.

Knitwear and woollens

The range of Scottish knitwear is huge: beautiful designer knitwear, cashmere pullovers and cardigans, and Shetland and Fair Isle sweaters. Tartan woollens can be bought by the yard, and you can see them woven at several woollen mills. Harris tweed and sheepskin rugs are also popular buys.

Jewellery

Look for sterling and enamel jewellery made from the designs of Charles Rennie Mackintosh. From Orkney and Shetland comes attractive silvercraft with designs inspired by Norse mythology. Celtic-designed jewellery, clan brooches and ornate kilt pins are often produced in pewter. For those with a romantic streak there's the delicately worked luckenbooth, a traditional Scottish love token.

Whisky

Scotch whisky is not less expensive in Scotland, but you'll find brands that you never knew existed, so take the opportunity to discover an unusual malt that suits your taste. The single malts are particularly good. Beautifully designed stainless-steel spirit flasks and little telescopic whisky tumblers can be ideal partners for that special bottle.

Value Added Tax (VAT)

Almost all merchandise and services are subject to a 17.5 percent Value Added Tax (VAT). For major purchases over a certain amount, overseas visitors can get a VAT refund. Note that this applies only to stores that are members of the Retail Export Scheme. When you make your purchase, request a signed form and a stamped pre-addressed envelope; have your form stamped by British Customs as you leave the country and mail the form back to the store. The refund should arrive in due course. You can also avoid the VAT if you do your shopping in duty-free stores – look for the sign.

Tourist Offices

For the definitive aid to locating tourist information centres and other information, see: www.visitmap.info. Visit Britain (formerly the British Tourist Authority) has offices worldwide. See www.visitbritain.com

UK

Inverness: Castle Wynd, Inverness IV2 3BJ; tel: 0845 22 55 121; e-mail: info@visitscotland.com; www.visithighlands.com

Glasgow: 11 George Square, Glasgow G2 1DY; tel: 0141 204 4400; fax: 0141 221 3524; e-mail: enquiries@seeglasgow.com; www.seeglasgow.com

Britain and London Visitor Centre: 1 Regent Street, London SW1Y 4XT; e-mail: blvcinfo@visitbritain.org; www.visitbritain.com

VisitScotland: the booking and information line has details of all tourist offices in Scotland: 01506 832 121.

19 Cockspur Street, London SW1Y 5BL; tel: 020 7321 5752.
3 Princes Street, Edinburgh EH2 2QP; tel: 0845 22 55 121; e-mail: info@visitscotland.com; www.visitscotland.com

US

VisitBritain, 551 5th Avenue, 7th Floor, New York, NY 10176-0799; tel: 800-462-2748; e-mail: travelinfo@visitbritain.org; www.visitbritain.com/usa

Telecommunications

It is usually cheaper to use public phones rather than those in hotel rooms as hotels make high profits out of this service.

British Telecom (BT) is the main telephone operating company. Its public telephones are by far the most plentiful, although a number of other telephone companies also have kiosks. Some public phones take

coins only, some plastic phonecards and/or credit cards, and some all three. Phonecards can be purchased from post offices and newsagents in varying amounts between £1 and £20.

Public telephone boxes are no longer ubiquitous now that so many people have mobile phones. Stations and shopping centres in particular are good places to look. In country areas, try a pub.

The most expensive time to use the telephone is 8am–6pm weekdays, while the cheapest is after 6pm on weekdays and all weekend. Calls are charged by distance, so a long-distance conversation on a weekday morning can eat up coins in a phone box.

Numbers beginning with the prefixes 0800, 0500, 0321 or 0808 are freephone lines. Those prefixed by 0345, 0645 or 0845 are charged at local rates irrespective of their distance. Those starting with 0891, 0839, 0640, 0660 and 0898 are very expensive.

Security and Crime

As everywhere, the crime rate in the UK is rising, but even Glasgow, with Scotland's highest crime rate, is not dangerous by world standards. Police warn that theft, particularly involving cars, is usually invited by carelessness – never leave anything on view in your car. In hotels, put your most valuable objects in the safe.

Useful and Emergency Telephone Numbers

Police, Fire and Ambulance: 999
Operator: 100
Directory Enquiries (UK): 118 500, 118 888 or 118 811
International Directory Enquiries: 118 505, 118 866 or 118 899

R IVER VESSEL LISTINGS

A GUIDE TO EUROPEAN AND NILE VESSELS WITH RATINGS

Vessel Design

There is some variety in the length and beam and height of river cruise vessels, although these differ according to the rivers on which the vessels will operate. This is due, in part, to the restrictions placed on a vessel's dimensions by the locks located on the various rivers. Almost all vessels are built on a monohull.

At present, only one vessel in Europe has two hulls *(Viking Primadonna)*, while one vessel has a monohull that has two sets of bows that give the impression of having twin hulls *(Mozart)*. While twin hulls mean that there is more room because the vessel will by necessity be wider than average, the problem of having such wide vessels is that the hull must flex more to accommodate the strong currents and water movements encountered in some parts of the river. Most vessel designers would, therefore, prefer to stay with the conventional monohull that is found as the base for most of the river cruise vessels in the world today.

DESIGN CHARACTERISTICS. Because of the necessity of their long, "low-slung" design, river cruise vessels have only a limited amount of space for public areas. There are, basically, only two major public rooms aboard those plying the waterways of Europe and Egypt, the dining room and the main lounge. However, in these two areas, there are several variations and differences between vessel designers (such as where to place the bar, and perhaps a small dance floor and baby grand or upright piano), and the degree of comfort and user-friendliness built into the design.

KEY
❶ = French (tiny) balcony
❷ = Real Balcony

BELOW: the "low slung" design of river vessels tends to limit the space available for public areas.

STEAUA DELTEI

							RIVER CRUISE VESSELS
VESSEL	OWNER/OPERATING COMPANY	RATING	BUILT	LENGTH (m)	BEAM (m)	CABINS	PRINCIPAL RIVERS
EUROPE							
A'Rosa Bella ❶	Arkona Reisen	★★★★	2002	124.5	14.4	100	Danube
A'Rosa Donna ❶	Arkona Reisen	★★★★	2002	124.5	14.4	100	Danube
A'Rosa Luna ❶	Arkona Reisen	★★★★	2004	125.8	11.4	86	Rhône, Saône
A'Rosa Mia ❶	Arkona Reisen	★★★★	2003	124.5	14.4	100	Danube
A'Rosa Riva ❶	Arkona Reisen	★★★★	2004	124.5	14.4	100	Danube
A'Rosa Stella ❶	Arkona Reisen	★★★★	2005	125.8	11.4	86	Rhône, Saône
Abel Tasman	Bonaventura Cruises	★★★		105	10.4	73	Danube, Rhine
Amadagio	Amadeus Waterways	NYR	2006	110	11.4	75	Danube, Elbe, Rhine
Amadeus	Luftner Reisen	★★★★	1997	110	11.4	73	Danube, Rhine
Amadeus Classic	Luftner Reisen	★★★★	2001	110	11.4	73	Danube, Rhine
Amadeus Princess ❶	Luftner Reisen	NYR	2006	110	11.4	83	Danube, Rhine
Amadeus Rhapsody	Luftner Reisen	★★★★	1998	110	11.4	71	Danube, Rhine
Amadeus Royal	Luftner Reisen	★★★★	2005	110	11.4	73	Danube, Rhine
Amadeus Symphony	Luftner Reisen	★★★★	2003	110	11.4	73	Danube, Rhine
Amsterdam	Feenstra Rhine Line	★		78	9.5	49	Rhine
Amur	Ukrainian Danube Shipping	★	1960	86	9	50	Danube
Arlene	Boonstra River Line	★★	1986	91.2	10.5	53	various
Avalon Artistry ❶	Avalon Waterways	★★★★	2004	130	11.4	89	Danube
Avalon Poetry	Avalon Waterways	★★★★	2005	130	11.4	88	Danube, Rhine
Avalon Tapestry ❶	Avalon Waterways	NYR	2006	132	14.4	84	Danube, Rhine
Azolla	Feenstra Rhine Line	★★		76.5	7.8	45	Rhine
Balkan Beauty	Danube Black Sea Shipping	★★	1968	83	14	46	Danube
Beethoven	CroisiEurope	★★★★	2004	110	11	88	Danube, Rhine
Belle de Cadix	CroisiEurope	★★★	2005	110	10	90	Guadalquivir
Bellevue ❶	Transocean Tours Touristik	★★★★	2006	135	11.4	97	Danube, Rhine, Moselle
Bizet	Grand Circle Travel	★★★★	2002	110	11.4	60	Seine
Blue Danube	Europe Cruise Line	★★★★	1995	117	11.4	72	various
Blue Danube II	Grand Circle Travel	★★★★	1998	110	11	72	various
Bolero ❶	Nicko Tours	★★★★	2003	126.7	11.4	90	various
Botticelli	CroisiEurope	★★★	2004	110	11.4	77	various
Calypso	Feenstra Rhine Line	★★	1978	75.6	10.5	49	Rhine
Camargue	CroisiEurope	★★★	1995	110	11	74	Seine, Rhône, Saône
Casanova	Peter Deilmann River Cruises	★★★★	2001	103	9.7	48	Po
Cezanne	Peter Deilmann River Cruises	★★★	1992	118	11.6	50	Rhône, Saône
Debussy	Grand Circle Travel	★★★★	2000	110	11.4	60	Rhône, Seine
Delta Star	Giurgiu Navigation Company	★★	1985	107	13.1	83	Danube
Der kleine Prinz	Swiss Cruises Basel	★★★	1992	93.3	11.2	44	Danube
Diana	Gota Canal Steamship Company	★	1931	31.6	6.7	28	Gota Canal (Sweden)
Dnepr	Ukrainian Danube Shipping	★	1971	106	16.1	80	Danube
Donauprinzessen (Danube Princess)	Peter Deilmann River Cruises	★★★	1983	111	15.4	95	Danube
Donaustar	Giurgiu Navigation Company	★★	1987	107	13	89	Danube
Douce France	CroisiEurope	★★★★	1997	110	10	80	Rhine
Douro Prince ❷	various operators	★★	1955	57	8.8	23	Douro
Douro Queen	Uniworld River Cruises	★★★★	2005	78.3	11.2	64	Douro
Dresden	Peter Deilmann River Cruises	★★★	1991	97.8	11.1	54	Elbe, Oder
Dunaj	Ukrainian Danube Shipping	★	1960	86	9	50	Danube
Elegant Lady	WT Cruises	★★★	2002	110	11.4	68	various
Erasmus	WT Cruises	★★★	1995	105	11.4	57	various
Esmerelda	WT Cruises	★★★	1995	90	11.4	63	various
Europa	WT Cruises	★★★	2000	82	9.5	42	various
Eurostar	various operators	★★★	1998	81	9.5	41	Elbe, Havel, Oder, Rhine
Fernão de Magelhães	CroisiEurope	★★★	2003	110	11.4	71	Douro
Fidelio	Klaus Sahr	★★★	1995	110	11.4	74	various
Filia Rheni	Holland River Line	★★	1980	90	11.4	62	various
Flamenco ❷	Nicko Tours	★★★★	2005	135	11.4	96	Danube
Florentina	Boonstra River Line	★★	1981	80	9.5	54	Danube, Main, Rhine
Fortuna	Boonstra River Line	★★	1974	66	8.9	46	Danube, Main, Rhine
Fluvius	Phoenix Reisen	★★	2001	70	5.6	20	Elbe, Oder, Havel
France	CroisiEurope	★★★★	2001	110	11	80	Rhine
Frederic Chopin	Peter Deilmann River Cruises	★★★★	2002	83	9.5	41	Elbe, Havel
Heidelberg	Peter Deilmann River Cruises	★★★★	2004	110	11.4	55	Moselle, Rhine
Invicta	Douro Azul	★★		68	8.6	40	Douro
Johann Strauss ❶	Austrian River Cruises	★★★	2004	126.7	11.4	80	Danube, Main, Rhine
Juno	Gotal Canal Steamship Company	★	1874	31.4	6.6	28	Gota Canal (Sweden)
Katharina von Bora	Peter Deilmann River Cruises	★★★★	2000	83	9.5	41	various
Kellerman	Boonstra River Line	★★	1972	74.4	10.1	48	various
Konigstein	Peter Deilmann River Cruises	★★★	1992	67	8.2	29	Elbe, Havel, Vltava
Kristina Brahe	Kristina Cruises	★★	1943	58	10	57	Kiel Canal

RIVER CRUISE VESSELS

VESSEL	OWNER/OPERATING COMPANY	RATING	BUILT	LENGTH (m)	BEAM (m)	CABINS	PRINCIPAL RIVERS
L'Esprit d'Europe	Continental Waterways	***	2003	60	9.1	19	Seine
L'Europe	CroisiEurope	NYR	2006	110	10	80	various
La Bohème	CroisiEurope	***	1995	110	10	80	Danube
Leonardo da Vinci	CroisiEurope	***	2003	110	10	72	Rhine
Liberte	CroisiEurope	***	1991	105	10	74	Rhine
Lord of the Glens	various operators	****	2000	45.7	10.5	27	Scottish rivers/waterways
Lord of the Highlands ❷	various operators	****	1995	50	14.5	27	Scottish rivers/waterways
Michelangelo	CroisiEurope/Phoenix Reisen	***	2000	110	11	74	Po
Mr Jan Elshout	WT Cruises	**	1991	87	9.5	59	Danube, Rhine
Mistral	CroisiEuope	****	1999	110	11	76	Rhône
Modigliani	CroisiEurope	****	2001	110	11	76	Danube
Moldavia	Ukrainian Danube Shipping/ Transocean Tours Touristik	**	1979	115.7	17	80	Danube, Dnieper
Mona Lisa	CroisiEurope	***	2000	82.5	9.5	50	Elbe
Monet	CroisiEurope	****	1999	110	11	83	Rhine
Mosel Star	Boonstra River Line	**	1966	63.5	7.7	40	various
Mozart	Peter Deilmann River Cruises	****	1987	120.6	22.8	100	Danube
Normandie	Boonstra River Line	***	1989	91.2	10.5	51	various
Oltenita	Danube Black Sea Shipping	**	1968	83	14	46	Danube
Patria	Boonstra River Line	**	1974	67	7.6	38	various
Picasso	CroisiEurope	***	2000	110	11.2	74	various
Poseidon	Feenstra Rhine Line	**		78	10.5	49	Rhine
Prince du Douro	CroisiEurope	***	2003	75	11.4	70	Douro
Princes Christina	Bonaventura Cruises	**		70.6	9.2	54	Rhine
Princess	Boonstra River Line	***	1984	80	9.5	50	various
Princess	Feenstra Rhine Line	**	1981	80	9.5	50	Rhine
Princesse de Provence	Peter Deilmann River Cruises	***	1992	110	11.2	71	Rhône, Saône
Princesse Sissi	CroisiEurope	***	1994	105	10	74	Rhine
Prinzessin von Preussen	Peter Deilmann River Cruises	***	1991	110	11.2	69	Danube, Main, Mosel, Rhein
Provence	Abercrombie & Kent	***	2002	89	9.4	27	Rhône
Queen of Holland	Holland River Line	***	1995	110	11.4	73	Danube, Main, Rhine
Rembrandt	Austrian River Cruises	***	2003	82	9.5	42	various
Ravel	Grand Circle Travel	****	2001	123.3	11.4	60	Rhône, Seine
Rembrandt von Rijn	Feenstra Rhine Line	***	1985	110	10.5	63	Danube, Main, Rhine
Renoir	CroisiEurope	****	1999	110	11	78	Seine, Rhône, Saône
Regina Rheni	Holland River Line	***	1993	109.8	11.4	73	Moselle, Rhine
Rex Rheni	Holland River Line	**	1979	90	11.4	79	Moselle, Rhine
Rhine Princess	Princess River Cruises	***	1992	83.2	13.7	60	Moselle, Rhine
Rhone Princess	CroisiEurope	***	2001	110	11	60	Rhône
Rigoletto	Viking Aquatel River Cruises	**	1987	105	10.5	60	various
River Adagio ❷	Grand Circle Travel	****	2003	125	11.4	82	various
River Aria ❷	Grand Circle Travel	****	2001	125	11.4	82	various
River Baroness	Global River Cruises/Uniworld	***	1997	110	11.4	70	various
River Cloud	Sea Cloud Cruises	****	1996	110	11.4	47	Danube, Main, Moselle, Rhine
River Cloud II	Sea Cloud Cruises	****	2000	103	9.7	44	various
River Concerto ❷	Grand Circle Travel	****	2000	110	11.4	70	various
River Countess	Global River Cruises/Uniworld	****	2003	110	11.4	68	various
River Duchess	Global River Cruises/Uniworld	****	2003	110	11.4	68	various
River Empress	Global River Cruises/Uniworld	****	2002	110	11.4	68	various
River Explorer	Vantage Deluxe World Tours	****	2001	125	11.4	85	various
River Harmony ❷	Grand Circle Travel	****	1999	110	11.4	70	various
River Melody ❷	Grand Circle Travel	****	1999	110	11.4	70	various
River Navigator	Vantage Deluxe World Tours	****	2000	110	11.4	70	various
River Odyssey	Vantage Deluxe World Tours	****	2002	125	11.4	85	various
River Princess	Uniworld River Cruises	****	2001	110	11.4	68	various
River Queen	Holland River Line	****	1999	110	11.4	70	various
River Rhapsody	Grand Circle Travel	****	1999	110	11.4	70	various
River Royale ❶	Uniworld River Cruises	NYR	2006	110	11.4	70	Rhône, Saône
River Symphony ❷	Grand Circle Travel	****	1999	110	11.4	70	various
Roland von England III	Holland River Line	***	1978	76	11.5	68	various
Rousse	Bulgarian Danube Shipping/ Luftner Reisen	**	1983	113.5	16	98	Danube
Rugen	Klaus Sahr	**	1982	82.5	9.5	52	Elbe
St Odile	CroisiEurope	***	1992	90	10	63	Rhine
Salvinia	Feenstra Rhine Line	**		91.5	10	65	Rhine
Saxonia	Scylla Tours	***	2001	82	9.5	45	Main, Mosel, Rhine, Saar
Seine Princess	CroisiEurope	****	2002	110	11	78	Seine
Serena	Boonstra River Line	*	1948	90	9.9	56	various
Sofia	Bulgarian Danube Shipping	**	1983	113.5	16	99	Danube
Statendam	Feenstra Rhine Line	**		104.3	11.6	96	Rhine
Swiss Coral	Scylla Tours	****	1998	82	9.5	44	Danube, Main, Rhine

VESSEL	OWNER/OPERATING COMPANY	RATING	BUILT	LENGTH (m)	BEAM (m)	CABINS	PRINCIPAL RIVERS
							RIVER CRUISE VESSELS
Swiss Corona ❶	Scylla Tours	****	2004	110	11.4	75	Danube, Main, Rhine
Swiss Crown	Scylla Tours	****	2000	110	11.4	75	Danube
Swiss Crystal	Scylla Tours	***	1995	101.3	11.4	63	Main, Moselle, Rhine
Swiss Diamond	Scylla Tours	***	1996	101.3	11.4	61	Main, Moselle, Rhine
Swiss Pearl	Scylla Tours	***	1993	110	11.4	62	Danube, Main, Rhine
Swiss Ruby	Scylla Tours	***	2002	85	10.6	43	Danube
Switzerland	Scylla Tours	***	1988	100	11.1	56	Danube
Switzerland II	Scylla Tours	***	1991	100	11.1	53	Danube, Main, Rhine
Symphonie	CroisiEurope	****	1997	110	10	80	Danube
Theodor Korner	KD River Cruises	**	1965	87	16.5	41	various
Ukraina	Ukrainian Danube Shipping	**	1983	116	17	79	Danube
Van Gogh	CroisiEurope	****	1999	110	11	80	Rhône
Vasco da Gama	CroisiEurope/Phoenix Reisen	***	2002	110	11.4	71	Douro
Venezia	Scylla Tours/Viking River Cruises	***	1984	88.25	10.5	51	Po
Victor Hugo	CroisiEurope	****	2000	82.5	9.5	74	Tisza
Victoria Amazonica	Bonaventura Cruises	***	2001	80	9.2	49	Rhine, Danube
Victoria Cruziana	Bonaventura Cruises	**	1960	88.5	11.6	60	Rhine, Danube
Viking Britannia	Viking River Cruises	**	1969	110	11.6	92	Rhine
Viking Burgundy	Viking River Cruises	****	2000	111.2	11.4	77	Rhône/Saône
Viking Danube	Viking River Cruises	****	1999	110	11.4	75	Main/Rhine/Danube
Viking Deutschland	Viking River Cruises	**	1971	110	11.6	92	Rhine, Main, Mosel
Viking Europe	Viking River Cruises	****	2001	114.34	11.4	75	Danube, Rhine
Viking Fontane	Viking River Cruises	***	1991	94.8	11	60	Elbe
Viking Helvetia	Viking River Cruises	NYR	2006	114.34	11.4	75	various
Viking Neptune	Viking River Cruises	****	2001	114.34	11.4	75	Danube, Rhine
Viking Normandie	Viking River Cruises	**	1989	91.2	10.5	53	Rhône, Saône
Viking Pride	Viking River Cruises	****	2001	114.34	11.4	75	Danube, Rhine
Viking Primadonna ❷	Viking River Cruises	****	1998	113.3	17.3	76	Danube
Viking Rugen	Viking River Cruises	**	1982	82.75	9.65	46	Havel, Oder
Viking Schumann	Viking River Cruises	***	1991	94.8	11	60	Elbe
Viking Seine	Viking River Cruises	****	2000	111.2	11.2	80	Rhône, Saône
Viking Sky	Viking River Cruises	****	2004	110	11.4	75	Danube, Rhine
Viking Spirit	Viking River Cruises	****	2001	114.34	11.4	75	Danube, Rhine
Viking Star	Viking River Cruises	****	2000	111.24	11.4	77	Danube, Rhine, Seine
Viking Sun	Viking River Cruises	****	2004	131	11.4	76	Rhine, Main, Danube
Vincent van Gogh	International River Cruises	***	1997	64	7	14	Rhine, Moselle
Viking Tell	Viking River Cruises	**	1987	95	10.5	47	Main, Moselle, Rhine
Volga	Ukrainian Danube Shipping	**	1970	116	17	79	Danube
Wilhelm Thamm	Gota Canal Steamship Company	*	1912	31.6	6.7	28	Gota Canal (Sweden)
							RUSSIA & UKRAINE
Aleksandr Pirogov	Russian/various	*	1963	77.9	15.2	39	Circular Waterways Route
Aleksandr Radishchev	Russian/various	**	1982	125	16.7	136	various Russian rivers
Aleksandr Shemagin	Russian/various	*	1962	77.9	15.2	39	Circular Waterways Route
Aleksey Surkov	Russian/various	**	1984	129.1	16.7	125	various Russian rivers
Aleksey Vatchenko	Russian/various	** +	1985	129.1	16.7	144	Volga
Avalon Anastasia (4)	Avalon Waterways	NYR	2006	98.5	16.7	60	Neva, Volga
Checkhov	Russian/various	**	1978	115.6	16.7	100	Yenisey
Demyan Bedniy	Russian/various	**	1986	90.2	15	90	various Russian rivers
Dimitriy Furmanov	Russian/various	**	1983	129.1	16.7	130	various Russian rivers
Dniepr Princess	Ukrainian/various	**	1976	129.2	16.7	152	var. Russian/Ukrainian rivers
Dniepr Star	Ukrainian/various	**	1988	129.2	16.7	156	var. Russian/Ukrainian rivers
Dostoyevskiy	Russian/various	**	1983	125	16.7	103	Volga
Fedor Shalyapin	Russian/various	**	1977	135.8	16.8	198	various Russian rivers
Felix Dzerzhinskiy	Russian/various	**	1978	135.8	16.8	198	various Russian rivers
General Vatutin	Ukrainian/various	**	1986	129.1	16.7	156	var. Russian/Ukrainian rivers
Georgiy Chicherin	Russian/various	**	1988	129.1	16.7	140	various Russian rivers
Georgiy Zhukov	Russian/various	**	1983	135.8	16.8	198	various Russian rivers
Glushkov	Russian/various	***	1985	129.1	16.7	120	Neva, Volga
Griboedov	Russian/various	**	1982	125	16.7	152	Volga
Karl Marx	Russian/various	*	1957	95.8	14.3	64	various Russian rivers
Kazan	Russian/various	***+	1999	122.3	11.3	75	Neva, Volga
Konstantin Fedin	Russian/various	*	1980	125	16.7	126	various Russian rivers
Konstantin Fedov	Russian/various	**	1985	129.1	16.7	170	various Russian rivers
Konstantin Korotkov	Russian/various	**	1976	125	16.7	129	various Russian rivers
Konstantin Simonov	Russian/various	**	1984	129.1	16.7	150	various Russian rivers
Koshevoy	Russian/various	**	1988	129.1	16.7	157	various Russian rivers
Kronstadt	Russian/various	**	1979	125	16.7	161	various Russian rivers
Lenin	Russian/various	**	1987	129.1	16.7	156	Neva, Volga
Leonid Krasin	Russian/various	**	1989	129.1	16.7	161	various Russian rivers

PLANNING THE TRIP

LIFE ON BOARD

A–Z

RIVER VESSEL LISTINGS

RIVER CRUISE VESSELS

VESSEL	OWNER/OPERATING COMPANY	RATING	BUILT	LENGTH (m)	BEAM (m)	CABINS	PRINCIPAL RIVERS
Leonid Sobolev	Russian/various	**	1985	129.1	16.7	147	various Russian rivers
Litvinov	Russian/various	**	1990	129.1	16.7	140	Neva, Volga
Marshal Rybalko	Russian/various	**	1988	129.1	16.7	145	Dnieper, Black Sea
Maksim Gorkiy	Russian/various	**	1974	110.1	16.7	88	various Russian rivers
Maxim Rylskiy	Russian/various	**	1979	125	16.7	140	various Russian rivers
Mayakovskiy	Russian/various	**	1978	125	16.7	140	Neva, Volga
Mikhail Frunze	Russian/various	**	1980	135.8	16.8	198	various Russian rivers
Mikhail Kalinin	Russian/various	**	1981	135.8	16.8	198	various Russian rivers
Mikhail Lomonosov	Russian/various	**	1979	125	16.7	140	various Russian rivers
Mikhail Svetlov	Russian/various	**	1985	90.2	15	71	various Russian rivers
Nikolai Bauman	Russian/various	**	1989	129.1	16.7	140	various Russian rivers
Nikolai Chernyshevsky	Russian/various	**	1981	125	16.7	138	Neva, Volga
Nikolai Karamzim	Russian/various	**	1981	125	16.7	170	various Russian rivers
Nizhni Novgorod	Russian/various	**	1977	125	16.7	133	Volga
Priboy	Russian/various	**	1983	129.1	16.7	156	Neva, Volga
Pushkin	Russian/various	**	1976	110	14.5	140	Volga
Rimsky Korsakov	Orthodox Cruise Company/ Phoenix Reisen	**	1955	80.2	14	42	various Russian rivers
River Voyager	Russian/various	*	1988	95.8	14.3	58	various Russian rivers
Russ	Russian/various	***	1987	129.1	16.7	140	various Russian rivers
St Petersburg	Russian/various	**	1974	125	16.7	140	various Russian rivers
Sergey Kushkin	Russian/various	**	1979	135.8	16.8	198	various Russian rivers
Semyon Budyonnyy	Russian/various	**	1981	135.8	16.8	198	various Russian rivers
Sergey Kirov	Russian/various	***	1987	129.1	16.7	120	various Russian rivers
Sergey Kushkin	Russian/various	**	1979	135.8	16.8	198	various Russian rivers
Sholokhov	Russian/various	**	1985	129.1	16.7	152	Neva, Volga
T. Shevchenko	Russian/various	** +	1985	129.1	16.7	115	various Russian rivers
Tchitscherin	Russian/various	**	1988	129.1	16.7	147	Volga
Tikhiy Don	Russian/various	**	1977	125	16.7	140	various Russian rivers
Tolstoi	Russian/various	**	1979	115.6	16.7	80	Neva, Volga
Valerian Kuybyshev	Russian/various	**	1976	135.8	16.8	198	various Russian rivers
Valeriy Bryusov	Russian/various	**	1985	90.2	15	114	various Russian rivers
Vasilij Surikov	Russian/various	**	1975	110	14.5	70	various Russian rivers
Viking Kirov	Russian/various	**	1987	129.1	16.7	103	Neva, Svir, Volga
Viking Lavrinenkov	Viking River Cruises	***	1989	129.1	16.7	125	Dnieper/Black Sea
Viking Pakhomov	Viking River Cruises	***	1990	129.1	16.7	115	Neva/Svir/Volga
Viking Peterhof	Viking River Cruises	**	1975	125	16.7	118	Neva/Svir/Volga
Viking Surikov	Viking River Cruises	**	1975	129.1	16.7	103	Neva, Svir, Volga
Vissarion Belinsky	Russian/various	**	1980	125	16.7	161	various Russian rivers
Vladimir Ilych	Russian/various	*	1976	125	16.7	120	various Russian rivers
Volga Prince	Russian/various	**	1988	129.1	16.7	140	Neva, Volga
Volga Queen	Russian/various	**	1990	129.1	16.7	140	Neva, Volga
Yesenin	Russian/various	***	1984	90.4	15	49	Neva, Volga
Yuriy Andropov	Russian/various	**	1986	129.1	16.7	156	Neva, Volga
Zoshima Shashkov	Russian/various	**	1986	129.1	16.7	157	various Russian rivers

THE NILE

VESSEL	OWNER/OPERATING COMPANY	RATING	BUILT	LENGTH (m)	BEAM (m)	CABINS	PRINCIPAL RIVERS
African Queen	Egyptian/various	**	1992	72	14	54	The Nile
Akhnaton	Egyptian/various	***	1987	65	11	44	The Nile
Al Nabilatan	Egyptian/various	***	1999	72.5	14.4	66	The Nile
Amarco I	Egyptian/various	***	2003	72	14.2	59	The Nile
Anni	Egyptian/various	*	1980	72	11.3	56	The Nile
Aton	Egyptian/various	**	1978	72	11.3	54	The Nile
Aurora	Egyptian/various	**	1995	72	13.5	41	The Nile
Cairo	Egyptian/various	*	1981	78	13.5	58	The Nile
Caprice	Egyptian/various	**	2001	72	13.5	63	The Nile
Cleopatra II	Egyptian/various	*	1968	68.1	10.1	43	The Nile
Crown Jewel	Egyptian/various	**	1999	72	14	80	The Nile
Crown Jubilee	Egyptian/various	****	2005	72	14	80	The Nile
Crown Prince	Egyptian/various	***	1999	72	14	80	The Nile
Dar Amy	Egyptian/various	*	1983	33.5	7	16	The Nile
Dar Jaqueline	Egyptian/various	**	1987	36	8	10	The Nile
Dar Mahassen	Egyptian/various	**	1997	40	7.6	16	The Nile
Dar Shaden	Egyptian/various	**	1983	31	5.6	8	The Nile
Dar Sultana	Egyptian/various	*	1975	38.5	7.5	15	The Nile
Dar Thebes	Egyptian/various	**	1984	27	6.2	10	The Nile
Diamond	Egyptian/various	***	1994	71.5	13	72	The Nile
Domina Prestige	Egyptian/various	***	2004	72	14.2	72	The Nile
Egyptian Princess	Egyptian/various	**	1985	72	11.85	61	The Nile
El Fostat	Egyptian/various	****	2002	72	14.3	81	The Nile

RIVER CRUISE VESSELS							
VESSEL	OWNER/OPERATING COMPANY	RATING	BUILT	LENGTH (m)	BEAM (m)	CABINS	PRINCIPAL RIVERS
El Mahrousa	Egyptian/various	***	1999	66	12	52	The Nile
El Tarek	Egyptian/various	**	1992	61	12	40	The Nile
Embassy	Egyptian/various	**	1989	46	9	30	The Nile
Etoile du Nil I	Egyptian/various	**	1990	72	13	65	The Nile
Etoile du Nil II	Egyptian/various	**	1990	172	13	51	The Nile
Eugenie	Egyptian/various	**	1993	24	11	110	Lake Nasser
Fleurette	Egyptian/various	**	1988	64	11.8	48	The Nile
Florence	Egyptian/various	***	2001	71	12	75	The Nile
Giza	Egyptian/various	*	1981	78	13.5	58	The Nile
Golden	Egyptian/various	*	1984	70	11.5	52	The Nile
Golden Moon	Egyptian/various	***	2005	72	14	38	The Nile
Gondola	Egyptian/various	**	1998	48	8.5	32	The Nile
Hamees	Egyptian/various	***	2000	72	14	72	The Nile
Hapi I	Egyptian/various	**	1989	57.3	11	15	The Nile
Helio	Egyptian/various	**	1983	71	11	48	The Nile
Helios Regency	Egyptian/various	**	1992	72	13.8	51	The Nile
Hotp	Egyptian/various	*	1979	71	11	54	The Nile
Iberotel Crown Emperor	Egyptian/various	***	2003	100	14	118	The Nile
Iberotel Crown Empress	Egyptian/various	***	2004	100	14	128	The Nile
Imperial	Egyptian/various	**	1991	72	13.5	50	The Nile
Isis	Egyptian/various	**	1963	70	11	54	The Nile
Karim	Egyptian/various	*	1971	46	10	17	The Nile
Kasr du Nil	Egyptian/various	**	1990	72	13.5	50	The Nile
Kasr Ibrim	Egyptian/various	**	1997	79	14	70	Lake Nasser
King Mina	Egyptian/various	**	1986	67.5	11	55	The Nile
King of Thebes	Egyptian/various	***	1998	72	13.5	65	The Nile
King Tut I	Egyptian/various	***	2002	72	14.3	81	The Nile
King Tut II	Egyptian/various	***	1998	72	14.3	81	The Nile
King Tut III	Egyptian/various	***	1999	72	14.3	84	The Nile
King Tut IV	Egyptian/various	***	2004	72	14.3	81	The Nile
La Traviata	Egyptian/various	**	2004	63	13.4	45	The Nile
Lady Christina	Egyptian/various	***	2001	72	14.3	74	The Nile
Lady Diana	Egyptian/various	**	1988	70.5	12.8	60	The Nile
Lady Mary	Egyptian/various	***	2002	72	11	72	The Nile
Lady Sara	Egyptian/various	*	1989	58	11.5	55	The Nile
Lady Sophia	Egyptian/various	***	2001	72	12	74	The Nile
Liberty	Egyptian/various	***	1993	72.5	14.5	72	The Nile
Magic I	Egyptian/various	***	2001	72		72	The Nile
Magic II	Egyptian/various	***	2002	72		72	The Nile
Mahrousa	Egyptian/various	**	1999	66	12	52	The Nile
Media	Egyptian/various	**	1999	72	13.7	62	The Nile
Melodie	Egyptian/various	*	1987	60	8	40	The Nile
Mirage	Egyptian/various	***	2002	72	14	62	The Nile
Miriam	Egyptian/various	**	1997	72	14	58	The Nile
Mojito	Egyptian/various	***	2005	72	14	70	The Nile
Monaco	Egyptian/various	***	2003	72	14.4	80	The Nile
Monte Carlo	Egyptian/various	***	2003	72	14	80	The Nile
Moon River	Egyptian/various	***	2004	65	11.6	55	The Nile
Napoleon	Egyptian/various	**	2002	72	11	72	The Nile
Nile Adventurer	Egyptian/various	**	1990	99	11	34	The Nile
Nile Angel	Egyptian/various	**	1997	58	11	48	The Nile
Nile Carnival	Egyptian/various	**	1999	72	14	68	The Nile
Nile Crocodilo	Egyptian/various	**	1989	72	14	55	The Nile
Nile Crown	Egyptian/various	**	1990	72	14	60	The Nile
Nile Dream	Egyptian/various	**	1983	52.5	9	45	The Nile
Nile Elegante	Egyptian/various	**	1990			65	The Nile
Nile Elite	Egyptian/various	**	1992	72	14	74	The Nile
Nile Emerald	Egyptian/various	**	1989	72	12	67	The Nile
Nile Empress	Egyptian/various	**	1989	42	10.5	29	The Nile
Nile Fantasy	Egyptian/various	**	1987	42	11	27	The Nile
Nile Monarch	Egyptian/various	**	1990	72	11	45	The Nile
Nile Odyssey	Egyptian/various	**	1995	72	14	74	The Nile
Nile Pearl	Egyptian/various	*	1986	52	9	23	The Nile
Nile Pioneer	Egyptian/various	***	1994	72	13	64	The Nile
Nile Princess	Egyptian/various	*	1979	40	8	56	The Nile
Nile Quality	Egyptian/various	***	1994	72	14		The Nile
Nile Rhapsody	Egyptian/various	**	1988	62	10.5	26	The Nile
Nile Ruby	Egyptian/various	***	1992	72.5	14.5	74	The Nile
Nile Sapphire	Egyptian/various	**	1993	72	14	72	The Nile
Nile Secret	Egyptian/various	**	1991	62.5	11.5	54	The Nile
Nile Stephanie	Egyptian/various	***	2004	72	14.3	68	The Nile

RIVER CRUISE VESSELS

VESSEL	OWNER/OPERATING COMPANY	RATING	BUILT	LENGTH (m)	BEAM (m)	CABINS	PRINCIPAL RIVERS
Nile Symphony	Egyptian/various	**	1988	72	13	75	The Nile
Ninfea	Egyptian/various	*	1989	61	11	34	The Nile
Noor	Egyptian/various	*	1983	72	11.2	69	The Nile
Oberoi Philae	Oberoi Hotels/various	***	1996	72	13	54	The Nile
Oberoi Shehrazad	Oberoi Hotels/various	***	1986	72	13	40	The Nile
Oberoi Sherayar	Oberoi Hotels/various	***	1986	72	13	40	The Nile
Osiris	Egyptian/various	**	1963	70	11	55	The Nile
Pharaos	Egyptian/various	**	1994	72	14	77	The Nile
Princess Amira	Egyptian/various	**	1988	72	12.8	66	The Nile
Princess of the Nile	Egyptian/various	**	1992	73	13.5	58	The Nile
Queen of Abu Simbel	Egyptian/various	**	2000	107	15.5	62	Lake Nasser
Queen of the Nile	Egyptian/various	***	2000	71.6	13.1	65	The Nile
Ra I	Egyptian/various	*	1988	72	11	72	The Nile
Ra II	Egyptian/various	**	1990	78	11.8	73	The Nile
Radamis I	Egyptian/various	**	1991	72	13	72	The Nile
Radamis II	Egyptian/various	***	2000	72.3	13.8	80	The Nile
Ramses King of the Nile	Egyptian/various	***	2000	71.6	13.1	65	The Nile
Ramses of Egypt I	Egyptian/various	**	1984	53	10.3	40	The Nile
Ramses of Egypt III	Egyptian/various	**	1989	71.8	14.3	84	The Nile
Regency	Egyptian/various	**	1992	72	13.8	52	The Nile
Regina	Egyptian/various	**	1992	72	13.8	60	The Nile
River Anuket	Egyptian/various	**	2000	70	14.3	70	The Nile
Rosa Bianca	Egyptian/various	*	1990	52.5	10.3	32	The Nile
Royal Lotus	Egyptian/various	***	2005	72	14	62	The Nile
Royal Regency	Egyptian/various	***	2005	82	11	70	The Nile
Royal Ruby	Egyptian/various	***	2005	72.5	14.8	70	The Nile
Royale	Egyptian/various	**	1992	72	13.8	52	The Nile
Safari Queen	Egyptian/various	**	1990	71.5	11	54	The Nile
Semiramis I	Egyptian/various	***	2001	72	15	70	The Nile
Semiramis II	Egyptian/various	***	2001	72	15	70	The Nile
Seti IV	Egyptian/various	**	1988	64	8.5	40	The Nile
Sherry Boat	Egyptian/various	***	1989	66	11	56	The Nile
Silver Moon	Egyptian/various	*	1988	52.5	10	38	The Nile
Solaris I	Egyptian/various	**	1990	72	14.5	66	The Nile
Solaris II	Egyptian/various	***	1999	72	14.4	68	The Nile
Soleil	Egyptian/various	*	1989	71	12	34	The Nile
Sonesta Nile Goddess	Sonesta Hotels/various	**	1989	77	13	65	The Nile
Sonesta Moon Goddess	Sonesta Hotels/various	***	2000	72	14.2	56	The Nile
Sonesta Star Goddess	Sonesta Nile Cruises	NYR	2006	72	14	66	The Nile
Sonesta Sun Goddess	Sonesta Hotels/various	**	1993	77	14	62	The Nile
Sudan	Egyptian/various	**	1885	40	7.6	23	The Nile
Sun Boat III	Egyptian/various	**	1993	61	10	20	The Nile
Sun Boat IV	Egyptian/various	***	1996	72	12.8	40	The Nile
Sun Ray	Egyptian/various	***	2002	72	14	66	The Nile
Sylvia	Egyptian/various	**	1995	72	13.5	41	The Nile
Tania	Egyptian/various	*	1995	72	14	33	The Nile
Tanis	Egyptian/various	**	1990	73	13	70	The Nile
Telestar II	Egyptian/various	**	1989	58	11.5	57	The Nile
Terramar	Egyptian/various	***	1999	71	11	20	The Nile
Tut	Egyptian/various	*	1978	71	11	80	The Nile
Userhat	Egyptian/various	**	1991	70	47	51	The Nile
Viking Premier	Egyptian/various	**	1995	74	14	58	The Nile
Vittoria	Egyptian/various	**	1995	72	14	58	The Nile

ART & PHOTO CREDITS

4Corners Images 160
Peter Adam/Zefa/Corbis 38
age fotostock/SuperStock
48, 74, 98, 212
Alamy 2/3, 26, 51, 67, 104,
120, 205, 242, 276, 284,
294
akg-images London 19, 20,
118, 122, 123, 126, 214,
215R
Jerry Alexander/Stone/Getty
Images 282
Paul Almasy/Corbis 87
Alvey & Towers 195
Stefano Amantini/4Corners
304
The Art Archive 96, 186T
Gonzalo M. Azumendi 56/57,
246/247, 248, 250R, 253,
255, 275, 277, 287, 307
Laszio
Balogh/Reuters/Corbis 91
D. Barnes/Scottish
Viewpoint 238/239
Baseltour 112/113
Pat Behnke/Alamy back flap
bottom,14, 135
Pete Bennett/Apa 101T,
102, 148T. 156T, 285T,
292T, 308T
Peter
Bialobrzeski/Laif/Camera
Press 40, 44L, 45,
Walter Bibikow/jonarnold 90
Bildarchiv Monheim 141T,
144/145, 161, 161T,
162L&R
Bomford & Borrill/Survival
Anglia 280
Bodo Bondzio 134, 151T
Massimo Borchi/4Corners
119R, 124, 130, 213
British Waterways 23
CSTK Bratislava 66
Sue Bryant 229, 231
Rex Butcher/jonarnold 71
Cephas 207
Chris Coe/Apa 118T, 166,
217T, 232/233
Luis Castameda/Image
Bank/ Getty 60/61
Corbis 6TR
David Crausby/Alamy 131
Cremona Mondomuisca 216
Derek Croucher/Corbis
52/53
Cubolmages/Alamy 212
Richard Cummins/Corbis
244
Fridmar Damm/4Corners 8/9
Stefan Damm/4Corners 138
Danita Delimont/Alamy front
flap T, 33
Jerry Dennis/Apa 119L, 127,
142, 171T, 176T, 181
Colin Dutton/4Corners 215L
Sindre Ellingsen/Alamy
288/289
Annabel Elston/Apa 217
Euro Waterways 30, 194
Foto World/Image
Bank/Getty Images 285
Wolfgang Fritz 73, 81
Gapys
Photo/Zyarescu/Alamy
172/173
Gil Galvin/Apa 229T, 230T,
232T
Alain Le Garsmeur/Apa 269
Glyn Genin/Apa 6BL, 76T,

146, 156, 206
Getty Images 204T
Günther Gräfenhain/4Corners
7C, 106/107, 108, 180
Dietmar Guth/FAN
travelstock/Alamy 7BR
M. Hallberg/4Corners 76
Gavin Hellier/jonarnold 136
John Heseltine 202
Michael Hetier 197
Dave G. Houser/Corbis 149
Johanna Huber/4Corners 290
Image100/Alamy 39
Images of France 31, 193,
196
Volkmar Janicke 281
Britta Jaschinski/Apa back
cover TL, 10/11, 187T
Ed Kashi/Corbis 69
Wolfgang Kaehler/Corbis 24
Catherine Karnow 175
Martin Kirchner/Laif/Camera
Press 159
David Kjaer/Nature Picture
Library 77
Holger Klaes/4Corners 12/13
Kobal 125
Axel Krause/Apa 291, 292T,
293, 298, 299, 302, 306,
308T, 309
Ralf Kreuels/Laif/Camera
Press 198
Kunstmuseum Basel 113T
Tom Le Bas back cover CL,
3BR, 4BR, 5C, 5BR, 21, 36,
49, 66T, 90T, 124T, 137T,
249, 250L, 251, 254, 257,
258T, 258, 259, 264T, 264,
266L, 267T, 275T
Klaus Leidorf/Zefa/Corbis
68
Lucerne Tourist Board 116T
David Lyons/Alamy 236
Mary Evans Picture Library
18, 221, 295
Colin McPherson/Scottish
Viewpoint 237
Jens Meyer/AP/Empics 158
Anna Mockford & Nick
Bonetti/ Apa 274
NHPA 65
Nagelstock/Alamy 163
National Portrait Gallery 305
Richard Nowitz 43
Richard Nowitz/Apa 251T,
252, 255T, 256T, 277T
Dietmar Okon/Image Bank/
Getty 139
Christine
Osborne/WWPL/Alamy 303
Rosey Pajak/Alamy 178
Erhard Pansegrau 109
Doug Pearson/jonarnold 58
Helge Pedersen/Alamy 279
Peter Deilmann River Cruises
22, 34, 47, 322, 360
Photolibrary.com 179
Pictures Colour Library 78R
Lesley Player 134T
Mike Potts/Nature Picture
Library 105
Sarah Louise Ramsay/Apa
297, 305T, 306T, 308, 309
Mark Read/Apa 81T, 86T,
157, 158T, 214T, 226, 230
Matthias
Rietschel/AP/Empics 147
Robert Harding Picture
Library 151, 174, 190/191,
228

Robert Harding/Alamy 266R
Robert Harding/Getty
Images 75
Mick Rock/Cephas/Alamy
177, 222T, 223
Roger-Viollet/Topfoto 17
Joern Sackermann/Alamy
116
Sebastiano
Scattalin/4Corners 20/201
Reinhard
Schmid/SIME/4Corners 72,
115, 137
Giovanni Simeone/4Corners
79, 181T, 188, 199,
218/219, 220, 227, 267
Jonathan Smith/LPI/Getty
286
Lee Snider/Photo Images/
Corbis 117
Jeroen Snijders/Apa 189,
189T, 194T
StockScotland 234/235
Geray Sweeney/Apa 243,
245T
George Taylor/Apa 198T
Liba Taylor/Corbis 265
Peter Titmuss/Alamy 192
Thomas Cook 16, 110
TopFoto 16T, 240
TopFoto/Kingsford 78L
Travel-Ink 141
The Travel Library 64
The Travel Library/Rex
Features 32
Craig Turp 103
Mireille Vautier/Apa 187
Vienna Tourist Board 86
Viking River Cruises back
cover TR, 4/5, 37, 41, 42,
140, 143, 283, 318
Mark Wadlow/Russian &
Eastern Images 268
Douglas Ward front flap B,
spine, back cover B, back
cover T, 1, 5BL, 25, 27, 29,
35, 44R, 46, 50, 79T, 111,
138T, 150, 203
Bill Wassman/Apa 113T,
238T, 240T, 241
Marcus Wilson-Smith/Apa
244T, 245
Adam Woolfitt/Corbis 99,
100, 101
Phil Wood/Apa 74T
Gregory Wrona/Apa 28,
102T, 105T, 167, 168, 168T,
169, 170, 171, 280T
Zoom/4Corners 54/55

PORTS OF CALL

Pages 82/85 Vienna: all
pictures Glyn Genin/Apa
except: Alamy 84TL; Mark
Read/Apa 83CL, BL.
Pages 88/89 Bratislava:
Michael Nicholson/Corbis
88/89T; Pictures Colour
Library 88CR; Jan
Sullivan/Alamy 88BL; Tom Le
Bas 88BR; TopFoto 89CL;
Michigan State University
89TC; Kevin Schafer/Corbis
89TR.
Pages 92/93 Budapest:
Gavin Hellier/jonarnold
92/93T; Apa 94T, 95CL;
Marcus Brooke 92TL, Mark
Read 92BR, 93BCL, CR, BR,

94CR, BR, 95C, CR; Douglas
Ward 93TR.
Pages 128/129 Cologne:
Ogando/Laif/Camera Press
128/129T; TopFoto/Image
Works 128CL, BR; H.P.
Merten/Robert Harding
128CR; Mervyn Rees/Alamy
129CL; Achim
Gaasterland/Laif/Camera
Press 129CR; Richard
Bryant/Arcaid Ed/Alamy
129TR.
Pages 132/133 Amsterdam:
Bill Wassman/Apa 132/133T;
Glyn Genin/Apa 132TL, BL,
133CL; M. Gotin 132CR. Lee
Foster 133TL; Gil Galvin/Apa
133CR, BL.
Pages 152/153 Prague:
Robert Harding 152/153T all
other pictures Glyn
Genin/Apa.
Pages 164/165 Berlin: Tony
Halliday/Apa 164/165T
164TL, 165TR; Berlin
Tourismus Marketing
(btm)/Koch 164CR, Chris
Coe/Apa 164BL; Cro
Magnon/Alamy 164BR.
Pages 182/185 Paris: David
Martin Hughes/Robert
Harding 182/183T; Andrea
Pistolesi 182CL; Jerry
Dennis/Apa 182BR, 183CL,
C, TC, TR, 184CR, BL, BR,
185TL, TR; Britta
Jaschinski/Apa 183CR, BL,
BR, 184T, CL, CB.
Pages 208/211 Venice: Anna
Mockford & Nick Bonetti/Apa
208/209T, 211TL, TR; Glyn
Genin/Apa 208BR, 209TCL,
TR, CL, CR, BR, 210 T, CL, BL,
211CR.
Pages 224/225 Porto:
Massimo Ripani/4Corners
224/225T; Chris Coe/Apa
225TL; TR; Mark Read 224TL,
CR, BL, 225CL.
Pages 260/263 Moscow:
Richard Nowitz/Apa 260/261,
260CR, 261TR, 261C,
261BL, 262T, BL, BR, 263CL,
TR; Tom Le Bas/Apa 260BL,
261BR, 263TL.
**Pages 270/273 St
Petersburg**: all pictures Anna
Mockford & Nick Bonetti/Apa.
Pages 300/301 Cairo: Axel
Krause/Apa 300/301,
301TR, CR, BL; Sarah Louise
Ramsay/Apa 300 CR, BL, BR.
Pages 310/313 Luxor: Pete
Bennett/Apa 310CR, 311TR,
B; Luc Chessex/Apa 310BL;
Axel Krause/Apa 310/311T,
311C, 312CR, BL, 313TL, TR.

Cartographic Editor:
Zoë Goodwin
Map Production:
James Macdonald and Mike
Adams
©2006 Apa Publications GmbH &
Co. Verlag KG, Singapore Branch

Book Production:
Linton Donaldson

INDEX